Creation's
Slavery & Liberation

Cascade Library of Pauline Studies

The aim of the series is to advance Pauline theology by publishing monographs that make original scholarly proposals in conversation with existing scholarly debates, and which have the potential to shape future trajectories in research.

As both the title of the series and the list of categories above suggests, it is their contribution to critical discussion of Pauline theology that will be the hallmark of books published in CLPS. However, the nature and scope of Pauline theology is intended to be understood in a somewhat expansive manner, with an openness to the use of methodologies (e.g., social-scientific or post-colonial approaches) that have sometimes been regarded as standing in opposition to theological modes of Pauline interpretation. The criterion by which the suitability of a study for inclusion in the series will be assessed is its theological interest. This judgment will be made on the basis of the potential benefits of a particular approach or methodology for our understanding of Pauline theology rather than on the basis of conformity to preconceived ideas of what constitutes an appropriately theological approach to Pauline interpretation. As such, CLPS will also be open both to studies that are broadly confessional in tone and to those that are more critical of perspectives expressed in the Pauline texts.

Series Editors:
Stephen Chester, Wycliffe College, Toronto
Dorothea H. Bertschmann, Abbey House Palace Green, Durham University

Editorial Board:
John M. G. Barclay, Durham University
Lisa Marie Bowens, Princeton Theological Seminary
Martinus C. de Boer, Vrije Universiteit Amsterdam
Andreas Dettwiler, Universite de Geneve
Susan Eastman, Duke Divinity School
Beverly Roberts Gaventa, Baylor University
David G. Horrell, University of Exeter
Jonathan Linebaugh, Beesen Divinity School, Samford University
Grand Macaskill, University of Aberdeen
Volker Rabens, Friedrich Schiller University Jena

Creation's Slavery & Liberation

Paul's Letter to Rome in the Face of
Imperial & Industrial Agriculture

Presian Renee Burroughs

CASCADE Books • Eugene, Oregon

CREATION'S SLAVERY & LIBERATION
Paul's Letter to Rome in the Face of Imperial & Industrial Agriculture

Cascade Library of Pauline Studies

Copyright © 2022 Presian Renee Burroughs. All rights reserved. Except for brief quotations in critical publications or reviews, no part of this book may be reproduced in any manner without prior written permission from the publisher. Write: Permissions, Wipf and Stock Publishers, 199 W. 8th Ave., Suite 3, Eugene, OR 97401.

Cascade Books
An Imprint of Wipf and Stock Publishers
199 W. 8th Ave., Suite 3
Eugene, OR 97401

www.wipfandstock.com

PAPERBACK ISBN: 978-1-7252-9487-5
HARDCOVER ISBN: 978-1-7252-9488-2
EBOOK ISBN: 978-1-7252-9489-9

Cataloguing-in-Publication data:

Names: Burroughs, Presian Renee, author.

Title: Creation's slavery and liberation : Paul's letter to Rome in the face of imperial and industrial agriculture / Presian Renee Burroughs.

Description: Eugene, OR: Cascade Books, 2022 | Series: Cascade Libarary of Pauline Studies | Includes bibliographical references and index(es).

Identifiers: ISBN 978-1-7252-9487-5 (paperback) | ISBN 978-1-7252-9488-2 (hardcover) | ISBN 978-1-7252-9489-9 (ebook)

Subjects: LCSH: Bible. Romans—Criticism, interpretation, etc. | Imperialism. | Industries—Rome. | Agriculture, Ancient—Rome. | Agriculture—Economic aspects—United States. | Human ecology—Religious aspects—Christianity.

Classification: BS2665.52 B877 2022 (print) | BS2665.52 (ebook)

03/14/24

*To my dear children,
Justus Steven and Makaria Grace,
whose love for justice and vitality give me great hope and joy.*

Contents

List of Tables and Figures | xi
Series Introduction | xiii
Acknowledgments | xvii
Abbreviations | xxiii

Introduction: A Convergence of Stories | 1

1. Creation's Interrelatedness: Nonhuman, Human, and Divine Relationships in the Tanakh | 27

   1.1 The Creation Accounts: Human Leadership and Care | 29

   1.1.1 Genesis 1 | 31

   1.1.2 Genesis 2 | 38

   1.2 Torah: Human Sin, Divine Covenant, and Creational Blessing | 41

   1.2.1 Genesis 3–9 | 41

   1.2.2 Genesis 12 and God's Covenants with Abram and Israel | 45

   1.2.3 Exodus, Leviticus, and Deuteronomy | 46

   1.3 Prophets and Writings: Creation's Restoration and the Messiah's Rule | 55

   1.3.1 Amos | 56

   1.3.2 Ezekiel | 59

   1.3.3 Isaiah | 61

   1.3.4 Psalms | 66

   1.4 Conclusion | 67

2. Creation's Subjugation: The Imperial Gospel in Action | 69

    2.1 Rome's Claims: Liberating People from Hunger | 70

    2.2 Environmental History's Report: Ecological Deterioration in North Africa | 89

        2.2.1 Land Preparation | 91

        2.2.2 Cultivation | 94

        2.2.3 Collection | 96

        2.2.4 Transportation, Processing, and Distribution | 97

3. Creation's Advocate: Paul, the Imperial Gospel, and His Letter to Rome | 102

    3.1 Paul's Ambit: Creation's Degradation in Asia Minor and Syria | 103

    3.2 Paul's Gospel: The God Who Makes Right and Makes Alive | 109

        3.2.1 Romans 1–4 | 112

        3.2.2 Romans 5–8 | 119

        3.2.3 Romans 9–11 | 127

        3.2.4 Romans 12–16 | 129

    3.3 Paul's Eco-Ethical Vision | 139

4. Creation's Slavery and Subjection: The Story of Human Sin in Romans | 145

    4.1 "Creation" in Romans | 147

    4.2 Romans 8:21: Creation's Slavery | 150

        4.2.1 The Genesis of Slavery | 152

        4.2.2 The Nature of Destruction | 155

    4.3 Romans 8:20: Creation's Subjection | 160

        4.3.1 Primary and Secondary Causes of Subjection | 161

        4.3.2 The Condition of Frustration | 163

5. Creation's Expectation and Liberation: The Story of Human Glory in Romans | 167

    5.1 Romans 8:19: Creation's Expectation | 168

        5.1.1 Apocalypse and the Coming Glory | 169

5.2 Romans 8:21: Creation's Liberation | 174

    5.2.1 Liberation Produced by Glory | 176

5.3 Romans 8:22: Creation's Co-Groaning and Co-Laboring | 179

    5.3.1 Co-Groaning | 181

    5.3.2 Co-Laboring | 184

    5.3.3 Co-Groaning and Co-Laboring Until Now | 187

    5.3.4 Creation as Tomb and Womb | 191

5.4 Conclusion | 193

6. Creation's Destruction: Industrial Agriculture in Action | 197

    6.1 Industrial Agriculture's Claims: Abundant, Safe, and Affordable Food | 202

    6.2 Environmental History's Report: Degradation of Soil, Water, Air, and Life | 206

        6.2.1 Land Preparation | 206

        6.2.2 Cultivation | 214

            6.2.2.1 Glyphosate, Agribusinesses, and Governmental Oversight | 219

            6.2.2.2 Glyphosate, Ecological Harm, and Mammalian Disease | 221

        6.2.3 Collection | 233

        6.2.4 Transportation, Processing, and Distribution | 241

    6.3 Conclusion | 249

7. Creation's Preliminary Liberation: Regenerative Agriculture at Work | 252

    7.1 The Land's Expectations: Regenerative Agriculture | 253

    7.2 The Land's Hope: Perennial Agriculture | 256

Conclusion: Cultivating Liberative Relationships with Human and Nonhuman Creation | 266

Appendix: Forgotten Truths: Synthetic Pesticides and Genetic Modification | 283

Bibliography | 289
Subject Index | 305
Modern Author Index | 321
Ancient Texts Index | 325

List of Tables and Figures

Tables

Table 1: Global Climate Change | 3

Table 2: The EPA's Glyphosate Residue Tolerances for Common Food Crops | 224

Figures

Figure 1: Silver Denarius of Augustus, Colonia Patricia, 18–17 BCE | 74

Figure 2: Silver Cistophorus of Claudius, Pergamum, 41–54 CE | 75

Figure 3: "Competent Threshing Here Will Hasten the Thrashing Over There" | 234

Figure 4: Roots Comparison | 261

Series Introduction

FOR THE APOSTLE PAUL, his own significance rested entirely on his commission as an apostle and his proclamation of the gospel of Christ ("by the grace of God, I am what I am," 1 Cor 15:10). For this reason, the heart of Pauline studies must lie in Paul's exposition of this gospel, which is to say his theology, as it comes to expression in his surviving letters. Here Paul expresses both his deepest convictions about the significance of Jesus Christ and his perspectives on their embodiment in the life of early church communities. The Cascade Library of Pauline Studies (CLPS) will focus squarely on engagement with the theological content of the Pauline letters, along with its impact on human thought and behavior throughout the centuries. The series aims to provide a home for research efforts that produce fresh insight into Paul's theology in its original contexts, its legacies and reception, and its significance today; efforts that therefore possess the potential to shape trajectories in future research.

To stake such a claim for the centrality of Pauline theology within its discipline implies both something about the current state of Pauline studies and also an aspiration for its future. For the discipline is simultaneously marked by impressive vitality and by fragmentation. A wide range of theoretical approaches are employed, and even among those adopting a more traditional approach, the list of different frameworks within which Paul is understood is substantial: the apocalyptic Paul, the covenantal Paul, the Paul of the New Perspective, the Paul of the Old Perspective, Paul within Judaism etc. It is easy for the scholarly discourses which result to feel like separate conversations. Forums are needed within which a shared focus on Paul's theological ideas can stimulate new thinking, promote dialogue, and help to map pathways forward beyond the reassertion of incommensurate conclusions. CLPS aims to provide such a forum.

Yet an insistence on the centrality of Pauline theology within Pauline studies ought not to mean imposing a forced uniformity or understanding the scope of Pauline theology in a narrow manner. For one thing, engagement with the theological content of Paul's message is impossible without the careful historical work necessary to understand Paul's ideas in their own ancient contexts. The study of Pauline theology cannot be advanced by the erection of artificial divides between theological and historical approaches to interpretation. Neither can our attempts to understand Paul's ideas in their own ancient contexts be detached from the influence upon us of our own historical location as interpreters. We are impacted both by previous traditions of interpreting Paul and by our own social and cultural contexts. They shape our concerns, and they both enable and constrain our understanding of the past. Implicit in even the most historical approaches to the study of Pauline theology are present day questions and horizons. Some theological interpreters simply take account of the impact of historical location upon their task, keeping their focus on Paul in his own time and place. Others instead embrace the constructive task of explicitly recontextualizing Paul's theology for contemporary readers, connecting the historical study of Paul's ideas in varied ways with the Christian tradition today.

There is thus considerable and appropriate diversity within the study of Pauline theology. For this reason, exegetical studies, studies comparing Paul's ideas with those of others in the ancient world, studies exploring Paul's ideas in their canonical contexts, studies of reception history, and studies bringing Paul's theological ideas into dialogue with contemporary theological concerns are all welcome within CLPS. Some of these types of studies may employ analytical tools drawn from the Christian theological tradition. Their methodology will be theological as well as their content. However, engagement with the theological content of Paul's message can also sometimes be served by inter-disciplinary methodologies that have not typically been understood as theological or have even been understood by some of their practitioners as antithetical to theological interpretation. Post-colonial interpretation, the use of various forms of political philosophy that prioritize liberation, and various kinds of feminist interpretation all provide examples of such inter-disciplinary methodologies. Where studies use such methodologies to engage with Paul's theological ideas or to recontextualize them for the contemporary world they too will be welcome within CLPS. It is the kinds of questions asked, the quality of the

Series Introduction

theological reflection offered, and the depth of critical engagement that we intend to be the hallmark of CLPS.

Dorothea H. Bertschmann
Stephen J. Chester
Series Editors

Acknowledgments

EIGHT YEARS AGO, MY dissertation committee—Drs. Susan Eastman, Ellen Davis, Douglas Campbell, and Norman Wirzba—approved what was, in a manner of speaking, a seedling. Since that time, the seedling has matured and grown into something much larger and more complex and, hopefully, something that will bear nourishing fruit. This book as it stands now is far different from the dissertation it once was, and I am indebted to many people for helping me further cultivate it.

I thank my dissertation committee for providing me with insightful and encouraging feedback, and I appreciate the ways in which Susan and Ellen continued to mentor me as I met the demands of teaching while also reworking this project. When I reconfigured my chapter on industrial agriculture, Ellen kindly connected me with her friend and renowned scientist Wes Jackson. I thank Wes for devoting time and energy to reading and offering recommendations on chapter 6.

I am supremely grateful for the many people who guided my learning prior to and during my doctoral work. Before studying at Duke, my understanding of Paul and his historical and theological contexts took on greater complexity at Trinity Western University, where my hermeneutical grid expanded under the influence of Drs. Peter Flint, Randy Radney, Larry Perkins, and other professors and friends. It continued to be challenged when Dr. Daniel Wallace introduced me to the complexities of New Testament textual criticism while I assisted him in Münster, Germany for six months. My most significant transformation took place at Duke University during my MDiv and ThD studies, when I received instruction from Drs. Richard Hays, Ed Sanders, Joel Marcus, Susan Eastman, Douglas Campbell, Ellen Davis, Norman Wirzba, Fred Edie, Stanley Hauerwas, Melvin Peters, Joshua Sosin, and many others. I cannot begin to describe my appreciation for all these scholars and their patience with me as I asked questions,

Acknowledgments

wrestled with new ideas, and practiced new skills. And I thank the friends who studied with me at Duke—especially Drs. Celia Wolff, Laura Rodgers Levens, Emily Peck-McClain, and Mindy Makant—for making the doctoral journey (and beyond) more bearable and even delightful.

I could not have completed my doctoral studies without the generous financial and spiritual support of the John Wesley Fellowship (A Foundation for Theological Education) and Duke Divinity School's ThD Fellowship and Edgar B. Fisher Memorial Grant. I thank them for investing in this project and in me.

My deep gratitude extends to my former students and colleagues at United Theological Seminary. United's faculty, especially Drs. Tom Dozeman, Joni Sancken, Anthony LeDonne, and Justus Hunter, kindly empathized with me and offered encouragement, help, and caring friendship. Of greatest relevance to this project was Tom's insistence that, according to the Tanakh, the condition of the land related intimately to human purity. His insights prodded me to investigate this topic and integrate it into my understanding of the Tanakh and its implications for Jesus's atonement. I can't thank Tom enough for being a senior scholar who—though very busy with his own work—nevertheless cared for and advised a lowly junior faculty member.

I also am truly grateful for the learning community at Wake Forest University's School of Divinity for welcoming me while my husband, Bradley Burroughs, serves in Wake Forest's Program for Leadership and Character. It is absolutely thrilling to engage in conversations with a group of faculty and students who recognize the theological, ethical, and practical importance of how we grow and receive our food. Dr. Katherine Shaner has become a welcome writing companion, and her insights, suggestions, and friendship have greatly enriched my work. I thank Drs. Neal Walls, Jill Crainshaw, and Kevin Jung for inviting me to teach several courses at the School of Divinity, including a course on the topic of this book. I deeply appreciate my students who enthusiastically and attentively engaged in my courses and those who even read earlier portions of this book. Their feedback has pushed me to make the book more comprehensible and precise.

I thank Dr. Sarah Blair, Brillie Scott, Ken Cochrane, Dr. Rychie Breidenstein, Mark Condy, and Caryn Dalton for having supplied me with books, interlibrary loans, and encouragement at United Theological Seminary's O'Brien Library. Similarly, the librarians and library resources at Duke University, Graduate Theological Union, University of California

Acknowledgments

(Berkeley), Wright State University, Allegheny College, and Wake Forest University have sated my hunger for more knowledge, especially as I engaged in research outside my primary field. They have my unending thanks.

My exploration of ecological interpretations of the Bible has been inspired and enriched by the Ecological Hermeneutics Section of the Society of Biblical Literature (SBL), whose co-chairs kindly include me on their steering committee. They have my deep gratitude for promoting stimulating conversations and providing me with helpful feedback as I have shared my ideas and learned from them and those who participated in the section's sessions. I am also grateful for the Pauline Theology Section of SBL who thoughtfully considered my reflections on Romans 5 and 8 in relation to the ecological crisis.

Words cannot express the appreciation I have for Dr. Michael Gorman, who has been a mentor to me since the early days of my doctoral studies at Duke. He has modeled Christ-like compassion to Brad and me as we have faced stressful circumstances and navigated the treacherous terrain between family values and career aspirations. He was even kind enough to read through my dissertation and offer feedback early on in my revision process. Although his written work is not cited in this book, his theological, spiritual, and exegetical sensibilities certainly have shaped its content.

I am indebted to Dr. Sylvia Keesmaat, who—as a scholar of Paul and practitioner of regenerative agriculture—gave me indispensable feedback on a late version of this project. Because of her insights and critiques, I reordered my chapters, sifted out (some!) extraneous details, and integrated the project more fully. Her own work has modeled for me how to engage in intertextual, political, and theological exegesis. I especially admire and appreciate the way in which Sylvia exemplifies Christian and academic integrity as she promotes creation's liberation in all facets of her life.

I thank Dr. David Horrell for reviewing the penultimate draft of this project, offering invaluable suggestions for its refinement, and recommending its inclusion in the new Cascade Library of Pauline Studies. I count it a true honor and privilege to receive the editorial board's endorsement and extend my thanks most especially to Stephen Chester and Dorothea Bertschmann, the series' co-editors, for overseeing this process so quickly and attentively.

Michael Thomson—Wipf and Stock's Acquisitions and Development Editor—has my deep gratitude for consistently cheering me on and advocating for my interdisciplinary work. And the publication of this contribution

ACKNOWLEDGMENTS

was made all the more possible and enjoyable by the attentiveness, patience, and helpfulness of Cascade's publishing team, most notably: Chris Spinks, Stephanie Hough, Mike Suber, Rachel Saunders, James Stock, George Callihan, and Matt Wimer. I thank them for their diligent and careful work.

Longtime friends—Ruthanne, Christa, Laurie, Tiffany, Meredith, and Edith—receive my undying appreciation and love for their constant compassion, fidelity, and forgiveness. I thank them for praying for me when I had no words to utter as I endured many moves; paralyzing fear; bouts of depression; questions of vocation; and struggles with being the follower of Christ, parent, spouse, and academic I desire to be.

My heartfelt thanks go to my dear mother-in-law, Cindy Burroughs, for constantly cheering Brad and me on as we pursue academic careers and always take on too many projects. I cannot thank Cindy enough for loving and enjoying our two children so passionately and caring for them in times when Brad and I needed to devote extra attention to our many responsibilities. I always know that I can count on her to help, listen, and care. She is a true gift.

I thank my dad, Steve Smyers, who taught me how to work hard, take chances, and not give up. He instilled in me a love for being outdoors and with animals, and he introduced me to the complexities involved in farming. I thank him and my stepmother, Rita Smyers, for generously supporting me, Brad, and our family in concrete ways. Their support has always helped us pursue our dreams and has substantially helped make this book a reality.

My deepest gratitude also goes to my mom, Linda Smyers, who taught me to ask questions, devote myself to learning, sit quietly in nature, and seek after God and goodness. Even though I was an incredibly active (and stubborn) child, her patience and focus eventually taught me the value of concentrating my energies on tackling academic pursuits. More recently, Mom has made our family's many moves more organized, less stressful, and far more feasible by her countless hours of packing, unpacking, and cleaning. My unbounded appreciation goes to her for all these forms of support and her tender care for Brad, me, and our children.

How can I adequately express my gratitude and love for Brad, who has partnered with me since our first year of divinity school? His expansive knowledge and astute questions have always enriched my thinking and writing. By his own example of perseverance, hard work, careful reading and writing, and courageous and critical thinking, he has prodded me to

ACKNOWLEDGMENTS

do what I did not think I could. He has devoted countless hours to combing through my writing and offering invaluable suggestions even though he knew I'd initially be defensive and discouraged. Brad so thoroughly believed in me and my work that he even was willing to sacrifice his first teaching position so that I could take mine. Brad's love, integrity, commitment to others' development and success, wisdom, perceptive critiques, and devotion to me, our kids, and our families have, more than anything else, made this book possible. I truly could not have done this without him nor would I have wanted to do so. I thank him for loving me so faithfully and believing in me so ceaselessly.

Finally, I thank our children, Justus and Makaria, for making me laugh and warming my heart. More than I'd like to remember, they endured being told "Mommy's working" with understanding and patience. Justus especially has helped me write this book by attending to and amusing his little sister and entertaining himself so that I could get "one more thing" done. His kind inquiries about how I'm doing never cease to amaze me, while his witty comments lighten my heart. And I'll treasure the memories of Makaria sneaking into the office, sitting on my lap, and playing by my desk when I was writing. Their compassion for others, concern for justice, and exuberance for life inspire me, and I hope with all my heart that during their lifetimes they will experience creation's liberation more than its destruction. It is to Justus and Makaria I dedicate this book.

Abbreviations

ABD	*The Anchor Bible Dictionary*
ANTC	Abingdon New Testament Commentaries
Aen.	Virgil, *Aeneid*
AB	Anchor Bible
BDAG	F. W. Danker, W. Bauer, W. F. Arndt, and F. W. Gingrich, *A Greek-English Lexicon of the New Testament and Other Early Christian Literature*
BDB	F. Brown, S. R. Driver, C. A. Briggs, *A Hebrew and English Lexicon of the Old Testament*
CDC	Centers for Disease Control and Prevention
CERA	Center for Environmental Risk Assessment
Ecl.	Virgil, *Eclogues*
EDNT	H. Balz and G. Schneider, *Exegetical Dictionary of the New Testament*
EPA / USEPA	United States Environmental Protection Agency
FAO	Food and Agriculture Organization of the United Nations
GM	Genetically modified
GBH	Glyphosate-based herbicide
IPCC	Intergovernmental Panel on Climate Change
ICC	International Critical Commentary
IFAD	International Fund for Agricultural Development
JBL	*Journal of Biblical Literature*

Abbreviations

JSNTSup	Journal for the Study of the New Testament: Supplement Series
JSOTSup	Journal for the Study of the Old Testament: Supplement Series
LSJ	H. G. Liddell, R. Scott, H. S. Jones, *An Intermediate Greek-English Lexicon*
LCL	Loeb Classical Library
LXX	A. Rahlfs and R. Hanhart, *Septuaginta*
Met.	Ovid, *Metamorphoses*
NESTA	National Earth Science Teachers Association
NETS	*A New English Translation of the Septuagint*
NIB	*The New Interpreter's Bible*
NOAA	National Oceanic and Atmospheric Administration
NH	Pliny, *Natural History*
NICNT	The New International Commentary on the New Testament
NICOT	The New International Commentary on the Old Testament
NTS	*New Testament Studies*
OTL	Old Testament Library
RG	Augustus, *Res Gestae*
RCO	Roman Climate Optimum
TDNT	G. Kittel and G. W. Bromiley, *Theological Dictionary of the New Testament*
TDOT	G. J. Botterweck and H. Ringgren, *Theological Dictionary of the Old Testament*
UNICEF	United Nations International Children's Emergency Fund
USDA	United States Department of Agriculture
USGS	United States Geological Society
WBC	Word Biblical Commentary
WFP	World Food Programme
WHO	World Health Organization

Introduction

A Convergence of Stories

And God said, "Let the land sprout vegetation—plants bearing seed, fruit trees bearing fruit with the seed in it according to its kind upon the land." And it was so. The land brought forth vegetation—plants bearing seed according to its kind, trees bearing fruit with the seed in it according to its kind. And God perceived it was good . . . And God said, "Let us make humankind according to our image and likeness, and let them rule over the fish of the sea, the birds of the skies, the animals, all the earth, and all the creeping things creeping on the earth." . . . God said, "Behold, I have given to you every seed-bearing plant with seed for sowing, which is upon the whole earth, and every tree that has seed-bearing fruit for sowing—for you they are food. And to every animal of the land and to every bird of the skies and to every thing creeping on the land with the breath of life in it [I have given] every green plant for food." And it was so.

—GENESIS 1:11–12, 26, 29, 30[1]

---

1. All English Scripture citations in this introduction are the author's own unless otherwise noted. The translation of Gen 1:11–12, 26, 29, 30 was done in consultation with the Hebrew and Greek texts (Elliger, Rudolph, and Schenker, *Biblia Hebraica Stuttgartensia*; Rahlfs and Hanhart, *Septuaginta*). My translation of Gen 1:26, in particular, resonates with the LXX and also finds guidance in Richard Friedman's translation of the Hebrew, in which he separates "all the earth" from the "domestic animals" in contrast with the NRSV's "all the wild animals of the earth" (Friedman, *Commentary on the Torah*, 12).

Creation's Slavery and Liberation

And to the man [God] said, "Because . . . you have eaten from the tree that I commanded, 'Do not eat from it,' the land lies cursed on account of your works . . ."[2]

—GENESIS 3:17

For the creation was subjected to frustration . . . [but] will be liberated from the slavery of destruction into the liberation of the glory of God's children.

—ROMANS 8:20, 21

EARTH'S STORY IS A story of life. Plants spring up across land and water with the amazing capacity to adapt, grow, and reproduce themselves. And because of their unrelenting work, they nourish countless other living things. This has been Earth's story for millions of years.

Yet, this story of life also entails death. And death often nourishes new life. Occasionally and increasingly, however, natural events and human actions intensify destruction and, therefore, increase death in ways that disrupt life. Over the past two or three centuries, Earth's story has turned into a story of extinction, a sixth mass extinction of life.[3] In such times, Earth's story reads like a tragedy. With moans and dismal silence, Earth's sundry members tell the tragedy.

Earth's atmosphere sighs and roars as its changing composition raises Earth's temperature, melts glaciers, dries fragile lands, inundates lowlands, and stirs up violent and frequent hurricanes. All because of human activity.[4] And the story of global climate change proceeds in uncanny ways.

---

2. The Greek text supplies the noun "works" (Rahlfs and Hanhart, *Septuaginta*). Whereas the Hebrew and Greek texts of Gen 3:17 lack a finite verb that would connect the "land" to its cursed condition, I supply the verb "lies" in order to reflect the ways in which the passive participle of the Hebrew and the adjective of the Greek do not refer to an agent. It may be, as Sigve Tonstad argues (Tonstad, *Letter to the Romans*, 250), that God here observes the land's condition (which is explicitly explained to be a result of Adam's action) and does not pronounce or enact a *divine* curse upon the land (contra Habel, "Reading as an Earth Being," 100–101). For further discussion, see 1.2.1.

3. Kolbert, *Sixth Extinction*.

4. Because people are burning fossil fuels and forests, spreading nitrogenous fertilizers, and raising thousands of livestock animals in concentrated animal feed operations (CAFOs) at unprecedented rates, unnatural amounts of greenhouse gases are filling the atmosphere. The National Oceanic and Atmospheric Administration (NOAA) identified

A Convergence of Stories

Table 1. Global Climate Change

May 2020: CO_2 levels reach 417.16 parts per million (ppm) at Mauna Lao[a]
July 2020: N_2O levels reach 333.99 parts per billion (ppb) at Mauna Lao[b]
N_2O is "three hundred times more powerful than carbon dioxide in creating climate warming," and its main source is agriculture[c]
Oceans absorb "about 30% of the anthropogenic carbon dioxide" that is released into the air, and this causes "ocean acidification" at levels the Earth has not seen for "the last 65 million years"[d]

---

[a] Keeling et al., "Exchanges of Atmospheric CO_2 and $13CO_2$."
[b] "Global N_2O Levels."
[c] Miller, *Farming and the Food Supply*, 80.
[d] Hoegh-Guldberg et al., "Impacts of 1.5°C Global Warming," 178.

Earth's waters whisper their tragedy as the atmosphere's increasing CO_2 levels acidify the world's oceans. The resulting carbonic acids prevent shellfish, plankton, and corals from creating and maintaining their protective shells and coral reef homes. And as global temperatures rise and corals die, coral reefs take on the pallor of death.

Earth's aquatic creatures offer obituaries written in protest as they suffocate in the ocean's dead zones.[5] Because unnatural amounts of fertil-

---

July of 2019 as the hottest month ever recorded, with the average "land and ocean surface temperature" "0.95°C (1.71°F) above the 20th century average." Keeping with this warming trend, the global surface temperature in July 2021 "was the highest for July since global records began in 1880" (NOAA, "Global Climate Report—July 2021"). "Nine of the 10 warmest Julys have occurred since 2010, with the last seven Julys (2015-2021) being the seven warmest Julys on record" (NOAA, "Global Climate Report-July 2021"). Even with COVID-19 causing global economies to slow in the first half of 2020, the "average global land and ocean surface temperature for January-July 2020" was "the second highest January-July period on record" (NOAA, "State of the Climate"). The economic slowdown has demonstrated that reducing global warming and recalibrating the balance of atmospheric gasses is not a quick or straightforward fix. Forster et al. explain that the economic slowdown in 2020 resulted in reduced NO_x (whether NO or NO_2) and SO_2 emissions. While NO_x acts as a greenhouse gas that traps the sun's warming rays, SO_2 can reflect the sun's rays back into space and ultimately cool the planet. When economies slow down, less NO_x and SO_2 is released, but the warming and cooling effects, respectively, of these chemicals nearly balance each other out. Forster et al. argue that large-scale reductions in CO_2 and NO_x emissions and increases in carbon sequestration in tandem with reductions in SO_2 offer the greatest chance in combating global climate change in the long term ("Current and Future Global Climate Impacts," 918).

5. Nitrogenous fertilizers collect in great quantities in the Mississippi River Delta and other river deltas throughout the world. Nitrogen promotes the growth of algae, which live for a short time, die, and then absorb dissolved oxygen as they decompose. The

izers inundate rivers, lakes, and oceans, algae populations explode, die, and then consume the water's limited oxygen stores. The tragic result is the destruction of aquatic life.

Earth's skin—the soil—wordlessly grieves its story with clouds of dust and rivers of mud, as it is swept away from its vital work of nourishing life.[6] Although people primarily feed themselves with the help of soil, they cast it to the wind and waters when they plow land, clear-cut forests, and otherwise remove soil's anchors: plants. The result is that, over the past 150 years, Earth has lost about half of its topsoil.[7] And, "if current rates of degradation" persist, "all of the world's top soil could be gone within 60 years."[8] Meanwhile, the soil that still remains silently objects its human-wrought fate.

While their soil footing gives way, Earth's living communities sing a dirge as about 1 billion pounds of deadly pesticides rain down upon them each year in the United States alone.[9] These insecticides, fungicides, and herbicides turn out to be equal opportunity destroyers that degrade ecological diversity; decrease populations of insects, birds, amphibians, and aquatic organisms; and increase human illnesses. Earth's story increasingly strikes those with ears to hear with silence.[10]

The buzz and hum of Earth's insects have become hushed in the presence of pesticides, as these poisons threaten the survival and diversity of their populations. Meanwhile, their food sources and breeding grounds have come under attack as herbicides kill the plants on which insects

---

decomposing and sinking layers of algae cause a low-oxygen region to develop in the water. This hypoxic area, dubbed the "dead zone," causes aquatic species to suffocate and die. While the size of the Gulf of Mexico's dead zone has been decreasing over recent years from its record size of 8,776 square miles in 2017, its five-year average size remains much higher than the target of 1,900 square miles, a target set by the Mississippi River/Gulf of Mexico Watershed Nutrient Task Force for the year 2035 (NOAA, "Smaller-Than-Expected").

6. David Montgomery describes topsoil as "skin" (Montgomery, *Dirt*, 9). While plowing encourages erosion, the application of synthetic chemicals and the planting of monocultures also degrade soil's fertility and structure.

7. World Wildlife Foundation, "Soil Erosion and Degradation".

8. Arsenault, "Only 60 Years of Farming Left." This is a dire situation since it takes 1,000 years for natural processes to create three centimeters of topsoil.

9. In the United States, "[c]ommercial pesticide applicators, farmers, and homeowners apply about 1 billion pounds of pesticides annually to agricultural land, non-crop land, and urban areas" (USGS, "Pesticides in Groundwater").

10. Creation's silence might have been far greater had it not been for the timely, captivating, and illuminating work of Rachel Carson in *Silent Spring*. The environmental movement owes much to her inspiration, tenacity, research, and courage.

depend.[11] Within a few more decades, as many as 40 percent of the "world's insect species" may no longer exist.[12] Their death notice communicates to the world that industrial agriculture's devotion to pesticides destroys entire populations of vital, beneficial insects.

The silence is deafening as Earth's avian chorus also becomes muted. Bird populations around the world are declining, with "[a]t least 40% of bird species worldwide" experiencing recent population decreases.[13] And the birds themselves suffer as they endure unintended debilitating effects from neurotoxic insecticides that farmers spray on crops to kill insects.[14] Their hush and anguish are ominous.

Silence haunts the amphibian world, as agricultural forces stifle the splashing, chirping, and croaking of amphibians. Agricultural chemicals poison waters and air, permeating amphibians' delicate skin.[15] As their kind dwindles, their vital place in the food web becomes eerily vacant.

In the midst of these wordless tragedies, Earth's human communities endure the destructive effects of toxic processes, including those used in industrial agriculture. The approximately 20,000 farmworkers in the US who "suffer acute pesticide poisonings annually" call out in pain and misery.[16]

11. Because habitat loss remains a chief factor in the demise of insects, the "application of *herbicides* to cropland has had more negative impacts on both terrestrial and aquatic plants and insect biodiversity than *any other* agronomic practice" (Sánchez-Bayo and Wyckhuys, "Worldwide Decline of the Entomofauna," 20. Emphasis added).

12. While "habitat loss and conversion to intensive agriculture and urbanisation" stand as primary causes of insect decline, the use of "synthetic pesticides and fertilisers" also destroys these important communities (Sánchez-Bayo and Wyckhuys, "Worldwide Decline of the Entomofauna," 8).

13. Since 1988 when global assessments began, scientists have tabulated "a steady and continuing deterioration in the status of the world's birds" (BirdLife International, "State of the World's Birds," 20). Human activities drive the decrease in bird populations and avian diversity, and "agricultural expansion and intensification" is the foremost among these human pursuits (30).

14. BirdLife International, "State of the World's Birds," 32. In addition to poisoning common birds, modern agricultural efforts negatively affect 74 percent of the world's "threatened birds" (30).

15. Agricultural chemicals, such as "pesticides, fertilizers, or supplements given to livestock," are at fault for contaminating amphibian habitats and bodies (National Amphibian Research and Monitoring Initiative, "Stressors").

16. Moore, "Hidden Dimensions of Damage," 139. Perhaps we will listen to farmworkers' voices since they tell Earth's story in forms of communication we readily understand. It is more probable, however, that many of their voices will be silenced within the food system, since it is "15 times more likely" than not that the poisoned farmworker is a migrant, who goes without adequate rights and protections (Kimbrell, *Fatal Harvest*, 17).

Farmers and farmworkers, entangled in herbicide-dependent modes of agriculture, groan from their increased experiences of Parkinson's disease and non-Hodgkin lymphoma.[17] And these producers of food sigh under the injuries and injustices they sustain.

Earth's damning testimony against human industrial food production—its disregard for the health and vitality of entire ecosystems—has been mounting for over 70 years.[18] Some argue that "agriculture is the 'largest threat to biodiversity and ecosystem function of any single human activity.'"[19] Earth's many members have offered their evidence. But will humanity listen?[20] And, if they do, what verdict will they pronounce?

For those willing to listen, the apostle Paul offers a verdict. His verdict also comes in the form of a story, a story of God and God's creation.[21] Paul's account of creation recognizes Earth's suffering and identifies it as slavery to destruction; and he considers humans are much to blame (Rom 8:21; 5:12–21; 3:9–18). But his judgment on the matter is surprisingly merciful. For, although his gospel condemns sin and decries injustice and

---

17. Kachuri et al., "Cancer Risks in a Population-Based Study"; Wang et al., "Parkinsonism," 486; Zhang et al., "Exposure to Glyphosate-Based Herbicides," 186. Glyphosate's small but deadly part of Earth's story has begun to catch people's attention as headlines about lawsuits against Bayer–Monsanto's Roundup® rage. It is becoming more and more likely that Roundup® and its active ingredient glyphosate promote the growth of cancer in mammals, and the National Cancer Institute estimates that farmers using industrial herbicides are six times more likely to develop non-Hodgkin lymphoma than those who do not use them (Kimbrell, *Fatal Harvest*, 11).

18. Robin Wall Kimmerer insightfully notes: "The story of our relationship to the earth is written more truthfully on the land than on the page. It lasts there. The land remembers what we said and what we did" (*Braiding Sweetgrass*, 341). Thus, we would be wise to listen.

19. Jackson, *Consulting the Genius of the Place*, 186.

20. Kimmerer beautifully captures the importance of Earth's story and of humanity's willingness to attend to it. She contends: "our relationship with land cannot heal until we hear its stories" (*Braiding Sweetgrass*, 9).

21. We might also name this concept of story "tradition." In her exploration of the foundational stories/traditions that shaped Paul's theological purview—in particular, the story of Israel's exodus from Egypt, Sylvia Keesmaat defines tradition as "*comprised of those events, stories, rituals and symbols that shape the collective identity of a community, that are passed down in a community from generation to generation and that are rooted in the foundational past of that community*" (*Paul and His Story*, 17; emphasis original). In a later piece, Keesmaat describes the ways in which Paul's reconfiguration of the Jewish scriptural tradition—especially the prophetic identification of "the sexual, economic, and creational abuse of their times"—functions as a judgment "whispered" in Rom 3 against "the powers of his own day" ("Land, Idolatry, and Justice," 96).

A Convergence of Stories

violence (Rom 8:3; 3:9–18), it nevertheless announces liberation to the whole creation. Paul's gospel announces God's world-transforming work of justification and *zōopoiēsis*, God's "making right" and "making alive." In and through Jesus Christ and the Spirit, God liberates people from their slavery to sin and death and liberates nonhuman creation from its slavery to destruction (5:12–21; 8:21). With the God who makes right and makes alive, hope therefore remains.

Hope not only remains but powerfully surges forth because the Creator God is on a mission to make wrongs right and to make the dying alive (5:6–9; 8:11).[22] While many Christians view God's work of making right—more commonly called "justification"—as the obvious and primary facet of salvation, God's project of "making alive"—endowing plants with vitality, creatures with life, and humans with resurrection life—figures prominently in Scripture as well. From Genesis through Revelation, the Christian Scriptures trace a story of creation, which is a story of God-given life.[23] Some interpreters understand Scripture's story to follow a plotline of *creation–fall–redemption–consummation*.[24] Yet, Paul's portrait in Rom 8:19–22 would suggest instead a plot of *creation–subjection–liberation–glorification*.[25] This storyline indicates that despite current forms of subjection and slavery in the world, liberation and glorification hover over the present and beckon all creation graciously into the future. This future glorification—emanating from God's own vivifying glory—will be marked by life.

Within Paul's plotline, we find ourselves in the midst of subjection. The persistence of subjection—a subjection Jesus Christ has nevertheless curtailed and ultimately alleviated—mirrors the current story told by both scientists and Earth's creatures. It is a story of deterioration, destruction, and extinction. The current moment contradicts the idyllic past narrated in Gen 1 as well as the glorious future envisioned in Rom 8:21. Earth's—or, using

---

22. Hope also rises out of the resilience and vitality that God instilled in the creation and its living members.

23. By "Christian Scriptures" I refer to the contents of both the Tanakh (called the Old Testament by many Christians) and the New Testament. My reading of Romans through the lens of Paul's Scriptures, the Tanakh, owes much to the exemplary work of Richard Hays, especially his *Echoes of Scripture* and *The Faith of Jesus Christ*.

24. See discussion in Middleton, *New Heaven and a New Earth*, 38.

25. I am grateful for and indebted to David Horrell, Cherryl Hunt, and Christopher Southgate for convincingly explaining that Paul sketches a basic narrative about creation in Rom 8:19–22. Their insights inspire my interpretation of this important passage (*Greening Paul*).

Creation's Slavery and Liberation

Paul's terminology, creation's—present chapter details a time of frustrated attempts at flourishing and destructive forms of slavery (8:20–21).[26] It illustrates for us that human ingenuity and action often, though not always, resist God's work of creational liberation and flourishing. We find this is especially the case since, today, creation's food base is under assault. Human agricultural endeavors inordinately destroy God's creational system in which plants—rooted in healthy soils—liberally grow according to their kind and bear fruit for their kind's future and for their animal kins' nourishment. In this moment, then, creation appears cursed, subjected, enslaved.

Creation's Slavery and Liberation attempts to elucidate these stories of human and nonhuman creation by retracing relevant passages in Paul's Scriptures, the Tanakh (ch. 1);[27] critically evaluating Roman imperial claims and practices pertaining to nature and the growing of wheat (ch. 2); elucidating God's work of making right and making alive proclaimed in Paul's letter to Rome (ch. 3), examining in detail creation's story of slavery (ch. 4) and liberation (ch. 5) in Rom 8:19–22; describing the destructive impacts of industrial wheat agriculture in the US Great Plains (ch. 6); offering signals of hope and liberation found in regenerative forms of agriculture (ch. 7); and, in the conclusion, suggesting how the Pauline story of creation reconfigures our identities, purposes, and practices so that Christians might more fully participate in God's work of liberation here and now.[28] By putting relevant

---

26. In chapter 4.1, I explain that Paul refers to nonhuman creation with the term κτίσις in Rom 8:19–22. Scientists use the term "E/earth" to refer to living and nonliving members of planet Earth, sometimes with an emphasis on nonhuman members. The Tanakh often employs the word "land" to refer to living and nonliving members of a region (especially the Levant), sometimes with a focus on nonhuman members and other times inclusive of human members. Historians of Rome and its rule typically use the word "nature" to refer to living and nonliving things, sometimes including humanity and sometimes not. Since there is significant overlap and inherent ambiguity involved in the terms Earth, creation, land, and nature, I use them somewhat interchangeably. However, when discussing Scripture, I typically use land or creation; when examining Roman history, I use nature; and when considering science, I often use Earth, land, ecosphere, or ecosystem.

27. The Tanakh includes three main parts: the Torah, or instruction, consists of Genesis through Deuteronomy; the Nevi'im, or prophets, consists of Joshua through 2 Kings as well as the so-called major and minor prophetic books (except Daniel); and the Ketuvim, or writings, includes a variety of other books such as Psalms, Proverbs, Ecclesiastes, and Daniel. I am choosing to use "Tanakh" to refer to the Hebrew Bible and its Greek and English translations rather than "Old Testament." My exegetical work, especially in chapter 1, draws heavily upon the Greek translations of the Tanakh since Paul seems to have made significant, if not primary, use of the Greek translations for his letter writing.

28. My focus on a Pauline narrative grows out of my education at Duke Divinity School and my work with Richard Hays (see Hays, *Faith of Jesus Christ*) and Douglas Campbell

A Convergence of Stories

religious, ecological, and political stories into conversation with one another at the place where they all meet—our food,[29] we may begin to see the ways in which they occasionally align and conflict. The process reveals a convergence of stories that discloses creation's slavery to destruction.

What is more, by putting these diverse streams of thought into conversation, we better perceive the ways in which our stories about creation/Earth affect our relationships with the human and nonhuman creation. This is because stories—whether they are told by scientists,[30] biblical prophets, imperial regimes, apostles, disciples, or modern food industries—lay claim to the past, advance a particular rendering of the present, and pronounce a likely future. Cosmologies, or stories providing accounts of the cosmos, "are a source of identity and orientation to the world. They tell us who we are."[31] In so doing, stories highlight what is important; they teach us to discern between good and bad; and they instill values and visions and even encourage actions. Because stories shape our realities, activate our impulses, and inform our actions, this book evaluates and elucidates ancient and modern stories with the hope they will move us toward *life-supporting* behaviors.[32]

(see Campbell, *Quest for Paul's Gospel*). More specifically, my interest in the narrative elements of Rom 8:19–22 rises out of the model set forth by David Horrell, Cherryl Hunt, and Christopher Southgate (*Greening Paul*, 49–59).

29. For an engaging theological illustration of this nexus, see Wirzba, *Food and Faith*.

30. By no means do I mean to imply here that all scientists will tell the same "story." Chapter 6 makes plain that scientists disagree, for instance, on how to construe the story of the herbicide glyphosate.

31. Kimmerer, *Braiding Sweetgrass*, 7. In comparing and contrasting the origin stories of the native peoples of the Great Lakes region and of the Judeo-Christian people who confiscated their land, she recognizes a clear distinction between the stories' ethical and relational import. "On one side of the world were people whose relationship with the living world was shaped by Skywoman, who created a garden for the well-being of all. On the other side was another woman with a garden and a tree. But for tasting its fruit, she was banished from the garden and the gates clanged shut behind her. That mother of men was made to wander in the wilderness and earn her bread by the sweat of her brow, not by filling her mouth with the sweet juicy fruit that bend the branches low. In order to eat, she was instructed to subdue the wilderness into which she was cast" (6–7). Her interpretation of Eve's story is a valid and prominent one. Yet, it is the contention of this book that Gen 1–3 along with other passages may be understood in more ecologically beneficial ways (see 1.1–2).

32. I interpret the Bible ethically by placing a strong emphasis on what Richard Hays calls a "metaphorical embodiment of narrative paradigms." This approach understands "the Bible as a *story* that narrates God's gracious action for the reconciliation of the world" (Hays, "Mapping the Field," 15). In this mode of ethical interpretation, interpreters discern a narrative in the Bible and allow it to establish a "symbolic world in which we

Creation's Slavery and Liberation

Although there are many ways in which we derive ethics from our interpretations of the Bible, science, history, etc., the approach taken here is to begin with the overarching biblical narrative of *creation–subjection–liberation–glorification* and, then, to compare and contrast human actions and perspectives with this narrative trajectory. When human actions and perspectives align with this scriptural/theological narrative by promoting God's work of liberation and glorification (or, in comparable words, justification and *zōopoiēsis*), they are deemed "ethical," "just," and/or "life-supporting." In contrast, when human actions and perspectives counter the theological trajectory of liberation and glorification, they are considered less ethical or unethical.[33]

While my interpretive gaze looks first and foremost through a scriptural/theological lens, it nevertheless gains greater focus and accuracy (at least for ecological purposes) as it looks through lenses shaped by ecological and biological sciences.[34] We might say that I read Scripture through at

---

are to find our orientation and identity" (16). The Bible consequently exercises formative power over readers for their transformation (16). Since the particular symbolic world that the reader sees at work in a passage affects the theological and ethical outcome of the interpretation, the entire process is admittedly fraught with ambiguity. I therefore approach the hermeneutical task with humility and *attempt* to understand and represent the perspectives of the biblical book's author(s) and intended readers in relation to their historical, political, and ecological contexts as much as possible. By interpreting the biblical texts in this way, I try to grasp the authors' understandings of God's work in the world and their expectations for human relationships with God, one another, and the rest of creation. Thus, my interpretive project tends to be descriptive and constructive more often than deconstructive. Among ecological interpreters of the Bible, then, my approach falls into the category of "readings of recovery" more than anything else. According to Horrell, Hunt, and Southgate, this method engages in "Rescuing the Bible from Misinterpretation and Recovering its Ecological Wisdom" (*Greening Paul*, 14). Even as I attempt to understand a biblical writer's theological vision and ethical impulse, I do not think Christians today must adopt those visions and impulses uncritically. Instead, we employ our reason in assessing our experiences with the divine and our histories, theologies, ecclesial traditions, and scientific studies to help us excavate and dismiss those elements encountered in Scripture that arise from unhealthy, unloving, or otherwise destructive beliefs and practices. When such beliefs and practices do not align (as best as we can ascertain) with the purposes of God's love, fidelity, vitality, relationality, etc., we do our best as corporate followers of Christ to discern a better, more God-honoring way forward.

33. There are ranges in ethical quality, from bad to better to best. "Best" is ideal but is not always feasible under systemic constraints. In such cases, I consider it more advisable to shoot for "better" than to stick with "bad."

34. This is the case with many ecological interpretations of the Bible. Eco-ethical interpretations of the Bible integrate—even if implicitly—insights from the ecological sciences, making use of modern scientific experiences of ecosystems and their

A Convergence of Stories

least two lenses simultaneously. The first and primary lens brings into focus Scripture's emphasis on the God who faithfully makes things right and alive in the world. The secondary lens—shaped by scientists like Aldo Leopold, John Muir, Rachel Carson, and Wes Jackson—reveals the ways in which ecosystems work interdependently.[35] This ecological lens, then, sharpens my/our perception of the relationships binding together "organisms and their environment"—their earth home.[36] In overlapping the scriptural and ecological lenses, we are enabled to perceive a convergence of Scripture's story of creation and science's story of Earth. They both reveal the importance of nonhuman vitality and health.[37]

Because the health and vitality of entire ecosystems is so important, ecology brings with it ethical mores, or rules for "home." Ecology, therefore, empowers our discernment between right and wrong. Aldo Leopold contends, "A thing is right when it tends to preserve the integrity,

---

understandings of ecosystem health and activities. A prominent ecological approach to biblical interpretation is manifested in The Earth Bible project, which blends ecological perspectives with religious and ethical concerns. Ernst Conradie explains that The Earth Bible project incorporates six interpretive principles: (1) "The universe, Earth and all its components have intrinsic worth/value"; (2) "Earth is a community of interconnected living things that are mutually dependent on each other for life and survival"; (3) "Earth is a subject capable of raising its voice in celebration and against injustice"; (4) "The universe, Earth and all its components, are part of a dynamic cosmic design within which each piece has a place in the overall goal of that design"; (5) "Earth is a balanced and diverse domain where responsible custodians can function as partners, rather than rulers, to sustain a balanced and diverse Earth community"; (6) "Earth and its components not only suffer from injustices at the hands of humans, but actively resist them in the struggle for justice" (Conradie, "Road Towards," 310). Conradie suggests that The Earth Bible principles function as a "small dogmatics" for ecological interpretations of the Bible (311). Although I do not self-consciously apply these principles to my interpretation, I certainly have been informed by them.

35. In addition to these well-known scientists, the teachers who invested in me at Cedarville University and Au Sable Institute have also shaped my perspectives. I especially thank John Silvius and Cal DeWitt for their passionate instruction during my undergraduate studies.

36. Smith, "Ecology." Ecology is essentially a science of *home*, our earth home. Inspired by the Greek term οἶκος, "home," Ernst Haekel developed the German word *oekologie* (in English, ecology) to describe the interrelationships between and among living and nonliving organic and nonorganic entities ("Ecology"). It is a "study of relationships between those who occupy a home" (Mason, "Ecology").

37. Aldo Leopold, the father of wildlife ecology, helpfully explains that "[h]ealth is the capacity of the land for self-renewal. Conservation is our effort to understand and preserve this capacity" (Leopold, *Sand County Almanac*, 185). I understand health and self-renewal as near synonyms to long-term vitality.

stability, and beauty of the biotic community. It is wrong when it tends otherwise."[38] Because the promotion of life on a grand scale—as a fundamental ethic—depends on relationships, we discover that ecological discernment simultaneously grows out of specific relationships and enhances those relationships. What Leopold considers to be "right," may otherwise be understood in terms of the common good, which "is the organic context in which each member of the community is enabled to achieve her good, which can only be done through relationship to others . . . The science of ecology speaks in terms of dynamic and systemic wholes, focusing not on creatures in isolation but on the relationships among them."[39] What is right, good, and ecologically ethical, then, grows out of and promotes the health and well-being of the whole.

In our overlap of lenses, then, we perceive the Christian Scriptures at times aligning with scientists when they stress the importance of relationality and interdependence for the well-being of the whole creation. The Scriptures often portray this relational and ethical dynamic with the term "covenant." Biblically, covenant describes the mutual responsibility and interdependence binding together God, humans, and nonhuman creation (see chapters 1 and 3). In somewhat different terms, Aldo Leopold speaks of a land ethic, which depends upon relationship. For, "[w]e can be ethical only in relation to something we can see, feel, understand, love, or otherwise have faith in."[40] "A land ethic, then, reflects the existence of an ecological conscience, and this in turn reflects a conviction of individual responsibility for the health of the land."[41] Together, the lenses shaped by the Christian Scriptures and ecologists allow our vision to converge on the importance of engaging in relationships of respect and care with the land/creation/Earth.

---

38. "Aldo Leopold"; Leopold, *Sand County Almanac*, 187.
39. Sheid, *Cosmic Common Good*, 17, 27.
40. Leopold, *Sand County Almanac*, 180.
41. Leopold, *Sand County Almanac*, 185. Leopold also explains: "An ethic, ecologically, is a limitation on freedom of action in the struggle for existence. An ethic, philosophically, is a differentiation of social from anti-social conduct. These are two definitions of one thing. The thing has its origin in the tendency of interdependent individuals or groups to evolve modes of co-operation. The ecological calls these symbioses . . . All ethics so far evolved rest upon a single premise: that the individual is a member of a community of interdependent parts . . . The land ethic simply enlarges the boundaries of the community to include soils, waters, plants, and animals, or collectively: the land" (172).

A Convergence of Stories

Because of the relational nature of the world, both Scripture and science assume that human activity necessarily affects the nonhuman creation/ecosphere. The stories of past, present, and future that science and Scripture very differently tell agree on the fact that human and nonhuman members of the earth community depend on one another and even (to some extent) determine one another's future. Of course, the primary difference between science and religion, between scientists and theologians concerns the role they claim supernatural forces play in the world. For Christians, the Creator God continues to participate in gracious, supernatural ways in the story of the universe/creation.

Consequently, the story of creation told in the Christian Scriptures is a *theological* story, a story of God engaging in relationship with the world. It is necessarily and unapologetically a confessional story. It proclaims that God was, is, and will be at work throughout creation's beautiful beginning, in the midst of its messy climax, and during its glorious denouement. It trusts God to make the wrongs of this world right and to make the dead alive. It expects God to liberate human beings from their slaveries to sin and death (Rom 5:12–21) and to liberate creation from its slavery to destruction (8:21). And it teaches God's people to be servants of righteousness and God, enabling them to reign in and for *life* (6:18, 22; 5:17). Unlike any scientific story, this theological story writes human beings into God's universal purposes of making right and making alive.

In this scriptural/theological story, all the characters have responsibilities as well as expectations. God takes care to establish the good creation as a fertile, biologically diverse, and interdependent system, and God expects human and nonhuman creation to maintain it. Humans are responsible for employing their minds and bodies and exercising their volitions in ways that support the long-term flourishing of the entire system even as they expect God's gracious assistance and creation's resilient cooperation. The nonhuman creation is responsible for making everyday life possible—the processes of respiration, nutrition, decomposition, recycling. And its expectations? What can the nonhuman creation, including inanimate rocks and waters, possibly expect of God and humanity? According to Paul, it expects a lot. Creation's "eager expectation" is for God to reveal the fully liberated and glorified children of God (8:19, 21)! It expects that *humanity's* liberation into glory will bring an end to *its* slavery to destruction. In other words, nonhuman creation expects humanity to live in line with God's work of liberation and life.

Although an ecological account of the world would render the characters, responsibilities, and expectations differently, certain ecological thinkers nevertheless maintain that nature expects certain things of its living communities. For example, an agrarian would emphasize the expectations of creation, or more precisely, the land. The "land" in this case encapsulates an entire terrestrial ecosystem that features specific soil types, weather conditions, plant varieties, and animal inhabitants. Its expectations flow out of and depend upon these specific features. The land expects all its inhabitants to live within the constraints of their home ecosystem, to live sustainably, to pursue long-term stability.[42] In other words, our ecosystem homes *order* (or, according to ecologists, *should order*) our creaturely lives and relationships.

As we order our lives within (and too often beyond) the contraints of our ecosystem homes we necessarily engage in forms of political activity. In a broad sense, political activity—or, politics—"refers to the mechanisms by which a polity orders the lives of its members."[43] In other words, a group of people—called a polity—works together to order their common lives in a common space, and they do this by various means and mechanisms. One such mechanism employs storytelling, in which narratives of the past, present, and future establish a polity's shared identity and narrates its relationships with the nonhuman world. The stories by which a polity describes its members' relationships with their home ecosystem(s) and how they follow the ordering of that ecosystem (or not) powerfully shape members' attitudes and actions.

We may recognize, therefore, that Scripture's stories about creation and at least some of ecology's stories about nature are politically interested stories. They not only tell a people/polity about its past, present, and future but also lay claim to how those people ought to conduct themselves in relation to one another and their environments.[44] Scripture and the sciences offer people (admittedly different) accounts of reality that, if heeded, function politically to order their lives in the world. In light of these political

---

42. Jackson, Berry, and Colman, *Meeting the Expectations of the Land*.

43. This is the understanding of politics that Christian political ethicist, Bradley B. Burroughs, works with in *Christianity, Politics, and the Predicament of Evil*. Bradley B. Burroughs, conversation with author, Winston-Salem, NC, November 4, 2021.

44. Human ecologist, Garret Hardin, portrays some of the ways in which the science of ecology—and, more particularly, human ecology which studies the ways societies live in their natural environments—is political in nature. Human ecology is especially political when it points out the ways in which human societies exceed the carrying capacity of their home ecosystems. Hardin, "Human Ecology."

implications, we discover the need for a third lens to be added to our hermeneutical glasses: the lens of politics.

As we apply this third, political lens to our reading of Romans, it brings into focus the wider socio-political context in which and to which Paul wrote. Some interpreters, however, question the extent to which Paul wrote his letters with specific political factors in view. At the risk of oversimplification, we may conceptualize the interpretive landscape as configured in relation to at least three sets of questions:[45] (1) How political or apolitical was Paul's message and practice? (2) If politically aligned, was Paul overtly and categorically anti-imperial; specifically anti-*Roman*-imperial or anti-*Jewish*-imperial; or politically inclined in some other direction? (3) To what extent did Paul write primarily with a view towards instantiating and/or critiquing Jewish perspectives and practices, on the one hand, or Roman ones, on the other hand; or, did he address both in his letters? Each of these questions can be answered along a continuum, creating a complex, multi-dimensional interpretive landscape.

In order to situate my approach in this landscape, it is helpful to consider the work of two scholars, John Barclay and Neil Elliott, with whom I share commonalities and differences.[46] While attending to Paul's political context, Barclay tends to emphasize Paul's Jewish interpretive horizon much more than a Roman one. In this I find I am with good company. However, he also often refrains from interpreting the Pauline epistles as purposely addressing claims and practices of the Roman Empire.[47] He con-

---

45. Here, I draw upon Neil Elliott's helpful map of political interpretations of Paul in his "Paul and the Politics of Empire." Another helpful guide to the field is Davina Lopez's "Roman Imperial Culture." She notes that scholars examine how New Testament "texts potentially model a 'pro-imperial' or 'anti-imperial' stance, reflecting a modern concern about the intersection of politics, religion, and theology as well as an inclination to 're-claim' biblical texts and traditions for politically liberal and progressive religious projects" (260). Many such scholars consider "whether early Christians may have performed in ways that suggest either accomodation or resistance to the Roman Empire" (260).

46. This is not a holistic overview of their significant contributions. Rather, I draw primarily from their own self-conscious discussions of the interpretive landscape: Barclay, "Why the Roman Empire" and Elliott, *Arrogance of the Nations*. I could also include Robert Jewett's work in this analysis. My interpretation often aligns with his *Romans* and "The Corruption and Redemption of Creation." However, unlike Jewett, I do not presuppose Paul knew imperial rhetoric about nature's restoration or that he recognized imperial forms of nature's degradation (Jewett, "Corruption and Redemption of Creation," 32, 37). Instead, I attempt to provide supporting evidence for these inferences.

47. Barclay asserts Paul did not attack "the Roman empire and/or the imperial cult as a particular target of his theological polemics" (Barclay, "Why the Roman Empire,"

tends that, according to Paul, the Roman Empire was not a primary actor in history; instead, other, more fundamental powers inspired and mobilized it. In Pauline terms those powers were "Sin, Death and the Flesh."[48] With this general perspective I agree, but I often describe the anti-God powers or influences as slavery to sin, death, and destruction (Rom 5–6; 8:21). In Barclay's view, the primary anti-God actors of the old age—Sin, Death, and the Flesh—attempt to coopt every social and political body, whether Greek, Roman, Jewish, or other.[49] Accordingly, Paul's account of reality goes behind and beneath all political systems so that he did not need to—and, as Barclay implies, Paul deliberately chose not to—mention the powers' manifestations in the Roman Empire.[50] In keeping with Paul's supposed approach, then, Barclay resists interpreting Paul's letters as discourses intentionally critiquing and countering the imperium.[51] Practically, Barclay's interpretation means Paul implicitly encouraged the Christian communities throughout the Mediterranean region neither uncritically to oppose nor naïvely to align themselves with the governments of the world, but he did this by instructing them to discern, oppose, and resist the powers of Sin, Death, and the Flesh (rather than the power and impulses of the imperial regime itself).[52]

---

363). Instead, Paul's writings actually ignore (and thus, perhaps, implicitly subvert) the Roman Empire by "relegat[ing] it to the rank of a dependent and derivative entity, denied a distinguishable name or significant role in the story of the world" (383–84). While I agree Paul did not explicitly name imperial events and figures, he did employ politically poignant terms in ways that pushed against certain values and tactics of the empire. For example, I understand Paul's reconfiguration of weakness and strength and shame and honor to be clear instances of transformative ministry that contradicted imperial modes of being and doing (Jewett, *Romans*, 46–59; Elliott, *Arrogance of the Nations*, 51).

48. Barclay, "Why the Roman Empire," 384.

49. Barclay, "Why the Roman Empire," 384–86.

50. Barclay, "Why the Roman Empire," 384–87.

51. Nevertheless, for Barclay, this does not mean that Paul was "apolitical"; such a conclusion would entail viewing his theology and practice as "privatised, confined to the level of individual piety" or as "spiritualised, detached from the social and political realities of everyday life" (Barclay, "Why the Roman Empire," 385). Paul cannot be deemed apolitical because, according to Barclay, Paul views "the Lordship of Christ" as "destined to operate in every sphere of existence (Phil 2.11)" so that "the Pauline gospel penetrates every dimension of life, including what we label 'political;'" and, at the same time, Barclay insists that Paul's gospel "declines to separate the political from the personal, the state-power of Sin from the interpersonal-power of Sin" (387).

52. Barclay explains: Paul's "stance towards the Roman empire is neither simple opposition nor obedience: it is a field of human reality criss-crossed and contested (like all

A Convergence of Stories

With less hesitation than Barclay, Elliott reads Paul as indirectly and subtly critiquing the Roman Empire in the idiom of his Jewish heritage that was filtered through his experience of Messiah Jesus. Elliott contends (and I concur), "[t]he rhetoric of Romans shows that Paul participated in a cultural transcript, drawing on the repertoire of Judean Scripture and apocalyptic writings, that was inescapably in conflict with the empire's absolutizing claims on allegiance."[53] Where Paul, in his letter to divided congregations in Rome, employed language and concepts that overlapped with "imperial propaganda," Elliott perceives these "invocations and allusions as evidence that the situation in the Roman assemblies was shaped" especially by "*perceptions* and *themes* in the broader ideology and culture of the Augustan and post-Augustan age."[54] In other words, problematic thinking and acting among Rome's Jesus followers arose not simply on account of different interpretations of the Tanakh and the theologies it inspired; they also resulted on account of and in relation to Roman imperial prejudices and practices.[55] Nevertheless, "[t]he empire as such is never [Paul's] direct target: his goal is to lay a claim on the allegiance of his listeners with which the rival claims of empire inevitably interfered."[56] While Paul's messianic claim countered Roman imperial claims, Elliott admits that Paul himself ministered and wrote in ways that perpetuated (consciously or not) some imperialist assumptions about human society and

---

others) by the opposing forces of Flesh and Spirit, and it is subject to powers far greater than itself in the battle created by the gospel" (Barclay, "Why the Roman Empire," 386). Paul's political theology, as it is portrayed by Barclay, implies that Jesus's followers had to exercise discernment so that they might recognize those ways in which people and societal institutions either followed the way of God's New Creation in Christ or resisted it (383–84). With an emphasis on discernment, Paul instructed Christians to resist conformation to any political regime guided by the powers of Sin, Death, and the Flesh, and instead have their minds, practices, and allegiances transformed by God's New Creation.

53. Elliott, *Arrogance of the Nations*, 12. Elliott draws upon the work of James C. Scott, *Domination and the Arts of Resistance* to explain Paul's subtlety.

54. Elliott, *Arrogance of the Nations*, 14. Elliott provides logical warrant for placing Paul's letter in conversation with imperial messages by applying Richard Hays's rubric for ascertaining the likelihood of intertextual echoes (43).

55. Elliott notes, "I read the letter not as a Christian critique of Judaism, or a defense of Gentile Christianity, but as a Judean critique of an incipient non-Judean Christianity in which the pressures of imperial ideology were a decisive factor" (Elliott, *Arrogance of the Nations*, 15).

56. Elliott, *Arrogance of the Nations*, 15.

leadership, especially in his insistence that Christ is Lord and the nations ought to pledge allegiance to him.[57]

When I place myself in this interpretive landscape, I must insist that Paul, as a Jewish follower of the Jewish man Jesus, wrote from a theological position within Judaism even as he navigated the theological, political, and ecological terrain of the Roman Empire. While sharing the gospel of Jesus Christ in synagogues and market squares with Jews and people of many nations, he necessarily encountered, considered, and even confronted Roman (and other) beliefs and practices that did not align with his understanding of God's justifying, life-giving, and liberative work in the world. The people he taught, organized, and pastored, in turn, existed at the nexus of these dynamic influences. He thus wrote for people immersed not only in the Scriptures but also in the imperial milieu, both of which held distinct expectations for those within their spheres. While I agree with Barclay's claim that Paul most explicitly critiqued the anti-God powers at work in the world and subsumed the Roman Empire under those powers, I take my interpretation a step further. Like Elliott, I understand Paul to be undermining and supplanting *particular* expressions of these anti-God distortions as they manifested themselves in and through Roman imperial practices and ideologies. This is because these distortions were destructive to God's people but could take on the appearance of seeming natural or inevitable. They, therefore, needed to be identified and resisted. Thus, when Paul employs a phrase or term that not only carries Jewish theological meaning but also overlaps with imperial rhetoric,[58] I am inclined to view his words as deliberately reinterpreting the concept in light of the gospel of Jesus Christ and, thereby, unveiling, resisting, or critiquing destructive imperial realities. At the same time, like both authors, I do not perceive Paul attempting to take down the imperium, for he adamantly believed the returning Son of God would fully and finally establish God's kingdom.[59]

---

57. Elliott, *Arrogance of the Nations*, 15, 18, 45–47. He asserts: Paul's "scenario of the nations turning in faithful obedience to Israel's Messiah was a peculiarly Israelite vision, informed by Israel's scriptures. Those scriptures explicitly identified the Messiah as the one 'who rises to rule the nations' (Isa 11:10), an irreducibly political phrase that Paul quotes at the climax of the chain of scriptures in Rom 15:7–13" (46).

58. All Paul's language simultaneously existed within and carried meaning in Jewish as well as Greco-Roman cultural spheres, but certain phrases held special weight because of their use in imperial proclamations. For example, son of g/God, gospel, and visitation (*parousia*).

59. For an illuminating discussion, see Elliott, *Arrogance of the Nations*, 50–57. I agree with Elliott that Paul appears to support "empire," specifically an empire that is

A Convergence of Stories

Assuming such convergences between Scripture/theology and imperial polity exist in Paul's epistle to Rome, I deliberately examine first-century imperial sources, history, and practices in chapter 2. I rely on the careful work of classicists to describe and interpret literary and material artifacts—such as coins, inscriptions, and imagery—and on environmental historians to understand ecological realities of Paul's era. Through these investigations, I notice how sin, death, and destruction manifested themselves in specific ways in the Roman Empire.[60] Taking this investigation a step further, I then compare and contrast imperial realities with Paul's statements in Romans in chapters 3–5. I first establish the likelihood that Paul would have been privy to imperial propaganda and practice before I interpret his letter as critiquing it (see 3.1). When the evidence suggests Paul had opportunities to encounter imperial rhetoric *and* when that rhetoric stands at cross purposes with specific statements Paul wrote, I intentionally consider how Paul and his letter critiqued imperial conceptualities. I feel this deliberate process is especially important when considering the topic of imperial environmental degradation since this particular concern is relatively new to biblical studies and depends, in part, on non-literary forms of evidence. Through this process, I find good reason to believe Paul wrote with the imperial horizon in view when he discusses creation's condition in Rom 8:19–22.

We may see this complex interpretive dynamic at work most obviously when we encounter Paul's mention of the "sons of God" in 8:19. Since "sons of God" not only interfaces with Jewish beliefs about Israel's leadership (e.g., 2 Sam 7:14; Ps 2:7) but also with Roman imperial claims about the emperors, I interpret Paul's meaning as multifaceted. His assertions

---

under the leadership of Jesus Christ, who rules over the nations as the root of Jesse, the Lord (Rom 15:12). Yet, I would also say, Paul's conception of empire differs in interesting ways from the empires of human history. For example, Paul believes Lord Jesus's siblings will share in his glory and inheritance and even, to some extent, reign in life (Rom 8:17; 5:17). Moreover, Jesus gains his position of leadership, power, authority, and dominion by way of self-giving and service (15:3, 8–9; Phil 2:5–11). Might these be hints of a more democratized form of empire, then?

60. Barclay too acknowledges the importance for readers today to learn about the political matrices in which Paul lived and ministered. He contends, "we should learn from classical scholars that the imperial cult was extremely important for most of Paul's contemporaries, in festivals, games, statues, coins, temples, and calendrical structures, even though, also under instruction from the classicists, I would want to give this picture a lot of nuance, expecting different kinds of imperial cult, in different places, at different times, with different effects, at different social levels" (Barclay, "Why the Roman Empire," 2).

about who the "sons of God" are and what they experience and even effect appears to me to contradict imperial rhetoric purposely. In other words, the imperial narrative claiming Augustus and Nero (in particular) had restored nature and refreshed the Golden Age was clearly false, since—according to Paul—nonhuman creation continues to suffer frustration and destruction (Rom 8:20–21). Moreover, rather than looking to the imperial sons of gods, creation still eagerly awaits the revelation of the glorified sons of God—Jesus's siblings from among the Jews and the nations—precisely because, at *that* point in the *future* all creation would experience liberation (8:19, 21). Even though, on its surface, the Roman Empire's account of its relationships with nature—in particular, that the imperial sons of gods had restored nature's fertility and abundance—may appear positive and directed towards life, Paul's version of creation's story scratches below the gilded surface. His words direct hearers to observe creation's actual condition and to resist the ways in which imperial activities perpetuated slavery to sin, death, and destruction. The letter's addressees, consequently, are trained to notice how imperial practices and proclamations resist God's justifying and life-restoring work in the world. Thus, Paul—on a mission to prompt the obedience of the nations (1:5; 15:18)—empowered Jesus's followers in Rome to discern the concrete ways in which individuals and polities succumbed to and perpetuated humanity's slavery to sin and death and creation's slavery to destruction (5–6; 8:19–21; 12:2).

It is precisely for this goal of discernment, I would contend, that readers today need to include in their purview the *particular* political (and ecological) spheres in which Paul ministered and to which he wrote. Because we are not now immersed in a Roman imperial context, we need to learn about this context deliberately. And as we perceive the practices and perspectives of the Roman Empire during Paul's day, we may discern how Paul's message censures any polities influenced by sin, death, and destruction in the first century *and* beyond. Thus, a political reading of Paul assists us in sharpening our vision so that we might conceive how his letter to the Romans addresses twenty-first-century socio-political and ecological contexts.

A political hermeneutical lens, then, assists us in perceiving how—nearly two thousand years ago—the nascent rule of Messiah Jesus over the nations created local polities (i.e., churches) that interfaced with other polities surrounding them. Because all these polities concerned themselves with ordering their members' lives, they employed various means to shape their members' attitudes and actions, both of which necessarily affected

A Convergence of Stories

the nonhuman creation. Just as the Roman Empire and its local manifestations employed imperial stories, actions, and values to shape its members' lives, Paul too offers church members messianic stories, actions, and values for their instruction. For Paul, this process of shaping conforms people to the image of Messiah Jesus himself (8:29; Phil 2:1–11) and strengthens God's people to resist the influential pressures of "the world" (Rom 12:2). To resist effectively, God's people must employ their minds to distinguish God's will from the enslaving forces of sin, death, and destruction as these are variously manifested in any and every political body (12:2). Paul's messianically inspired formation, therefore, conflicts occasionally with imperial attempts of formation.[61]

By cautiously employing a political lens in our reading of Romans, we may perceive some of the tangible, concrete ways in which the *ecclesia* in Rome not only had to navigate *ecclesial* political formation but also *imperial* Roman formation. Such a hermeneutic assumes that Paul perceived, interpreted, and subtly addressed the complex political landscape of the Roman Empire not only because that empire had a vested interest in shaping people's lives but also because it, at times, promoted the values of sin and death in contradistinction to the values of God's liberative work in Christ manifested in life under the guidance of the Spirit.

With the use of scriptural/theological, ecological, and political hermeneutical lenses, this book attempts to describe several different, overlapping stories and bring them into conversation with one another—stories of creation in the Tanakh and Romans; stories of nature, religion, and empire in early imperial Rome; and stories of people and land in the industrialized US Midwest. In so doing, I believe we might more accurately grasp the truths and possible shortcomings of each, and we may begin to see more clearly the path(s) toward liberation that God intends for all. It is, of course, impossible for us to consider all these stories exhaustively, and I will inevitably leave out information or (unintentionally) oversimplify complex topics that specialists might find aggravating.[62] Yet, I press bravely forward

---

61. While I acknowledge the likelihood of this conflict, I would not categorize Paul's ecclesial formation as radically subversive. See my discussion of Rom 13 in 3.2.4.

62. My interdisciplinary work attempts to mimic what human ecologists do as they analyze and describe the ways in which people groups live in their natural environments. Garret Hardin indicates that such work depends on collaboration among scholars in different disciplines and is necessarily interdisciplinary and synthetic. But he warns the human ecologist: "this approach seldom has a happy outcome. Great though the personal risks may be, it is the individual who must carry out the work of synthesis. Individuals

in the hope that some illumination might be gained through the endeavor. In order to facilitate the expansiveness of this interdisciplinary project, I confine much of my focus to Paul's epistle to Rome, especially 8:19–22, and a few of the Scriptures that likely informed his perspectives there. I also narrow my gaze to view primarily the reigns of Augustus and Nero and their management of the North African grain trade in the effort to see the ways in which their political and ecological stories unfolded. Finally, I also confine the political and ecological stories I tell about our contemporary ecological moment by focusing on wheat agriculture in the US Great Plains.

The first chapter examines the ways in which Paul's scriptural heritage (the Tanakh) portrays human beings as standing in interdependent solidarity with the whole creation and as those commissioned to nurture creation's flourishing. The first section interprets the creation accounts of Gen 1–2, illustrating how their portraits of God's relationship with creation define human "dominion" (or, better, "servant leadership") and establish boundaries for humanity's proper relationship with nonhuman creation. Section two traces stories of human sin and increasing violence in Gen 3–6; God's covenants of healing and blessing made with Abram and Israel in Genesis; and God's commitment to life and liberation in Exodus and consequent instructions for liturgical intercession and life-supporting living in Exodus, Leviticus, and Deuteronomy. Ps 72 and the prophets Amos, Ezekiel, and Isaiah figure prominently in section three as those who called God's people to account for their unjust and destructive ways and meanwhile promised restoration and creational peace and flourishing in what may be called the New Creation.[63] The chapter concludes in section four by proposing six eco-theological principles that rise out of the reviewed passages and, in all likelihood, informed the apostle Paul.

Because Paul and those in Rome to whom he wrote not only knew the Scriptures but also would have regularly encountered an imperial gospel

---

must be prepared to make mistakes and be castigated by the narrow specialists. Every statement made by a daring synthesizer will tread on someone's toes. Controversy is unavoidable" (Hardin, "Humany Ecology," 102).

63. I rarely refer in this book to the concept of "New Creation" but instead employ Paul's terminology in Rom 8:19–22 of a liberated creation. Because this passage anticipates creation's liberation (as it enters the liberation produced by the glory of God's children, see 5.2), I understand Paul's eschatological vision as involving the restoration, rather than dissolution and re-creation, of creation. Thus, when I do write "New Creation" I refer to a restored, renewed creation rather than an entirely different and new creation. For a fine analysis of "new creation" concepts in Paul's letters and the writings undergirding them, see T. Ryan Jackson's *New Creation in Paul's Letters*.

A Convergence of Stories

announcing Rome's success at establishing peace and bringing about natural abundance, chapter 2 describes key features of this imperial story and traces the ways in which abundance in the capital depended on exploitation and destruction of people and lands elsewhere. Section one outlines common Roman beliefs about nature and humanity's relationship with nature and how these perspectives, in turn, shaped specific religious practices that Roman farmers and politicians (including the emperor) thought would ensure agriculture's success as they confronted the variable climates of the Mediterranean. As the empire's chief patrons and—at times—its principal priests, the emperors were heralded by imperial poets, coin-makers, artisans, and builders as those who renewed the Golden Age; secured abundant, reliable, and consistent supplies of food (at least for certain people); and re-established natural fertility. Because Emperors Augustus and, most especially, Nero brought the productive lands of Egypt and North Africa under their control by military might and political dominance, as section two goes on to explain, they made the imperial story of abundance more tangible and believable. Yet, even as the preparation of land in North Africa and wheat's cultivation, collection, transportation, and distribution gave the illusion of abundance, the empire's abundance depended on processes that catalyzed ecological degradation in North Africa.

With imperial accounts of nature clearly in view, chapter 3 traces the ways in which Paul and his Roman audience may have encountered imperial forms of ecological degradation. Although some biblical scholars simply assume that Paul subverts the imperial gospel in his statements about creation in Rom 8:19–22, section one offers compelling reasons from archaeology and environmental history for believing that Paul was aware of and resistant to imperial claims and practices pertaining to nature. With a strong sense of Paul's ecological context in view, section two builds upon the theological foundation laid in chapter 1 by examining the twin themes of justification and *zōopoiēsis* ("making alive") in Romans. Each of the four main sections of Paul's letter reveal that God is the one who makes wrongs right and makes the dying, dead, or not-yet-existing alive. The theological vision presented in Romans meanwhile indicates that Paul subtly critiques imperial propaganda. Because God's work in the world necessarily shapes the theological perspectives of God's people, section three reconfigures the six eco-theological principles from chapter 1 into seven principles in conversation with Romans. It then offers seven eco-ethical principles by which Jesus's followers might collaborate with God in the divine mission of making right and making alive.

The foregoing theological, political, and ecological contexts prepare us to grasp Paul's story of creation, especially its slavery and subjection, discussed in chapter 4. As a preliminary investigation, section one argues that κτίσις in Rom 8:19–22 primarily refers to nonhuman creation. Section two, then, contends that creation's slavery to destruction (8:21) refers not simply to its susceptibility to death and decay and its moral contamination by human sin but also to its experience of active forms of destruction. More broadly, creation's slavery of destruction mirrors humanity's own slavery to sin and death that came about, according to Rom 5:12–21, because of Adam's disobedience. In light of the underlying scriptural matrix of Gen 3–6, "slavery of destruction" results, in part, from human sin while creation's liberation is linked to human righteousness and glory. This chapter's third section turns back to Rom 8:20 to consider its complex depiction of creation's predicament, particularly the way in which "creation was subjected to frustration" "by the one subjecting it in hope" (8:20). These references to subjection expand the scriptural matrix found in Rom 5 to include not only Gen 3 but also Gen 1. Paul's two descriptions of creation's "subjection" point towards God's primary responsibility in placing creation under the "dominion" of humanity and to humanity's secondary culpability in exercising that power in ways that render creation's attempts at flourishing ineffective or frustrated. These exegetical claims suggest that Paul perceives human sin to have damaging effects not only on humanity but on the rest of creation as well.

On account of its subjection to frustration and slavery to destruction, creation eagerly looks forward to and expects humanity's resurrection so that it too might be liberated (Rom 8:19), as the first section of chapter 5 explains. Because distorted human "dominion" brought about distortions in creation, true liberation requires human beings to be liberated from sin and death through rectification and glorification. This, in turn, depends upon Jesus's righteous, faithful, and self-giving love and resurrection life. Creation's expectation will be met, as section two argues, when God ultimately liberates God's children from the influences of sin and the forces of death at the resurrection; consequently, creation too will experience its own form of liberation (8:21). Despite the central role that God's justification and *zōopoiēsis* of humanity plays in creation's liberation, section three emphasizes the cooperative role of nonhuman creation. In light of intertextual traditions that portray nonhuman creation as laboring and delivering forth humanity *to* God and *with* God for judgment and resurrection, I break with conventional interpretations of 8:22 by claiming Paul's image here suggests that creation cooperates with God in the miraculous work of resurrection. This chapter concludes with section four in which we confirm the seven eco-ethical principles earlier presented in chapter 3. Most especially, Paul's story of creation in Romans directs Jesus's followers to maintain creation's fertility and biodiversity so that it can flourish. Thus, Christians are to shape their daily activity and social lives in accordance with God's work of creational liberation.

With a Pauline vision of flourishing, interdependence, and mutual liberation in place, the sixth chapter evaluates the story of US industrial agriculture, especially of wheat production. Section one highlights the rhetoric of industrial agriculture, particularly its promises of abundant, safe, and affordable food. During the first half of the nineteenth century, the US Great Plains took the stage as the breadbasket of the Western world when farmers fulfilled their leaders' calls to expand production in every possible way. They used tractors, synthetic fertilizers, and pesticides to create an illusion of never-ending abundance. However, as section two discloses, the industrial agricultural food system exploits and degrades people and lands by the ways in which it prepares land in the Great Plains and cultivates, collects, transports, processes, and distributes wheat and wheat products. Environmental history and current scientific research, thus, reveal horrifying realities: the near decimation of Bison; the subjugation of Great Plains Tribal Peoples; soil compaction and erosion; decreases in soil fertility; hypoxic dead zones in the Gulf of Mexico; increases in the use of deadly synthetic pesticides and herbicides; consequent decreases in ecosystem and individual health; loss of native prairie grasslands and species; decreases in aquifer levels; increases in agribusiness control and profit; unjust farmer incomes and unsustainable farm viabilities; acceleration of global warming and greenhouse gas emissions; and injustices in food safety, food security, and food access. Although industrial agriculture has indeed provided necessary food for many people, it has also brought degradation and even destruction to ecosystems and people. While these deleterious effects arguably flow out of a distorted construal of human dominion that endorsed colonization, westward expansion, and unrestrained consumption in the United States, creation's story now demands that God's people find alternative, more just and life-supporting ways to grow and distribute their food.

Better farming alternatives do exist, and chapter 7 briefly describes some of the methods that safely and plentifully feed people and safeguard ecosystems. Regenerative, organic, conservation, or natural systems agriculture are different names for agricultural approaches that attempt to do as little harm to an ecosystem and even to benefit it while farmers grow food. Section one presents the central principles involved in regenerative forms of agriculture and, according to projections, suggests that its approaches can feed the world sustainably. Taking regenerative approaches to their ideal extreme, a few scientists are developing other promising alternatives to growing staple crops conventionally by breeding perennial staple crops instead, as section two explains. Since perennial crops endure drought and diseases more successfully, require less tilling, and promote greater biodiversity and soil health than annuals, they would provide humanity with alternative forms of agriculture that more closely approximate a Pauline vision of liberation for the whole creation.

With these portraits of creation's slavery and liberation in place, the conclusion reflects theologically and practically on how people might cultivate more liberative relationships with human and nonhuman creation. In particular, the conclusion focuses on how ecclesial communities might reshape their identities, practices, and purposes in ways that help them collaborate with God in the work of liberation, justification, and *zōopoiēsis*. As a central Christian practice, Eucharist provides one means by which people might remind themselves of creation's story, their true identities, and their relational obligations. Eucharist integrates people into God's story with and for the creation and, when done holistically, mobilizes them to align their lives with the creational, liberative purposes of God.

CHAPTER 1

Creation's Interrelatedness

Nonhuman, Human, and Divine Relationships in the Tanakh

THE RICH NARRATIVE ARC undergirding Paul's brief references to creation in Rom 8:19-22 might elude readers when interpreted apart from the Tanakh—an acronym for the entirety of Israel's and Paul's Scriptures: the Torah, Prophets, and Writings. The Tanakh introduces the central characters we later encounter in Paul's own writings, namely, the Creator God, Israel, the nations, and nonhuman creation. The Tanakh's narratives, instructions, prophetic pronouncements, and liturgies provide the broad outlines of a theological drama in which God establishes a good, blessed, and flourishing creation; human righteousness supports creation's flourishing or their transgression corrupts and destroys creation's flourishing; God provides restoration and liberation through actions and covenants; and God glorifies the entire creation so that it might enjoy peace and uninterrupted life. While different variations of this main storyline appear in the Tanakh, this chapter examines a small selection of the passages that likely informed Paul's own vision of creation's theological drama.

In general terms, we might summarize the Tanakh's story of creation as follows. Torah's creation accounts of Gen 1-2 reveal God as one who creates life in cooperation with the water and land, cultivating a world that is fertile, diverse, interdependent, and very good (section 1). These creation narratives display God's human creatures as those who exercise servant leadership and bear the divine image, an impression that should fundamentally shape their relationships with the rest of creation in conformity with God's nurturing ways. Yet, the stories of increasing sin and destruction in Gen 3–6 expose the ways in which humans often fail to conform to God's design and instead pursue violent and destructive paths (section 2). Despite humanity's distorted ways of being in the world, Torah's narrative of Abram and the call of Israel illustrates how God remains committed to humanity and the flourishing of the whole creation. For, God provides a covenant of blessing, instructions for liturgical intercession, and regulations in the Torah that guide God's people to embody proper relationships with God, each other, and the creation (sections 2–3). The Prophets and Writings, in turn, remind the covenant people of God's life-supporting expectations for their relationships with God, one another, and the creation, and they announce God's coming restoration of creation in the face of ongoing desecration and destruction (section 3).

Plotting these formative stories along an arc from creation to restoration, biblical interpreters commonly demarcate four key movements in the story of the world: *creation–fall–redemption–consummation*.[1] If we perceive this theological arc through a Pauline lens formed by Rom 8:19–22, however, we might rename these movements as *creation–subjection–liberation–glorification*. In this case, we find that although God made creation "good" and subjected nonhuman creation to human dominion or leadership (Gen 1; Rom 8:20), humanity's oversight went askew as humans became enslaved to sin and death (Gen 3–6; Rom 5:12–21). The creation's subjection to sinning humans—who should have nurtured and preserved creation's health and well-being—frustrated or interrupted its flourishing (Gen 1:28–30; 2:15; Rom 8:20) and led creation to be enslaved to destruction (Gen 6:11; Rom 8:21). Yet, despite these aberrations, God unswervingly committed to liberating humanity from its bondage to sin and death and to liberating creation from its bondage to destruction (Gen 6–9; Rom 8:20–21), first through the Torah and its covenants (Gen 12:1–3; Lev 25–26; Exod 20; 23; Deut 11; 28), then through the just and atoning work of the messiah (Isa 11:1–9; Ps 72; Rom 3:21–26; 5:12–21; 6:1–4; 8:1–11, 29–34). Ultimately, God will liberate the whole creation by fully and finally liberating human beings from sin and death by glorifying them and conforming them to the image of Jesus Christ, God's Son (Rom 5:1–2, 17–21 6:17–23; 8:17–18, 23, 29).[2]

1. Middleton, *New Heaven and a New Earth*, 38.
2. All too often interpreters have focused on the ways in which the biblical tradition displays God's salvation of humanity to such an extent that they lose sight of God's salvation or restoration of the nonhuman creation. Ryan T. Jackson illustrates the way in which this phenomenon plagues the study of "new creation" in Paul's letters. Scholars

Creation's Interrelatedness

Along with this plot line, three central themes weave their way through this theological story. These themes also arguably underlie Paul's perspectives on creation. The first asserts humans stand in interdependent solidarity with the whole creation. Since God created humans as one type of living being among many, but one which uniquely reflects God's image, God expects them to nurture creation's flourishing by exercising hospitable servant leadership, or "dominion" (Gen 1:26, 28).[3] The second theme claims that human injustice, unholiness, and exploitation cause creation's desecration, degradation, and even destruction (all of which, in turn, negatively affect human societies; Gen 3; 6; Deut 11; 1 Kgs 14; Jer 3; 11; Ezek 36; Isa 24; 65; Amos 8; Hos 4). On the flip side, human acts of justice, holiness, and care lead to creation's fertility, abundance, and harmony (Lev 23; 25; 26; Exod 23; Deut 20; Ps 72; Isa 11; 65; Ezek 36). Despite human sin and creation's consequent deterioration, the third theme claims that the Creator God restores the health and fertility of creation; cleanses, forgives, and sanctifies God's people; and raises up a messiah to establish justice, vitality, and peace. These theological perspectives provide the complex narrative matrix for making sense of Paul's observation that creation is subjected to frustration and enslaved to destruction and for comprehending his abiding hope that God will soon liberate the creation at the coming apocalypse of God's glorified children, the siblings of Jesus the Messiah.

1.1 The Creation Accounts: Human Leadership and Care

Stories depicting creation's origin and the origin of humans, including their social structures, powerfully shape people's understandings of themselves and their relationships with each other and the rest of creation. Such cosmologies, as they may be called, existed throughout the ancient world and functioned (and continue to function) in ways that might oppress or liberate members of creation, including humans. In the context of ancient Mesopotamia, Israel established its own cosmologies that, according to certain interpretations, pointed towards the mutual flourishing of human and

---

have commonly examined either the anthropological facets or the cosmological facets of God's work of salvation, sometimes encapsulated in the phrase "new creation" (*New Creation in Paul's Letters*, 3–6). It is my goal, like Jackson, to avoid and ultimately correct such tunnel vision.

3. All English Scripture translations are from the New Revised Standard Version (NRSV) in this chapter unless otherwise noted.

nonhuman creation even as human beings were uniquely stamped with the image of God.

Ancient Near Eastern (ANE) societies, including Israel, assumed that at least certain human beings acted as images of the divine. In ancient Mesopotamia the king functioned as a priest and the image of god and, as such, was divinely appointed to rule all others.[4] Such a worldview, sometimes labeled "royal theology," also claimed that the *royal* divine image bearers could establish social peace and creational abundance when they performed their duties rightly. The opposite was true as well since "an offence in the legal realm obviously has effects in the realm of nature (drought, famine) or in the political sphere (threat of the enemy). Law, nature, and politics are only aspects of one comprehensive order of creation."[5] Ancient Near Eastern royal theology, then, assumed that creational fertility and abundance were linked to political order, and the divinely appointed ruler forged this link.

Ancient Mesopotamian creation myths meanwhile held that common human beings were created to serve the gods, by giving them shelter, food, and drink.[6] The stated purpose of humanity was to relieve the gods of agricultural work, especially of digging and maintaining irrigation systems. In the words of J. Richard Middleton, the creation myths functioned to "legitimate the social role of vast numbers of human beings as vassals of the gods and servants of the temple and the priesthood in ancient Sumer, Babylon, and Assyria, thus bolstering a sociopolitical arrangement characteristic of ancient Mesopotamian civilization for close to three thousand years."[7] These social arrangements depended upon intensive forms of agriculture, especially irrigation systems. It was the hard agricultural labor of the vast majority of human subordinates that actually made it possible for the king to achieve so-called creational abundance. Without their labor, the blessings of creation were understood to be scarce.

---

4. Middleton, *Liberating Image*, 94. For example, *Eridu Genesis*, also known as the *Sumerian Flood Story*, illustrates that the king functioned as a mediator between the world and the gods (119).

5. Schmid, "Creation, Righteousness, and Salvation," 105. Schmid refers to the Code of Hammurabi and ANE wisdom texts in support of his observation.

6. Middleton, *Liberating Image*, 151–66. Of particular relevance are the *Atrahasis Epic* 1.240–41, 337–39 and *Enuma Elish* 6.5–8, 31–38, 113–18 (Middleton, *Liberating Image*, 152–53, 65–66).

7. Middleton, *Liberating Image*, 170.

Creation's Interrelatedness

1.1.1 Genesis 1

Whereas Mesopotamian mythology proclaimed the Mesopotamian king to be the divine image bearer and all others his servants,[8] Israelite theologians resisted, subverted, and recalibrated these marginalizing messages through their Scriptures and practices. Gen 1, most likely written during the demoralizing experience of the Babylonian exile, expresses in poetic form Israel's own subversive, democratizing theology of creation. Middleton explains that "Genesis 1 . . . constitutes a genuine democratization of the ancient Near Eastern royal ideology. As *imago Dei*, then, humanity in Genesis 1 is called to be the representative and intermediary of God's power and blessing on earth."[9] So understood, this first of the canonical creation accounts commissioned *all* humans to exercise "dominion" in a world that was naturally fertile and teeming with abundance.[10]

When Gen 1 narrates the creation of humankind, it stresses their identity as divine image-bearers. On day six, immediately after the land "brings forth" and God "makes" land animals (1:24–25), God invites "*us*" to create humankind, declaring:[11]

> "Let us make humankind in our image, according to our likeness; and let them have dominion over the fish of the sea, and over the birds of the air, and over the cattle, and over all the wild animals of the earth, and over every creeping thing that creeps upon the earth." So God created humankind in his image, in the image of God he created them; male and female he created them. God

---

8. Middleton, *Liberating Image*, 186–89.

9. Middleton, *Liberating Image*, 121.

10. Instead of understanding the early narratives of Genesis as illustrating a universal and liberative message, Dora Rudo Mbuwayesango argues that the primeval history in chs. 1–11 underwrites an exclusivistic message illustrated through God's choice of Abram and his descendants (Gen 12–50) (Mbuwayesango, "'Canaanites Were in the Land,'" 84–86). Understood in this way, the book of Genesis legitimates Israel's violent and deadly occupation of the promised land as depicted in Joshua. Although I agree the biblical narrative could be read along these lines, I find the early chapters of Genesis to resist and counter these exclusivistic and nationalistic movements in the drama.

11. The "us" in "let us make humankind in our image" suggests that God addresses another entity that would participate in God's act of creating humans. Commonly, scholars identify the addressee(s) as a heavenly council (of angels or other gods). However, for contextual and historical-critical reasons, I identify the addressee as the land (which God invited to bring forth land creatures earlier on that same day of creation) (see footnote 18 for more discussion as well as Burroughs, "In the Image of God and Earth" and Burroughs, "Liberation in the Midst of Futility and Destruction," 52–60).

blessed them, and God said to them, "Be fruitful and multiply, and fill the earth and subdue it; and have dominion over the fish of the sea and over the birds of the air and over every living thing that moves upon the earth." (Gen 1:26–28)

In contrast to other ANE cosmologies, Gen 1 insists that all of humankind is impressed with God's own image. Although this passage begins by noting that humans will be made in "our" image, the stress of verse 27 on the creation of humankind in *his* image emphasizes the way in which humans uniquely bear the image of God.[12] As those who bear *God's* image, then, humans are expected to conduct themselves in ways that mirror God's own way of being.[13]

Throughout Gen 1, God's way of being is co-creative and life giving. God interacts cooperatively with land and water in the initial creation of living things. While the creation account of Gen 1 portrays the Creator God as establishing the elements of creation by a powerful word (rather than through violence or coercion as is the case in some ANE creation narratives), it also depicts God as inviting the water and land to cooperate with God in creating living things.[14] On days 4–6, God speaks to the water and land using invitational commands.[15] God invites the waters to swarm

---

12. Although the image of God has become an important theological concern in Christian thinking, Davis notes that the Tanakh refers to it only five times. She indicates that, to grasp the meaning of "image of God," the reader must attend to the depictions of God that occur throughout the Scriptures (Davis, *Scripture, Culture, and Agriculture*, 55–56).

13. Sigve Tonstad insightfully notes: "The 'image of God' confers on humans the responsibility to act toward the rest of creation according to God's character and intention" (Tonstad, *Letter to the Romans*, 191).

14. Fretheim, *God and World*, 38. Drawing on the work of Fretheim, Norman Habel portrays the cooperative dynamic between God and the land by explaining, "the life forces within Earth are activated by a word of *Elohim*. The Earth, supported by waters and the sky, brings forth flora and fauna as living realities. Earth is a subject, a character who participates with *Elohim* in the creation process" (Habel, "Geophany," 45).

15. Throughout Gen 1, God speaks indirectly to various elements of nonhuman creation by means of jussives, verbs that function as polite commands or invitations. It is a matter of some debate whether the jussive verb form in Hebrew functions as an invitation or command. Terence Fretheim claims that the jussive verbs in Gen 1 depict God as creating the heavens and the earth not by command but by invitation (Fretheim, *God and World*, 42–43). However, Gordon Wenham understands the jussive verbs to be commands (Wenham, *Genesis*, 6). Nahum Sarna calls the jussive of 1:14 a "pronouncement" (Sarna, *Genesis*, 9). As a side note, the Greek translations of Gen 1 use third-person imperative verbs, a form which is unavailable in biblical Hebrew.

with aquatic creatures and invites birds to fly over the land (1:20). According to the priestly poet, God then actively creates the sea creatures and birds (1:21). The next day God invites the land to bring forth land creatures (1:24). And again the poet explains God makes terrestrial animals on the sixth day. In this collaborative portrait of the creative process, "the earth is depicted as the mediating element, implying that God endows it with generative powers that He now activates by His utterance."[16] In this complex way, God cooperates with the earth to make living creatures alive.

God's cooperation with the land arguably continues on the sixth day when God announces, "Let us make humankind in our image" (1:26). However, in the transition between verses 25 and 26, interpreters often perceive a disconnect between the preceding creation of nonhuman things and the proceeding creation of humans. This disconnect occurs primarily because 1:26 presents God as employing the first-person plural pronoun, "us," for the first time in the account. While many interpret this pronoun as referring to a heavenly or divine council with whom God confers in the creation of human beings,[17] within the context of Gen 1, the plural pronoun more naturally gestures toward the land itself as God's creative partner.[18]

As we interpret humanity's image bearing in light of Gen 1, several themes rise to the surface. First, this creation account's portrait of God as

---

16. Sarna, *Genesis*, 9.

17. Habel illustrates this perspective, stating, "The 'us' seems to refer to beings in a celestial realm that is not part of the cosmos as construed thus far in the story (von Rad 1961: 57). *Elohim* apparently moves from being a breath and voice within the cosmos to being the head of a heavenly council beyond the cosmos of the Earth story" (Habel, "Geophany," 46). For others who take "us" to refer to a divine or heavenly council, see: Fretheim, *Genesis*, 345; Fretheim, *God and World*, 42–43; Sarna, *Genesis*, 12; John Skinner, *Genesis*, 31; von Rad, *Genesis*, 58–59; Wenham, *Genesis 1–15*, 1:28.

18. The cohortative, "let us make," as spoken to the land, garners textual and contextual support in several important ways. First, since God invites the land to produce the nonhuman living things in cooperation with God (1:24), the passage already presents the land as a subject, actor, and addressee. Second, interpreting God as speaking to the land rather than to divine or angelic beings maintains the theological perspective of the Priestly tradition, of which Gen 1 is a part. Because the Priestly tradition does not elsewhere suggest that other divine or angelic beings even exist (see Wenham, *Genesis 1–15*, 1:21; von Rad, 55; Garr, *In His Own Image and Likeness*, 90–91) the assumption that Gen 1:26 addresses a heavenly/divine council contradicts priestly theology. Third, interpreting the land as God's addressee views the events on the sixth day of creation as more integrated, with God inviting the land to put forth land creatures early in the day and, then, inviting the land to collaborate with God in making human beings later that same day. For a fuller explanation of this reading, see Burroughs, "In the Image of God and Earth," forthcoming.

eliciting life from the land and water—of working with them to make them teeming with life—models for God's image bearers life-giving and life-supporting modes of relating to the rest of creation. By endowing each of the plants and animals with the ability to reproduce after their kind (1:11, 12, 22), moreover, God demonstrates the importance of fertility. The reproductive capacity of plants and animals ensures the ongoing vitality and diversity of the earth. Protecting and nurturing that capacity is of central importance to humanity's divine image bearing.

In tandem with honoring and nurturing divinely bestowed fertility, God's image bearers learn, secondly, of the fundamental importance of plants in the world. Gen 1:11–12 and 29, especially in the Hebrew and Greek texts, poignantly depict the fertile capabilities of plants as "seeding seed" and of trees as "making fruit with the seed in it."[19] Their fertility, as becomes apparent in 1:29–30, mobilizes the vitality of earth's animal and human creatures as well. Thus, plants occupy a central and critical place in God's very good creation. And, notably, plants are to be *shared*, for God tells the male and female humans and then all the animals, birds, and creeping things that the plants are gifted to them as food (1:29–30).[20] By filling the creation with abundant, diverse plants on which animate living things depend and also endowing all types of living things with the ability to reproduce,[21] God ensures creation will remain nourished, fertile, and diversified for countless generations. God's image bearers, then, best conform to their Creator as they too nurture diverse and bountiful botanical systems on which all depend.

---

19. Much more could be said about the importance of seeds. For insightful discussions, see Davis, *Scripture, Culture, and Agriculture*, 48–53; Tonstad, *Letter to the Romans*, 295–99. Tonstad eloquently states: "Seed is the ecological marvel in God's original economy of abundance, corroborating, metaphorically speaking, that the divine command 'was for life' (Rom. 7.11)" (296).

20. Some interpreters assume humans and nonhuman animals are assigned different categories of plants to eat in the first creation account. Gen 1:29 indicates God gave the seed bearing *plants* (kāl-ēʿśeb zōrēʿa zeraʿ) and fruiting trees to humans for food. But at 1:30, God gave terrestrial animals green *plants* (kāl-yereq ēʿśeb). Granted the slight difference regarding the "seed bearing" plants versus the "green" plants, a significant distinction does not separate human food from animal food. In fact, it may be that animals receive the much broader category of "green" plants, whereas humans receive a more limited selection of plants.

21. This is not to say that each individual is ensured reproductive capacity (as the narratives about infertility in the Scriptures poignantly illustrate) but that the group as a whole will have members who can reproduce.

Creation's Interrelatedness

In view of these two themes and also within this context of fertility, diversity, and cooperation, God commissions humans to exercise "dominion" as those who bear the image of the Creator God.[22] Whatever human "dominion" is, it must reflect God's cooperative relationship with creation as well as safeguard and support its ongoing fertility and diversity. The latter constraint upon human "dominion" is especially clear in light of God's commission to the water creatures to "be fruitful and multiply and fill the waters in the seas" and the birds to "multiply on the earth" (1:22).[23] Although God also commissions human beings to "fill" and "subdue"[24] the earth and "have dominion" (1:28), they must do so in ways that allow for the simultaneous multiplying of God's aquatic and avian creatures (whose multiplying is explicitly encouraged in the text). We might perceive, then,

---

22. Throughout the account, God identifies the creation as "good" (1:10, 12, 18, 21, 25) and ultimately designates the entire work of creation as "very good" (1:31). Thus, we might add "goodness" to the list of fertility, diversity, and cooperation.

23. Tonstad beautifully captures the idea of God's blessing by stating: "The compassionate God is not absent in creation or at creation. When God confers a blessing on non-human creatures in the Genesis story of creation, we see a God who cares for, and takes delight in, the well-being and flourishing of all sentient beings (Gen. 1.20-22)" (*Letter to the Romans*, 294).

24. The term "subdue," along with dominion, suggests to some that humans stand in an adversarial relationship with creation and must make it obey the human will. Habel, for example, indicates that the verb *kabash*, "subdue," elsewhere connotes "forceful subjugation, including enslavement (Jer. 34.11; Neh. 5.5), the crushing of hostile nations (2 Sam. 8.11) and the rape of a woman (Est. 7.8)" and that "[t]here is nothing gentle about the verb *kabash*" (Habel, "Geophany," 46–47). In contrast to this interpretation, Richard Bauckham suggests, "when 'land' (*'eretz*) is the object, the meaning seems more like 'to occupy' or 'to take possession' (Num. 32:22, 29; Josh. 18:1; 1 Chr. 22:18). The action, in these cases, requires defeating the enemies who previously occupied the land, but the land itself has only to be possessed. It is not itself an enemy to be forcibly subjugated" (Bauckham, *Bible and Ecology*, 16–17). Davis interprets "subdue" in the context of the Priestly tradition, of which Gen 1 is one portion. Since Leviticus insists that the land/earth is the Lord's possession and God's people must ensure its ongoing health, any form of "subduing" must be implemented accordingly (Davis, *Scripture, Culture, and Agriculture*, 59–63). To be sure, the translation of *kabash* with "subdue" (NIV, KJV, NRSV, NASB) suggests to many readers that humans are to relate to the land in ways that are domineering, if not violent. While the verb *kabash* may connote violent and oppressive forms of interaction, depending on its context, it is my understanding that its meaning in Gen 1:28 is constrained by other features in the immediate and wider context. I suggest we must intentionally resist conclusions that claim this passage underwrites human violence, exploitation, and oppression towards the rest of creation. Instead, within the wider context of Gen 1, the priestly tradition, the historical context, and the narrative arc of Scripture the verse may be interpreted as encouraging humans to inhabit the entire earth in ways that support its biodiversity and health.

that "God endows non-human creation with a bill of rights, empowering non-human beings to flourish (Gen. 1.20–22)."[25] Even the land creatures that most obviously compete with humans for food are divinely provided green plants that will help them flourish (1:30). In modern parlance, then, we might say that all God's creatures—nonhuman and human—have a basic right to food and the land and water that produce it. Gen 1 presents humans as one species among many others and expects them to live in ways that support God's commission to other creatures to multiply and fill the creation (1:22). In order for this abundant fertility and diversity to continue, therefore, humans must share (rather than hoard) creation's food supplies with all others, including land animals and birds (1:30).

While this first creation account places human beings squarely in the midst of other living creatures that are also commissioned to flourish, humans are given the unique responsibility of tending the relationships in and among creation. This responsibility has often been named "dominion,"[26] but "servant leadership" may capture the meaning of Gen 1:28 in its scriptural context more accurately.[27] For, both Judaism and Christianity portray

---

25. Tonstad, *Letter to the Romans*, 18.

26. Although the phrase in Gen 1:26, 28 is commonly translated as "dominion *over*," the preposition attending this verb "can mean 'among'" so that humanity's dominion might better be understood as "mastery among" (Davis, *Scripture, Culture, and Agriculture*, 55). Translated this way and interpreted in view of God's own way of relating to creation, we find that humanity's relationship with the rest of creation is not one of unbounded domination. It is constrained by communal ties. Ellen Davis also suggests that "the verbal phrase as a whole may denote rule that is characterized by firmness rather than harshness (see Ps. 72:8)" (55). She also explains that the verbal form for "have dominion," *r-d-h*, conjures up images of shepherding.

Richard Bauckham notes that Christian theology often interprets this dominion as stewardship. Yet, for several reasons the idea of "stewardship" is problematic. Chief among these problems is the idea that a steward is supposed to exercise control on account of his or her thoroughgoing knowledge of the realm. Yet, "[t]he whole of the modern scientific-technological project of dominating nature and exploiting its resources for the good of humanity presumed that total mastery of the Earth's natural processes was within human grasp. It exaggerated what was known and turned a blind eye to what was not" (Bauckham, *Bible and Ecology*, 4). As humans, we simply do not know enough to envision ourselves as creation's stewards. If stewardship "means that humans consider themselves to have controlling charge over the Earth, then it is indeed hubristic, consciously or not, since the facts of human knowledge and power do not measure up to such a role" (5–6).

27. After reviewing an earlier draft of my book, Sylvia Keesmaat insightfully suggested that I consider using the idea of servanthood to describe humanity's relationship with creation. This suggestion brings many themes together, so I employ the phrase "servant leadership" to capture the precise nuance of "dominion" that are depicted in the

godly, lawful "dominion" as service. Israel's kings and the messiah himself are supposed to rule in ways that serve the interests of God and the whole community (see 1 Sam 12; Isa 11). Paul presents Jesus himself as a minister or servant (Rom 15:8).[28] In this servant role, Jesus rules over the nations (15:12; Isa 11:1) and thereby establishes peace and harmony in all God's creation (Isa 11:1–9).[29] Although Jesus is the principal servant leader, Paul depicts Jesus's followers simultaneously as serving righteousness and reigning in life (Rom 5:17; 6:18). Norman Wirzba poignantly explains the ecological implications of this correlation between leadership and service, stating:

> Surely the ancient Israelite notion of royal kingship as entailing responsibility for the well-being of the ruled and Christian claims that 'Jesus is Lord,' that he is 'the image (*eikon*) of God' (2 Cor. 4:4; Col. 1:15), ought to call into question all notions of dominion as exploitation, particularly when we recognize the hallmark of Christ's lordship and mastery was his servanthood to all.[30]

This idea of servant leadership, rather than dominion, gains greater clarity in the second creation account as well as in the rest of Torah and the Prophets.[31]

By portraying humans as bearing the image of God and inhabiting an influential position of servant leadership in God's creation, the creation account of Gen 1 mirrors some elements of an ANE royal theology and,

---

Tanakh and Romans.

28. The term Paul employs to describe Jesus is διάκονος rather than δοῦλος; he identifies Jesus as a servant (rather than slave) to those who are circumcised and those who are not.

29. Wagner, "Christ," 481–82.

30. Wirzba, *Paradise of God*, 124.

31. Middleton illustrates some aspects of this message, stating, "every element of the account of human creation on the sixth day (image and rule, fertility and food) articulates a vision of the human role in the cosmos that is diametrically opposed to that of ancient Mesopotamia. In contrast to an ideology that claims that humans are created for a relationship of dependency, to meet divine need, God in Gen 1 creates for the benefit of the creature, without explicitly asking for a direct return of any kind. And humans, in God's image, I suggest, are expected to imitate this primal generosity in their own shared rule of the earth" (Middleton, *Liberating Image*, 204–5). Middleton highlights the fact that Israel's primeval history also includes a critique of human beings by portraying them as murderers and polluters of the earth (Gen 4, 6) (219–20). Moreover, he suggests that God shares power by inviting the nonhuman creation into God's creative work (287). Robert Murray also suggests that the democratization of the image of God brought with it the responsibility to exercise justice (Murray, *Cosmic Covenant*, 98–99).

as chapter 2 will describe, later Roman imperial ideologies. Chief among these elements is the assumption that human wrongdoing diminishes creation's abundance and flourishing while human right-doing supports (if not enhances) its abundance and flourishing.

Yet, even as Gen 1 shares these commonalities with ANE perspectives, Israel's counternarrative of creation identifies *all humans* as commissioned to serve creation as its leaders and as those who bear the image of the Creator God. All humans, then, are designed to reflect their Creator, who created not out of conflict and violence but out of cooperation and generosity and with attention to the vitality, flourishing, and needs of all creatures.[32] Thus, Gen 1 establishes human persons as creatures who reflect God most especially as they carry out their servant leadership in ways that promote life.

1.1.2 Genesis 2

The second creation account adds depth and color to this portrait of human beings by highlighting their organic commonality with other creatures. Meanwhile, this story includes God's explicit commission to humanity to tend the creation. According to Gen 2, God models this tangible, creative tending by forming humans and other living beings out of the soil (2:7, 19). By describing God's creation of *Adam* and every animal and bird with the same verb, "form" (*y-ṣ-r*), and identifying each as a *nefeš hyah*, "living being," the text indicates that humans and other land creatures share a common origin and identity. God's reason for creating the animals, moreover, reveals the underlying intention that the human should form close relationships with the other creatures. They are formed to be the man's partners or friends and alleviate his "aloneness" (2:18–20).[33] Strikingly, they are not depicted as competitors for limited resources since their garden home meets everyone's needs. The human's close relationship with the other creatures becomes actualized when *Adam* names them (2:19–20). Even so, although *Adam* shares a common creatureliness with the animals, he nevertheless stands distinct from them since YHWH uniquely places in *Adam's* nostrils "the breath of life" (2:7).

Unlike the other living beings, *Adam* is also assigned a set of responsibilities on behalf of the creation. The reader gets a hint of what these

---

32. Middleton, *Liberating Image*, 263–66.
33. Fretheim, *God and World*, 56–57.

responsibilities are when the story explains that no "produce of the field" or "vegetation of the field" had yet grown, because "there had been no human [*Adam*] to work the ground" (2:5).³⁴ The soil in this situation awaits humanity's nurturing care so that it might support a flourishing garden. It is as though "humans are created for the sake of the earth and not the other way around."³⁵ And after God molds the human out of the soil, God personally plants a garden full of trees "good for food" and places the human in the garden to "till it and keep it" (2:8–9, 15). Even as the text commissions humans to be farmworkers, it also portrays God as a gardener, which effectively elevates the hard work of gardening to a divine rather than servile status, the latter of which was common in ANE cosmologies.

As divinely made farmworkers, humans are expected to serve.³⁶ While the English word "till" in 2:5 and 15 (NRSV) specifically connotes an agricultural meaning, the underlying Hebrew verb *'avad* more generally means "serve, work." This Hebrew verb applies to a wide range of activities, from doing various forms of work, serving another person or deity, and performing the duties of a priest.³⁷ As it occurs in the context of Gen 2:5 and 15, tilling the soil is done "in the *service* of the nonhuman world, moving it toward its fullest possible potential."³⁸ It is perfectly reasonable to understand this type of garden work as benefitting not just humans but the animals and plants with whom they share the earth.

By commissioning the human being also to "keep" the garden, God intends this first human to nurture and maintain the garden's richness throughout the generations. The verb š-*m-r*, "keep," is the same verb used throughout the Torah to describe Israel's appropriate response to the Covenant—that they should *keep it*, observe it, maintain it.³⁹ Ellen Davis in-

---

34. Friedman, *Commentary on the Torah*, 6. Middleton indicates that God "delayed the garden until there was a human to work it (vv. 5b, 7–8). This suggests that the garden in Genesis 2 is not simply a 'natural' phenomenon, but rather a cultural project in which humans are to participate. Not only are humans made *from* the ground (v. 7), but also they are made *for* the ground, with a specific task or vocation in mind" (Middleton, *New Heaven and a New Earth*, 41–42).

35. Tonstad, *Letter to the Romans*, 191.

36. Fretheim insightfully notes that God even chooses to serve the well-being of the man by making him animal friends and a female partner (Fretheim, *God and World*, 57).

37. BDB, 712–13. The Greek translation of "till" employs the verb ἐργάζομαι, which similarly holds a generalized meaning of "work."

38. Fretheim, *God and World*, 53.

39. Davis, *Getting Involved with God*, 192. The Greek translation of Gen 2:15 uses the verb φυλάσσω, which is also the typical Greek verb used for keeping God's covenant,

sightfully explains that "there are divinely established rules and constraints attached to our use of the soil, and it has always been so. 'Observe it'—learn from it and about it; 'keep it'—from harm and violation," as if the soil itself is a vulnerable member of the covenant community.[40] Freitheim further notes that keeping Torah's "commandments has both positive and negative dimensions, namely, to promote the well-being of others and to restrain violence and the misuse of others."[41] Within this wider scriptural matrix, God's intentions for the human to "till [the garden] and keep it" (NRSV), then, do not entitle the human to hoard or degrade the land's resources. God expects the human to observe and maintain the garden home in all its rich, God-given complexity. In covenantal fashion, the human "serves and maintains" the fertile soil and all the living things that it supports. In other words, the human is not free to use up and deplete the garden's natural resources and then move on to another location to follow the same exploitative cycle. He is to keep it healthy for the longhaul. In the words of Norman Habel, "The mission of the first Earth being . . . is to serve and sustain the fertile forests of Mother Earth."[42]

After establishing an arboreal garden home for the living creatures and commissioning the human to serve and maintain it, God establishes generous boundaries within which the human might flourish. Although God had planted numerous trees from which the human might nourish himself (2:7–8), God designates as off-limits to humanity the tree of the knowledge of good and evil (2:17; 3:11). Thus, although *Adam* had the freedom to eat of every tree (including the tree of life) except one, he was not given unbounded "dominion."

Taken together, as the two foundational accounts of creation, Gen 1 and 2 indicate that God created humankind to reflect God's own being and to engage in servant leadership. Humans are to serve and keep the earth in ways that maintain creation's vitality, fertility, and diversity. In so doing, they mirror God. God's work of cooperating with the land and water in order to create and nourish life[43] and laboring in order to plant arboreal

---

commandments, Sabbaths, and festivals (for example, Exod 19:5; 20:6; 23:15; Deut 4:2, 40; 6:3).

40. Davis, *Getting Involved with God*, 193–94.

41. Fretheim, *God and World*, 53.

42. Habel, "Reading as an Earth Being: Rereading Genesis 2–3—Again," 97.

43. We find this motif affirmed throughout the Tanakh when God continues to maintain a nurturing and life-giving relationship with creation, providing food for the baby ravens (Job 38:41), breathing life into creatures (Ps 104:30), and renewing the face of the

Creation's Interrelatedness

gardens, establishes the divine pattern the human image-bearers ought to follow. They are to serve the vitality of the whole.[44]

1.2 Torah: Human Sin, Divine Covenant, and Creational Blessing

While the creation narratives of Gen 1–2 provide the broad outlines for positive forms of human identity and responsibility, the narratives and instructions throughout the rest of Torah flesh out human responsibilities more concretely. Sometimes Torah does this through prohibitions and negative examples, such as in Gen 3. Immediately after the idyllic creation accounts, the story turns to humanity's first and—according to Paul—its world-transforming failure to conform to God's pattern (Rom 5:12–21). Soon thereafter people failed to conform to God's purposes to such a degree that the land became corrupt, ruined, destroyed (Gen 6:11, 13). Despite these and other failures, God's mercy, grace, and life-giving purposes prevailed. For, God rectified the situation by making a binding covenant with Earth, Abram, and Israel (9:9–17; 12:1–3; Exod 19–23; Deut 29–30). In the covenant with Israel, God provided specific guidance for how God's people should care for the land and each other; live into their God-given identity and responsibility; and make atonement for their sins and impurities.

1.2.1 Genesis 3–9

The Torah is very clear that the relationships between humanity and God and between human creatures and the rest of creation are not as they should be.[45] While creation was subjected to human dominion for good, their

---

ground (Ps 104:30).

44. In somewhat different and more Pauline terms, we may thus infer from the creation accounts what "original righteousness" and God's ultimate plan for the New Creation might look like, as Ellen Davis suggests (Davis, *Getting Involved with God*, 191).

45. Looking beyond the Tanakh, Harry Alan Hahne demonstrates the ways in which Genesis' concept of creation's distortion or "corruption" was interpreted in Second Temple Jewish apocalyptic literature. He notes, "Jewish apocalyptic writings agree with Genesis 1 that God originally made the creation good. But something went wrong and now the created world is damaged. In the apocalyptic writings studied, however, neither the created world nor matter are inherently evil" (Hahne, *Corruption and Redemption of Creation*, 154). Instead, he argues, "Creation is corrupted due to (1) human sin (2 *En*; 4 *Ezra*; 2 *Bar*; *Apoc. Mos./LAE*), (2) the sins of fallen Watchers (BW 6–16; En. Noah) or

servant leadership became mutated by human sin. Poignant illustrations of that fact occur repeatedly throughout the Tanakh, with their canonical debut coming in Gen 3. Although God forbade *Adam* ("man") from eating only the fruit of the tree of the knowledge of good and evil, the serpent implicitly called into question God's generosity and provision in the garden (Gen 2:17; 3:1). Because Eve acted on this misperception and Adam and Eve misappropriated the forbidden tree's good fruit (3:6), a fracture developed between the humans and their Creator.[46] Meanwhile, a fissure tore through the mutually beneficial relationship between humanity and the rest of creation. For, the humans took that which was not God-given, and they ate—not for nourishment—but self-glorification (3:6).

As a consequence of transgressing God's prohibition, the Genesis account indicates the humans introduced a host of negative consequences into the world.[47] In addition to death (3:19), which Paul will stress in Rom 5, God announced to *Adam* that the *adamah* ("land") now stood "cursed . . . because of" his disobedience (Gen 3:17). This cursed condition contradicts the blessedness God identifies in the creation in Gen 1. Human action—rather

---

(3) the sins of both humans and Watchers (BW 17–36; AA; AB 80; *Jub*; BP III)" (154). In this chapter I do not discuss Second Temple apocalyptic literature but instead focus on texts viewed as sacred "scripture" by the apostle Paul. In chs. 4–5, nevertheless, I attend to the most relevant Second Temple apocalyptic texts in my discussion of Rom 8:19–22.

46. In describing Gen 3 as background to Rom 5, Tonstad insightfully notes: "When Adam 'disobeys' the divine command, he acts in response to a malicious misrepresentation of the command so as to make his disobedience the violation of a command God did not give" (Tonstad, *Letter to the Romans*, 189). Norman Habel proposes a less antagonistic reading of Gen 3, perceiving the snake as an earth creature that helps Eve gain greater "enlightenment" by asking her questions that lead her away from her simplistic view of God and God's world (Habel, "Reading as an Earth Being, 98–99). While I agree that the snake led Eve towards a greater understanding of good and evil, the shape of this narrative—particularly the cursed condition of the snake that results from its actions—suggest the snake acted in ways that were dishonoring or disobedient to God.

47. As a result of their disobedience, several undesirable consequences follow, including (among others): the woman would have great difficulty in childbearing (πληθυνῶ τὰς λύπας σου καὶ τόν στεναγμόν σου, ἐν λύπαις τέξῃ τέκνα, Gen 3:16 LXX); the man would harvest produce from the land after much toil and ultimately would become part of the land again through death and decomposition (3:17–19); and the land itself would enter a condition of cursedness rather than blessedness so that it readily produced thorns and thistles rather than the edible fruit it originally brought forth (3:17–18; 1:11–12, 29; 2:9). Thus, Gen 3 stresses the theme that human action—whether righteous or sinful—affects the well-being of the rest of creation. We also find that creation's own condition affects human well-being. This two-way relationship is nicely captured by the term "interdependence."

than God's decree—subjects the land to a less than ideal condition,[48] in which the land would produce inedible plants ("thorn and thistles," Gen 3:18-19) and the human would resort to tearing up these unwanted living things, cutting into the soil, and laboring endlessly to cultivate the food on which he and his family depended. Rather than tending and keeping the garden in accordance with God's boundaries, Adam and Eve became the source of the land's affliction.[49] The fertile soil was now an aggrieved partner in a covenantal relationship. To some extent, the humans and the soil became adversaries on account of human action rather than mutual nurturers; they experienced cursedness and alienation rather than blessedness.

In the chapters that follow this cursed condition, humans, as well as other living things, engaged in increasing violence. Out in the field, Cain killed his brother Abel whose blood cried out to God from the *adamah* (4:10). And Cain ended up being "cursed from the ground" itself so that when he would "till the ground, it [would] no longer yield... its strength" to him (4:11, 12).[50] The fertility and diversity that saturated the creation just a few chapters before now stood threatened on account of human villainy.

Violence, destruction, and deterioration escalated among humankind and "all flesh" (6:5, 11-12) to such a degree that the earth was itself judged to be "corrupt" (6:11). This English term "corrupt" may convey the idea that the earth was morally contaminated, but the underlying Hebrew verb *š-ḥ-t* more directly connotes the idea of something being ruined or destroyed.[51] Because the immediate context associates this verb with *ḥamas*, "violence,"[52]

48. As a passive participle in the Hebrew, "cursed" leaves open the question of what or who placed the curse on the ground. Certainly the humans' disobedience initiated this consequence, but did God determine the consequence and, therefore, actively curse the land? Drawing upon Eugene Combs's work, Tonstad denies that God enacted the curse. Instead, God diagnosed the condition. Tonstad suggests, "human agency is primary with respect to disruption, and God's role is descriptive and confirmatory, but the verb centers on what happens to the earth more than on agency" (Tonstad, *Letter to the Romans*, 250; Combs, "Has God Cursed the Ground?").

49. Genesis 3 also places blame on the serpent although Paul does not in his retelling of this story in Rom 5:12-21.

50. Although this passage does not identify murder as causing the perpetrator as well as the land to become morally impure, the Torah later names these effects to be the case, as will be discussed in 1.2.3. Yet, moral impurity is not simply some abstract, spiritual state. Rather, Gen 4 orients us to recognize the larger scriptural theme in which human action—especially physical violence, such as murder—can negatively affect nonhuman creation's physical condition.

51. BDB, 1007-8.

52. Richard Bauckham suggests that the text's reference to violence likely refers, at

š-ḥ-t may more accurately be translated with "ruined" or "destroyed" than corrupted. Accordingly, "[t]he earth is 'ruined before God' (Gen 6:11), because 'all flesh had ruined its way on the earth' (v. 12); only when the fact of ruin is fully established (v. 13a) does God resolve to 'effect-their-ruination' (v. 13b)."[53] The Hebrew text repeats the same verb four times, making it clear that "[t]he ruin that God effects is no more than the full manifestation of what 'all flesh' has already done to itself and the earth."[54] Thus, the earth's "ruin," stemming from human moral corruption and violence, entailed physical destruction. Interestingly, the LXX—Paul's Scriptures—translates š-ḥ-t with the verb φθείρω, "to destroy" (6:11). As we shall see in 4.2, Paul employs a cognate of this word when he describes creation's bondage in Rom 8:21, suggesting that we should understand creation's "bondage of corruption" (KJV) as a bondage of "ruin" or "destruction."

Despite God's decision to "make an end of all flesh" (Gen 6:13) with a flood, God remained committed to preserving the creation and thus employed the man Noah and his family to ensure the ongoing survival of land and avian creatures (Gen 6–9). After this diluvial judgment, God entered into a covenant relationship with all "living beings" (*nefeš haḥyah*, 9:10; author's translation), promising never again to exterminate life in such a way (9:9–17).[55] God also recommissioned the humans to multiply and fill the earth and meanwhile extended the boundaries of their relationship with creation by allowing humans to eat not only green plants but also animal flesh (9:3).[56] Nonhuman creatures too may have received divine permis-

---

least in part, to the violence and killing that is part and parcel of eating meat. He explains, "The account has to be read against the background of the way Genesis 1 portrays humans and animals as originally vegetarian. God gave them only plants for food (Gen. 1:29–30). In view of the change that is recognised after the Flood (Gen. 9:2–3, 5–6), we are probably to understand that the violence that led to the Flood included killing for food" (Bauckham, *Bible and Ecology*, 23).

53. Davis, *Biblical Prophecy*, 95. The New English Translation of the Septuagint (NETS) also uses "ruin" rather than "corrupt" in this passage.

54. Davis, *Biblical Prophecy*, 95. Davis also explains, "With four iterations of the verb, the narrator shows a punishment that not only fits the crime but is essentially identical with it."

55. Much more could be gleaned from this passage. For further discussion, see Murray, *Cosmic Covenant*.

56. It is interesting to note, however, that God did not recommission the fish and birds to be fruitful and multiply, nor did God commission the land animals to do the same. We may therefore wonder whether the narrative assumes the commissions from Gen 1 were still in play.

sion to eat other, nonhuman creatures (9:5). Interpreted theologically, we may infer God gave "plants and animals to every living creature for food," and "this giving is a reflection of the self-offering that characterizes God's creative and sustaining life from the beginning."[57]

1.2.2 Genesis 12 and God's Covenants with Abram and Israel

Although humans continued at times to act disobediently, the biblical narrative suggests they could enjoy divine blessings as a result of God's covenantal relationship with Abram and, eventually, with the nation of Israel. At several points in Genesis, God called and blessed Abram and promised to bless all people through him and his offspring (Gen 12:1–3; 18:18–19; 22:18; 26:4). The first such announcement states:

> Now the LORD said to Abram, "Go from your country and your kindred and your father's house to the land that I will show you. I will make of you a great nation, and I will bless you, and make your name great, so that you will be a blessing. I will bless those who bless you, and the one who curses you I will curse; and in you all the families of the earth shall be blessed." (Gen 12:1–3)

H. H. Schmid suggests that this foundational promise of "increase, fortune, and prosperity" reflects a typical ANE perspective on what it means to be a nation.[58] The national deity—here, YHWH—provides land, the increase of the human population, and blessing for the establishment of a nation, Israel. God's special covenant with Abram also transcends this common ANE trope, however, by proclaiming that YHWH will bless those outside Abram's family through him.

Thus, according to Genesis, the covenant that God made with Abram and codified for his descendants in the Mosaic Covenant begins to restore humanity's right relationships with God and creation. God's original promise to Abram and the ongoing covenant with Israel includes the promise of land, provided that the people follow God's commandments (Gen 12:1, 7; Deut 5:33). While the majority of these commandments pertained to the people's relationship with God and their relationship with fellow human beings, a striking number directly address their relationships with nonhuman creation, both living and nonliving. We find, then, that Torah, the Law,

---

57. Wirzba, *Food and Faith*, 133.
58. Schmid, "Creation, Righteousness, and Salvation," 109.

is "creational in its orientation" and is given "in the service of life," "the life, health, and well-being of individuals in community."[59] In other words, "[t]he law is given because God is concerned about the *best possible life* for *all* of God's creatures."[60] God's Law focuses upon preserving the goodness of creation and expanding creational well-being.

1.2.3 Exodus, Leviticus, and Deuteronomy

Exodus, Leviticus, and Deuteronomy contain the core elements of Israelite Law, by which God's people could know how to maintin their covenant with God. The stipulations contained therein correlate obedience to God with the land's health and provision, a perspective also found in other ANE texts. Ellen Davis insightfully notes: "Taken as whole, biblical law seeks to inculcate a precise awareness of physical being: of human life in a particular place, the land of Canaan, shared with other creatures—trees (Deut 20:19) and birds and animals (Deut 22:4, 6-7; 25:4)—whose own lives are precious and vulnerable."[61] Additionally, the book of Leviticus "articulates . . . a theologically profound vision of the complexity and interdependence of the created order."[62] Leviticus especially fleshes out what it might mean for humans to serve and keep the land (Gen 2:15) in ways that honor and mirror the Creator.

Before the giving of the Law, however, God demonstrates God's fidelity and grace to Abraham, Sarah, and their heirs by liberating the Hebrew nation from slavery and the forces of creational destruction in Egypt, as narrated in Exod 1-15.[63] This divine, redemptive act of God—sometimes mediated by

---

59. Fretheim, *God and World*, 134.

60. Fretheim, *God and World*, 135. Emphasis original. Fretheim suggests, in relation to New Testament Christianity, this understanding of Law means that specific "food laws," for example, "may no longer be applicable," but "food laws will still be needed for the sake of the health and well-being of the community"; this is because, according to Fretheim, "every law of God continues to have value for present-day communities *at some level*, especially at the level of concern that generated the law in the first place" (155). As suggested by the passages reviewed here, the concern of Torah is creational life and well-being.

61. Davis, *Scripture, Culture, and Agriculture*, 82.

62. Davis, *Scripture, Culture, and Agriculture*, 83.

63. Fretheim demonstrates that, by attempting to "close down God's work of multiplication and fruitfulness" in the killing of Hebrew baby boys, Pharaoh engages in "oppressive measures against Israel [that] are antilife and anticreation" (Fretheim, *God and World*, 113, 115). Moreover, "Pharaoh's antilife measures against God's creation have

human servant leaders (especially Moses and Aaron) and even nonhuman creation (most spectacularly, the Red Sea)—establishes a foundational story by which God's people, Israel, shape their identity as well as their expectations for the future.[64] Because God's covenant people remembered and, in a sense, relived the exodus each year in their *Pesaḥ*/Passover celebrations, the story of God's liberation of Israel and creation from slavery were continually revived. In *Paul and His Story*, Sylvia Keesmaat describes the ways in which the exodus story functioned in these formative ways not only in the biblical canon (especially the Prophets) but also in Second Temple Jewish writings and the Pauline epistles. She concludes: "The exodus was recalled every year in the passover ritual; in that ritual it was actualized and made present for every generation. The exodus was recalled as having been experienced by every Israelite in the present day. As such it became a symbol of what God had done in the past, is doing in the present and will do in the future."[65] The exodus communicates to God's people that God is a God who liberates humans and all creation from destructive forms of slavery.[66]

After the foundational event of the exodus and on its basis, God reveals to the people, by way of Moses, the ways in which they are to live into their liberation from slavery. Although some may have interpreted God's liberation of the people from slavery and God's provision of the Promised Land as removing all constraints, God's covenant with Israel makes it clear that such is not the case. In fact, God's gracious liberation of and commitment to Israel comes with obligations. The covenant assumes the people of Israel are now God's servants (Lev 25:55) and that the land of promise is actually God's possession (25:23).[67]

---

unleashed chaotic effects that threaten the very creation that God intended" (119). God's liberation of Israel out of Egypt is creational in focus, for "God's work in and through Moses, climaxing in Israel's crossing of the sea on 'dry land,' constitutes God's efforts of re-creation" (119).

64. Keesmaat, *Paul and His Story*, 34–48.

65. Keesmaat, *Paul and His Story*, 36.

66. Much more could be gleaned from the story of Israel's exodus from Egypt. For example, Ellen Davis illustrates the ways in which the economy of Egypt was one of extraction, exploitation, and extreme inequity whereas the wilderness or manna economy taught Israel to practice self-restraint and trust by taking only what was needed day to day (Davis, *Scripture, Culture, and Agriculture*, 66–79).

67. Davis recognizes a clear correspondence between "farmer and field" "in the laws of redemption (Leviticus 25)," since these laws "treat analogously the enslaved farmer and alienated land." She goes on to explain that through the restoration enacted in the Jubilee, poor Israelite families who had become landless through debt would be re-established on

On the basis of this fundamental perspective, Lev 26 correlates human obedience with creational blessing. This chapter explains that if Israel obeys God's stipulations it will have agricultural success, for God declares:

> If you follow my statutes and keep my commandments and observe them faithfully, I will give you your rains in their season, and the land shall yield its produce, and the trees of the field shall yield their fruit. Your threshing shall overtake the vintage, and the vintage shall overtake the sowing; you shall eat your bread to the full, and live securely in your land. And I will grant peace in the land, and you shall lie down, and no one shall make you afraid; I will remove dangerous animals from the land, and no sword shall go through your land. You shall give chase to your enemies, and they shall fall before you by the sword . . . I will place my dwelling in your midst, and I shall not abhor you. And I will walk among you, and will be your God, and you shall be my people. (Lev 26:3–7, 11–12)

God's instructions here indicate that Israel's obedience to God's teaching—the "Torah"—would elicit God's sending of nourishing rains upon the land and the provision of abundant crops (see also Deut 11:13–15; 28:1–14). The Torah, then, assumes that human behavior affects the condition of creation. Israel's obedience to the liturgical, ethical, and practical stipulations of the Law elicits God's blessing: the people would be rewarded with agricultural abundance by doing what is right and lawful.

In order to enable the Israelites, later called the Judeans and Jews, to experience security and abundance and avoid agricultural and political disintegration, God provided Israel with specific agricultural instructions. Underlying these instructions is the assumption that the land is the Lord's to which God has the right, not humans, and that "human beings are to treat it accordingly, as gift not possession."[68] Because of God's covenantal relationship with the land—as illustrated by God's commitment to "remember the land" (Lev 26:42)[69]—God presented the people with specific guidelines for its care.

---

ancestral lands. Consequently, farmers and land would no longer be estranged. Part of the theological motivation for this came from the notion that God owns the land and redeemed Israel from slavery in Egypt (Davis, *Scripture, Culture, and Agriculture*, 92–94).

68. Fretheim, *God and World*, 139.

69. Davis points out from this verse that "[i]t is within the context of *covenant relationship* that God considers and values—'remembers'—the land" (*Scripture, Culture, and Agriculture*, 83).

Creation's Interrelatedness

For example, God enjoined the people to give the land rest from tilling, planting, and pruning every seventh and fiftieth year (Exod 23:10–11; Lev 25:3–7, 11–12). Interpreted through a lens of rights, Leviticus presumes the land has a right to these forms of rest.[70] Incidentally, we know today that allowing fields to lie fallow for a year helps the soil replenish its nutrients, moisture, and organic matter.

Additionally, passages in Torah illustrate God's care for the lives of plants and animals and therefore provide guidance for Israel's relationships with them. For example: God's people were instructed to protect and properly care for fruit trees (Deut 20:19–20; Lev 19:23–25). On every Sabbath, while the Israelites/Judeans gave themselves and their servants rest, they were to rest their animals, suggesting that domestic animals had certain rights (Exod 20:10; 23:12; Deut 5:14). Torah meanwhile enjoined the Israelites/Judeans to share agricultural produce with wild animals (Exod 23:11; Lev 25:7). It also instructed them to harvest in such a way that allowed the poor and sojourner to share in the abundance (19:9–10), which would also decrease pressure on marginal and uncultivated lands. By performing these and other commandments, Israel better ensured that the "land [would] yield its produce" (26:4).

Managing their fields and flocks according to God's stipulations was not the only avenue by which God's covenant people could pursue agricultural success, however. God's people were also instructed to observe special agricultural festivals in which they thanked the Creator God for agricultural blessings and petitioned God for nourishing rains and salutary growing conditions in the coming season. In this way, the people of Israel functioned as "priests" by mediating between God and creation so that the whole region might be blessed.[71] The feast of Unleavened Bread, the Festival of Trumpets, and the Festival of Booths strikingly illustrate the correlation between proper Israelite/Judean worship and agricultural well-being.

In the early spring, God's people performed liturgical services in order to express thanksgiving to the Creator God for the gifts of ripening grain

---

70. Fretheim, *God and World*, 139.

71. Milgrom attests, "To be sure, H [Holiness source], no differently from P [Priestly source], presumes that sacrificial service is conducted exclusively by priests. However, maintenance of the public cult and, presumably, supervision over the priestly order are ultimately the people's responsibility" (*Leviticus*, 275). As a gesture toward considering how the liturgical activities presented in Torah could have shaped what Paul envisioned should be the Christian's reasonable service of worship (Rom 12:1), I briefly discuss these ideas in the conclusion to this book.

and to petition God for the grain's continued flourishing during a particularly vulnerable period of its lifecycle. These liturgies took place at the end of *Pesah* (literally, "protection" and often called "Passover" in English).[72] In addition to the festivities of *Pesah* itself, the people gathered for a sacred assembly on the seventh day of the Festival of Unleavened Bread when God's people would present the earliest ripening sheaves of grain to the Lord (Lev 23:8). In the Levant, this assembly correlated with the beginning of the dry season, when winds threatened to destroy spring grain crops by drying up necessary water.[73] In order for the grains' kernels to ripen fully, the crops needed at least daily dew, making the time between *Pesah* and Pentecost especially vulnerable to crop failure. Israel's sacred assembly during the Festival of Unleavened Bread functioned, in part, as a prayer service "to supplicate God for a 'safe passage' [or, 'protection'] on behalf of the crops."[74] In the days and weeks following this pilgrimage festival, God's people also offered God the first sheaves of their harvested barley and wheat crops (23:9–14).[75] They did this to express gratitude as well as ensure ongoing salutary conditions.[76] Although the agricultural focus of these rituals had diminished somewhat by the first-century CE, the practical function of the firstfruits offerings was understood during Paul's day and beyond, as attested by Tosefta Sukkot 3:18, which states, "The Holy One Blessed Be He has said: Bring before me a sheaf on the Festival of Protection *so that* you will be blessed with grain in the fields."[77] God's people perceived that their agricultural labor and liturgical activity were intimately related, since their actions—in concert with the Creator and creation—affected the well-being of the nonhuman world.

During the autumn preparations for the next spring's harvest of grain, Israelites/Judeans again took an active role in mediating between creation and Creator. Having already harvested the summer crops in the early fall,

---

72. Milgrom asserts that the LXX translation πάσχα, which gave rise to the English "Passover," is "erroneous." Instead, as the rabbis in *Mekilta Bo'* par. 7 declare, *Pesah* means protection, protection from the "Destroyer" (Exod 12:13, 23) (Milgrom, *Leviticus*, 276).

73. Milgrom, *Leviticus*, 277.

74. Milgrom, *Leviticus*, 277.

75. It was likely during the last spring festival, Pentecost, that Paul delivered the generous gifts from Macedonia and Achaia to the poor saints in Jerusalem (Acts 20:16).

76. Milgrom, *Leviticus*, 278. Milgrom explains, "the cereal offering of the barley (and of the wheat) not only functions as a sign of thanks for the new crop, but also expresses the hope that God, in turn, will bless the new crop (Ezek 44:30; Prov 3:9–10)."

77. Milgrom, *Leviticus*, 278–79. Emphasis added.

they then observed during the seventh month two feasts (the Festival of Trumpets and the Festival of Booths or *Sukkot*) and one fast (the Day of Atonement) (Lev 23:23–36). The seventh month happened to be "the only month [in the Levant] that follows the harvests and precedes the rains."[78] And, according to Jacob Milgrom, these autumn liturgical activities are closely linked to the provision of water:

> All three festivals of the seventh month—the alarm call on the first day [the Festival of Trumpets], the fast day on the tenth [the Day of Atonement], the circumambulation of the altar with waving fronds and other vegetation for seven days [the Festival of Booths], from the fifteenth through the twenty-second, as well as the tradition of a water libation offering during these days—combine into a single-minded goal: to beseech God for adequate and timely rain in the forthcoming agricultural year.[79]

The agricultural agenda of the Festival of Booths, in particular, is confirmed in Zechariah when the prophet mandates that "all who survive of the nations that have come against Jerusalem shall go up year after year to worship the King, the Lord of hosts, and to keep the *festival of booths*. If any of the families of the earth do not go up to Jerusalem to worship the King, the Lord of hosts, *there will be no rain upon them*" (Zech 14:16–17, emphasis added). Here, even the gentiles were expected to participate in *Sukkoth*, dependent as they too were on the land's fertility.[80] This festival at the end of the annual fall harvest and the beginning of the new growing season functioned not simply to thank God for the agricultural success of the past but also to petition God to continue such conditions into the future. In essence, *Sukkot* taught (and continues to teach) people about their utter dependence on God's generosity that is materially manifested in and through creation.

Because timely and sufficient rains in the semi-arid region of the Levant benefitted not only humans but all plants and animals living in the region, the intercessory activity of Israel/Judea functioned as one means by which God's people exercised servant leadership by which they "served and maintained" their garden home (Gen 1:26; 2:15; author's translation).

78. Milgrom, *Leviticus*, 280.

79. Milgrom, *Leviticus*, 281.

80. Zechariah's requirement that gentiles participate in the Jewish festival of *Sukkoth* stands in tension with what the Pauline epistles appear to teach gentile Christians (Gal 4:8–11; Rom 14:5; Col 2:16). Whether or not gentile Christians could—in Paul's view—appropriately embrace the Jewish agricultural festivals is a question I plan to consider in the future.

In such ways, we find that "Israelite worship is a means by which the world is created and re-created in every new ritual activity."[81]

Despite all these positive activities the Torah mobilized among God's people, human impurities and destructive conditions nevertheless endangered Israel's well-being and the land's vitality. Individual and corporate impurities and sins repeatedly threatened to repel God's presence with the people and reduce the productivity of the land (1 Kgs 14:15–16; 2 Kgs 17:22; Isa 1:4; 24:5; Jer 11:10; Hos 14:1). The Tanakh frequently indicates that if Israel acted unfaithfully and disobediently, the land would become polluted and God would allow pestilence, wild animals, and enemies to diminish Israel's population and destroy its land (Lev 26:14–32; Deut 11:16–17; 28:15–68; Jer 3:2–3; Hos 4:1–3).[82] Human wickedness, according to this biblical perspective, clearly and almost necessarily resulted in the degradation and sometimes the destruction of the nonhuman creation.[83]

Since Israel understood God to be holy and pure, human impurities repelled God's presence. Purgation of impurities—impurities we would today categorize as both ritual and moral in nature—was therefore of central importance. Thus, Torah also instructed the people on how to cleanse impurities and make atonement. For, if left without appropriate cleansing, atonement, and repentance (for moral impurities), Israel's defilement would separate God's people from the blessing and presence of God (Lev 26:14–33).[84] Although ritual impurities—such as genital discharge, child-

81. Fretheim, *God and World*, 145.

82. The situation could become so bad that the land itself could "vomit out its inhabitants," as—according to Leviticus—it did to the nations who occupied the Promised Land before the people of Israel (Lev 18:25). As Davis describes it, Leviticus portrays the land as "a semi-autonomous moral agent." As such, its responsibility to God means it "must finally expel the unhealthful presence and make up the Sabbath years that Israel failed to observe" (*Scripture, Culture, and Agriculture*, 100).

83. Davis would thus add: "Leviticus draws a direct threefold connection among Israel's obedience, the 'fruitfulness' of both people and earth, and the immediate presence of God to both" (*Scripture, Culture, and Agriculture*, 60).

84. Jacob Milgrom states, "Because the quintessential source of holiness resides with God, Israel is enjoined to control the occurrence of impurity lest it impinge on his realm" (*Leviticus*, 13). Jewish Priestly and Holiness traditions thus maintained that humans could act in ways that secured divine blessings in the land, while it was the power of humans, rather than demons or malevolent gods, that could cause harm (9). This Jewish perspective, then, stands in contrast with what might be called "pagan" religion. According to Milgrom, pagan religion promoted belief in: gods who are under the direction of other god(s), good and bad forces at work in the world, and the human ability to manipulate these forces if done according to the correct rituals (8). As chapter 2 discusses, several Roman religious practices demonstrate these "pagan" perspectives.

birth, and corpse contact—were natural parts of human life, generally were not correlated with sin, and did not negatively affect or defile the land, they could pollute sacred places and objects. Thus, if a ritually impure person came too close to its holy precincts, the Temple would become polluted.[85] Consequently, God's covenant people had to cleanse all ritual impurities by "sacrifices, sprinklings, washings, and bathings" and with the passage of designated amounts of time.[86]

In contrast, moral impurities (as we might categorize them) were considered sinful and could not simply be washed away. Moral impurities included "sexual sins (e.g., Lev. 18:24–30), idolatry (e.g., Lev. 19:31; 20:1–3), and bloodshed (e.g., Num. 35:33–34)."[87] In his extensive examination of the topic, Jonathan Klawans explains that "[m]oral impurity is best understood as a potent force unleashed by certain sinful human actions. The force unleashed defiles the sinner, the sanctuary, and the land."[88] These sins or moral impurities caused the land and Temple to be polluted and the sinner to be degraded, and they could only be cleansed through "punishment" or, when possible, "atonement."[89] Israel's transgressions—its moral impurities—could accumulate to such an extent that negative consequences would undermine the flourishing of life in the land, ranging in severity from sickness, crop failure, and civil unrest to war, destruction, and banishment from the land (Deut 11:13–17; Hos 4:1–7).[90] The power of hu-

---

85. Klawans, *Impurity and Sin*, 23.

86. Klawans, *Impurity and Sin*, 22–23.

87. Klawans goes on to explain: "These three sinful behaviors are also frequently referred to as 'abominations' ([tv'bot]). They bring about an impurity that *morally*—but not *ritually*—defiles the sinner (Lev. 18:24), the land of Israel (Lev. 18:25, Ezek. 36:17), and the sanctuary of God (Lev. 20:3; Ezek. 5:11). This defilement, in turn leads to the expulsion of the people from the land of Israel (Lev. 18:28; Ezek. 36:19)" (Klawans, *Impurity and Sin*, 26. Emphasis original.).

88. Klawans, *Impurity and Sin*, 29. For many people today, the Israelite belief in moral impurities conveying deleterious effects on the land seems unfounded and superstitious. However, as we attempt to see the world and the work of God through Paul's eyes, it may be important to remember this often neglected aspect of his religious context. As chapters 3–5 demonstrate, Paul understood Jesus's atoning life, death, and resurrection as having powerful, cleansing, liberatory effects on the nonhuman creation. Perhaps one of these effects, from Paul's perspective, included cleansing the unseen but potent contaminations that human murder, sexual sin, and idolatry inflicted upon the land.

89. Klawans, *Impurity and Sin*, 26–27.

90. In response, various authors in the Tanakh envision the Lord summoning the mountains and hills, the earth and the heavens to judge and witness against human corruption and abuse in the divine courtroom (Mic 6:1–2; Deut 30:19; 31:28). In these cases,

man immorality was so great that people could even "drive God out of the sanctuary by polluting it with their moral and ritual sins. All that the priests [could] do is periodically purge the sanctuary of its impurities and influence the people to atone for their wrongs."[91] Such atonement was especially important because God had chosen to dwell in Jerusalem (according to the Deuteronomistic tradition), and the health of the surrounding territory was dependent on God's presence there. Designated priests, then, worked to maintain the purity of Israel and its land so that God could continue to abide in the temple and bless the people in their homeland.[92]

Although atonement, especially the atonement enacted on the Day of Atonement, purged impurities from the holy center of Israel, the Torah offered no means of atonement for the grave moral impurities that degraded the land itself.[93] Sexual sins (Lev 18:24–30; Jer 3:1), murder (Num 35:33–34), and idolatry (Jer 2:7; Ezek 36:18) were understood to contaminate the land with "a noncontagious degradation."[94] Moreover, "[t]he ultimate result of this defilement, if it remain[ed] unchecked, is the exile of the land's

---

nonhuman creation stands as an aggrieved member in a covenantal relationship, in its relationship with the people of Israel and with the Creator God. Perhaps the destructive consequences the land, in particular, would endure on account of Israel's transgression resulted not from God's direct command but as a result of those transgressions repelling God's life-giving presence in the temple.

91. Milgrom, *Leviticus*, 9.

92. Davis highlights the importance of discernment in the process of maintaining holiness or purity. She states, "what enables Israel to live with God in its midst is precisely a refined ability to distinguish the holy from the 'profane' (*profanus*, literally, that which remains 'in front of the temple,' outside the sacred precinct), and further, to distinguish between different levels of holiness" (Davis, *Scripture, Culture, and Agriculture*, 86). Because the land itself was considered holy to the Lord, "there is no place in the land that ordinary Israelites are not obliged to revere. Only by constant mindfulness of the holy in its varying intensities can this people live fittingly on the land with which it is entrusted" (86).

93. Although nations other than Israel were not considered to be members of God's covenant people, their lands were occasionally perceived to be contaminated by moral sins. Klawans contends, "It is not only the land of Israel that is subject to this moral defilement; a few biblical traditions refer to the idea that foreign lands were considered to be defiled. Amos 7:17 threatens the insolent Israelites with exile to a polluted land. Joshua 22:19 suggests that tribal holdings east of the Jordan River are impure from idolatry. In my view, the traditions that refer to foreign lands as impure are to be understood in the context of moral impurity" (*Impurity and Sin*, 30).

94. Klawans, *Impurity and Sin*, 30. Klawans also highlights Ezek 22:1–4 and Ps 106:34–40 as passages that pinpoint the ways in which murder and idolatry (in contrast to ritual impurity) pollute the land.

inhabitants."⁹⁵ In contrast to the atonement available for ritual impurities and less grave moral impurities:

> [t]he Holiness Code gives no indication of any methods for the removal of [grave] defilements. Ablutions . . . are not efficacious here. The Day of Atonement service involves the purgation of the altar and shrine, which removes the stain left by sin upon the sanctuary (Lev. 16:11–19). This service also includes other sacrifices which atone for the people (16:20–22). But these sacrifices do not appear to purify grave sinners, or the land upon which the grave sins were committed.⁹⁶

Consequently, "[t]he land . . . suffers permanent degradation."⁹⁷ In other words, there was little hope for a full restoration of the land's pure status by means of the day-to-day and year-to-year liturgical activities of Israel.

This is not to say that there was no hope at all. The prophet Ezekiel envisioned God's eschatological atonement of the land and its people. Similarly, the prophet Isaiah looked forward to the coming of a descendant of Jesse and a time of creational renewal. While God's people exercised servant leadership in attempting to maintain the integrity, purity, and fertility of the land with the help of the priests, they also anticipated a unique provision of atonement or cleansing given by God as well as the advent of the anointed one, the messiah. This messiah, according to the Prophets and Writings, would institute the justice and goodness required for creational health. Thus, at least from the perspective of the land, the coming of the messiah and the atonement of God in the eschatological age offered a unique possibility of liberation from the destructive effects of sin.

1.3 Prophets and Writings: Creation's Restoration and the Messiah's Rule

Although God had established guidelines for the ways in which the covenant people were to live fruitfully in the land of promise, the development of a monarchy often contradicted these guidelines and threatened the well-being of God's people and land. Much of the Latter Prophets criticize Israel's monarchs (the anointed rulers) and upper classes for exploiting

---

95. Klawans, *Impurity and Sin*, 30.
96. Klawans, *Impurity and Sin*, 30.
97. Klawans, *Impurity and Sin*, 30.

poor farmers (the majority of Israel's population) and confiscating their land (tribal inheritances). Ellen Davis explains that

> the prophetic movement gained traction in the eighth century, a nodal point in the history of ancient Israel's agricultural economy, when the traditional system of independent family farms was yielding to a system of state-controlled agriculture. As the crown and the aristocracy were growing rich through trade in the three commodities of the Levant—grain, wine, and oil—the smallholders, virtually everyone else in the population were (literally) losing ground.[98]

The canonical prophets exposed and condemned the unchecked and unlawful "dominion" exercised in the kingdoms of Israel and Judah. Yet, it is within this context of aberrant dominion that the prophets most poignantly depict God's intentions to restore justice, fertility, and peace in and for the created order. Although we might consider more of the Tanakh's Prophets and Writings from which Paul draws inspiration (most especially Habakkuk),[99] we will limit our focus to Amos, Ezekiel, Isaiah, and Ps 72.

1.3.1 Amos

While the apostle Paul does not explicitly quote Amos, this prophetic book elucidates some of the destructive dynamics at work in Israel's relationship with the land. It signals some of the ways in which creation was enslaved to destruction and portrays the context in which Israel's hope for creational liberation took root. In a time of relative political stability and peace, the prophet Amos warned the Northern Kingdom of Israel of impending divine

---

98. Davis, *Biblical Prophecy*, 86.

99. Habakkuk 2:4 is a foundational text for Paul, as Richard Hays eloquently demonstrates in *Faith of Jesus Christ*. Also recognizing this text's central role in Paul's thought, especially in Romans, Keesmaat elucidates the connections between Habakkuk and Romans in their critique of idolatry, greed, and oppression and their simultaneous insistence on the faithfulness of God. She explains, "Habakkuk's affirmations of the faithfulness of God occur in a context of judgment against the Chaldeans for their arrogance, their greedy grasping of the property of others (2:6), their economic exploitation of the poor (2:6), their shedding of human blood, and their profanation of the earth, the cities, and all who live in them (2:8) . . . The verbal echoes with shame, greed, and profanity (usually translated ungodliness in Rom 1:18) in Rom 1 are striking" (Keesmaat, "Land, Idolatry, and Justice," 92). She goes on to indicate: "Habakkuk's affirmation of life for the just, therefore, quoted by Paul, occurs in a context of bloody idolatrous economic exploitation, with deadly effects for humanity, animals, and, as is stated repeatedly, the earth" (93). As will be discussed more in chapters 2 and 3, Paul's first-century Roman imperial context holds striking similarities to the historal context of Habakkuk.

judgment and disaster on account of its unfaithfulness to God's covenant.[100] During the eighth century BCE, God justly condemned Israel's leaders for instituting systems of oppression and forsaking God-given constraints on agricultural production and consumption.[101] Amos portrays Israel's injustices in vivid, agricultural hues:

> Hear this, you that trample on the needy, and bring to ruin the poor of the land, saying, "When will the new moon be over so that we may sell grain; and the sabbath, so that we may offer wheat for sale? We will make the ephah small and the shekel great, and practice deceit with false balances, buying the poor for silver and the needy for a pair of sandals, and selling the sweepings of the wheat." (Amos 8:4–6)[102]

The agriculturally based economic system Amos here portrays involves exploiting the poor; observing holy days as one form of law observance even while salesmen broke the law by using inaccurate and exploitative measurements for their sales (Lev 19:35–36);[103] buying impoverished people who had finally resorted to selling themselves into slavery;[104] and selling grain whose weight was artificially increased by dirt and other debris.

---

100. Douglas Stuart indicates that Amos's prophetic critique of Israel mirrors the stipulations and consequences outlined in the Mosaic covenant, explaining: "The crimes Amos identifies are those the Sinai covenant defines as crimes (e.g., oppression of the poor, denial of inheritance rights, failure to observe sabbatical and jubilee laws, etc.)" (Stuart, *Hosea—Jonah*, 288, 83–84).

101. Stuart, *Hosea—Jonah*, 383. Ellen Davis explains, Amos's "words expose the ideology and inner workings of a complex social system that alienated ordinary Israelites from their inherited land. It took out of their hands, if not always the land itself (although that happened frequently enough), then at least crucial decisions about its cultivation, and also much or most of its marketable produce" (Davis, *Scripture, Culture, and Agriculture*, 127–28). These dynamics also marked Roman imperial actions as well.

102. See also Amos 5:11, which states: "Therefore because you trample on the poor and take from them levies of grain, you have built houses of hewn stone, but you shall not live in them; you have planted pleasant vineyards, but you shall not drink their wine."

103. Stuart, *Hosea—Jonah*, 384. Stuart explains that although God had intended for all the covenant people (excepting the Levites) to have direct access to the land and its produce, the developments of the eighth century BCE—with increased urbanization and control of land by the rich—made the landless poor extremely vulnerable to exploitation and abuse. "The increasingly powerful upper class secured more and more land for themselves, particularly by foreclosing mercilessly on loans to poor farmers (2:6–8; 5:12; Isa 5:8; Exod 22:24) and by ignoring the covenant's gleaning laws (e.g., Lev 19:9–10; Deut 24:19–21)" (387). Because the landless and urban poor had no alternative access to food, those who sold food could often demand high prices (284).

104. Andersen and Freedman, *Amos*, 801.

According to Amos, such abuses and covenantal transgressions were seen and remembered by the Creator God and would bring about cosmic consequences. The effects of Israel's injustices would result in what appears to be the dissolution of creation itself since "the absence of justice in Israel disrupts not only the social order but also the cosmic order."[105] Amos warns those who participated in and benefited from the disordered economic system, declaring:

> The Lord has sworn by the pride of Jacob: Surely I will never forget any of their deeds. Shall not the land tremble on this account, and everyone mourn who lives in it, and all of it rise like the Nile, and be tossed about and sink again, like the Nile of Egypt? On that day, says the Lord God, I will make the sun go down at noon, and darken the earth in broad daylight. I will turn your feasts into mourning, and all your songs into lamentation; I will bring sackcloth on all loins, and baldness on every head; I will make it like the mourning for an only son, and the end of it like a bitter day. (Amos 8:7–10)[106]

Amos knows what it is for the land literally to tremble since he ministered when an earthquake took place (Amos 1:1), and here he correlates the land's tumult with the unrighteous and unjust deeds of God's people. The sun setting at noon and darkness covering the earth during the day further represents a disturbance in the order of creation in which God had established the sun to "rule the day" (Gen 1:16). Amos makes it clear that the injustices disrupting human society would destabilize the most reliable aspects of creation.

By the end of Amos, the prophet nevertheless directs Israel's attention to God's future salvation and restoration, and this restoration includes creational fertility, justice, and peace.[107]

---

105. Fretheim, *God and World*, 170.

106. See also Amos 5:7–9: "Ah, you that turn justice to wormwood, and bring righteousness to the ground! The one who made the Pleiades and Orion, and turns deep darkness into the morning, and darkens the day into night, who calls for the waters of the sea, and pours them out on the surface of the earth, the Lord is his name, who makes destruction flash out against the strong, so that destruction comes upon the fortress."

107. Although scholars debate whether verses 11–15 are authentic to the prophet Amos, Stuart claims the text is original to the prophet because of linguistic reasons (Stuart, *Hosea—Jonah*, 397). See also Andersen and Freedman who think Amos 9:11–15 does not reflect post-exilic times but resonates with other "general predictions of restoration that we find scattered through the Primary History and major prophets" (Andersen and Freedman, *Amos*, 893).

> The time is surely coming, says the Lord, when the one who plows shall overtake the one who reaps, and the treader of grapes the one who sows the seed; the mountains shall drip sweet wine, and all the hills shall flow with it. I will restore the fortunes of my people Israel, and they shall rebuild the ruined cities and inhabit them; they shall plant vineyards and drink their wine, and they shall make gardens and eat their fruit. I will plant them upon their land, and they shall never again be plucked up out of the land that I have given them, says the Lord your God. (Amos 9:13–15)

Instead of the famine-like experiences of 4:6–9, the end of Amos envisions agricultural abundance at an unimaginable scale, when the work of harvesting does not end even by the time of the next planting season, just as Lev 26:3–7 promised would happen if Israel obeyed God's commands.[108] Israel's return to its land would allow God's people to labor productively and reap the rewards of their diligent and faithful labors. According to Fretheim, this vision implies that "*the natural order* will be rid of the adverse effects of human sinfulness. Even more, the creation will function in ways that outstrip God's original creational intentions."[109] While God's people would have the renewed opportunity to "serve and maintain" their garden home (Gen 2:15), emphasis in this passage clearly lies in God's gracious work of planting the people in the land and restoring its health.[110]

1.3.2 Ezekiel

Again, although Paul makes little explicit use of Ezekiel, this prophet's correlation of human sin with creational degradation and hope for resurrection are instructive. The prophet Ezekiel portrays Israel's past, present, and future in ways that clearly illustrate the ancient Israelite beliefs that immoral human action degrades creation but divine intervention restores

---

108. Stuart explains: "The harvests will be so abundant that harvesters will still be trying after many months to finish collecting one crop when it will already be time to plant the next one. Barley and wheat are ripe in Palestine by early May; grapes by early September. Ploughing begins in October, followed immediately by sowing" (Stuart, *Hosea—Jonah*, 398–99).

109. Fretheim, *God and World*, 171.

110. Although other prophetic books—such as Habakkuk and Hosea—offer similar theological perspectives and arguably inform Paul's theological imagination, time and space constraints compel me not to discuss them here.

it.[111] Although Ezekiel does not focus on a messianic figure, the prophet's vision of God's future cleansing of the people and their land powerfully shapes biblical expectations, in which the land's own restoration happens as a result of God's commitment to its good and in conjunction with human forgiveness, cleansing, and restoration.[112]

This cleansing of people entails the land's restoration because human sin degraded creation in the first place, as Ezek 36:17, 18 make plain: "Mortal, when the house of Israel lived on their own soil, they defiled it with their ways and their deeds... So I poured out my wrath upon them for the blood that they had shed upon the land, and for the idols with which they had defiled it." Their moral sins of murder and idolatry defiled the land in ways that only God could cleanse.[113] Yet, by cleansing the land's occupants of their sin and impurities, God will revive creational abundance one day. By the mouth of Ezekiel, God promises:

> I will sprinkle clean water upon you, and you shall be clean from all your uncleannesses, and from all your idols I will cleanse you. A new heart I will give you, and a new spirit I will put within you; and I will remove from your body the heart of stone and give you a heart of flesh. I will put my spirit within you, and make you follow my statutes and be careful to observe my ordinances. Then you shall live in the land that I gave to your ancestors; and you shall be my people, and I will be your God. I will save you from all your uncleannesses, and I will summon the grain and make it abundant and lay no famine upon you. I will make the fruit of the tree and the produce of the field abundant, so that you may never again suffer the disgrace of famine among the nations. (Ezek 36:25–30)

---

111. Aldo Leopold insightfully notes: "Individual thinkers since the days of Ezekiel and Isaiah have asserted that the despoliation of land is not only inexpedient but wrong. Society, however, has not yet affirmed their belief" (*Sand County Almanac*, 172).

112. We encounter God's commitment to the land, when God announces: "But you, O mountains of Israel, shall shoot out your branches, and yield your fruit to my people Israel; for they shall soon come home. See now, I am for you; I will turn to you, and you shall be tilled and sown... I will multiply human beings and animals upon you. They shall increase and be fruitful; and I will cause you to be inhabited as in your former times, and will do more good to you than ever before. Then you shall know that I am the LORD" (Ezek 36:8–9, 11).

113. In light of the fact that Ezek 36 correlates Israel's impurity with their shedding of blood and idolatry (36:18), Ezekiel's vision almost certainly presupposes the Levitical worldview in which murder and idolatory degrade the sinner(s) and the land (Klawans, *Impurity and Sin*, 30–31).

Creation's Interrelatedness

In the proceeding chapter, the prophet announces an even more breath-taking scene in which God's breath or Spirit vivifies the dry bones, the dead bodies, of God's people so they might live again on their land (Ezek 37:1–14).[114] In these passages ripe for Paul's later pneumatology and emphasis on resurrection, we find "the removal of Israel's uncleanness is accompanied by natural abundance and a new day for the land and its various creatures (see 36:8–12; 34:25–31; 47:7–12)."[115] According to Ezekiel, it is only the special justifying and vivifying acts of God that bring forgiveness of grave sins, cleanse impurities, restore life, and heal the land.[116]

1.3.3 Isaiah

Paul depends heavily on the book of Isaiah, and the prophet's words in Isa 11:1–9 provide an especially striking witness to the ways in which human righteousness could positively affect the whole of creation.[117] This passage, a portion of which Paul quotes in Rom 15:12, reflects a common ANE trope in which a monarch was considered to have profound influence on the well-being of human subjects and the rest of creation. In what was considered to be a divinely instituted order of the cosmos, the monarch (typically a male) occupied a highly responsible and representative role, and his actions directly affected the health (or lack of health) of the

---

114. Ezekiel, then, provides inspiration for the nascent Jewish hope in human resurrection. Somewhat similarly, Dan 12:1–3 offers God's suffering and persecuted people a hope for future, bodily resurrection when God will right all wrongs. Matt O'Reilly points to these prophetic texts and concludes, "Resurrection thus provides hope for justice and functions to sustain those who suffer unjustly with the hope that God will, at some future point, put the world to rights" (O'Reilly, *Paul and the Resurrected Body*, 13).

115. Fretheim, *God and World*, 196.

116. Klawans, *Impurity and Sin*, 31. Klawans explains Ezekiel's comparison of Israel's status and that of the menstruating woman thusly: "By conjuring the image of ritual purification, Ezekiel may be figuratively describing the ease with which God will be able to bring about a change in the people's moral status. Just as a menstruating woman can cleanse herself quickly and easily from her ritual impurity, so too will God purify the people from the defiling force of their sins. Then again, Ezekiel's vision may have been meant to be taken more literally: that God will, as the prophet says, purify the people from sin by dousing them with clean water. Whether Ezekiel envisions a literal purification of the people by God, or (more likely) is figuratively describing God's power of forgiveness, the fact remains that what is envisioned here is a future hope" (31).

117. The prophet Isaiah was a near contemporary of Amos, but Isaiah's ministry took place primarily in the Southern Kingdom, Judah, during the eighth century BCE.

created order.[118] In a biblical worldview, a king's reign of justice and peace answered, from the human side, God's eternal covenant with the earth.[119] We find this representative relationship most clearly illustrated in Isaiah's vision of the reinstated Davidic king who would establish justice and, as a result, usher in creational peace and fertility (Isa 11:1-9). Isaiah anticipated that the messiah, the "shoot ... from the stump of Jesse" for whom "righteousness shall be the belt around his waist, and faithfulness the belt around his loins," would establish a peaceable kingdom in which "[t]he cow and the bear shall graze, their young shall lie down together; and the lion shall eat straw like the ox" (11:1, 5-7).

Although scholars debate the literary and, therefore, causal connections between Isa 11:1-5, which focuses on humanity, and 11:6-9, which focuses on nonhuman creatures, these verses stand together and thereby function canonically to form a cohesive unit in which "the new scenario for 'nature' is made possible by the reordering of human relationships in verses 1-5."[120] Brevard Childs argues that these verses display a "conceptual unity" and reflect sentiments already expressed in Isaiah: "The themes of the restoration of Zion (1:26), the eschatological assembly of the nations of the world at the sacred mountain (2:1-4), and the establishment of a righteous rule by a future messianic ruler (9:1ff.) are reiterated by means of intertextual references throughout 11:1-9."[121] Isa 11:1-9 anticipates the

---

118. Undergirding this relational complex is an assumption that what one does in this world matters. Righteousness elicits peace, fertility, and more righteousness. Injustice, oppression, and destruction warrant punishment and further destruction. Despite accepting the basic claims of this worldview—what we might call an act-consequence model of creation—Israel also recognized the ways in which appropriate consequences did not always follow correlating acts. The righteous and compassionate acts of Job did not automatically lead to consequences of life-long *shalom*. The wicked and violent acts of the Assyrian army did not immediately receive divine punishment and restraint. Perhaps in response to these discontinuities some Israelites developed a belief that the consequences of their (and others') acts would be met in the life hereafter.

119. By "eternal covenant," I here echo Robert Murray's depiction of the "Cosmic Covenant," typified by "the belief in a divinely willed order harmoniously linking heaven and earth ... Human collaboration in this task was effected by maintaining justice with mercy and by ritual actions, in which kings played the leading part" (Murray, *Cosmic Covenant*, xx).

120. Brueggemann, *Isaiah 1-39*, 102; see also Blenkinsopp, *Isaiah 1-39*, 19:263-65.

121. Childs, *Isaiah*, 100. While it is unclear whether Isa 11:1-9 is an early Isaianic text or was later adjusted in light of the new creation concepts of Isa 65, some maintain that the vision of chapter 11 in fact influenced 65 (Childs, *Isaiah*, 100-102). Even if 11:6-9 was added to 11:1-5 at a later stage, canonically these verses stand together, and their collective meaning should be taken seriously.

Creation's Interrelatedness

harmony between humanity and animals that Gen 2 itself had envisioned for God's creation, and this new harmony would be realized when Jesse's descendant rules in righteousness and faithfulness.[122]

While prophetic texts, such as Amos 9:13-15 and Ezek 36, often portray God as the central actor in the restoration of creational peace and fertility, Isa 11:1-9 places the Davidic ruler at the center of this activity. Healthy human and nonhuman relationships would be reestablished primarily by the leadership of the messiah, who "with righteousness . . . shall judge the poor, and decide with equity for the meek of the earth" (Isa 11:4). The anointed leader's compassionate attention to and care for the poor stands in striking contrast with many of Judah's monarchs and, later, Rome's emperors. The latter attended to male, able-bodied plebs in the giving of free grain, the *frumentationes*, in order to establish and maintain political control (see 2.1). Rather than concentrate his attention primarily on the well-off, Israel/Judah's messiah would administer justice to the neediest in society and even would usher in an age when "[t]he wolf shall live with the lamb, the leopard shall lie down with the kid, the calf and the lion and the fatling together, and a little child shall lead them" (Isa 11:4, 6). As Isaiah foresaw it, the peace among persons and nonhuman creation would culminate in the messiah's raising "a signal for the nations, and assembl[ing] the outcasts of Israel, and gather[ing] the dispersed of Judah from the four corners of the earth" (11:12).[123] In this vision, the Spirit-filled, truly just messiah would establish a reign of peace so remarkable that former enemies—whether human or animal—would live in harmony with one another (11:2, 6-9).[124] Thus, we might conclude that in Isa 11:1-9 "[t]he prophetic picture is not a return to an ideal past, but the restoration of creation by a new act of God through the vehicle of a righteous ruler."[125]

---

122. The interruption of this harmony, as illustrated by Gen 3, nevertheless lurks behind Isa 11 since "*[t]he distortion of human relationships* is at the root of *distortions in creation*. . . . it is a *human* violation of God's order that produces the enemies of *nature*" (Brueggemann, *Isaiah 1-39*, 102. Emphasis original).

123. The Greek translation of 11:10, which Paul quotes in Rom 15:12, changes the Hebrew *Vorlage* in an important way: "On that day there shall be the root of Jesse and the one *who rises to rule the nations*. In him the nations shall hope, and his rest shall be glorious" (emphasis indicates the translational change of the phrase "a signal for the nations").

124. Admittedly, Isaiah's messiah also exacts fatal judgment on the wicked. The verses omitted above (vv 11, 13-16) are more militaristic than my interpretation of Romans encourages.

125. Childs, *Isaiah*, 104. It may be that Isa 11:1-9 consequently gestures toward the idea of "new creation," which Isa 65:17 describes as a new heavens and new earth; for

The necessity of God's work of restoration becomes all the more obvious when considered in light of Isaiah's Apocalypse, particularly chapter 24. Employing similar language as Gen 6:11–13 and Rom 8:21, the Greek translation of Isa 24:1, 3, 4 exclaims: "Behold, the Lord is destroying (καταφθείρει) the inhabited world (οἰκουμένην) and will make it desolate (ἐρημώσει) . . . The earth will be destroyed in destruction (φθορᾷ φθαρήσεται) . . . The earth mourned (ἐπένθησεν), and the inhabited world (οἰκουμένη) was destroyed (ἐφθάρη)."[126] Isaiah's reasons for this destruction of earth and the inhabited world (οἰκουμένη) become apparent in verses 5 and 6, where human transgression is blamed. Differing somewhat from the Hebrew Masoretic text, the Greek translation of 24:5–6a declares, "The earth was lawless (ἠνόμησεν) on account of its inhabitants, because they transgressed the law and exchanged the commands, an eternal covenant. Therefore, a curse eats the earth, because its inhabitants sinned (ἡμάρτοσαν)."[127] This Greek rendering, even more powerfully than the Hebrew, correlates human sin with creational deterioration.

While sin in general might stand behind the earth's degradation, the wider context suggests that God's people specifically transgressed in their relationships with the land, particularly in their overconsumption of the land's products. Intertextual echoes between Isa 24 and chapters 5 and 22 suggest the "city of chaos" (24:10) may have been a place where the inhabitants drank the fruit of the vine to the point of drunkenness.[128] In an exposition attentive to the agricultural context of Isaiah, Daniel Stulac stresses the way in which Isa 24:1–7 correlates "agro-ecological annihilation" with the people's rejection of Torah and their "excessive consumption, moral degeneracy, blasphemous pride, and military destruction."[129] The land

---

an insightful discussion of the literary, theological, and political background to Paul's notion of "new creation," see Jackson, *New Creation in Paul's Letters*.

126. Author's translation. I render οἰκουμένη as "inhabited world," with the implication that it refers primarily to those living in the world, most especially humans (see BDAG, 699–700).

127. This contrasts with the English translation of the Hebrew: "The earth lies polluted under its inhabitants; for they have transgressed laws, violated the statutes, broken the everlasting covenant. Therefore a curse devours the earth, and its inhabitants suffer for their guilt" (Isa 24:5–6a).

128. Daniel J. Stulac offers this perspective and also explains that the townspeople in Isa 22 perform "faithless slaughter of large and small cattle so that the people may gorge on meat while awaiting their doom (22:13)" (Stulac, *History and Hope*, 95).

129. Stulac, *History and Hope*, 95, 106, 97. Jackson similarly reads Isa 24 as indicating that "the earth itself is defiled by the sinfulness of the people against YHWH (24:5–6).

experiences ruin and destruction not only because God brings about judgment on its sinful inhabitants but also because of the ways in which those inhabitants had related to each other, God, and the land.[130]

Despite Israel's failures to comply with God's ways, as typified in the people's idolatrous practices of consumption (Isa 24:1–7; 65:1–8), Third Isaiah nevertheless presents God's faithful servants as inheriting the land and receiving its nourishing produce (65:9–10, 13–14). Along with Israel, the prophet portrays gentiles, the people of the nations, as one day worshipping "the God of Israel as the Lord of the universe" and turning away from "their false gods" (Isa 2:2–4; 56:5–6).[131] According to this vision, the gentiles "worship Israel's God, but they are not expected to become members of Israel or . . . convert to Judaism."[132] Of course, the apostle Paul perceived the fulfillment of this inclusive vision in his own ministry to the nations (Rom 1:5; 3:29–30; 15:8–21; 16:25–27).

In addition to God's restoration of an inclusive human community, Isa 65 offers a poem rich with images of creational well-being. Isa 65:17–25 expresses God's intention to rectify all things, particularly the "[h]uman sin [that] leads to natural destruction."[133] According to the Hebrew text, God declares: "I am about to create new heavens and a new earth; the former things shall not be remembered or come to mind" (Isa 65:17).[134] Mirroring

---

Creation strains under the awful weight of guilt from this rebellion against God (24:20)" (*New Creation in Paul's Letters*, 25).

130. Stulac, *History and Hope*, 95. Jonathan Moo insightfully explains the cause and effect dynamic as resulting, in part, from Israel's transgression of the Law, the "everlasting covenant" (Isa 24:5 NETS). He then correlates this complex dynamic with Rom 8:19–22, stating: Paul "considers creation to be enslaved to the effects of ongoing human sin and divine judgment. This slavery itself can be considered the result of God's decision to link the fate of the natural world and humankind through what Isa 24.5 calls an 'eternal covenant'" (Moo, "Romans 8.19–22," 74).

131. Shahar, "Jewish Views of Gentiles," 641.

132. Shahar, "Jewish Views of Gentiles," 641.

133. Jackson, *New Creation in Paul's Letters*, 19.

134. The NRSV's wording, which explicitly portrays God as creating anew, correlates God's restoration of creation with the original work of creation depicted in Gen 1:1. Yet, as Ryan T. Jackson indicates, the Greek translation of Isaiah with which the apostle Paul was likely familiar replaced the active verb of the Hebrew with a substantive clause: "For heaven will be new, and the earth will be new" (Isa 65:17a NETS). Scholars speculate on why the Septuagint's translators would have altered the text in this way (*New Creation in Paul's Letters*, 27–30). No matter the motivation, the Greek translation nevertheless illustrates that "the promise of a new heaven and earth is not a disregarding of the created order" but upholds the Tanakh's consistent vision that "the fate of humanity and the world are intertwined" (30).

First Isaiah's extraordinary vision of restored creation, a few verses later Third Isaiah presents God as promising that "[t]he wolf and the lamb shall feed together, the lion shall eat straw like the ox; but the serpent—its food shall be dust! They shall not hurt or destroy on all my holy mountain" (65:25). Here we find God's intention to reverse the destruction human idolatry and infidelity have brought upon the earth and instead to establish peace, flourishing, and harmony in a new (or, renewed) creation.[135] While attending to the nonhuman creation in these ways, God simultaneously provides joy, long life, and abundance to God's people (65:19–23).[136]

1.3.4 Psalms

Like Isa 11, the Psalms associate righteous human leadership with agricultural success.[137] Correlating a monarch's righteousness with the integrity and flourishing that occurs in the wider creation, Ps 72 begins by petitioning God to: "Give the king your justice, O God, and your righteousness to a king's son. May he judge your people with righteousness, and your poor with justice. May the mountains yield prosperity for the people, and the hills, in righteousness" (72:1–3). The psalmist pleads with God that the king might exercise "dominion from sea to sea" (72:8) and rule over the surrounding nations (72:9–11) *because* he "delivers the needy" and "has pity on the weak" (72:12–13). After extolling the king's covenantal ways of compassion and righteousness the psalmist continues: "[m]ay there be abundance of grain in the land; may it wave on the tops of the mountains; may its fruit be like Lebanon; and may people blossom in the cities like the grass of the field" (72:13, 16). Finally, in keeping with Israel's call to live at peace with nonhuman creation as well as the nations, the psalmist echoes

---

135. Admittedly, the passage gestures toward an *almost* complete restoration. The serpent appears to continue in its cursed condition on account of its words with Eve in Gen 3.

136. Perhaps such a scene reminds us of Lev 26:42 where God remembers the land and thereby preserves Israel during its exile so that the chosen people might be led back to the land of promise. All of this leads the land to rejoice over Israel's salvation (Isa 44:23) (Fretheim, *God and World*, 250).

137. Even though Paul does not quote this psalm, we find in it a reiteration of previous themes. Admittedly, more passages from the Writings could be discussed, such as several from Ecclesiastes. However, the focus of this chapter does not depend on further exposition.

God's covenant with Abram: "May all nations be blessed in him" (Ps 72:17). This Psalm, then, ties together many of the theological themes explored throughout this chapter.

1.4 Conclusion

From the Law to the Prophets to the Writings, Israel's Scriptures testify to God's intention for humans to embody their servant leadership and bear the divine image in ways that lead to flourishing, biodiversity, justice, and well-being for God's good creation. To lead in this charge, God calls upon Abram/Abraham and all his heirs to function as intercessors, servants, and keepers of creation, as people who bring blessing upon all the nations (Exod 19:6; Isa 42:6; 49:6; 60:3). The covenant, then, comes with obligations. "Dominion" comes with responsibilities. Relationship comes with expectations. God's particular relationship with Israel naturally expands into a saving and liberating relationship between and among God, the nations, and creation.

According to this overview of select portions of the Tanakh, at least six eco-theological principles offer themselves for consideration:

1. God cooperated with land and water to create living things; commissioned the creation to be diverse and interdependent so that all living things would have adequate access to food;[138] and instructed people to share land and food justly and equitably, even with other creatures.

2. God created humans to be creation's servant leaders but also gave them freedom to disobey and sin.

3. God created a world in which human activity necessarily affects the vitality, flourishing, and well-being of human and nonhuman creation.

---

138. On the basis of Gen 1, we might also add that God gave living things the ability to reproduce so that their kind might exist throughout time. God's people, then, ought also support this capacity among God's creatures. Yet, of course, the question of how we respond to the reproduction and spread of micro- and macroorganisms that destroy the health of humans and nonhumans requires the implementation of other theological and ethical principles. For example, since some viruses and bacteria may cause fatal illnesses, the principle of Spirit-endowed life (number 6) suggests that humans might employ their minds to restrain and prevent the life-destroying effects of such viruses and bacteria. Principle number 7, developed in 3.3, also suggests as much.

4. God provided God's people with the means to atone for impurities and minor sins and promised to cleanse the people and land fully in the future.

5. God promised a messiah to make things right/just.

6. God promised the Spirit to make things alive.

These principles and the story of creation underlying them arguably influenced the apostle Paul's interpretation and proclamation of the gospel, especially as he expresses it in Romans. Paul demonstrates that he—like the writers of the Tanakh—perceived human and creational well-being as interdependent. For, Romans not only portrays human beings as enslaved to sin and death (Rom 5:17; 6:6, 17) but also depicts the creation as subjected to frustration and enslaved to destruction (8:20–21). These negative conditions result, according to Paul, in large measure because of human sin. Thus, like his scriptural heritage, Paul recognizes that human activity drastically affects the rest of creation (5:12–21; 8:21). Nevertheless, in step with the hopes and promises expressed in the Tanakh, Paul came to trust that Jesus was Israel's long-expected Messiah who would not only liberate Jews but also gentiles from sin and death and would establish justice, making wrongs right (5:15–21). What is more, in fulfillment of God's covenantal faithfulness and righteousness, this Messiah and his people would ultimately lead the whole creation into its liberation (8:21), and God's Spirit would enliven humanity and creation. In the meantime, however, Paul invites all God's people to align themselves with God's work of making the world right and alive.

While this rendition of Paul's eco-theological context provides interpreters today with vital lenses for reading his story of creation well, his lived experience within the first-century Roman Empire affords us with an even more holistic view of this story. Naturally, we do not know what his day-to-day experiences in the empire entailed; yet, as we come to understand the empire's messages and methods more fully, we can better envision Paul's place within it. Consequently, we turn now, in chapter 2, to consider the ways in which the early Roman Empire proclaimed its emperor as the one who restores nature, establishes peace, and provides abundance. Then, in chapters 3–5, we will reflect on the ways in which the apostle Paul engaged the theological, political, and ecological contexts of the Tanakh and Roman Empire in his letter to Rome.

CHAPTER 2

Creation's Subjugation

The Imperial Gospel in Action

FROM THE START OF Emperor Augustus's reign to the birth of the church and continuing on after Saint Paul's execution, people throughout the Roman Empire regularly encountered an imperial gospel announcing the empire's success at establishing peace and natural abundance in the Mediterranean region. This peace and abundance was good news to many people since peasant farmers, estate owners, and imperial rulers all faced the difficult ecological challenge of producing sufficient, reliable, and consistent food in the variable climates and turbulent social milieus of the Mediterranean. The political stability and peace, which the Roman Empire secured through military might and vigilant oversight, allowed farmers (particularly those of military age) to tend their fields and terraces more effectively than during times of war. Peace and safety also facilitated trade between places of plenty and dearth. Because the productive lands of Egypt and North Africa were brought under imperial control, Roman emperors secured massive amounts of grain to feed Rome's inhabitants more consistently than ever before.[1] Political control, colonial expansion, and consistent food supply all made it appear that Rome's first emperor had successfully renewed the Golden Age. Imperial poets, coin-makers, artisans, and builders lauded Emperor Augustus's alleged achievements in

---

1. Drawing upon the work of Gerhard Lenski, Neil Elliott identifies the Roman Empire of this time as an "agrarian tributary empire" (Elliott, *Arrogance of the Nations*, 28). As such, a significant gap existed between the governing few who ruled and received tributes and those who were subjected and relinquished those tributes, taxes, and services (Lenski, *Power and Privilege*, 189–296).

restoring nature's bounty through his pious administration and superior dominion, and they consequently directed all peoples to pledge fidelity to him. However, when viewed holistically, the empire's so-called Golden Age cast an expansive shadow over the plight of farmers and sharecroppers, particularly those in North Africa, and the long-term environmental health of the Mediterranean region.

In his letter to the imperial capital, the apostle Paul seems to counter the imperial gospel when he declares that creation remained subjected to frustration and enslaved to destruction (Rom 8:20–21). His words rouse us to examine whether another reality—one that contradicted imperial claims—existed for some members and locations of the empire. In other words, his testimony regarding creation's condition prompts us to consider whether imperial rhetoric did not always line up with ecological realities. As this chapter argues, the agricultural regime that Rome's leaders developed in North Africa (2.2) enabled its emperors to appear as those who liberated the people from starvation and renewed a Golden Age of abundance, peace, and piety (2.1). Yet, that regime also catalyzed significant ecological degradation throughout the region and depended on human exploitation (2.2).

2.1 Rome's Claims: Liberating People from Hunger

In striking similarity to the Tanakh's creation account in Gen 2, the prominent first-century CE Roman mythology, the *Metamorphoses*, held that the earth was once so fruitful that people could eat freely and effortlessly from the land. A masterpiece of Roman mythology completed in 7 CE by the Roman poet Ovid, the *Metamorphoses* portrayed the human as "one who could have dominion over all the rest" of earth's creatures (Ovid, *Met.* 77).[2] Initially, the earth was liberally fertile:

> Golden was that first age, which, with no one to compel, without law, of its own will, kept faith and did the right . . . The earth herself, without compulsion, untouched by hoe or plowshare, of herself gave all things needful . . . Anon the earth, untilled, brought forth her stores of grain, and the fields, though unfallowed, grew white with heavy, bearded wheat. (Ovid, *Met.* 89–90, 100–101, 109–10)[3]

The Age of Gold, an age ruled by the god Saturn, consisted of peace, abundance, an obedient and fecund earth, and humans who were "content with

---

2. Ovid, *Metamorphoses*, 1:ix–x, 9.
3. Ovid, *Metamorphoses*, 1:8–11.

food which came with no one's seeking" (Ovid, *Met.* 103).[4] But the Golden Age faded when "Saturn had been banished to the dark land of death, and the world was under the sway of Jove [Jupiter]" (Ovid, *Met.* 113–14) so that the age turned to silver, which subsequently devolved to an Age of Bronze, and finally to an Age of Iron (Ovid, *Met.* 114, 125, 127).[5] People followed greedy passions, destroying each other and digging up the earth in pursuit of iron and gold (Ovid, *Met.* 128–43).[6] By tracing the devolution of human society in such a way, Ovid not only echoed Greek mythologies prior to him but also portrayed the world in ways that mirrored the difficult realities of life during the late republic and early empire.

Several decades before Ovid wrote his *Metamorphoses* and during the tumultuous times around 37 BCE that followed Julius Caesar's assassination (44 BCE), the Roman poet Virgil expressed hope for a better era in his *Eclogues* ("Selections").[7] Reflecting a similar worldview as Ovid, Virgil hoped for a cyclical (rather than ultimate and permanent) renewal of former glories.[8] He envisioned that this renewal would come from the wise dominion of an unnamed man.[9] Virgil highlighted the remarkable character of his hope by noting the shadow side of contemporary life, which involved sin, fear, and strife:

> Leading us, you'll erase all traces of our sins
> Remaining, freeing earth from endless fear and strife.
> (Virgil, *Ecl.* 4.13–14)[10]

---

4. Ovid, *Metamorphoses*, 1:9.

5. Ovid, *Metamorphoses*, 1:11.

6. Ovid, *Metamorphoses*, 1:13. Immorality, injustice, and impiety were understood to cause widespread problems in the ancient world. Some Romans also believe "disorderly barbarians and rebels caused the corruption of nature" (Jewett, "Corruption and Redemption of Creation," 31). Meanwhile, some upper class, land-holding Romans blamed the poor and low-class people in their own lands as causing disarray (Elliott and Reasoner, *Documents and Images*, 161–62).

7. Virgil, *Eclogues*, vii; Galinsky, *Augustan Culture*, 91–92. William Dunstan sees the context of the poem as "reflecting the false hope stemming from the temporary reconciliation between Mark Antony and Octavian at Brundisium in 40 BCE" (Dunstan, *Ancient Rome*, 265).

8. Virgil, *Eclogues*, 10.

9. Some historians identify the unnamed person as Pollio (Galinsky, *Augustan Culture*, 92). Arguing against sweeping claims that this poem set the agenda for Augustan art and politics, Galinsky explains that Virgil later developed the themes present in the fourth Eclogue into a more politically robust ideology (93).

10. Virgil, *Eclogues*, 52.

Through the new leader's exercise of political governance, the earth's sufferings—both of human and natural origin—would cease and would transform into experiences of peace. Virgil, then, looked forward to the greater natural fruitfulness he believed Rome's new leader would establish.

The new leader would not only eliminate warfare but would overcome creation's reluctance to give its bounty. Creation would freely bring its generous offerings to people. *Eclogues* 4.21–22, 38–40 exclaim:

> All by themselves, the goats shall bring milk-swollen udders
> Home, and herds faced with mighty lions shall not shudder . . .
>
> The sailing merchants and their pine-built ships will stop.
> There'll be no trading goods; all lands will bear all crops.
> The soil will never suffer hoe, nor vine the hook.[11]

Admittedly poetic in their ideal picture of a paradisiacal future, these verses illustrate a Roman dream of human forgiveness and leisure in the midst of natural peace, abundance, and ease.[12] So total is this peace that even the soil is spared the violence of tilling.[13]

Although this Roman ideal depicted humans at their leisure, poets and artists during the late republic and early empire increasingly recognized that material prosperity and political peace continually depended on human labor and occasionally on the use of force. Rome's first emperor, Augustus, later noted in an autobiographical exposition of his life's work, the *Res Gestae*, that during his reign "there was peace, secured by victory" (Aug., *RG* 13).[14] This peace and victory, moreover, flowed out of the gods'

---

11. Virgil, *Eclogues*, 52, 54.

12. Castriota, *Ara Pacis Augustae*, 124.

13. Several years after writing the *Eclogues*, during the civil wars involving Julius Caesar, and before the ascension of Augustus to *princeps*, Virgil altered his tone. This was a time when politicians confiscated the lands of rural farmers in order to favor faithful adherents and when Virgil wrote the *Georgics* ("Farming") (Virgil, *Georgics*, xiii). The political injustice of land redistribution may have touched Virgil personally since his own farming family may have lost its land to Antony, who allegedly confiscated it in order to reward his soldiers. Later, after writing *Georgics*, "Virgil supposedly regained it through the influence of acquaintances who were well connected to Octavian," later named Augustus; yet, "[e]ven if this story is not true, Virgil certainly knew farm families who had been made landless and homeless" (xvi). Instead of envisioning the provision of food without human work, as in the fourth *Eclogue*, in the *Georgics* Virgil more realistically depicts human labor as "the only barrier between the farmer and ruin" (xvii).

14. Augustus, *Velleius Paterculus*, 365.

ordaining the Romans and their leader to world dominion.[15] Yet, this renewal of past glories also depended on Roman morality and virtue.[16] These acknowledgements of human intentionality and agency demonstrate that "[t]he actual realities of Roman life" led people, especially writers, to adjust "the original Golden Age concept in literature into one where ongoing *labor* is the prevailing virtue."[17] The Golden Age no longer appeared as an effortless paradise, nor could Rome convincingly claim to have achieved *that* kind of era, and "no specific iconography exists that would point to a 'Golden Age' of easy bliss."[18] Instead, by the time Augustus received the title imperator and the republic had become an empire, Augustus and his supporters portrayed the Golden Age that he had ushered in as depending on human action and divine beneficence even as "traces (*vestigia*) of the crime-ridden Iron Age . . . overlap[ped] with the commencement of the Golden."[19] Consequently, imperial claims of ushering in the Golden Age and renewing earth's fertility and abundance appear with subtlety and, in comparison with images of dominion and threats of violence, infrequently. Nevertheless, the images depicting material abundance quietly pervaded imperial coins, art, and architecture.

The image of the cornucopia, for example, repeatedly appeared alongside depictions of military and naval might.[20] Imperial artisans employed the long-standing cornucopia to depict the material prosperity that Roman dominion of the Mediterranean had established. Statues, sculptures, mosaics, paintings, and coins portrayed members of the imperial family

---

15. Neil Elliott explains, "the increasing expansion of the Roman economy through the conquest and enslavement of subjected peoples was effectively represented as the inevitable, divinely ordained, and indeed salutary destiny of the Roman people" (*Arrogance of the Nations*, 29).

16. Galinsky, *Augustan Culture*, 107. While we may point to the celebration of the Secular Games of 17 BCE as the start of the renewed Golden Age (Jewett, "Corruption and Redemption of Creation," 27–28; Beard, North, and Price, *Religions of Rome*, 1:203), Galinsky explains that these games "did not celebrate the advent of millennial, passive bliss but took place only after one of the cornerstones of the Augustan program, the legislation on marriage and morals, had been passed in 18 B.C. The health of the new *saeculum* was not merely an automatic, god-given blessing but was to depend on the moral effort of the Romans, the ruling classes in particular" (Galinsky, *Augustan Culture*, 100).

17. Galinsky, *Augustan Culture*, 120.

18. Galinsky, *Augustan Culture*, 118.

19. Virgil, *Eclogues*, 10.

20. Galinsky, *Augustan Culture*, 111–20.

alongside goddesses who held a cornucopia or even a double cornucopia. Because Augustus's birth sign was the Capricorn, a goat sometimes appeared with a cornucopia as a representation of Augustus's rule. Classicist Karl Galinsky explains, "[o]n coins, the association with world rule is steadily maintained by the inclusion of globe and rudder in the depiction of the cornucopia-bearing Capricorn," as on a denarius that was minted in Spain between 17–15 BCE (fig. 1).[21]

Figure 1. Silver Denarius of Augustus, Colonia Patricia, 18–17 BCE. *Above left,* Head of Augustus; *right,* Capricorn, holding globe, carrying cornucopia. *Source:* Curtesy of the American Numismatic Society, http://numismatics.org/collection/1944.100.39167.

Another coin from 7 BCE placed "Victoria who holds both a cornucopia and a laurel crown, the traditional sign of the triumphator," beside Augustus's head.[22]

Emperor Augustus's heirs also employed the cornucopia on their coins in order to communicate abundance and provision. A coin the apostle Paul likely handled and interpreted during his ministry in Asia Minor was minted in Pergamum during Claudius's reign, between 41–54 CE (fig. 2).

---

21. Galinsky, *Augustan Culture*, 115–16.
22. Galinsky, *Augustan Culture*, 117.

Creation's Subjugation

Figure 2. Silver Cistophorus of Claudius, Pergamum, 41–54 CE. *Above left*, Head of Claudius; *right*, Claudius, standing front, left, being crowned by female figure, right, holding cornucopia. *Source*: Curtesy of the American Numismatic Society, http://numismatics.org/collection/1955.21.4v.

This coin displays "a distyle temple of Roma and Augustus with the standing figure of the Emperor (Claudius?) on the left being crowned by a female figure (a personification of Asia?) on the right. The Emperor holds a spear in his right hand while the female figure holds a cornucopia in her left."[23] If the female figure indeed symbolizes Asia, her cornucopia may represent Asia's many goods that she would be expected to surrender to her imperial lord. Like so many other similar imperial coins, this coin communicated a clear message: Roman control and martial victory brought an abundance of food in its train.

However, this message of abundance at times conflicted with everyday realities. The Mediterranean region has an erratic climate, which varies season-to-season and year-to-year. This climate makes agriculture highly susceptible to crop failure.[24] In ancient times, many Mediterranean farmers responded to the challenges of procuring daily bread by implementing farming practices that diffused agricultural risk, especially by crop diversification and ritual intercession.

23. Kreitzer, *Striking New Images*, 106. Scholars debate about where this coin was minted. Formerly, scholarly consensus claimed Ephesus, but more recent studies suggest the coin was created in Pergamum since it, rather than Ephesus, had a temple dedicated to Roma and the divine Augustus (106–7). Kreitzer claims that "it appears that the issue was politically motivated and designed to help consolidate Claudius's authority and power within the province" (107).

24. Horden and Purcell, *Corrupting Sea*, 78.

Farmers—along with Roman society as a whole—petitioned their gods for agricultural success. Both city dwellers and rural people could take an active part in agriculture's success through religious devotion, for the Roman people believed that every step of the agricultural process required a religious rite by which they might procure the help of beneficent gods and restrain malevolent ones, since growing food involved factors out of their control yet under the control of various gods.[25] The devout farmer "who knows the cycle of tasks to be done to ensure that the seed germinates, the shoot forms, the ear ripens undamaged, and that the crop is harvested, threshed, garnered, and stored, invokes in turn the qualified deities who are appropriate to the successful outcome of each process."[26] Roman farmers accordingly performed private, familial religious practices, and these practices set the pattern for the corporate, public religious rites of Roman society as a whole.[27] Agriculture, far from being a merely secular or rural activity, necessarily involved the gods and all people—both urban and rural, both slave and emperor—who depended on agriculture's success for their daily bread. In fact, "there was probably never a time when the city of Rome ceased to think of agricultural concerns as central to its way of life."[28] Roman religious traditions thus provided people a cultic means of responding to unreliable climatic and agricultural realities, inviting them to perceive such variability as under the direction of supernatural powers even as imperial rule attempted to provide security and abundance.[29]

In the burgeoning empire, the Roman Emperor held significant religious responsibility for procuring favorable agricultural conditions from the gods. Because of his supreme piety (it was believed), the first emperor, Augustus, obtained the success of military campaigns and agricultural seasons, mediated the blessings of salutary gods, restrained the fury of antagonistic deities, and ultimately established an era of peace and prosperity for Rome.[30] Roman advocates of Caesar Augustus applauded these successes and claimed his political leadership generated natural fertility and

25. Turcan, *Gods of Ancient Rome*, 3. Cicero grasps the vulnerability and impotence of farmers in the face of natural processes, admitting: "Farming is throughout a thing whose profits depend not on intelligence and industry but on those most uncertain things, wind and weather" (*2 In Verrem* 3.227) (Erdkamp, *Grain Market*, 145).

26. Turcan, *Gods of Ancient Rome*, 3.

27. Turcan, *Gods of Ancient Rome*, 12, 14.

28. Beard, North, and Price, *Religions of Rome*, 1:46.

29. Horden and Purcell, *Corrupting Sea*, 411.

30. For an insightful explanation of piety, *pietas*, see Galinsky, *Augustan Culture*, 88.

Creation's Subjugation

abundance. Augustus publicly demonstrated his piety by renovating sacred buildings and revitalizing the Roman cult by serving in "all four major priesthoods."[31] Augustus's membership in the Arval Fraternity (a college of priests), in particular, illustrates the religious role he played in attempting to secure agricultural success.

During the Republican Era, the Arval Fraternity was an inconspicuous religious order that made "public sacrifices so that the fields bear fruit."[32] The order's activities illustrate the intimate connection between public and private worship, for the fraternity "performed once a year at the public level the kind of ritual the Roman farmer would conduct privately with his *familia*. That was the Ambarvalia, a procession around the boundaries of the field."[33] Augustus joined this society and thereby endowed the fraternity with prestige and elevated its cultic worship of Dea Dia (the goddess of growth) to a more public and institutional level. In so doing, Augustus upheld "the traditional values of an agricultural society in the midst of a time of intellectual and material sophistication."[34] The fraternity, after Augustus's death, also honored the late emperor and priest by incorporating holy days into its ritual calendar in honor of *divus Augustus*.[35]

In concert with his prominent role in revitalizing the Roman cult, Augustus appeared to some as the divinely favored son of god who wielded his political dominion in ways that ushered in a renewed Golden Age. Poets Virgil and Horace perceived Augustus's pious leadership as prompting a shift in the ages, from an age of violence and dearth to one of peace and plenty. A particularly poignant paean by Virgil, the *Aeneid*, anticipates the peace and prosperity that would come in the late Roman Republic. After Augustus ascended to power in the Republic in 27 BCE and before his transition to emperor, Virgil created this hopeful epic in which he lauded Augustus for establishing peace in the previously fractious and warring

---

31. Galinsky, *Augustan Culture*, 313. The priesthoods included the pontiffs, augurs (those who took auspices for social and political activities), *quindecimviri* ("guardians of the Sibylline Books"), and *fetials* (those who "controlled and performed the rituals" of war) (Beard, North, and Price, *Religions of Rome*, 1:27). In his *Res Gestae*, Augustus declares: "I have been pontifex maximus [ἀρχιερεύς], augur, a member of the fifteen commissioners for performing sacred rites, one of the seven for sacred feasts, an arval brother, a *sodalis Titius*, a fetial priest" (Aug., *RG* 7) (Augustus, *Velleius Paterculus*, 355–57).

32. Galinsky, *Augustan Culture*, 292. See Varro 1.1.5.

33. Galinsky, *Augustan Culture*.

34. Galinsky, *Augustan Culture*, 293.

35. Galinsky, *Augustan Culture*.

Republic.³⁶ Virgil presented Augustus Caesar as a son of god who would usher in the Golden Age:

> Here is the man, he's here! Time and again
> you've heard his coming promised—Caesar Augustus!
> Son of a god, he will bring back the Age of Gold
> to the Latian fields where Saturn once held sway . . .
> (Virgil, *Aen.* 6.913–16)³⁷

Presuming the Roman cyclical view of time, the *Aeneid* portrayed the Age of Iron as leading into a renewed Age of Gold that would positively affect Italy's fields. This transition, according to Virgil, took place under the leadership of Augustus, who was identified as a son of god.

Virgil could consider Augustus a son of the god Julius Caesar, since more than a decade earlier—after Julius's death—the Senate declared in 42 BCE that Julius had ascended to the gods and became a *divus*.³⁸ As a *divus*, Julius became an honorary god (in contrast with the official gods of the pantheon, who were identified by the Latin term *deus*, a distinction that does not carry in Greek or English).³⁹ As the adopted son of *Divi Iuli*, Augustus appeared to have a direct line to the gods as a *divi filius*, "son of a god."⁴⁰ Augustus and his imperial heirs made frequent use of this phrase and placed it in abbreviated fashion on imperial coins. For example, around 41 BCE "Octavian [later named Augustus] issued his own coins with his image as *divi filius* on the obverse and Fortuna (possibly the Fortuna Caesaris), a rudder, and cornucopiae on the reverse."⁴¹ Since Augustus himself would be said to have ascended to the gods after his death, his heir Tiberius also emphasized his filial relationship with the gods. Tiberius minted a coin that read "Tiberius Caesar, Augustus, son of the divine Augustus."⁴² Still later, in an inscription after Claudius

---

36. Dunstan describes Virgil as "[i]ntensely patriotic" while at the same time rejecting "any role as a crude purveyor of imperial propaganda"; "Virgil shared Augustus' view that the ongoing process of restoring traditional values and principles would produce a harmonious social order" (Dunstan, *Ancient Rome*, 265).

37. Virgil, *Aeneid*, 208.

38. Beard, North, and Price, *Religions of Rome*, 1:208.

39. Galinsky, *Augustan Culture*, 322.

40. Kleiner, "Semblance and Storytelling," 207; Elliott and Reasoner, *Documents and Images*, 141.

41. Galinsky, *Augustan Culture*, 114.

42. Elliott and Reasoner, *Documents and Images*, 138.

died and was divinized, Emperor Nero also heralded himself "son of the divine Claudius, descendant of Tiberius Caesar Augustus and Germanicus Caesar, [themselves] sons of the divine Augustus."[43] The aforementioned coins circulated along with many others that proclaimed the emperor as a son of god, an identity that was broadly understood to establish beneficial relations between the gods, people, and nature.

In addition to coins, monuments throughout the empire also reminded Rome's subjects of the emperor's divine sonship. For example, the large gate of Mazaeus and Mithridates in Ephesus, which these freedmen built in honor of Emperor Augustus "between 4 and 2 BCE," held an imperious statue of Augustus, and the gate's inscription proclaimed Augustus as the son of god.[44] As a ubiquitous title for the emperor, the apostle Paul would have been well aware of its imperial meaning as he read the inscription while passing the Gate of Mazaeus and Mithridates during his ministry in Ephesus.

In addition to having his status elevated by being related to a divinized father,[45] Octavian's bestowed name, "Augustus," carried divine overtones that imply a particular power over the natural world.[46] "The etymology is ultimately based on the root *augos* that connotes the power, bestowed divinely, to foster growth; an Augustus, therefore, is 'the holder of that power,

---

43. Elliott and Reasoner, *Documents and Images*, 144. The editors cite Inscriptiones Graecae 5.1.1450.

44. Scherrer, "City of Ephesos," 6.

45. Although some in the Greek east wanted to honor Augustus as a god and worship him directly, Augustus simply allowed his status to be elevated by association and did not encourage direct worship of himself. He permitted Roman citizens to dedicate a temple not only to Roma but also to his adoptive father Divus Julius in Nicaea and Ephesus (Galinsky, *Augustan Culture*, 322).

46. The Senate did this in 27 BCE. Augustus recalled and memorialized this event in his *Res Gestae*, stating: "In my sixth and seventh consulships [28 and 27 BCE], when I had extinguished the flames of civil war, after receiving by universal consent the absolute control of affairs, I transferred the republic from my own control to the will of the senate and the Roman people. For this service on my part I was given the title of Augustus by decree of the senate, and the doorposts of my house were covered with laurels by public act, and a civic crown was fixed above my door, and a golden shield was placed in the Curia Julia whose inscription testified that the senate and the Roman people gave me this in recognition of my valour, my clemency, my justice [δικαιοσύνην], and my piety [εὐσέβειαν]. After that time I took precedence of all in rank, but of power [ἐξουσίας] I possessed no more than those who were my colleagues in any magistracy (Aug., *RG* 34)" (Augustus, *Velleius Paterculus*, 399–401). For reflections on these events in relation to Paul's letter to Rome, see Elliott, *Arrogance of the Nations*, 28–30, 44–47.

one who awakens life and dispenses blessings.'"[47] As a divinely empowered man, Augustus was perceived as wielding the god-like powers of fertility, growth, and life.

The Roman assertion that a supreme political leader could affect natural fertility finds literary expression in the writings of Horace, who explicitly proclaimed that Augustus had brought about an abundant supply of food and a remarkable time of peace:

> Your rule, Augustus,
> Has brought bounty to our fields, restored
> To our gods those standards stripped from proud
> Parthian columns, closed the iron doors
> To the temple of war . . . (Hor., *Odes* 4.15)[48]

It is as if Augustus himself transformed infertile fields into fertile ones. Yet, the political tenor of the passage indicates greater realism than magical fertility. Horace correlated the fields' new bounty with a renewal of piety and the expansion of Rome's borders. For, Augustus

> Reined in the recklessness of those who would swerve
> From the straight course, banished wickedness,
> And called us back to those ancient ways
> By which the Latin name,
>
> The power of Rome, the fame and majesty
> Of her empire have been gloriously extended
> From where the bright sun first rises
> Even to its westernmost bed.
>
> While Caesar stands guard, no turmoil at home,
> No arms abroad can unbalance the peace,
> And no wrath that forges swords
> Shall beset our cities. (Hor., *Odes* 4.15)[49]

---

47. Galinsky, *Augustan Culture*, 316.
48. Horace, *Odes*, 288.
49. Horace, *Odes*, 288.

Creation's Subjugation

According to Horace, Rome's political dominion and its consequent social peace were crucial to agricultural prosperity.[50]

Augustus and his imperial descendants promoted and propagated this message not only through coinage, inscriptions, and literature but also entire building campaigns. A particularly striking tribute to Augustus's political feats stood near the Pantheon and the Field of Mars (Campus Martinus) and celebrated his defeat of Spain and Gaul. The "Altar of Peace," *Ara Pacis Augustae*, unveiled in 9 BCE by Augustus and the Roman Senate, was dedicated "to the *Pax Augusta*, the era of peace and stability established by the reign of Augustus."[51] Through the figural and floral reliefs on its sides and walls, the monument told a story of Rome's transition from "war" and "impiety" during the Roman Republic to "peace and prosperity" under Augustus "in which piety [was] the ultimate virtue."[52] At the eastern entrance to the inner altar, the wall to the left portrayed a motherly figure that was both fertile and reposed. She sat "holding two babies on her lap, surrounded by symbols of fecundity" and was "likely a composite figure comprised of, at least, Venus, Ceres [goddess of cereal grains], Tellus [goddess of Earth], and Pax. Whoever she may be, it is clear that she represents peace and fertility."[53] This woman appeared in contrast to the woman on the right panel. There, the victorious goddess Roma sat erect and alert with weapons of war. Since the altar celebrated "Augustus' return from Spain and Gaul after pacifying the region," the relief of a peaceful and fecund mother provided a visual representation of Horace's literary claim that Augustus had "brought bounty to our fields" (Hor., *Odes* 4.15).[54] Yet the mother's clear juxtaposition with the victorious, warring Roma suggests that it was precisely through Rome's dominion over "barbarians" that prosperity came to the "civilized" world.

Although the human yet god-like figures sculpted on the altar would have captured much of an observer's attention, botanical features carved throughout the altar also arrested the eye. One scholar describes the floral

---

50. In his discussion of "new creation" concepts in Paul's letters, Jackson offers a similar conclusion: "The connection between the physical and political order meant that what happened in the cosmos was directly related to the state (and vice versa). During the time of Augustus, the earth itself was thought to respond to the peace Rome offered the world" (*New Creation in Paul's Letters*, 64).

51. Castriota, *Ara Pacis Augustae*, 3.

52. Armstrong, "Sacrificial Iconography," 351.

53. Armstrong, "Sacrificial Iconography," 351.

54. Horace, *Odes*, 288.

friezes "as a visual embodiment of the returning Golden Age, a new era of blessedness in which the limitless flowering of the earth is contingent upon the efficacious presence of a divinely appointed sovereign, Augustus himself."[55] The flowering vines growing in orderly yet abundant fashion at the base of all the figural reliefs, communicates in visual form the twin themes of political leadership and natural fertility. The *Ara Pacis* thereby proclaimed loud and clear the Augustan gospel of peace and natural abundance in a language understood by literate and illiterate alike.[56] Among the altar's interpreters was a probable community of Christians living near the Field of Mars about half a century after its dedication.[57] Even as they absorbed the imperial gospel from the *Ara Pacis*, these early Christians received Paul's correspondence to Rome.

---

55. Castriota, *Ara Pacis Augustae*, 5.

56. As Gail Armstrong explains, "Poetry touting a new golden age found concrete expression in the sparkling materials of the new buildings [in Rome]. Simply, Augustan propaganda was pervasive in the city, and in the lives of all residents . . . [A]ll were able to comprehend the Augustan system of ideas and ideals. For example, learned observers interpreted the intricate mythological figures carved on the Ara Pacis, while the uneducated surely appreciated the accessible and universal message of prosperity depicted by the carvings of lush plants" (Armstrong, "Sacrificial Iconography," 351). Through his building campaigns, Augustus expressed a clear imperial message and transformed the Roman landscape. Ironically, however, the very buildings that lauded Augustus for bringing natural harmony and abundance exacted a tremendous toll upon the earth. The new infusion of marble into Rome during the late first century BCE and throughout the first century CE came from Luna, a large quarry on the northwestern coast of Italy. Transported by ships to the port at Ostia, the marble was then taken up the river Tiber to Rome, "where special wharves were constructed to receive it" (Kleiner, "Semblance and Storytelling," 5). Art historian Diana Kleiner explains, "[i]t was the full-scale exploitation of the Luna quarries in the age of Augustus that made possible the emperor's boast that he had found Rome to be a city of brick and transformed it into a city of marble (Suet., *Aug.*, 28)" (5).

57. Lampe, *From Paul to Valentinus*, 65–66. This community lived near a grain distribution center (Porticus Minucia Frumentaria), where enlisted plebs could receive their free portions of grain each month (62). Another wealthy congregation of Jesus followers lived further south on the Aventine hill, probably less than a mile from Augustus's forum and near the city's center, where the imperial message of peace and prosperity was constantly displayed and enacted (Jewett, *Romans*, 63). Within close proximity of the Temple of Ceres, these Christians would have witnessed—at least from afar—important agricultural rites. They also lived near the silos where imported grain was stored (Lampe, *From Paul to Valentinus*, 60–61). It is likely, then, that both of these congregations, one of which Prisca and Aquila probably hosted (Rom 16:5), frequently encountered the imperial message that the Roman Empire had established natural fertility and abundant food supplies through its pious and powerful efforts.

Creation's Subjugation

Although the apostle Paul had not yet traveled to Rome and had not yet encountered its architecture prior to writing his epistle to its Christ followers, he probably envisaged comparable iconography in the Forum of Corinth, where an imposing statue of the deified Augustus was erected and an altar much like the *Ara Pacis* stood.[58] Donated early in Tiberius's reign by citizens who demonstrated explicit "support for the deified emperor," the statue stood in front of the Julian Basilica, which either functioned as a law court for the province or as a place of worship of the *genius Augusti*.[59] This prominent statue, itself standing 2.5 to 3 meters high aloft a 2.2 to 2.7 meter high base, faced a temple at the opposite end of the forum that likely functioned as the "official center of the imperial cult at Corinth."[60] The inscription on the statue's base states, "sacred to the deified Augustus," which "unequivocably sacralizes the monument to Augustus as a god." The statue did not necessarily function "as a cult image although it clearly connects the dedication to emperor worship."[61] In front of this statue stood an altar "resembling the Ara Pacis."[62] During his ministry in Corinth, we can imagine Paul encountering these figures and then underminding their religious significance with the gospel of Jesus Christ.

Soon after Paul wrote his epistle to Rome, Nero reiterated the message conveyed by the *Ara Pacis* and identified himself with its claims on bronze coins minted sometime between 64–67 CE. "The coins show the altar, including ornamentation on the top and decorations on the front panels which stand on either side of the central double doors. The words ARA PACIS stand at the base of the scene."[63] By correlating his own reign with Augustus's celebrated role as the one who brought peace and plenty to the

---

58. Laird, "Emperor in a Roman Town," 84.

59. Laird, "Emperor in a Roman Town," 82, 89.

60. Laird, "Emperor in a Roman Town," 91.

61. Laird, "Emperor in a Roman Town," 78, 81–82.

62. Laird, "Emperor in a Roman Town," 91. Another altar strikingly similar to the *Ara Pacis* stood in the colony of North Africa in Carthage. Local inhabitants likely designed and built it during Augustus's time. One side of the altar displays "a seated female figure, with children in her arms, her lap full of fruit, animals at her feet. This figure is closely based on the scene of 'Earth' on Augustus' Ara Pacis in Rome" (Beard, North, and Price, *Religions of Rome*, 1:331). It is unclear how artisans in Carthage came to mimic the altar in Rome, yet it is clear that the "*colonia* [of Africa] was expressing its own version of Roman identity" (333).

63. Kreitzer, *Striking New Images*, 121.

Roman Republic-turned-Empire, Nero communicated that he too secured Rome's dominion and prosperity in the world.[64]

Although the artistic expressions of poems, coins, monuments, and inscriptions impressively articulated the emperors' success in establishing Rome's peace, prosperity, and abundance, this message took on more concrete and convincing form when Rome's leaders provided the masses with food.[65] Augustus and subsequent emperors (especially Nero) powerfully exhibited their positive effects on nature by supplying abundant grain for the Roman populace. Through the provision of free grain, called *frumentationes*,[66] Rome's emperors demonstrated that, as divine sons, they had subdued a recalcitrant human and nonhuman world so that it would peacefully, willingly, and abundantly provide daily bread for the gloriously civilized people of Rome.

At times, however, natural forces disturbed Rome's peace and abundance. When a flood of the Tiber River in 22 BCE destroyed a great deal of stored grain in Rome, "[a] mob besieged the senate house, threatening to burn it down, and then beseeched Augustus to become dictator and take charge of the grain supply."[67] Augustus recounted this incident in his *Res Gestae*, avowing: "I did not decline at a time of the greatest scarcity of grain the charge of the grain-supply, which I so administered that, within a few days, I freed [ἐλευθερῶσαι] the entire people, at my own expense from the fear and danger in which they were" (Aug., *RG* 5).[68] He went on to emphasize his regular contributions of money and grain to Roman plebs:

> in my eleventh consulship I made twelve distributions of food
> from grain bought at my own expense . . . These largesses of mine

---

64. Kreitzer, *Striking New Images*, 121. However, Nero's success depended on excessive exploitation, noted by his contemporaries. For discussion, see Elliott, *Arrogance of the Nations*, 34–36.

65. Although my focus in this chapter and book is on wheat, much could be said about meat and its central role in imperial festivals. For some discussion, see Tonstad, *Letter to the Romans*, 255. Even as Rome provided thousands of people with food for the support of life, it functioned by the terror of death, especially crucifixion. Thus, in addition to provisions of food, "[t]he imperial economy of death was aided and abetted by relentless propaganda, an attempt to create a narrative of beneficence, peace, and prosperity that had little or no basis in reality" (124).

66. Rickman, "Grain Trade," 263.

67. Aldrete, *Floods of the Tiber*, 132.

68. Augustus, *Velleius Paterculus*, 352–53. Although there is a lacuna at the point where the monument reads "grain-supply," the editors of the text have deemed it likely that it originally read "frumenti," the free supply of grain.

> reached a number of persons never less than two hundred and fifty thousand ... When consul for the thirteenth time I gave sixty denarii apiece to the plebs who were then receiving public grain; these were a little more than two hundred thousand persons. (Aug., *RG* 15)[69]

By providing free grain and reminding his subjects of these acts of generosity, the emperor showed himself to be the supreme liberator and patron of Rome as well as the cultivator of agricultural abundance.

After Augustus's death and ascension to the gods, Tiberius—Augustus's heir to the imperial throne—etched the *Res Gestae* in both Latin and Greek on Augustus's mausoleum in the Field of Mars in Rome. Tiberius also inscribed these reminiscences on sacred monuments throughout the empire, including Pisidian Antioch and Ancyra, Galatia.[70] During his travels through Pisidian Antioch (Acts 13:14) and possibly Ancyra, Galatia, Paul may have taken the opportunity to read the *Res Gestae* for himself.

Even before Augustus, Julius Caesar had provided *frumentationes* to the Roman populace. During Julius's and Augustus's reigns, the *frumentationes* "rose to the point where they were being issued, even if only briefly, to some 320,000 recipients at the rate of 5 *modii* [about 1.23 bushels] per month. For these men alone more than 19 million *modii* a year were needed, that is, over 120,000 tons."[71] Wheat was "by far the most important, and the cheapest, source of calories," and 5 *modii* provided "a calorific value equivalent to between 3,000 and 3,500 calories a day" for one person for an entire month, although the grain was probably shared among family members.[72] Assuming a population of about one million people, the total annual grain requirement in Rome ranged between 30 and 60 million *modii*.[73] Taking 40 million *modii* as a median figure, Rome's total grain need would have amounted to roughly 250,000 tons of grain per year,[74] and the *frumentationes* provided somewhere between 32 percent and 63 percent of

---

69. Augustus, *Velleius Paterculus*, 368–71.

70. Augustus, *Velleius Paterculus*, 332–37. The primary source for the text of *Res Gestae* comes from the Temple of Rome and Augustus in Ancyra (338).

71. Rickman, "Grain Trade," 263.

72. Rickman, "Grain Trade," 262.

73. Dennis Kehoe gives the lower figure of 30 million (Kehoe, *Economics of Agriculture*, 4); Lionel Casson gives the higher figure of 60 million (Casson, "Role of the State," 21); G. E. Rickman suggests 40 million (Rickman, "Grain Trade," 263); and Paul Erdkamp proposes 30 to 40 million (Erdkamp, *Grain Market*, 230–35).

74. Rickman, "Grain Trade," 263.

Rome's grain needs. The rest of its grain requirements were met through the market and rural estates.

Most scholars assume that the list of people receiving free grain (the group known as *plebs frumentaria*) included mostly or only free men, inferring from the evidence that "only residents of Rome were eligible, that freedmen were included, that male citizens could receive from the age of 14" and that "citizenship was the main criterion of eligibility—and that poverty was not a criterion at all."[75] In other words, "informally manumitted slaves, foreigners, and even perhaps transient citizens were all deprived of corn [grain] rations."[76] With all these specifications, the *plebs frumentaria* totaled about 200,000 inhabitants of Rome during Augustus's reign and probably hovered around that same number throughout the first century.[77] Since grains likely provided 65–70 percent of first-century Mediterranean people's nutritional needs,[78] consistently supplying grain to a metropolis such as Rome was a central concern. By doing so, the emperor presented himself as chief patron (πατέρα πατρίδος, Aug., *RG* 35) and a powerful agent who transformed his people's experience of dearth into plenty.[79] All of this testified to the imperial narrative of a politically wrought abundance.[80]

By supplying so many people with essential food sources, the Roman Emperor captured—and perhaps colonized—his people's imaginations so that, through their experience of abundant, accessible food, they would easily believe that the Roman Emperor had ushered in the Golden Age.[81]

---

75. Garnsey and Rathbone, "Background to the Grain Law," 20. However, Coen van Galen argues that some women may have been included in the original list of recipients when Gracchus instituted the grain dole in 123 BCE (Galen, "Grain Distribution and Gender," 331).

76. Rickman, *Corn Supply*, 188.

77. Erdkamp, *Grain Market*, 241–43.

78. Horden and Purcell, *Corrupting Sea*, 201.

79. See Augustus, *Velleius Paterculus*, 400–401.

80. It is not just modern cynics that would suspect that Augustus's generous provision of grain was motivated by political aims. In fact, Tacitus, the late first century historian who found fault with the early emperors, believed the same, stating: "Augustus won over the soldiers with gifts, the populace with cheap corn [grain], and all men with the sweets of repose, and so grew greater by degrees, while he concentrated in himself the functions of the Senate, the magistrates, and the laws" (Elliott and Reasoner, *Documents and Images*, 163).

81. Rome's citizens, inhabitants, and slaves may have believed there were no good alternatives for supplying Rome with its necessary food. If that was the case, then—like American farmers and consumers today—they may have succumbed to something like the

Yet, hundreds of thousands of tons of grain did not magically spring forth from the storehouses in Rome. This abundance depended on the exploitation of people and lands across the sea.

Augustus procured consistent grain supplies from Egypt and North Africa, which produced large harvests of grain and were obliged to relinquish much of the produce in the form of taxes and forced purchases. In 30 BCE, after his defeat of Antony, Augustus brought Egypt under direct imperial control, and this province was "treated as the personal domain of the emperor."[82] Concurrently, an area west of Egypt, called Africa Procunsularis—often identified in scholarly literature as North Africa (much of which now stands in present-day Tunisia)—swore allegiance to Augustus (Aug., *RG* 25).[83] With both Egypt and North Africa under his thumb,[84] the emperor could extract enormous amounts of grain and direct it for sale and free distribution in the capital city of Rome, which approached one million people during the first centuries BCE and CE.[85] Thus, during imperial times the majority of Rome's grain supply issued from North Africa and Egypt even though elite citizens continued to receive produce from their rural Italian estates[86] and common people could buy Italian-grown grain or grain products at markets.[87] Consequently, whether or not they were

---

Stockholm Syndrome (Jackson, "Phone Conversation with Wes Jackson"; for more discussion see 7.2). They lauded and identified with the regime that oppressed them and others.

82. Augustus, *Velleius Paterculus*, 391nb.

83. Augustus, *Velleius Paterculus*, 384–87.

84. Erdkamp explains that grain from the province of Sicily played a much smaller role than grain from North Africa and Egypt but was a more proximate source. As a tithe-paying province, Sicily was obligated to Rome in two ways: first, it had to pay a tax from its grain crops, amounting to an imperial income of 9 percent of Sicily's grain harvest from taxed locales. The official tax rate was 10 percent, but the tax collector would collect 10 percent of that amount, leaving the government with 9 percent of the produce from "tithe-paying communities" (Erdkamp, *Grain Market*, 215). Second, Sicily had to sell grain to Rome in two different arrangements (the first involved about 3,000,000 *modii* of grain at 3 sesterces per *modius* and the second involved about 800,000 *modii* at 3.5 sesterces) (214). Erdkamp claims, then, that the Roman government received 20 percent of Sicily's grain harvest by these means, a total of 6,850,000 *modii* of grain (216). Possibly about one third of this total (2,283,333) reached Rome itself with most of the rest supplying the Roman military and government officials (217).

85. Erdkamp, *Grain Market*, 207.

86. An important source of grain was the private estates owned by inhabitants of Rome. Such owners would have some of the produce of their estates shipped to their urban dwellings (Erdkamp, *Grain Market*, 120).

87. Cancik and Schneider, *Cura Annonae*; Rickman, "Grain Trade," 263–64; Casson, "Role of the State," 21.

aware of it, Rome's masses directly depended on the empire's control of Africa and Egypt for their daily bread.

At the same time that Augustus solidified his control over imperial estates in Africa Procunsularis, other elite Romans procured land there as well. Thus, both private and imperial estates checkered the fertile valleys and hills of the region. Moreover, Augustus and his heirs added to and then bequeathed their imperial estates to their successors. Thus, by the time Paul wrote to Rome, Emperor Nero had inherited extensive imperial estates in Egypt and Africa that were already possessed by the Julio-Claudian house.

Nevertheless, Nero employed murderous tactics to confiscate even more land. After Nero ordered Seneca's suicide, he appropriated the Egyptian landholdings of Seneca, "whose possessions in Egypt were surpassed only by those of Nero himself."[88] Nero also expanded his ownership in North Africa by appropriating the "estates of six great landowners, who, according to Pliny, owned half of the province."[89] In a passage that criticizes this centralization of land ownership, Pliny states, "half of Africa was owned by six landlords, when the Emperor Nero put them to death" (Pliny, *NH* 18.35).[90] By killing land-owning opponents and taking their possessions, Nero demonstrated his imperial success of increasing Rome's grain supply, and he did this to a greater extent than did his immediate predecessors. His success was so impressive early in his reign that a member of his court could exclaim: "Amid untroubled peace, *the Golden Age springs to a second birth.*"[91] Natural abundance and political dominion thus appeared to be in great supply late in Paul's ministry.

Yet, as already suggested, Rome's abundance of food and expansive political control depended on notable forms of subjugation and degradation both of human life and ecological health. In order to see beyond the imperial claims and unmask the forms of social and ecological destruction that attended Rome's distribution of grain, we will follow the path of wheat from the hills of the Roman Province of Africa to the granaries in Rome.

---

88. Erdkamp, *Grain Market*, 221.

89. Erdkamp, *Grain Market*, 221.

90. Pliny, *Natural History*, 213. Kehoe notes, "Pliny may be exaggerating, but his testimony does suggest that the extent of imperial ownership of land in Africa increased substantially under Nero" (Kehoe, *Economics of Agriculture*, 11).

91. Siculus, "Eclogue 1," 221. Emphasis added. See also Elliott and Reasoner, *Documents and Images*, 144.

CREATION'S SUBJUGATION

2.2 Environmental History's Report: Ecological Deterioration in North Africa

While the Roman grain trade incurred real ecological and social costs, which this section displays, environmental historians reveal to us that the Mediterranean did in fact experience increases in verdure during the early period of the Roman Empire.[92] Environmental historians have demonstrated that many of the advances in agricultural productivity during the early imperial period resulted from climatic factors outside human control. From about 100 BCE to 200 CE, during what is now called the "Roman Climate Optimum" (RCO), the Mediterranean Basin experienced "exceptional climate stability," and "certain regions enjoyed unusually favorable conditions."[93] North Africa, Egypt, the Levant, and Italy received unusually generous amounts of rain (or flood waters in Egypt) and warmth during this time, which in turn enabled these areas to produce sufficient grains for the growing Roman population.[94] Thus, the decades spanning the reigns of Augustus to Nero, and almost a half-century beyond, were indeed marked by atypical natural fertility in the Mediterranean. While supporters of the empire would credit this fertility to the emperor's piety and the gods' favor, climate scientists point to "high and stable solar activity," low volcanic activity, and "high levels of [atmospheric] insolation."[95]

Since climatic changes during the Roman Climate Optimum (RCO) supplied beneficial conditions for agriculture, the "sustained temperature changes on the order of those experienced during the RCO let farmers carve entirely new landscapes of grain cultivation at higher elevations."[96]

---

92. Fortunately, the new field of environmental history has developed, which brings together scientists and historians. Their research unearths and describes the ecological context of various periods and places. For our study of Paul and his audience, the contributions of environmental history are invaluable for providing snapshots of the ecological conditions of cities and regions in ancient times. Some snapshots reveal ecological conditions before, during, and after the early decades of the Roman Empire. A helpful resource in this type of research is "Mapping Past Societies," https://darmc.harvard.edu/.

93. McCormick et al., "Climate Change," 174.

94. McCormick et al., "Climate Change," 180, 83.

95. Harper, *Fate of Rome*, 44–45.

96. Harper, *Fate of Rome*, 52. The first-century contemporary of Paul, Pliny the Elder, demonstrates his preference for Italian varieties of wheat and meanwhile exposes the unusual circumstance in which wheat was grown in the mountains by stating: "For my own part I should not rank any of [the several kinds of wheat] with Italian wheat for whiteness and for weight, for which it is particularly distinguished. Foreign wheat

The temperature increased by about 1°C in Italy during the RCO, which allowed about 5 million more hectares of land in higher elevations in Italy to come under new cultivation. This, in turn, facilitated the growth of enough wheat "to feed 3–4 million hungry bodies."[97] This expansion into higher elevations of the Italian hills and mountains required the clearing of forests and, when possible, the formation of terraces. Deforestation on the sloping terrain of Italy, however, increased the processes of soil erosion and decreased water retention, the effects of which were sometimes felt in Rome as the Tiber River flooded.[98]

While Italian-grown wheat provided a local and respectable supply of food for Italy's people,[99] Rome's leaders increasingly imported grain from Egypt and North Africa.[100] Wheat was a particular favorite among the Romans,[101] and the political importance of securing such food for its

---

can only be compared with that of the mountain regions of Italy" (18.12.63–66) (Pliny, *Natural History*, 231).

97. Harper, *Fate of Rome*, 52. Harper claims, "The RCO turned the lands ruled by Rome into a giant greenhouse. If we *only* count the marginal land rendered susceptible to arable farming in Italy by higher temperatures, on the most conservative estimates, it could account for more than all the growth achieved between Augustus and Marcus Aurelius" (53).

98. Harper, *Fate of Rome*, 47–49.

99. While the climate helped productivity greatly, the political peace established by Augustus created a stable and secure society such that farmers could tend their lands more effectively while also reaping the rewards of their labor by maintaining possession of greater portions of their harvests (rather than relinquishing them to armies or thieves). The political and social peace of the *Pax Romana* also promoted the agricultural productivity of Roman farms since men no longer served as soldiers but farmers (Casson, "Role of the State," 21).

100. One might expect that the imperial government would have protected the agricultural interests of its local farmers, but instead "[t]here were no export bonuses or import barriers"; local farmers competed on a level playing field with the large shipments of provincial grain (Erdkamp, *Grain Market*, 5). Rather than concerning themselves with the economic well-being of local farmers, Roman leaders simply worried about providing food for Rome's inhabitants, no matter the food's origin.

101. Despite this preference for wheat, Roman agronomist Columella insisted in the first century CE that farmers "should keep in store [various] kinds of wheat and emmer because it is unusual indeed to find a property which is situated so that we can make do with a single type of seed: some waterlogged or arid part is sure to get in the way" (*On Agriculture*, 2.6.4 quoted in Horden and Purcell, *Corrupting Sea*, 202). Polycultures increased the odds that farmers would reap at least some harvest when unfavorable weather, pests, or social unrest faced them. By growing a variety of crops, including cereals, olives, grapes, nuts, and vegetables, farmers diminished the risks of catastrophe, even as local and regional trade provided additional safety nets (Horden and Purcell, *Corrupting Sea*, 79–80).

CREATION'S SUBJUGATION

populace and troops cannot be overstressed.[102] As already indicated above, both Augustus and Nero went to extravagant lengths to control both Egypt and North Africa for this purpose.

Although Egypt continued to be an important breadbasket, Africa Procunsularis likely sent even more grain to Rome.[103] As "the granary of Rome,"[104] North Africa sent between 20–27 million *modii* of tax grain from its imperial and private estates to Rome.[105] From this collection of grain, the *plebs frumentaria* received their 5 *modii* of wheat. In order to uncover some of the negative social and ecological effects of Rome's North African grain trade, we shall trace the necessary steps involved in producing Rome's wheat, including the preparation of land and the cultivation, collection, transportation, and distribution of wheat.

2.2.1 Land Preparation

On account of imperial taxes, people in the Roman province of North Africa (primarily in present-day Tunisia) increasingly expanded agricultural efforts into hilly regions during the early empire. Political and economic pressures prompted this expansion and warmer and wetter conditions facilitated agriculture at higher elevations between 100 BCE and 150 CE. Although the precise dynamics of agricultural intensification are debated, it is clear that people who happened to live on imperial land were required now to pay rent in the form of produce.[106] The Fiscus, who collected the agricultural taxes, indirectly required the sharecroppers to increase their

102. Erdkamp, *Grain Market*, 240–42; Rickman, "Grain Trade," 262–63.

103. It is to be noted, that during the first centuries of the empire, "Egypt's productive farms seem to have enjoyed better Nile floods and therefore better harvests and fewer failed harvests" (McCormick et al., "Climate Change," 189). The authors explain, "The most favorable floods [of the Nile] occurred more frequently between 30 B.C. and 155 A.D., as clearly shown when contrasted with those of the following period" (189).

104. Harper, *Fate of Rome*, 49. Harper goes on to note, however, that North Africa must now import much of its grain.

105. Erdkamp, *Grain Market*, 221. This figure is calculated on the basis of a ratio provided by Josephus and the estimated grain need of the (estimated) Roman population.

106. By the time of Hadrian, wheat fields in Africa that had not been productive in the previous 10 years could be planted with grape vines. However, if farmers planted grape vines on imperial lands without permission or apart from these conditions, they were forced to tear them out (Erdkamp, *Grain Market*, 223). These stipulations illustrate the emperor's primary concern for wheat production but also expose the realities of soil exhaustion.

production so that they could meet their tax obligations as well as feed their families and save seed for the next year's plantings.[107] Providing food for an extractive economy meant that farmers had to expand their cultivation efforts to new, uncultivated lands. Estimating the size of typical families during early imperial times and likely wheat yields, Dennis Kehoe suggests that a family in North Africa who had to pay one third of its produce to the Fiscus as rent and tax would have had to farm "sixty percent more land than a family paying no rent or taxes at all," in other words a family not living on imperial property.[108] These increased demands on sharecroppers are attested in six extant inscriptions discovered in the hilly region of the Medjerda (*Bagrada*) River valley, though they are from the early second century CE.[109]

These increases in demand meant that previously forested hills were cleared, at least partially, in order to make more arable land available. Many farmers approached this task circumspectly since they also depended on forests for fuel, nuts, and other essential resources.[110] In upland areas near the headwaters of the major river, the Medjerda, farmers cleared native trees for grain cultivation but sometimes did so in order to replace them with olive groves.[111] While scientists debate the complex factors involved in North Africa's deforestation and later desertification, it is likely that "[t]he loss of forest cover suppresse[d] rainfall in the Mediterranean." Ultimately, this could have meant that "Roman deforestation interacted with natural patterns of late Holocene climate change to tip the circum-Mediterranean climate toward a regime with less summer precipitation."[112] The anthropogenic decrease in forest cover in North Africa, in other words, could have intensified the processes of desertification and climatic aridity that this region has ultimately undergone.

107. Kehoe, *Economics of Agriculture*, 14.

108. Kehoe, *Economics of Agriculture*, 16. Kehoe suggests that a typical family would have depended on 6 hectares of arable land, cultivating 3 hectares every other year while allowing the other 3 to remain fallow. The family paying rent on an imperial estate, however, had to cultivate 5 hectares each year.

109. Kehoe, *Economics of Agriculture*, 5, 7.

110. Testifying to at least some careful administration of forests, Harris notes, "The Roman Empire witnessed the serious depletion of some woodland resources, and the effective management of others" (Harris, "Defining and Detecting Mediterranean Deforestation," 184, 90–92).

111. Faust et al., "High-Resolution Fluvial Record," 1771.

112. Harper, *Fate of Rome*, 52.

Creation's Subjugation

In the short-term, however, Roman farmers made every effort to mitigate soil loss that otherwise would happen when sloping hillsides were deforested. Primarily, they built terraces to decrease erosion and slow the movement and loss of water downhill so that it might be used beneficially for their crops.[113] These efforts illustrated Roman "power over nature" and were "highly visible capital-intensive projects."[114] To their great credit, these terraces did indeed stabilize soil movement, as recent studies in the Medjerda region reveal. Notwithstanding these short-term gains, however, erosion greatly increased once Roman control of this region declined and the unattended Roman terraces washed away.[115] After Vandals invaded and took control of this region in the fifth century, Roman terraces and planting efforts were abandoned; this, along with cooling temperatures and increasing aridity that came after the Roman Climate Optimum (RCO), accelerated soil loss and the siltation of rivers.[116] Because of these diverse factors, North Africa no longer has the capacity to export grain and, instead, depends on imported grain to meet its needs in modern times.[117]

Although the Medjerda River valley received adequate rain during the RCO,[118] areas just beyond this region did not. Yet Romans encouraged the cultivation of those lands by building "aqueducts, wells, cisterns, terraces, dams, reservoirs, and subterranean fogaras (long channels that transport groundwater from higher elevations to cultivated lowlands) . . . By these devices water was assiduously collected and exploited in a semiarid region, where human occupation burgeoned as never before," as in North Africa.[119] Such technologies enabled farmers to carve out new areas of cultivation in high-risk and ecologically fragile zones in order to meet increased demands.

Those who had been forced off their lands because the emperor had confiscated them perhaps resettled in these fragile zones. It is a sad reality

---

113. Although it is often assumed that ancient Romans did not replace the fertility of their soils, there is evidence that manure was sometimes applied in the imperial period (Horden and Purcell, *Corrupting Sea*, 234).

114. However, if war, labor shortages, or a lack of economic resources led farmers to neglect their farms, terracing ultimately increased landscape degradation (Horden and Purcell, *Corrupting Sea*, 236–37). Horden and Purcell note, however, that assessing this effect is highly complex.

115. Faust et al., "High-Resolution Fluvial Record," 1770–71.

116. Faust et al., "High-Resolution Fluvial Record," 1771.

117. Harper, *Fate of Rome*, 49.

118. Kehoe, *Economics of Agriculture*, 12.

119. Harper, *Fate of Rome*, 49.

at this time that "[t]he idea that a whole community had been replaced by an estate was a commonplace of the literary tradition."[120] Since the empire's confiscation of lands at times displaced human populations, they had to depend on other sources of food and, by implication, to cultivate lands that were not currently cultivated or not cultivated as intensively. Even when inhabitants were not displaced from Roman landholdings but were conscripted as sharecroppers, they often had to increase their agricultural efforts by cultivating marginal areas in order to meet the demands of the emperor as well as their own food requirements.[121] The ecological impacts of these secondary effects of Roman control and the provision of Rome's wheat demand remain unquantifiable.

2.2.2 Cultivation

Once land was cleared of trees and shrubs and terraces were put in place, farmers could sow their wheat seeds. Since, on average, one measure of wheat seed rarely yielded four full measures of harvested grain in ancient times (a "yield-seed ration of 4:1"), one pleb's 5 *modii* of harvested wheat required the planting of 2 *modii* of seed on about an eighth of a hectare.[122] When viewed as whole, the conservative figure of 20 million *modii* of North African wheat for Rome required the cultivation of about 5 million hectares of land each year.[123] This equals over 19,000 square miles, a land area nearly the size of West Virginia. In order to work this large expanse of land, perhaps as many as 200,000 local sharecropping families would have served the North African imperial grain supply.[124] Although the primary agricultural workforce in North Africa consisted of free families, there is evidence that slaves also "worked alongside tenants cultivating small plots" of land.[125]

120. Horden and Purcell, *Corrupting Sea*, 280.

121. Kehoe, *Economics of Agriculture*, 227–28.

122. Kehoe, *Economics of Agriculture*, 15–16.

123. Figures derived from estimates presented in Kehoe, *Economics of Agriculture*, 15–16.

124. Kehoe, *Economics of Agriculture*, 16–17.

125. Kehoe, *Economics of Agriculture*, 27, 24–25. The use of slave labor for agriculture in Africa was significantly lower than in Italy at this time. Kehoe explains, "a landlord seeking to cultivate land would have the choice of investing in capital by purchasing and maintaining slaves, or else by employing free labor, either as wage-laborers or tenants. The landlord's ability to exploit his land profitably in the Roman world depended not

Creation's Subjugation

In order to facilitate so vast an agricultural effort, farmers needed strong tools not only to clear the land but also plow and harrow it. Advances in mining and metallurgy during the early empire improved the metal tools that, in turn, facilitated agricultural expansion. Across the Mediterranean, "the spread of metal tools, better ploughs, new harrows, and a novel kind of reaper from Gaul accomplished real improvement" in agriculture.[126] However, the forging of these implements necessitated high ecological costs.

Metallurgy depended on "the truly lavish use of wood fuel in the Roman world."[127] During its height, the "Roman Empire is likely to have produced 80– to 85,000 tons of iron a year. Eighty thousand tons would have required the fuel produced by approximately 26,000 km^2 of coppiced land."[128] While coppicing trees (which involved cutting the trunks of particular types of tress and leaving a sizeable stump to grow saplings again) did not cause soil erosion to the same degree as removing trees entirely, the metallurgical process led to other ecological ills.

The mining and smelting of metals released large amounts of poisonous lead into the atmosphere and environment. Although the empire purposely produced about 80,000 tons of usable lead annually, this process and the smelting of other metals released as much as 4000 tons into the atmosphere as a by-product.[129] Over time this lead settled on land and water, possibly poisoning inhabitants along the way. Quantities of airborne lead were preserved in peat bogs, such as those found in the Hautes Fagnes Plateau of southeastern Belgium, and on the ice sheets of Greenland. Belgian peat core samples contain the highest concentrations of lead for the era "between 50 BC and AD 215," the height of imperial growth.[130] Similarly,

---

only on competition among free farmers, but also on the availability of slave labor and his willingness to use it" (77).

126. Harper, *Fate of Rome*, 36. Harper also notes that "[a]gricultural processing experienced quantum leaps, with better screw presses, water-lifting machines, and salting vats in the vanguard. Water mills, it is now appreciated, were widely dispersed for the first time."

127. Harris, "Defining and Detecting Mediterranean Deforestation," 176.

128. Harris goes on to explain, "80–85,000 tons of production is unlikely to be a greatly exaggerated figure (the evidence of the Greenland ice-cores suggests that the production of metals in Europe did not reach Roman levels again until the Industrial Revolution), and it may well be too low" ("Defining and Detecting Mediterranean Deforestation," 176).

129. Allan et al., "Reconstruction of Atmospheric Lead Pollution," 2.

130. Allan et al., "Reconstruction of Atmospheric Lead Pollution," 14. The study examined cores that spanned 500 BCE to 500 CE.

Greenland ice core samples disclose a fourfold increase in lead deposition during Roman times (from about 500 BCE to 300 CE).[131]

Thus, even before farmers cut into the soil with their plows, ecological damage had been done to make cultivation possible. And once soil was laid bare and before the wheat's roots could stabilize it, wind and rain could easily remove precious topsoils. Nevertheless, agricultural efforts proceeded, and after several months farmers gathered their ripened wheat grains for collection and storage.

2.2.3 Collection

With Rome's wheat having been grown and harvested, it now had to be transported by oxen-drawn wooden wagons from the farms in the westernmost reaches of the Atlas Mountains to the lowland port of Carthage, present-day Tunis. For all the African grain destined for Rome to be transported this way, "literally hundreds of thousands" of wagonfulls would have traveled the Roman road through the Medjerda valley to the sea.[132] The amount of wood and metal necessary to build such a large caravan of wagons is bewildering.

The Fiscus, the manager of all imperial estates in the region, oversaw the collection of grain from the sharecroppers by employing local managers.[133] It was the Fiscus's chief aim to provide consistent and sufficient food supplies to Rome as well as to the local government in Africa Proconsularis.[134] Therefore, in addition to threating tenants that they would be pushed off their rented land if any refused to render sufficient payments of grain, the Fiscus could have resorted to "police power of the state in

---

131. Hong et al., "Greenland Ice Evidence," 1841. The scientists estimate that across the "whole Greenland ice cap . . . the net deposition [of lead] is about 400 tons during these 800 years. This estimate is as much as [approximately] 15% of the cumulative fallout of Pb to Greenland during the past 60 years that is linked to the massive use of Pb alkyl additives in gasoline" (1843).

132. Rickman, "Grain Trade," 264.

133. Kehoe explains the collection in detail: imperial properties were "cultivated by sharecroppers, *coloni*, who paid rent of generally one third of their produce to middlemen called *conductores*. The *coloni* raised a variety of crops, including wheat, barley, beans, wine, olive oil, honey, figs and other fruits. The *conductores*, who held temporary leases for the imperial estates, also cultivated land not occupied by *coloni*" (Kehoe, *Economics of Agriculture*, 5).

134. Kehoe, *Economics of Agriculture*, 166.

order to enforce its will (as it did during the conflicts of the 180's)."[135] Under the threat of violence, then, the sharecroppers surrendered about a third of their family's wheat crop to Rome.

2.2.4 Transportation, Processing, and Distribution

After farmers surrendered their grain to the Fiscus in Carthage, as much as 27 million *modii*[136] would have stood ready for transport to Rome. An enormous armada was needed to carry this grain from Africa.[137] Depending on the size of the ships used to transport this grain, between 800 and 4000 ships consequently serviced the grain trade from Africa as well as Egypt during "a relatively short 100-day period falling mostly during the summer."[138] The largest ships likely carried 340 tons whereas smaller ships carried about 70 tons of grain.[139] Although the layout of such grain ships is uncertain, great care needed to be taken when loading the wheat in the ship's hull since wheat's liquid-like movement could exert a great deal of force in a rocking ship and could capsize it. Additionally, since harvested wheat breathes—taking in oxygen and releasing carbon dioxide, water, and heat—the hull's temperature and humidity was of great concern since fires could kindle.[140] Storms and fire constantly threatened to thwart the ships' progress to Rome.

In addition to the tremendous effort and care involved in loading the grain and navigating the ships northeast from Carthage to Puteoli in Italy (a port south of the mouth of the Tiber River), the labor and natural resources necessary for building the grain ships in the first place were colossal. These ships required timber from tall and, therefore, old trees of distinct species—such as fir, pine, cedar, oak, ash, mulberry, and elm.[141] As early as the reign of Augustus, Italy's domestic supply of long timber for shipbuilding had dwindled.[142] By the first half of the second century, during

---

135. Kehoe, *Economics of Agriculture*, 154.

136. Kehoe, *Economics of Agriculture*, 4, fn. 8. Again, this figure depends on the ratio provided by Josephus and the estimated grain need of the (estimated) Roman population.

137. Rickman, "Grain Trade," 263.

138. Rickman, "Grain Trade," 263, 61; Aldrete, *Floods of the Tiber*, 134.

139. Rickman, "Grain Trade," 263.

140. Rickman, "Grain Trade," 261.

141. Harris, "Defining and Detecting Mediterranean Deforestation," 179.

142. Harris, "Defining and Detecting Mediterranean Deforestation," 181. Prior to the rise of the Roman Empire, "most but not all of mainland Greece, Sicily, the Aegean

Emperor Hadrian's reign, the tall trees of Syria were under significant threat so that Hadrian had erected "at least 800" markers to designate "four types of trees as imperial property."[143] Mediterranean forests experienced heavy pressures not only for old growth wood from extensive shipbuilding for the grain trade but also for new growth wood from the daily demands of a growing Roman population. Consequently, "[a]t the height of the Roman Empire, many areas that had been more or less heavily wooded in 800 BCE were farmland with scattered trees, or scrub-land, or in some cases heavily eroded land."[144] Such losses in forest cover not only decreased ambient humidity but also increased siltation of rivers and erosion of topsoil.

Because Rome was not a port city, grain ships often docked at Puteoli. At this port, the grain was transferred by hand—being measured along the way—to one of thousands of smaller boats that could navigate up the coast, into the Tiber River, and at last to Rome.[145] In order to expedite and simplify the shipping process, Emperor Claudius had harbor facilities built at Ostia, at the mouth of the Tiber. He celebrated this feat by minting a coin with the goddess Ceres, seated on a throne and holding two ears of wheat and a long torch, on the one side and his bust on the obverse.[146] However, in 62 CE under Emperor Nero's watch, "almost 200 ships with grain for Rome sank within the harbour in a storm."[147] Although Nero renovated Claudius's harbor from 62–64 CE,[148] several decades later, Emperor Trajan more successfully established this harbor and built granaries for the precious imported goods.[149] These facilities, in contrast with comparable ones near Vesuvius, were *not* built using long timbers, suggesting the rarity of tall trees at this time.[150]

Once the grain had been painstakingly transported up the coast and into the Tiber River, it was towed up river on one of perhaps 4000 boatloads

---

islands and the west coast of Asia Minor had lost most of their tall trees by about 310 BC, leaving them with simply enough coppiced trees and shrubs to provide fuel" (180).

143. Harris, "Defining and Detecting Mediterranean Deforestation," 182–83.
144. Harris, "Defining and Detecting Mediterranean Deforestation," 190.
145. Rickman, "Grain Trade," 267.
146. *Roman Imperial Coinage*, 1:127.
147. Rickman, "Grain Trade," 267.
148. Sutherland, *Roman History and Coinage*, 82.
149. Rickman, "Grain Trade," 267. See also, Kehoe, *Economics of Agriculture*, 5.
150. Harris, "Defining and Detecting Mediterranean Deforestation," 182.

Creation's Subjugation

of grain.[151] The boats likely docked and were unloaded near the Aventine Hill in the district called the Emporium (or *Vicus Frumentarius*), where dozens of specially designed warehouses stored that year's grain.[152] The warehouses (*horrea*) had elevated floors in order to keep grain away from ground moisture and potential flood waters, thick walls—perhaps one meter wide—to withstand the pressure of the standing grain, and ventilation windows high above the ground in order to prevent overheating as well as thieving.[153] It is unknown how large these facilities were during the apostle Paul's life, but the enormous warehouse called the *Horrea Galbana* eventually covered 20,000 m^2.[154] The amount of natural resources—especially quarried stone from which they were built—required for this and other warehouses in Rome is staggering.[155]

Rome's supply of wheat was now near at hand and ready for distribution to a "privileged section of the capital's populace."[156] As already indicated, most of the people eligible to receive the grain dole were free adult males. Prior to 123 BCE, wealthy Romans would give free or reduced-price grain to inhabitants of Rome in order to curry political favor.[157] However, in 123 BCE, tribune Gaius Gracchus convinced the Senate to remove the grain dole from private hands and place it under the administration of the Roman government.[158] The *frumentationes* consequently could not be used by just anyone as a political tool. Nevertheless, the Roman Republic and Empire continued to view the free supply of grain to registered persons as of chief political importance. Given that the grain dole provided food for the hardiest of Rome's populace, the ultimate goal of the *frumentationes* appeared to be the prevention of their unrest. Those who were most

---

151. Rickman, "Grain Trade," 267; Aldrete, *Floods of the Tiber*, 134.

152. Rickman, "Grain Trade," 267–68. Rickman suggests that the grain was probably unloaded in Region XIII, where—by the fourth century CE—35 *horrea* (public warehouse facilities) stood.

153. Aldrete, *Floods of the Tiber*, 135.

154. Aldrete, *Floods of the Tiber*, 135. The *Horrea Galbana* is mentioned in an inscription during Augustus's reign (Kaufman, "Horrea Romana," 50).

155. Kaufman, "Horrea Romana," 52.

156. Erdkamp, *Grain Market*, 242; Garnsey and Rathbone, "Background to the Grain Law," 20.

157. Paul Erdkamp explains, "From about the mid-second century BC, distributions of cheap grain became more frequent, as politicians came to recognise it as an opportunity to gain popularity" (Erdkamp, *Grain Market*, 241).

158. Erdkamp, *Grain Market*, 240–41.

vulnerable and powerless, in contrast, often went without or, if lucky, received portions from an enlisted male family member.

Even after the *frumentationes* were distributed, a great deal more African grain stood ready for purchase from Rome's granaries. Whether or not the grain was received freely from the emperor or purchased at the market, it needed to be processed into an edible form. Since most city-dwellers would have had no access to mills for grinding grain or ovens for baking bread, they depended on artisans who did these tasks.[159] In fact, it is likely that many city dwellers simply by-passed purchasing grain altogether and bought bread instead. The retail market, according to some scholars, centered on bread rather than grain; meanwhile, the wholesale market primarily sold grain to bakers. Since the price of grain fluctuated throughout the year in response to supply conditions and since it was difficult to make monetary change in small denominations at the point of sale, the *weight* rather than the *price* of bread varied according to market conditions.[160] As the price of grain went up, the weight of bread went down so that the price of the loaf remained the same. Bakers at times abused this system, but the government—at least when grain was scarce and expensive—protected consumers by issuing a mandatory minimum loaf weight for the set price. The bakers, then, were forced to take a financial hit, receiving less profit in times of grain shortage since the price of grain would be comparatively high.[161] Consequently, the government played an important role in regulating the consumer market so that the Roman populace could afford bread in times of crisis and could continue to perceive the emperor as the great patron and liberator from starvation.

The distribution of grain in Rome, which depended on Rome's control and exploitation of North Africa and the intensification and expansion of agriculture there, undoubtedly benefitted many people. Nevertheless, it has become increasingly clear that these economic and material benefits came with lasting ecological costs. Although the cultivation of North African lands likely increased the risk of soil exhaustion, the most damaging processes in the grain trade occurred in support of land preparation and grain transportation. Because the grain trade depended so heavily on clearing forests for fields, shipbuilding, and making agricultural implements, it unintentionally resulted in the erosion and depletion of soils, the silting of

159. Erdkamp, *Grain Market*, 294.
160. Erdkamp, *Grain Market*, 300–301.
161. Erdkamp, *Grain Market*, 301–2.

rivers, the release of lead, and perhaps even the alteration of climate, especially the availability of water in the form of precipitation. These forms of ecological destruction hardly match the image that the empire attempted to project about itself. While the Mediterranean did indeed experience unusual verdure prompted by warmer, wetter weather, it simultaneously suffered a slow process of degradation. The appearance of abundance gilding the surface of Roman imperial life masked an eroding ecological foundation.

CHAPTER 3

Creation's Advocate

Paul, the Imperial Gospel, and His Letter to Rome

For the creation expectantly awaits the apocalypse of the sons of God. For the creation was subjected to frustration, not willingly but on account of the one subjecting it in hope that the creation itself will be liberated from the slavery of destruction into the liberation of the glory of God's children. For we know that the whole creation is collectively groaning and laboring together even till now.

ROMANS 8:19–22[1]

DESPITE THE CLAIMS OF the imperial gospel, Paul testified to Jesus's followers in Rome that creation was subjected to frustration and enslaved to destruction. As an interpreter of *Israel's* story in the shadow of the empire, Paul simultaneously acted as an interpreter of *creation's* story. He considered it to be a story of human culpability and responsibility but also a story saturated by God's grace (Rom 5:12–21). Because Paul believed God created the world good and commissioned it to flourish, he stood as creation's advocate, logging his testimony about creation's condition in Rom 8:19–22. As his version of creation's story was told in Rome, his words functioned as a form of witness against destructive human powers—including powers wielded by the empire itself—that subjugated creation in Paul's day.[2] Thus,

---

1. All English Scripture translations are the author's own in this chapter unless otherwise noted.

2. As discussed in the introduction, Pauline scholars disagree over the degree to

as creation's advocate, Paul implicitly testified against the imperial gospel and boldly offered a contrasting account of creation's current condition and future hope. Not only did Paul's theology direct him towards this alternative portrayal of creation but his travels throughout Asia Minor arguably inspired him to witness against the imperial appetites that accelerated creation's degradation.

In order to support this interpretation of Romans, the first section of this chapter presents evidence from archaeology and environmental history that suggests the apostle Paul was aware of the imperial gospel and also had several opportunities to witness environmental degradation. Section two then examines the ways in which Paul—as creation's advocate—throughout his epistle to Rome proclaimed God as the one who makes right and makes alive. This section traces creational themes throughout the letter and is necessarily selective in its scope. Section three revises the eco-theological principles set forth in chapter 1 in light of what Paul writes in Romans and, then, offers eco-ethical principles that correspond with Paul's vision of a liberated humanity and a liberated nonhuman creation.

3.1 Paul's Ambit: Creation's Degradation in Asia Minor and Syria

While Rome announced the emperor's success in renewing the earth's fertility, freeing his subjects from starvation, and ushering in the Golden Age, Paul proclaimed a very different reality. Instead of being in a state of renewed fertility, Paul explained creation was subjected to frustration and enslaved to destruction (Rom 8:20–21). Why so? Did Paul base this belief solely on his interpretation of Scripture?[3] Or, might he also have witnessed

---

which Paul had the empire and imperial claims in view when he wrote his letters. It is important to realize that Paul's use of terms in common with imperial propaganda, for example "son(s) of G/god" (Rom 8:19), does not by itself necessarily convey disagreement with Rome or critique of its claims (Barclay, "Why the Roman Empire," 376–79). However, because in Rom 8:19–22 Paul describes the present condition of creation and its expectations for the future in ways that clearly disagree with imperial claims about nature—and the emperors' effects on nature in particular—I put their accounts in conversation with one another and perceive between them notable disagreement. On the basis of archaeological evidence, I also contend that Paul described creation's condition with an awareness of contrary imperial claims and did so, in part, to guide the Jesus followers in Rome to conform their lives to God's mission of liberation rather than to the empire's mission of dominion.

3. In addition to the Tanakh's passages offered up for consideration in chapter 1,

and perceived the destructive effects of human activity in his everyday world? Answering these questions takes us beyond his letters and, admittedly, into a realm of speculation and deductive reasoning. This realm is nevertheless grounded in the environmental realities of Paul's time, and these realities have recently come to light through the work of environmental historians. Journeying with environmental historians to the cities and regions Paul visited allows us to see the Roman Empire the way Paul might have seen it. By learning from environmental history, we may more confidently claim that Paul witnessed against imperial propaganda and instead offered a different account of creational reality.

It is important to take this journey into environmental history in order to substantiate what some scholars simply suppose. Robert Jewett, for example, contends that "Paul's formulation" in Rom 8:21 "*simply assumes, without arguing the point,* that the Caesarian view about the presence of a peaceful, magically prosperous gold age is illusory."[4] Yet, even to say that Paul assumes the imperial Golden Age was illusory goes beyond what Paul explicitly wrote. Jewett, therefore, takes it for granted that Paul was aware of and countered the imperial gospel. Is it possible to find corroborating evidence that would make such an assumption more reliable? It is the contention of this section, that archaeology and environmental history provide convincing forms of supporting evidence.

Along with the question about Paul's own ecological experience of the world, we might also ask whether the congregants in Rome had reason to doubt Rome's success in subduing and vivifying nature. Jewett suggests that—on the basis of their knowledge of Jewish prophetic traditions and Paul's letter—the Jesus followers in Rome

> could well have thought about how imperial ambitions, military conflicts, and economic exploitation had led to the erosion of the natural environment throughout the Mediterranean world,

---

Jewish apocalyptic perspectives current in the Second Temple period also arguably shaped Paul's understanding of creation's past, present, and future conditions. Second Temple apocalypticism marks a number of written works, and in his examination of this literature, Harry Alan Hahne demonstrates that Rom 8:19–22 and Jubilees, *4 Ezra, 2 Baruch, Apocalypse of Moses,* and *1 Enoch* share theological beliefs about creation. He suggests, "Paul's basic perspective of the present state and future hope of creation follows that strand of Jewish apocalyptic writings that sees the world as corrupted by the fall of Adam and looks forward to the eschatological transformation and perfection of creation through a decisive divine act" (Hahne, *Corruption and Redemption of Creation,* 226–27).

4. Jewett, "Corruption and Redemption of Creation," 32. Emphasis added.

leaving ruined cities, depleted fields, deforested mountains, and polluted streams as evidence of this universal human vanity. That such vanity in the form of the *pax Romana* had promised the restoration of the age of Saturn appears utterly preposterous in the light of this critical, biblical tradition.[5]

While listing these various forms of ecological degradation, Jewett provides no specific examples in support of these claims and refers to no publications that do so. Yet, in order for more scholars to take ecological and political readings of Romans seriously, these forms of evidence are necessary. What, then, is the evidence that readers in Rome had the opportunity to witness the empire's degradation—rather than renewal—of nature?

Archaeological information demonstrates both Paul and his Christian siblings in Rome would have had ample opportunities to see and interpret the imperial gospel. Roman coins (such as the coin honoring Claudius that was minted in Pergamum in 41–42 CE, fig. 2), the displays of Augustus's *Res Gestae* (both in Rome and Pisidian Antioch), and monuments like the *Ara Pacis* (at the Field of Mars in Rome and the Forum of Corinth) proclaimed the imperial gospel of abundance to the followers of Christ in Rome and to Paul as he traveled throughout the imperial provinces.[6] More specifically, while ministering for three years in Ephesus, the apostle might have passed by the gate of Mazaeus and Mithridates that honored and identified the emperors as sons of god(s).[7] At the Forum in Corinth, Paul might have interpreted the imposing statue of the deified and ascended Augustus, heralded both as a son of god and a god.[8] As Paul gazed upon the altar in Corinth that simulated Rome's *Ara Pacis* or viewed Roman imperial coins with cornucopia, he almost certainly would have grasped the imperial proclamation that Augustus had restored the Golden Age.[9] All together, these and other tributes to the imperial gospel make it highly probable that Paul and his addressees in Rome would have been aware of Rome's gospel: the Roman Empire, through its imperial leaders, generated peace, justice, and natural abundance.

Beyond countenancing these political declarations, Paul almost certainly would have encountered concrete instances of environmental

---

5. Jewett, "Corruption and Redemption of Creation," 37.
6. Kreitzer, *Striking New Images*, 106.
7. Scherrer, "City of Ephesos," 6.
8. Laird, "Emperor in a Roman Town, 91."
9. Laird, "Emperor in a Roman Town."

degradation—especially the removal of old growth forests and other forms of deforestation—in Syrian Antioch, Ephesus, and Miletus.[10] Because other Mediterranean people before him correlated deforestation with erosion, it is reasonable to suppose that Paul too understood the consequences of deforestation, including bare hillsides, erosion, and siltation of rivers.[11] We know from first-century literary sources as well as modern scientific analyses that such factors affected many areas around the Mediterranean. Imperial demands for old growth trees for ships and harbors, for example, exploited the forests of Syria and strained the region's long-term health. Syrian Antioch—a city the apostle Paul inhabited for a time and then later visited—placed increasing stress on its local hilly forests even as its more remote, upland forests were cut down for imperial naval purposes. Even though Syrian Antioch had functioned as the capitol of the Seleucid Empire over a hundred years prior to Paul's time, the Greek Empire did not cause substantial forms of environmental degradation. It was not until the early Roman Empire that this region underwent significant deforestation, which eventually allowed "severe erosion" to take place "from about 150 CE onwards" whenever heavy rains fell.[12]

Similarly, the harbor at Asia Minor's principal city, Ephesus, experienced the effects of erosion and became increasingly filled with silt, especially between 44 BCE and 52 CE, when the city underwent significant growth. Although volcanic activity may have increased the processes of siltation, scientists have found that Ephesus's Küçük Menderes delta was increasingly filled with silt during this era because of human population pressures.[13] Consequently, "[t]he landscape changed with a degradation

---

10. We might add other regions to this list as well. For example, drawing on the work of J. Donald Hughes (Hughes, *Environmental Problems*), Keesmaat concludes that, especially on account of his travels in Galilee and Judea, "Paul would have seen the effect on the land of decades of military occupation, the expansion of imperial estates with the loss of familial land, and the despair that accompanied such violence" (Keesmaat, "Land, Idolatry, and Justice," 100).

11. For an insightful understanding of these processes, see Plato's Critias 111 B-D (Plato, "Critias," 272–75).

12. Harris, "Defining and Detecting Mediterranean Deforestation," 186–87.

13. Delile et al., "Demise of a Harbor," 208. The authors note that the sudden increase in sediment may have been catalyzed by an earthquake, and three major earthquakes are dated to 17, 23, and 47 CE (Delile et al., "Demise of a Harbor," 209). However, because geological and biological markers in core samples from the river basin beside Ephesus are "dominated by human impact," "it is very difficult to trace evidence of the climate" and its possible deleterious effects, according to a different study (Stock et al., "Human Impact," 992).

of the hillslopes due to deforestation (for agriculture, fuel, construction of houses and ships) and grazing."[14]

To the south of Ephesus, the ancient bay abutting Miletus (which Paul may have visited early in his ministry and very likely visited on his way to Jerusalem according to Acts 20:15) became increasingly blocked off by sedimentation on the eastern side so that an inland lake developed during Roman rule. Deforestation and erosion from livestock grazing during Roman occupation was so heavy in this watershed that it caused sedimentation at rates almost six times greater than those taking place during Hellenistic control.[15] It does not strain reason to believe Paul would have learned about these environmental ills (and the economic forces catalyzing them) from Miletus's residents and perceived them as forms of human wrought destruction.

Along with Paul, the Jesus followers in Rome also would have had opportunities to observe anthropogenic forms of degradation. Rome was situated in a floodplain and, since it experienced wetter weather during the Roman Climate Optimum (RCO), it flooded in unusual ways during the first centuries BCE and CE (see 2.2 for more discussion of the RCO). Typically, the Tiber flooded in the winter, but during the unusually wetter conditions of the RCO it frequently flooded in the spring and summer, with extreme flooding recorded in the years 22 and 13 BCE and 5, 12, 15, 36, and 69 CE.[16] Because much of Rome's grain warehouses stood near the Tiber River (in order to expedite unloading of boats), they were under constant threat of being inundated with floodwaters. When this occurred, precious stores of grain spoiled and the populace had to pay more for the same amount of bread. Those of low economic status, in particular, consequently faced greater threats of malnutrition and even starvation.[17]

Although we might blame the wetter climate of the RCO for these repeated and unseasonable floods during the early empire, climate alone was not their cause. For, "the problem of disastrous flooding in the Roman Empire was exacerbated by the ravages inflicted on upland forests. The Roman Empire consumed fuel and material voraciously, denuding

---

14. Stock et al., "Human Impact," 992.

15. Knipping, Müllenhoff, and Brückner, "Human Induced Landscape Changes," 374, 78.

16. Harper, *Fate of Rome*, 48; Aldrete, *Floods of the Tiber*, 24–27. Harper also notes a few other dates before and after this span.

17. Aldrete, *Floods of the Tiber*, 132.

hillsides of the once dense sylvan texture that slowed and absorbed the rush of rainwaters."[18] Rome depended on wood from upstream forests, since "[t]he easiest way by far to transport felled trees is by water, and the forests along the banks of the Tiber and its tributaries would have been the first places where Roman loggers concentrated their efforts."[19] Julius Caesar recognized Rome's extreme forms of flooding originated further upstream, but he was murdered before he could implement a plan to redirect the upstream sources of the Tiber.[20] A century later, Emperor Claudius attempted to redress the problem of flooding in Rome by digging channels downstream from Rome in 42–46 CE.[21] This approach facilitated the freer movement of water at a bottleneck in the river several miles from Rome so that the excess water in the Tiber would flow more readily into the Mediterranean Sea near Claudius's new harbor facility at Portus.[22] In so doing, the emperor claimed that "Tiberius Claudius Caesar, son of Drusus, . . . freed the city from the danger of flooding by leading canals from the Tiber into the sea in connection with the building of the harbour."[23] Two decades later, Nero further improved the harbor facilities and commemorated his beneficence on coins that "rank among the most splendidly detailed architectural and topographical designs in the imperial series" with "a [b]ird's-eye view of the harbour of Ostia."[24] Despite these extravagant efforts, the Tiber severely flooded in 69 CE.[25] Because a primary anthropogenic cause of flooding in Rome—namely deforestation upstream—was not sufficiently redressed, digging canals downstream did not correct the problem. In fact, Rome's ongoing exploitation of forests upstream actually undermined its

18. Harper, *Fate of Rome*, 47–48.

19. Aldrete, *Floods of the Tiber*, 76. Aldrete goes on to explain that the floods of 202 BCE, 13 BCE, 12 CE, and 217 CE (which certainly occurred during the summer) also happened "when the logging of the Tiber basin was probably most intense" (Aldrete, *Floods of the Tiber*, 77).

20. Wilson, "Mediterranean Environment," 270.

21. Sutherland, *Roman History and Coinage*, 82.

22. Wilson, "Mediterranean Environment," 270.

23. Wilson, "Mediterranean Environment," 271. Wilson notes the quotation may be found in *Inscriptiones Latinae Selectae* 207, edited by H. Dessau.

24. Sutherland, *Roman History and Coinage*, 81–82.

25. Wilson, "Mediterranean Environment," 271. Several decades later, Emperor Trajan went to great lengths to establish an additional spillway for the Tiber in order to mitigate the potential of summer floods. For, during his reign such a strong flood hit Rome that "the furniture of the aristocracy and the tools of the peasantry" drifted through town (Harper, *Fate of Rome*, 47).

extravagant attempts at maintaining dry land in the city and providing dry, abundant stores of grain for its people.

Throughout these decades of unseasonal flooding and imperial intervention, many Roman Christians lived and worked in the swampy, lowland slums of Trastevere and Porta Capena.[26] While it is by no means certain that these followers of Christ would have perceived these floods as happening on account of upstream deforestation, they would have felt the pangs of hunger that these floods brought and witnessed their consequent destruction. It is likely, then, these Jesus followers could readily agree with Paul that the nonhuman creation suffered under destructive forces. Consequently, they may have been more inclined to question the empire's rhetoric (encountered in coins, festivals, and imperial proclamations) claiming *the emperor* had successfully controlled nature, established abundance, and ushered in the Golden Age.

These examples of environmental degradation stand among many others in the Mediterranean region, significant portions of which Paul himself saw firsthand. By bringing them forward, I do not claim that Paul perceived the processes of ecological destruction to the same degree or in the same light as present-day scientists. However, his testimony about creation—in particular, that it still awaits liberation from slavery to destruction—demonstrates he did not accept the imperial gospel and instead maintained a more honest, alternative view of reality. When we read his statements in Rom 8:19–22 in light of the political and ecological contexts in which they occur, Paul's rendition of creation's past, present, and future take on sharp political bite. With these ecological and political realities more clearly in view, we now turn to consider Paul's creation-attuned gospel as it appears throughout his letter to Rome.

3.2 Paul's Gospel: The God Who Makes Right and Makes Alive

As Paul ministered throughout the Roman Empire, he proclaimed a gospel that pointed to the Creator God as the One who makes right and makes alive through Jesus Christ and the Spirit.[27] Of the artifacts we have from Paul's life, his letter to the Christians in Rome most fully and clearly

---

26. Lampe, *From Paul to Valentinus*, 42, 46; Jewett, *Romans*, 62.

27. Some elements in 3.2 and its subsections first appeared in Burroughs, "Christlike Feasting."

articulates this gospel message. To be sure, Paul's overriding theological claim in Romans is that God makes all things right.[28] God is the justifier (Rom 3:26; 4:5; 8:33), who justifies/makes right human beings through God's Son, Jesus the Messiah.[29] Yet, God not only forgives and reestablishes right relationships with people, God also fills them with life. Restored life is necessary because human wrongdoing results in destruction and death (5:12–21). "Death," for Paul, entails not only the "cessation of an individual's biochemical function" but also a form of "sinful self-regard" that defies God's creational purposes.[30] Thus, God's liberatory work atones for sin and impurities ("justification") and, correspondingly, *restores life* to human beings. In other words, God engages in a process to make them alive, a process captured by the word *zōopoiēsis*.

Beyond human liberation from sin and death, however, God's liberation extends even further to the nonhuman creation. Since the effects of human sin, namely destruction and death, reach throughout the creation (see chapter 1 and 4.2–3), God's justification and *zōopoiēsis* also ultimately liberate the nonhuman creation from its slavery to destruction (8:21). Through Jesus Christ and the Spirit, God not only deals with human sin by means of justification but also fills human and nonhuman creation with life by means of *zōopoiēsis*, "making alive."[31] And Paul refers to this composite

---

28. Robert Jewett notes: "The main theme of Romans, 'God's righteousness,' which [i]s announced in 1:16 and reiterated in 3:5, appears primarily in the sense of God's saving activity in the crucified Christ that sets the world right" (Jewett, *Romans*, 272). Leander Keck explains that through the resurrection, "the making right of all things (and all people) is now under way because God's rightness is activated definitively. In other words, God's rightness, God's righteousness, God's rectitude rectifies whatever is not right and therefore not rightly related to God" (Keck, *Romans*, 35).

29. The English verbs justify and make right (and their corresponding parts of speech) translate the same underlying Greek verb δικαιόω. This Greek word group connotes both "justice" and "righteousness"—of right (or just) relations with human and nonhuman creation and right relations with God. Thus, the Greek word group suggests a much more holistic and integrated meaning than "make right" or "justify" express alone. I do my best to represent the complexity of this Greek word group by using terms deriving from "right" as well as "just."

30. Wirzba, *Food and Faith*, 112–13. For a robust theological discussion of death in relation to creation, see 110–43.

31. As will be discussed in 3.2.1, Paul correlates God's work of *zōopoiēsis* with God's calling "the things that do not exist into being" (Rom 4:17; author's translation). In light of this correlation and the Tanakh's emphasis on God as Creator and life-giver, we may understand *zōopoiēsis* in relation to God's neverending work of endowing creation with life and, thus, not simply with human resurrection.

divine work in each of the four main sections in the body of his letter: chapters 1–4, 5–8, 9–11, and 12–16.[32]

As we have seen from our review of the Tanakh in chapter 1, God's restoration of human and nonhuman creation's rightness, health, purity, and life involves a unique and gratuitous act of God. This is partly because the forms of atonement available under the stipulations of the Mosaic covenant did not remove the corrupting effects of moral sins (such as murder, idolatry, and certain sexual acts) that contaminated the people at fault and the land implicated. Consequently, human and nonhuman creation depended upon and hoped for God's gratuitous cleansing, reconciliation, and restoration to life—in other words, God's justification and *zōopoiēsis*. While God provided such forms of mercy at the behest of God's people throughout the ages, God most universally and abundantly poured out this grace, according to the apostle Paul, through Jesus Christ. On account of his encounter with the risen Jesus Christ, Paul becomes convinced that God's exceptional acts of justification and *zōopoiēsis* happen in and through the life, death, and resurrection of Jesus Christ and the vivifying work of the Spirit. In accordance with an Isaianic vision (Isa 2:2–4; 56:5–6),[33] Paul considers these acts to be universal in scope, providing liberation from sin and death to Jews as well as gentiles. And he perceives them to be creation-wide in extent, catalyzing creation's liberation from subjection to frustration and slavery to destruction.

While the contours of God's *justifying* work run clearly throughout Romans, God's work of making alive (*zōopoiēsis*) at first glance appears less distinct. Yet, this theological concern for restoring life marks every section of the letter. This is because, at least from Paul's perspective, the interwoven stories of humanity and the rest of creation have become stories not only of sin and alienation but also of destruction and death. Throughout Romans and especially in chapters 5 to 8, Paul narrates a story of human and nonhuman creation that consists of four movements: *creation–subjection–liberation–glorification*. These movements find their origins in the Tanakh and meet their fulfillment, according to Paul, in the justifying and vivifying activity of God, Messiah Jesus, and the Spirit.

Consequently, as Paul unfolds a timely exhortation to the Roman Christians (especially seen in Rom 12–15), he simultaneously highlights

---

32. Of course, the contents of this letter could be organized in different ways, but here I follow the general layout suggested by Robert Jewett (Jewett, *Romans*).

33. See discussion in 1.3.3 as well as Shahar, "Jewish Views of Gentiles."

the divine goals of justification and *zōopoiēsis*. In broad outlines, Paul addresses the work of *zōopoiēsis* in each major section in the following ways: he highlights the importance of Abraham's faith in the God who makes alive and resurrects in Rom 1–4 (3.2.1); he draws out the implications of Jesus's experience of death and resurrection as well as believers' participation in Jesus's resurrection life through the Spirit in Rom 5–8 (3.2.2); Paul points to Israel's destiny of reconciliation and, thereby, its possible role in ushering in the resurrection of the dead in Rom 9–11 (3.2.3); and, finally, he accentuates the ways in which the lives of Jesus's followers are to be conformed to the Living, Resurrected Lord in Rom 12–16 (3.2.4).

3.2.1 Romans 1–4

In the first section of the letter, Paul heralds Jesus Christ as the true Son of God on account of his resurrection from among the dead (1:4). This Son of God, the descendant of the Jewish King, David, stands in stark contrast to the Roman Empire's sons of gods, especially on account of his crucifixion by the imperial governing authorities.[34] Yet, despite and even because of his horrific, though atoning, death, Jesus is also the righteous/just one who lives from faith/trust (1:17, quoting Hab 2:4).[35] As Paul explains more fully in chapters 3 and 4, God's Son Jesus is the righteous/just human who trusts in God's life-giving and life-restoring power, God's work of *zōopoiēsis*.[36]

---

34. Elliott highlights the distinction between God's justice and the justice promulgated by Rome. In Romans, Elliott understands Paul to be "driving a rhetorical wedge between the justice of God and the false claims of mortals who pretend at justice, but deserve God's wrath instead" (Elliott, *Arrogance of the Nations*, 62).

35. Two key word groups Paul employs throughout Romans, namely πιστεύω and δικαιόω, typically receive inconsistent renderings in English, primarily because English does not provide translation options stemming from the same root words for all parts of speech. Thus, the verb πιστεύω often appears in English translations as "believe" (which is arguably overly cognitive) while the noun πίστις is rendered "faith" or "trust." The verb, δικαιόω, is usually translated as "justify," but the nouns, δικαιοσύνη and δίκαιος, variously occur as "righteousness" or "justice" and "righteous" or "just," respectively. I attempt to capture the implications of the Greek by rendering the πιστ- word group with phrases referring to active fidelity and the δικ- word group with words conveying rightness and justice.

36. My interpretation of Romans aligns with those who understand πίστεως Ἰησοῦ Χριστοῦ (Rom 3:22, *et al.*) as a subjective genitive (faith *of* Jesus Christ) rather than an objective genitive (faith *in* Jesus Christ) (see, especially, Hays, *Faith of Jesus Christ*; for a discussion of the debate, see Howard, "Faith of Christ"). Interpreting the phrase as a subjective genitive enables us to recognize the ways in which Paul highlights Jesus Christ's own fidelity, trust, and faith in the God who is just and who makes alive. What

Creation's Advocate

In contrast, in Rom 1:19–32 and throughout the letter many other humans fail to trust God and live accordingly. In Paul's Second Temple Jewish critique of the world's problems in 1:19–32, the importance of faith and the necessity of justification and vivification therefore become apparent.[37] Although this passage indicts human beings with a wide range of errors, we will focus here on the ways in which it pinpoints a disruption between human creatures and nonhuman creation.

Romans 1:19–21 implies that Paul believed God created the world in ways that manifest God's existence.[38] God so valued and relied on creation that God gave it an important role of revealing God's invisible characteristics, such as eternal power and divinity (1:20).[39] As humans received evidence of God's existence in the material gifts of creation, they were expected to act in ways that honored God and rendered thanks to God (1:21). Creation's role in revealing God, on the one hand, and humanity's responsibility in receiving this revelation in ways that lead to proper worship of God, on the other hand, together indicate that God established an important relational triad among God's self, the nonhuman creation, and the human creation.[40]

---

is more, Paul employs the catchphrase ἐκ πίστεως throughout Romans to portray the righteous/just person's living "from faith," which most especially is exemplified by Jesus Christ himself (3:22) but also by Abraham (4:16) and all those having peace with God through Jesus Christ (especially "we" in 5:1 and the believing gentiles in 9:30).

37. Other Second Temple Jewish texts, such as Wisdom of Solomon, similarly critique the nations/gentiles.

38. Although Douglas Campbell calls into question whether Rom 1:19–32 presents Paul's own perspective on humanity and instead argues that this passage mimicks the teaching of Paul's opponent(s), I am not entirely convinced by his conclusion that 1:19–32 does not offer some of Paul's perspectives (Campbell, *Deliverance of God*, 519–46). I do agree with Campbell that Paul's clearest analysis of the human problem comes in Rom 5, where sin appears not so much as a human choice but as a dominating power. I also agree that Paul employs 1:19–32 as a foil for his own argument and as a means of undermining his opponents' perspectives. Nevertheless, I take it as a theological given that Paul would have considered God to be Creator and the creation as, at least in some ways, revealing the Creator.

39. Jewett explains that, in ways reminiscent of Hellenistic Judaism, Paul likely combines Jewish theology and Greco-Roman philosophy in his correlation of divine revelation and creation (Jewett, *Romans*, 154–55).

40. This is not to say that through the creation people come to know the fullness of God's redeeming love, which is revealed in God's covenant with Israel and the new covenant through Jesus Christ (Keck, *Romans*, 63; Jewett, *Romans*, 154–55; Dunn, *Romans: 1–8*, 57–58; and Moo, *Epistle to the Romans*, 105). Rom 1 nevertheless suggests: "God has revealed something of himself in and through the created world" (Matera, *Romans*, 49).

Creation's Slavery and Liberation

Yet, according to the critique embedded in 1:19-32, people did not properly feast their eyes on the magnificence of creation. They therefore missed or misconstrued the magnificence of the Creator. They became futile in their thinking, and by the sin of idolatry people distorted creation's revelatory testimony about God's eternal power and divinity (1:20-23).[41] They "venerated and worshiped through cultic service [ἐλάτρευσαν] the creation rather than the Creator" (1:25).[42] Thus, people not only neglected the Creator God by failing to "honor him as God or give thanks to him" (1:21 NRSV),[43] but they also misapprehended creation itself.[44] This erroneously led them into making created things into idols or gods (1:23). People no longer directed their adoration and thanks to the indestructible God—"from [whom] and through [whom] and to [whom] are all things" (11:36)—but instead adored and served destructible things (1:23).[45]

In misperceiving the Creator and creation, humans interrupted—and, arguably, continue to interrupt—the generous movement of God towards creation and creation's own movement back to God by focusing their attention on the creation itself rather than directing their gaze *through creation*

---

41. The verb Paul uses in 1:21 to describe the consequence of human ingratitude is ἐματαιώθησαν ("they were made futile"), a verb that repeatedly appears in the Greek translation of the Tanakh to describe the vanity of human idolatry (Jewett, *Romans*, 158). Paul uses the related noun in 8:20 to explain why creation so eagerly anticipates the revelation of the sons of God: it was subjected to futility/vanity. That futility may be related to idolatry specifically, but it more likely has a more expansive connotation in 8:20. Jewett suggests the term in 8:20 (in tandem with 1:21) "describe[s] the frustration and destructiveness of persons or groups who suppress the truth and refuse to recognize God" and that "Paul has in mind the abuse of the natural world by Adam and his descendants. The basic idea is that the human refusal to accept limitations ruins the world. By acting out idolatrous desires to have unlimited dominion over the garden, the original purpose of creation—to express divine goodness (Gen. 1:31) and reflect divine glory (Ps 19:1-4)—was emptied" (513).

42. Jewett suggests that the verb "venerated" might allude to veneration of the emperor in the imperial cult (Jewett, *Romans*, 170).

43. Romans and Jews alike understood that expressing thanks to God was a central aspect of human devotion and piety (Jewett, *Romans*, 157-58). "Early Christianity gave particular prominence to this idea, not only in following the tradition of Hellenistic Judaism of giving thanks at mealtime but also in naming its principal ritual the 'Eucharist'" (158).

44. Edward Adams contends, "[i]t is not the κτίσις which seduces and tempts human beings away from God. If human beings stand in an ambiguous relation to creation, it is due to *their* misperception and misappropriation of it, to *their* distortion of its true character" (Adams, *Constructing the World*, 158. Emphasis original).

45. For more discussion of "indestructible" versus "destructible," see 4.2.2.

onto the life-creating and life-sustaining God, who is the giver of good things.[46] Perhaps as a result of this misperception, people impose upon creation inordinate expectations, assuming somehow that created things—whether people, empires, animals, or inanimate objects—can deliver God-sized blessings, meaning, and results.[47] Especially in the context of the idolatries present during early Roman imperial times, such "[i]dolatry prevents knowledge of the true creator, it is rooted in falsehood, and results in futility and foolishness. There is in idolatry a loss of glory, and a misunderstanding of creation."[48] As so often happens—whether in ancient or modern forms of idolatry—God's human creatures end up misappropriating creation in order to satisfy selfish appetites.[49] For, at its root, idolatry "is blind to the gift that the creator has offered, and attempts to seize the abundance and fertility of the gift on its own terms—terms that result in economic exploitation, control, and death . . . This is where an inability to see the earth as gift will lead."[50] Paul's proceeding portrait of humanity's existence under the powers of sin and death in chapters 3–8 flesh out some

---

46. In his theological account of food, Norman Wirzba puts flesh on how people might direct their gaze through creation to the Creator, explaining that "what a theological approach to eating does is enable the perception of food within a context that stretches *through* the many ecological and social relationships of this world *to* the divine creator and sustainer of it" (Wirzba, *Food and Faith*, 29).

47. Wirzba, *From Nature to Creation*, 48–49.

48. Keesmaat, "Land, Idolatry, and Justice," 94.

49. Wirzba, *From Nature to Creation*, 87–94. While interpreting the ascetic traditions of Christian monasticism, Wirzba describes the ways in which sinful human passions distort our vision of and consequent relationships with creation: "Asceticism is all about attending to customary ways of approaching others that lead to distortion because what we see is dominated by the anxiety or hubris or insecurity we so often feel" (89). In order to counteract and correct this distortion, we must engage in a rigorous process of self-examination (with the assistance and encouragement of a community) (89). This process "begins with attention to how personal ambition, fear, and boredom get in the way of seeing things for what they are, that is, expressions of God's love, and as such, the material manifestations of God's goodness and delight" (91).

50. Keesmaat, "Land, Idolatry, and Justice," 95. Regarding 1:28–31, Keesmaat perceptively explains: "Of the twenty behaviors that manifest a 'debased mind and improper conduct' (v. 28), the first nine are used to describe economic injustice in the LXX (injustice, wickedness, greed, evil, envy, murder, quarreling, treachery, malice; v. 29), three describe the deceit that the Psalms link to economic oppression (informers, slanderers, inventors of evil; vv. 28, 29), three characterize those who inhabit superior socioeconomic situations, a link between riches and pride also found in the LXX (conceited, arrogant, boastful; v. 30), and the last three describe attitudes that shape an ethos of injustice (faithless, heartless, and without mercy; v. 31)" (96).

of the ways in which idolatrous perspectives and practices—whether practiced by gentiles or Jews—result in the destruction of life and well-being.

We may be inclined to conclude that the way in which we avoid idolatry is to concentrate all our attention on the Creator God. Yet, because we are embodied beings that depend upon the creation for air, water, shelter, and nourishment, we cannot entirely disregard creation; we must continue to toil and till the ground in order "to eat of it all the days" of our lives (Gen 3:17 NRSV). If we dualistically separate our spiritual attention from our material concerns, we will continue to misperceive and misappropriate creation. Concentrating solely upon God would ignore the value of that which God has made and the divinely derived claim that it has upon us. Thus, ignoring creation's witness about God and creation's story about itself would almost certainly lead us to cultivate destructive rather than healthy relationships with each other and the rest of God's creation.

Especially in light of how Paul narrates creation's story in Rom 8:19–22, proper worship of the Creator and appropriate relationships with God's creation requires us to attend to creation's story in God honoring ways. This means we not only must remain alert to how creation points toward the gracious provision of our Creator (even as we acknowledge creation's limits), but it also means we pay heed to how our activities harm creation. It turns out, Paul's letter offers us some starting points for our examination in chapter 3.

After indicting anyone who would judge others for the failures listed in 1:19–36 but who would also fail to recognize similar mistakes in themselves (Rom 2), Paul provides a litany of Scriptures in chapter 3 detailing the ways in which human sin—a power under which all people exist—reaps destruction and death. People, both of Judean and gentile descent, destroy others with their words (3:13), their bodies (3:15), and their life trajectories (3:16). On top of these destructive and perhaps even murderous behaviors, they express no fear of God (3:18) and do not seek God (3:11). While Paul's string of quotations provides little insight into the concrete contexts in which people practiced these destructive behaviors, many of the quotations originate in Scriptures that bemoan and condemn the economic exploitation of God's people, which in turn led to their loss of inherited land.[51]

51. Keesmaat notes: "As [Paul] describes the unjust who have no understanding and do not seek God—those whose mouths are full of death-dealing and poisonous lies that create a curse and bitterness, whose way of walking only leads to death and who create ruin and misery for the innocent who get in their way, who have no knowledge at all of what makes for peace because they do not know or seek God—we hear echoes of classic

Paul's litany in chapter 3, therefore, underscores the dire need for a servant leader who would establish justice and rectify wrongs.

Beyond humanity's need for tangible forms of rectification, 3:1–20 also alludes to the land's need for purification and restoration on account of those human practices that degrade the land's status. As chapter 1 of this volume explained, the Tanakh designates murder and idolatry as moral sins. These sins were understood to contaminate the human persons involved and, by implication, the lands on which these moral forms of impurity were committed. No cultic or ritual means could remove the contaminations caused by moral impurities. These impurities/sins therefore required a novel, gracious, divine act of forgiveness and atonement (for more discussion, see 1.2.3). Because God's covenant people, Israel, as well as countless gentiles occasionally committed these and other sins, they and their lands stood in need of purification. The litany especially indicts the Roman Empire for employing violence and deceptive speech as it conquered the world. For, "[t]he illusory *Golden Age* was built by 'feet swift to shed blood' (Rom. 3.15)."[52] All lands, then—according to Jewish tradition—needed atonement in order to be freed from the contaminating effects of moral impurities.[53] Read from this theological perspective, sin's pervasive presence among Jews and gentiles (3:9–18) makes it all the more apparent that atonement was needed—even for the nonhuman creation. And Paul's insistence that people could do little but trust God for making this dire situation right follows quite logically (3:19–22).

While God had provided people with various means of offering sacrifices to atone for human impurity and sin by way of Torah, the atonement through Jesus Christ that Paul describes in 3:21–26 is an offering that was not prescribed by the Law.[54] It goes beyond the atonement available through the Mosaic covenant by providing universal right-making, a form of justification that extends beyond the historic covenant people of Israel, in fulfillment of some Jewish expectations (e.g., Isa 65–66). The atonement also went beyond the legislation of Torah by employing an atoning sacrifice

---

texts that describe idolatry in Israel . . . where the faithful cry out to God for justice in the face of economic oppression that results in loss of land" (Keesmaat, "Land, Idolatry, and Justice," 96–97).

52. Tonstad, *Letter to the Romans*, 122. Tonstad also insightfully notes: "While the government of the Roman Empire cast itself as a benefactor and caring father, it was government by conquest and military rule," as we observed in chapter 2 of this volume (122).

53. For a related discussion, see Klawans, *Impurity and Sin*, 30.

54. For discussion, see Keck, *Romans*, 104–5.

not prescribed by the Law, namely, a willing human person, a righteous martyr (Rom 3:22, 30).[55] With connotations of liberation, the redemption Jesus brings through his willing death not only delivers people from slavery to sin, as Paul makes plain in chapter 5, but also implicitly fulfills God's promise to cleanse people of their impurities, especially idolatry (Ezek 36:25; 37:23; see also Jer 33:8; Zech 13:1).[56] Because this divine cleansing and forgiveness are not received through the liturgical practices set forth in the Law, the benefits of God's gracious atonement through Jesus are appropriated not by liturgical works (ἐξ ἔργων) but by way of faith or trust (ἐκ πίστεως). What is more, this atonement and redemption, as Rom 8:21 suggests, effect cleansing and renewal for the nonhuman creation as well as for humanity (see Ezek 39:16).[57] The reconciliation Jesus effects (Rom 5:11) between humanity and God also encompasses creation so that Adam's children are no longer creation's adversaries (Gen 3:17-19; see 1.2.1).

Even prior to the atonement of Jesus Christ, this mode of trusting God was the means to a right relationship with God, as made clear from Israel's foremost patriarch: Abraham (4:1-25).[58] While Paul's focus on Abraham is

---

55. Scholars debate over which sacrificial ritual from the Tanakh Jesus's atoning death most closely mimics and, therefore, fulfills. The Passover lamb could be one option, especially in light of Paul's statement in 1 Cor 5:7, "our Paschal lamb, Christ, has been sacrificed" (NRSV). Another main option for understanding the dynamics in Rom 3:21-26 is the Day of Atonement sacrifice, especially the scapegoat. Rather than pinpointing one paradigm, I would suggest instead that Jesus's atoning death reflects all these images but does not correspond fully to any one of them. Perhaps, we might also interpret the redemption and cleansing that Jesus brings as fulfilling the divine cleansing promised in passages like Ezek 36.

56. Many first-century Jews likely viewed gentiles as *morally* rather than *ritually* impure. Because gentiles were not under the Jewish Law, they were not obligated to maintain the ritual purity codes of Leviticus. Thus, gentiles did not accumulate ritual impurities (for discussion, see Fredriksen, *Paul*, 52-54; Klawans, *Impurity and Sin*, 150-55). Yet, from a common Jewish perspective, all people could accumulate moral impurities through acts of idolatry, murder, and certain sexual acts (cf. Lev 18:24). Thus, gentiles—along with Jews—needed God's gracious purification/cleansing; and according to Paul, this takes place through Christ. For texts relating to moral impurity and purification in Paul's undisputed letters, see, Rom 1:24; 6:19; 2 Cor 7:21; 12:21; Gal 5:19; 1 Thess 4:7.

57. Recognizing the creation-wide implications of Jesus's atonement, Jewett explains: "'making upright' is much broader than the usual idea of 'justification.' It is not so much the individual soul that is at stake in the revelation of divine righteousness that occurred in Christ and the subsequent preaching of the gospel, but rather the restoration of the entire cosmic order, including each group and species distorted by sin" (Jewett, *Romans*, 273).

58. Keck, *Romans*, 124.

meant to convince people that faith rather than works has always been the divinely approved means to justification, he meanwhile elucidates a prime eco-theological principle. Paul identifies Abraham as one who had faith in "the God who makes the dead alive (ζῳοποιοῦντος) and calls the things that do not exist into being" (4:17).[59] Here we find the first of two references in Romans to God as the one who makes alive (ζῳοποιέω), a composite verb that combines the adjective ζωός (alive, living) with the verb ποιέω (to make). This verb refers occasionally to natural processes (see 1 Cor 15:36) but most often, in biblical literature, to supernatural acts that instill life in something.[60] Thus, Abraham trusted in the Creator God who gave him and Sarah a beloved offspring in their old age (Rom 4:17–21). It is this life-giving and life-restoring God who is at work making all things right in a world where deception, idolatry, and violence multiply (3:9–18). This life-giving Creator—as Parent, Son, and Spirit—acts as Liberator, Justifier, and Creator of life in a world where, as Paul goes on to explain, sin enslaves and death dominates (5:14, 17, 21; 6:12, 16–18).[61]

3.2.2 Romans 5–8

The second section of Romans presents Paul's analysis of the world's fundamental problem: the dominion of sin and death.[62] Death's dominion does not simply concern biological death but also "death-in-life."[63] As he explains Jesus's atoning death and resurrection life in greater depth, Paul also announces God's gracious solution: the new dominion of righteousness

---

59. In this section, Paul also correlates Abraham's faith with the faith of all those who "trust in God who raised Jesus our Lord from the dead" (4:24).

60. BDAG, 431; LSJ, 345. James Dunn indicates this verb may not only refer to resurrection but also "can denote God's creative, sustaining (keeping alive) or renewing power (see Neh 9:6; Job 36:6; Eccl 7:12; *Jos. As.* 8.9; John 6:63; 2 Cor 3:6; Gal 3:21)" (Dunn, *Romans: 1–8*, 217).

61. Although Paul frequently refers to Jesus and the Spirit in ways that closely associate them with God, I typically do not refer explicitly to the Trinity since this theological signifier developed many years later.

62. By using the framework of problem and solution, I self-consciously echo the contributions of E. P. Sanders (Sanders, *Paul and Palestinian Judaism*, 442–47).

63. Tonstad, *Letter to the Romans*, 160. Tonstad insightfully points out that Paul's view of death as enemy and oppressor contrasts significantly with Socratic philosophy, which considered death as liberating the eternal soul from its imprisonment in the body (161–67). This Greco-Roman perspective fundamentally contradicts Genesis' view of creation—and embodied human life—as "good."

Creation's Slavery and Liberation

and life that flows forth from God's love (5:8).[64] We encounter in Rom 5–8, therefore, the heart of Paul's gospel and the backbone of his story of creation.

In chapter 5, Paul correlates the world's problems with the creational boundary crossing of Adam. As he renarrates Gen 3 in Rom 5:12–21, Paul reminds his readers that Adam transgressed God's command, and he asserts that this transgression allowed sin and death to gain dominion in the world. While he does not state explicitly that Adam ate fruit from the tree God had designated as off limits, Paul's use of the Gen 3 narrative nevertheless situates this human trespass at the nexus of the creation-human-divine triad of relationships.[65] And Paul explicitly describes Adam's disobedience as bringing about cosmic effects, explaining, "the many [humans] became sinners" (Rom 5:19); they consequently experience condemnation (5:18) and death (5:12, 14, 15, 17, 21).[66] These Adamic effects, Paul later intimates, likewise cause havoc throughout creation (8:19–22).

Even as Adam's transgression introduced sin and death into God's good and life-filled creation, God ultimately remediates this problem through the good and life-filled Messiah. Throughout Romans and especially in 5:12–21 and 6:6–23, Paul portrays Jesus's obedient, righteous life and death as God's world-transforming solution to the reign of sin and death.[67] Beyond the cleansing and reconciliation effected by his death, Jesus's resurrection life provides new life to those who unite themselves in death, burial, and resurrection with Christ (5:6–21; 6:1–11). Their identification with and

---

64. Timothy Eberhart notes: "God's holiness is God's perfect love, and in the convivial bonds of the Holy Spirit, the superabundant love of God overflows out into the creation as wholly harmonious love, which nurtures health" (Eberhart, *Rooted and Grounded in Love*, 76).

65. Tonstad indicates that Adam's (and humanity's) core problem is that they misperceive God as a God who deprives them of good things (i.e., the forbidden fruit) rather than as the God who graciously gives an abundance of good things (Tonstad, *Letter to the Romans*, 174). Put somewhat differently, it is as if Adam's transgression flowed from "a way of life that [wa]s not attuned to life with and for others but a life of self-enclosure and self-magnification" (Wirzba, *Food and Faith*, 114).

66. For more discussion of this important passage, see 4.2.1.

67. We may rightly wonder how death could function in both negative and positive ways according to Paul. Wirzba helpfully suggests: "death is evil insofar as it is a force that degrades life. It is not evil if it follows a fulfilled life, a life enriched by the kenotic, self-offering love that is the mark of God's own life" (Wirzba, *Food and Faith*, 115). More specifically, "Jesus' death speaks to God's way of being with the world and thus also to creation's inner meaning. On the cross Jesus encountered the alienating and violent death of this world and transformed it into the self-offering death that leads to resurrection life" (125).

participation in Jesus's own story of life from death, grants Jews as well as gentiles "the abundance of grace and the gift of righteousness" and empowers them to "reign in life through the one Jesus Christ" (Rom 5:17).

Paul's reference to reigning in life here may indicate that those who experience liberation now will rule alongside Christ in the eschaton.[68] Yet, it may also suggest that, even before the eschaton, God is at work restoring people's capacity to "exercise dominion" properly. Those gifted with grace and righteousness "reign in life," which—when understood in light of key passages in the Tanakh—entails "exercising dominion" as creation's servant leaders. As they are graciously conformed to the image of God's Son and thereby more fully experience God's work of making alive (Gen 1:26–28; Rom 8:29), they are enabled to live in life-supporting ways.[69] Their experiences of justification, sanctification, *zōopoiēsis*, and glorification ultimately will alleviate creation's experience of destruction, as becomes clear in 8:21 where Paul explains that the whole creation will be liberated *into* the glory of God's children (see 5.1–2).

Paul's expectation for those in Christ to undergo a process of transformation prior to the eschaton becomes all the more obvious in Rom 6. Paul expresses this most clearly when he declares that Jesus's saving grace does not excuse people from living in righteousness now (6:1–4). God's work of making them right—making them just—has practical and embodied consequences.[70] Because they have died and risen with Christ through baptism

---

68. Jewett, *Romans*, 384; Dunn, *Romans: 1–8*, 282.

69. Douglas Harink insightfully points out how the Pauline conceptions of inheriting the world (Rom 4:13) and reigning in life (5:17) are potentially dangerous. The lens of politics quickly reveals many destructive horrors inflicted on the world by the hands of "Christian" nations. Harink insists that "world-inheriting and reigning in life are promised always and only *in Jesus Messiah*" and this "fundamentally qualifies, or rather constitutes, what world-inheriting and reigning in life are and what they look like for those to whom they have been promised.... *There is a single road to messianic world-inheriting and glory; it is the paschal road of the Messiah, the way of the cross*" (cf., 8:17) (Harink, "Messianic Anarchy: The Liberating Word of Romans 13:1–7," 202. Emphasis Original.).

70. In commenting on Paul's notion of the "body of sin" (Rom 6:6), John Barclay insightfully explains that, according to Paul and apart from Christ, "the body has been commandeered by sin, such that its dispositions, emotions, speech-patterns, and habitual gestures are bound to systems of honor, self-aggrandizement, and license that are fundamentally at odds with the will of God" (Barclay, *Paul and the Gift*, 508). Yet, through "the physical rite of baptism," humans may undergo "a transition from death to life" with the result that they now "are committed to instantiate a new embodied *habitus*" (508). In and through the body, Jesus's followers live out their faith, as Matt O'Reilly also notes in his monograph on the social and ethical implications of resurrection in Paul's thought. He

and because of the eternal life to come, followers of Christ are to walk in newness of life now, as 6:1–5 attests:

> What shall we conclude, then? Shall we continue in sin in order that grace might multiply? Absolutely not! The ones who have died to sin, how shall they still live in it? Or are you ignorant that as many of us that were baptized into Messiah Jesus, we were baptized into his death? Therefore, we were put in the tomb with him through this baptism into death, in order that just as the Messiah was raised from the dead through the glory of the Father, thus also we might walk in new life. For if we have become conformed to the likeness of his death, so also shall we be conformed to his resurrection.

According to Paul, participation in Jesus Christ's life, death, and resurrection empowers and obligates people to live in righteousness consistently and in accordance with the new life of resurrection.[71] The future goal of faith in Christ—glorious resurrection life—necessarily defines ethical behavior in life now.[72] Thus, Christians' reign in life, their servant leadership, must align with this goal of vitality.

The responsibility of achieving this goal, however, does not rest on the Christ followers alone, for Paul stresses the Spirit's central role in guiding and empowering this transformed living (8:2–14; see also Gal 5:16–26).[73]

---

states, "it is somatic language in particular that connects the theology of [Rom] chapter 6 with the ethical material beginning in chapter 12 (σῶμα, 12:1) and extending to Paul's expectations for table fellowship in chapters 14 and 15" (O'Reilly, *Paul and the Resurrected Body*, 139–40). See also, Tonstad, *Letter to the Romans*, 194–202.

71. Paul specifies some of the practical implications of participation with Christ in 6:11–13, commanding, "Reckon yourselves dead to sin but living for God in Messiah Jesus. Therefore, do not allow sin to rule over your dying body so that you obey its passions. Do not offer your embodied selves as tools of injustice for sin, but offer yourselves to God as those alive from the dead and your embodied selves as tools of righteousness/justice for God." In discussing these verses, John Barclay explains: "The very location where sin once had most visible sway, and where its grip still draws believers' bodily selves towards death, is now the location where the 'newness of life' breaks through into action, displaying in counterintuitive patterns of behavior the miraculous Christ-life that draws their embodied selves toward the 'vivification' (8:11) or 'redemption' (8:23) of the body" (Barclay, *Paul and the Gift*, 505–6).

72. O'Reilly similarly concludes: "The cocrucifixion of the 'old self' with Christ liberates the believer from the reign of sin and makes possible the resulting present condition in which the believer's bodily life is no longer characterized by habits and patterns of sin" (O'Reilly, *Paul and the Resurrected Body*, 141).

73. Paul does not propose that Christians simply follow Jesus by their own strength. Douglas Campbell explains: "Just as Jesus faithfully endured suffering to the point of death and then received a triumphant and glorious resurrection, so too Christians who

After describing the ways in which the power of sin hijacks the good and guiding purposes of God's Law in Rom 7, Paul declares: "The guiding principle of the Spirit—who is characterized by life—has liberated you in Christ Jesus from the guiding principle of sin and death" (8:2).[74] The "Spirit of life," in other words, assists God in making people truly right/just (8:4), and the Spirit also empowers God's work of making alive by liberating people from the dominating rule of sin and death. Paul emphasizes the Spirit's role in making alive yet again when he declares: "And if the Spirit who raised Jesus from the dead dwells in you, the one who raised Christ from the dead will make alive (ζῳοποιήσει) even your dying bodies through his Spirit dwelling in you" (8:11). While interpreters are often inclined to understand the Spirit's vivifying work as solely eschatological in nature (as a work of resurrection), the trajectory of what Paul expresses in chapters 5–8 also points to a holistic, this-worldly reading. The Spirit fills God's people with life now, directing them to live a life-supporting life, a *zōopoietical* life, just as much as the Spirit empowers them to live a righteous, justified life (8:4, 6).

By yielding to the Spirit's work of "making alive" and fulfilling their commission to "reign in life" (8:11; 5:17), God's people most faithfully take on a form of life that no longer inflicts destruction upon themselves, other people, or the nonhuman creation (8:21). Instead, life in the Spirit mobilizes them to live now in accordance with God's eternal purposes of life. In the words of Jewett, "Sons of God demonstrate their sonship by exercising the kind of dominion that heals rather than destroys."[75] God's form of domin-

---

maintain their loyalty to God and to Christ until the end will receive a resurrection. Moreover, in so doing, God is not asking them to imitate Christ—perhaps an impossible task—so much as to inhabit or to indwell him. That is, any such endurance through duress is evidence that the Spirit of God is actively reshaping the Christian into the likeness of Christ, and that they are therefore already part of the story, a story that will result in eschatological salvation!" (Campbell, *Quest*, 93).

74. Of course, "guiding principle" here could be translated as "law" (BDAG, 677–78). In Rom 8:2, I take the second genitive in the phrase τοῦ πνεύματος τῆς ζωῆς to be a descriptive genitive (with a meaning of "characterized by"), although other options certainly make contextual sense as well (see Wallace, *Greek Grammar Beyond the Basics*, 79). The New English Translation (NET) offers the translation, "life-giving Spirit" for this phrase in 8:2 (Burer et al., *New Testament*, 422).

75. Jewett, "Corruption and Redemption of Creation," 46. In more ecological terms, Tonstad states: "Ecological demise is . . . a feature of loss of dominion, and ecological healing is possible when the recipients of grace are restored to the lost dominion, bringing with them the economy of life that was lost" (Tonstad, *Letter to the Romans*, 193). However, because misconceptions of "dominion" have easily perverted human relationships with creation, I would rephrase this quotation to refer to humanity's "servant leadership" instead.

ion—what I would call "servant leadership" (see chapter 1)—demands the attentive nurturing of a diverse creation so that it might support the flourishing of life. We might conceptualize this line of thinking by paraphrasing the logic of Rom 6 in light of 8:19–22 (see further discussion of 8:19–22 below and in chapters 4–5). A Pauline query might ask: "Since the Spirit of life has liberated people in Christ from their slavery to the law of sin and death (Rom 8:2), shall they continue in sin and death by enslaving the rest of God's creation to untimely destruction (8:21)?" Pauline Christians might respond, "Absolutely not! Now, in Christ and by the power of the Spirit, the possibility exists for us to break the cycle of violence and destruction that plagues the world—at least to a limited extent. Just as we cooperate with God in the process of sanctification, we cooperate with God everyday in the liberation of creation." Such cooperation encapsulates "reigning in life."

Despite the Spirit's current vivifying work, God's people and, in fact, the whole creation continue to wait for something more. Even as those walking in the Spirit may become ever more sanctified in this life and in some sense become glorified now (6:22; 8:30), they still await bodily glorification, the redemption of the body (8:17, 23).[76] The fullness of salvation therefore still depends on a future decisive and divine action in which God resurrects human persons, liberating them fully and finally from the influences of sin and death (8:10–11, 23). From other Pauline epistles, we learn that this future resurrection will be correlated with Christ's *parousia*, his return to earth in victory, judgment, and glory (1 Thess 2:19; 3:13; 4:15; 5:23; 2 Thess 2:1, 8; 1 Cor 15:23).

While acknowledging the suffering that God's people must endure as they wait for resurrection (Rom 8:17–18), Paul insists that this future, collective resurrection and ultimate glorification has significant creational implications. Even as those in Christ await the ultimate redemption of their body (8:23), the nonhuman creation also longingly and expectantly awaits their resurrection (8:19). For, by way of humanity's ultimate glorification, the onslaught of sin and death will be removed, and the creation will no longer be subjected to frustration or enslaved to destruction (8:19–21). These perverted forms of subjection and slavery result, according to the logic of Rom 5–8, from human trespass and the ongoing dominion of sin and death. Consequently, creation cannot be free from frustration or destruction while human sin and the threats of sin, destruction, and death remain in the world. The whole of creation will only experience the full

---

76. Keck, *Romans*, 212–13; Jewett, *Romans*, 518; Dunn, *Romans: 1–8*, 491.

liberation made available through the atoning life, death, and resurrection of Jesus when God's children are truly just and glorified. At that point, creation too will enter the glory that Jesus's siblings enjoy (8:21). But, for now, creation longingly anticipates this future (8:19).

The suffering, waiting, and groaning the nonhuman creation and God's children must endure together reveals an important aspect of Paul's account of creation. Not only is human and nonhuman creation interdependent but God's human creatures are invited to stand in solidarity with the rest of creation. Because their histories and destinies intertwine, humanity and creation experience a solidarity of suffering as well as liberation. Solidarity expresses the fact that humanity and the rest of God's creation are interdependent; they currently share in suffering and ultimately will share in the experience of salvation. So intertwined are they that creation's suffering goes hand in hand with humanity's slavery to sin. Yet, when humans receive their ultimate liberation from sin and death at the resurrection, the rest of creation will be right there experiencing liberation as well.

Placed within the first-century context, creation's longing and waiting for this liberation stands diametrically opposed to imperial proclamations. For, Paul insinuates that creation certainly has *not* been liberated and restored by the appearance and administration of a Roman son of god, the emperor. Creation still anticipates the liberation that comes with the apocalypse of the "sons of God," and these sons/children are markedly different from Rome's sons of gods (and many other governing authorities).[77] God the Creator's "sons," who might more properly be called "children" (8:16,

---

77. The similarities and differences between imperial proclamations about the sons of god(s) and Paul's is made all the clearer in the Latin translation of Rom 8:19 and 21. Paul's references to "sons of God" and "children of God" in these verses both appear as *filiorum Dei* in the Vulgate, as compared with the imperial references to *filius divi* (*Biblia Sacra*, 1759; for more discussion of the Latin terms for "god," see 2.1). While imperial rhetoric portrayed the heirs of the Julio-Claudian line as intimately related to honorary gods (*divis*) and thereby as sons of gods, Paul instead argues that all those "in Christ Jesus" and led by the Spirit are the adopted "sons" of the high God (*filiorum Dei*) (8:1, 14). Therefore, much like Gen 1:26-28 subverted Mesopotamian claims that the king was the deity's image bearer, so too Rom 8:19-22 counters Rome's imperial perspectives. For, the writers of Genesis considered the image of God to be impressed upon all humans so that they all held positions of honor and responsibility in God's creation. Similarly, Paul contradicts imperial suggestions that the imperial family held primary responsibility for renewing creation as sons of honorary gods. Instead, the honor and responsibility for liberating the creation is shared by people of any heritage, socio-economic situation, or relation who are children of the One, True God. According to Paul, these children are Jesus Christ's siblings and co-heirs (8:17, 29).

21), endure sufferings with Christ now but will be glorified with him in the future (8:17). It is for *these* sons/children, asserts Paul, creation waits (8:19, 21).

The reigning in life of God's children, moreover, falls in step with their risen Lord by resisting the elitist, exclusivist, consumptive, and anthropocentric approaches to ruling that the Roman Empire (and plenty of other societies) embodied (see Rom 12–16 below). Consequently, the imperial gospel claiming that Emperors Augustus and then Nero had restored the Golden Age becomes far less convincing and even farcical when considered in light of Paul's gospel. For, the truly just and reconciling Liberator is the crucified and risen Jewish Messiah, Jesus Christ, who serves the circumcised and uncircumcised (15:8–9). Descended from King David (1:3) as Son of the Creator God (1:4, 20; 11:36), Messiah Jesus has saved, reconciled, justified, and liberated all those who identify with him (5:9–11; 6:22; 8:2). This Son of God, the root of Jesse (15:12; Isa 11:10), rises to rule the nations with justice and to establish the conditions for creational peace and flourishing (Isa 11:6–9, following the LXX). For the fullness of these conditions, however, the creation continues to wait.

In its waiting, we may expect creation to anticipate the return of the victorious Lord. Yet, Paul startles his readers by claiming instead that creation waits for the resurrected children of God.[78] Put more starkly, Paul does not explain that the creation primarily waits for the *parousia* of Jesus Christ so it can at last experience liberation. Instead, creation's attentive focus is on the appearance of Jesus's glorified siblings (Rom 8:17, 29). The reason this is the case, according to Paul's story of creation in Rom 5–8, is that (outside of life in Christ) all people are enslaved to sin and death and thereby may often act in ways that are destructive to others, including the nonhuman creation (Rom 5:12–21; 3:9–19; 8:20–21). Human creatures must undergo glorious transformation before nonhuman creation can receive its full liberation. Such a perspective contrasts with imperial claims. For, "[w]hereas the Roman premise was that *disorderly barbarians and rebels* caused the corruption of nature, Paul argues that all humans reenact Adam's fall."[79] Adam's consequent disease of sin, according to Paul, infects the "pious," "civilized" Romans along with all others, even Jesus's

---

78. Tonstad identifies this unexpected dynamic by saying, "Expectation does not run in a straight line directly to God but by way of '*the children of God*'" (Tonstad, *Letter to the Romans*, 246).

79. Jewett, "Corruption and Redemption of Creation," 31. Emphasis added.

followers who would wrongly choose to use their bodies for injustice and destruction (cf., 6:13). Until humanity's universal problem of sin, destruction, and death is rectified, therefore, creation cannot truly be free from its subjection to frustration and slavery to destruction. Creation waits for God fully to rectify and glorify Greek and barbarian, wise and foolish, slave and free, Jew and gentile. Creation waits for the glorification of humanity as a whole.[80] And God's covenant people, Israel, remains an important part of this whole.

3.2.3 Romans 9–11

In the third section of his letter, Paul grapples with the fact that many Jews in his day had not accepted Jesus as their Messiah; yet he argues that, despite this reality, God remains righteous as well as faithful to Israel. Throughout this discussion, Paul of course highlights God's work of justification, of making things right. By the end of this section, however, he also touches on the corresponding divine project of making alive (11:15).

In the first few verses of this section, Paul identifies the glory and adoption that he previously discussed in chapter 8 as rightfully belonging to God's covenant people, the Israelites (9:4). They are the ones from whose flesh the Messiah was born (9:6). This Messiah, as Paul suggests in his quotation of Isa 11 in Rom 15, is the long-expected root of Jesse whose rule over Israel and the nations would establish societal and creational peace, justice, and flourishing (Rom 15:12; Isa 11:1–9). Read in accordance with the rich contours of Isaiah, these passages point to Messiah Jesus as God's servant who makes things right for Israel, the nations, and the nonhuman creation.

Although Paul will discuss Jesus's servant leadership in more detail in Rom 15, we will consider it now in relation to God's promises to Israel. After Paul insists that the Jesus followers in Rome welcome one another (Rom 15:7), Paul describes the way in which Jesus—as an Israelite/Judean according to the flesh—served God's covenant people. Jesus's way of self-giving and peace-making demonstrates God's never-ending commitment to the covenant people, Israel. For, "Jesus became a servant of the circumcision people on behalf of God's truth in order to confirm [God's] promises to the fathers" (15:8). By his clear-sighted judgment and self-giving justice during his life, Jesus represented the just God and thereby fulfilled, in these

---

80. Tonstad is wary of saying creation's liberation depends on humanity's liberation, but he admits the correlation is suggested by Paul (Tonstad, *Letter to the Romans*, 246).

respects, the heart of Jewish Messianic expectations (Isa 11:1-10).[81] Yet, even in his role as David's ruling son, Jesus did not lead a revolt against Rome in order to take back Abraham's geographical inheritance for his descendants.[82] Rather, Jesus submitted in humility to Jewish and Roman authorities, rejecting coercion and violence while choosing self-giving love (Rom 5:8; 15:3). Thus, Jesus's righteous piety led not to divinely blessed military victories but to service and a divestment of power.[83]

Paul invites Jews as well as gentiles to confess Messiah Jesus—God's ruling servant, whom "God raised . . . from the dead" (10:9)—as Lord. Through this process of invitation and commitment, God extends eschatological salvation to Israel. Even though many of Paul's "kindred according to the flesh" (9:3 NRSV) had thus far rejected Jesus, Paul trusts that more of God's covenant people would indeed accept Jesus as their resurrected, living Lord. In a suggestive query, Paul even identifies Israel's future adjustment of loyalties as intimately related to resurrection life, for "[i]f a portion of Israel's discarding [of the gospel] is the reconciliation of the world, what will their acceptance be but life from the dead?" (11:15).[84] Here, Paul's "un-

81. For a helpful analysis of Rom 15, see Tonstad, *Letter to the Romans*, 358–83.

82. Although Paul does not specifically refer to God's promise of land to Abraham, Sarah, and their descendants, Paul's reference to the "promises" in 9:4 may allude to it. It may be that any eschatological inheritance of the land through the Messiah's administration, however, would include not only the territory promised to Abraham but also the entire "cosmos" (4:13). For more discussion, see Harink, "Messianic Anarchy," 198–203.

83. Following this pattern, Paul too rejected the violence and subjugation that typifies imperial regimes and instead gained the obedience of faith of all nations through proclamation, service, and signs of wonder by the Holy Spirit (Rom 15:19). The liberation that Jesus's atonement effects is not thrust upon the world compulsorily according to Paul. Instead, God employs human beings to announce the good news of liberation and to invite people to pledge their fidelity and obedience to the Lord Jesus Christ (1:1, 5, 14–17; 10:14–17; 15:15–19). Jewett suggests a similar dynamic: "In Paul's case the avenue of divine action is the conversion of humans rather than their enslavement under a ruler pretending to be a god. So what the creation awaits with eager longing is the emergence of this triumph of divine righteousness (see Rom 1:17), which will begin to restore a rightful balance to the creation, overcoming the Adamic legacy of corruption and disorder that fell as a calamitous curse upon the ground (Gen 3:17–19)" (Jewett, "Corruption and Redemption of Creation," 35–36). Similarly, Jewett states, in contrast to "imperial celebrations and administration as the hinge of the golden age, Paul tout[ed] the power of the gospel to convert the world" (31). As the mediator between the Creator God and all descendants of Adam and of Abraham (the father of *many* nations, Rom 4:13; see also 3:29–30; 4:11–12, 17–18; 8:28–30), Jesus the Son of God summoned the obedience of all nations through his emissaries, such as Paul (5:12–14; 1:5–6).

84. Because Paul has already indicated that he has a portion of Israel in view—the portion that he is trying to provoke towards jealousy (11:14)—I replace Paul's general

paralleled expression 'life from the dead' probably refers to the resurrection at the end of time, to which the completion of [Paul's] mission was thought to lead."[85] While this verse and the eschatological process it presupposes certainly raises many questions about how Christians (whether gentile or Jewish) relate to non-Christian Jews, Paul's ruminations about Israel throughout this section indicate that salvation, reconciliation, and life from the dead stand as primary divine goals in God's work for both ancestral Israel and the nations, the work we may otherwise identify as making right and making alive.

3.2.4 Romans 12–16

Paul applies the theological vision of justification and *zōopoiēsis* to the lives of Rome's Jesus followers in the fourth section. Although chapters 12–16 do not refer explicitly to creation, these chapters begin to flesh out some of the ways in which God's people are to live corporate lives on earth. The practical suggestions Paul highlights not only support healthy, good, and holy ecclesial and political relationships but also, incidentally, less destructive relationships with the nonhuman creation.

A foremost implication of God's *zōopoiēsis* is that God's people reciprocate by offering themselves to their merciful God as *living* sacrifices.[86] Recognizing the importance of the body and its activities to the Creator God, Paul urges the Christians in Rome to present their individual bodies (τὰ σώματα ὑμῶν) to God. In so doing, they would "present their bodies in exclusive orientation to God,"[87] offering God a sacrifice that is living

---

pronoun "their" with "a portion of Israel" (see Keck, *Romans*, 272). Jewett suggests that ἀποβολή be translated as "throwing away" or "discarding" and argues convincingly that this "discarding" is done by Israel and not to Israel (Jewett, *Romans*, 680–81). Paul, then, does not say here that God rejects or throws away Israel. He unequivocally denies this is possible in 11:1. Instead, he indicates that some members of Israel have thrown away Paul's ministry or gospel (11:13). This perspective counters Keck's exegetical decision regarding ἀποβολή (Keck, *Romans*, 272).

85. Jewett, *Romans*, 681.

86. The mercies of God identify God as merciful, echoing a key story in the Tanakh, in which God proclaims God's self as merciful (Exod 33:18–19; 34:6–7). Sigve Tonstad notes, "God is in this representation a Person who accelerates and magnifies the momentum of good in the world and, conversely, slows and minimizes the momentum of evil" (Tonstad, *Letter to the Romans*, 288).

87. Barclay, *Paul and the Gift*, 509.

(ζῶσαν), holy (ἁγίαν), and acceptable (εὐάρεστον) to God (Rom 12:1).[88] They may engage in this form of liturgical service, or worship, even while they are far from Jerusalem and its temple.[89] Whether in Rome or anywhere in the world, their liturgical service occurs continually since the sacrifices—their own bodies—do not die on the altar but remain alive on the earth.[90]

God's people, moreover, are expected to attend to the ways in which they are being influenced. Paul tells the Jesus followers to resist being conformed to "this age" (12:2), an age—we may understand from 5:12–21—that has been shown to be under the dominion of sin and death.[91] Instead of conformation, the Jesus followers in Rome deliberately undergo transformation into creatures of the new age, the age of the living Lord, by a process of mental renewal.[92] As they allow their minds—their thinking and assumptions about the world—to be shaped by the new age's dominion of life, grace, and righteousness (5:17, 21; 6:18), they will be able to discern that which is good, pleasing, and perfect (12:2). Practically, this means that God's people are to be shaped by God's mercy and love (12:1, 9), with divine love providing "a life-orientation that is self-giving, dedicated to the good of others and to the building up of the community."[93] Meanwhile, God's people are to avoid evil (12:9, 17, 21), establish peace (12:16, 18), and even

---

88. This form of sacrifice appears to be new though in keeping with the spirit of Jewish liturgical service outlined in the Tanakh. The service is not meant just for Jews or gentiles but all people.

89. Paul uses the noun λατρείαν in Rom 12:1 to refer to the worshipful service in which God's people are to engage. The corresponding verb λατρεύω occurs in the Greek translation of the Tanakh and refers to Israel's worship and even to the priests' service in the Tabernacle (for example, Exod 3:12; 8:1; 23:25; Num 16:9; Deut 6:13; 10:12).

90. We may wonder what ways their liturgical service may have been directed towards the well-being of nonhuman creation, especially in relation to agriculture. Might their liturgical service concern itself with petitioning the Creator God for timely, gentle rains and the safe passage of grains? See chapter 1.2.3 and the conclusion for more discussion.

91. The term Paul uses here is "age" rather than "world," contra the NRSV.

92. Tonstad, *Letter to the Romans*, 289–90. Barclay contends that this renewing of the mind "will not clash at every point with the modes of behavior common in their surroundings: there will be some overlap in the recognition of what is 'good' and 'bad' (12:17; 13:3) and no *inevitable* clash with the interests of the governing authorities (13:1–7). But the new orientation to the Lord (12:11) will involve a mindset whose assumptions, priorities, and dispositions are newly configured, in differentiation from 'this age' (12:2)" (Barclay, *Paul and the Gift*, 509). I take from this insight that Christian communities must engage in ongoing discernment *with* as well as ongoing critical dialogue *with* those outside the Christian community.

93. Tonstad, *Letter to the Romans*, 292.

share food and drink with those considered to be enemies (12:20). In light of the fact that war often leads to ecological degradation and its methods may include destroying a people's food supply as a means to gain control of them, Paul's admonitions prove ecologically significant in a warring world.

As a people devoted to overcoming evil with good and constantly paying their never-ending debt of love to everyone (12:21; 13:8),[94] Paul expects the Jesus followers in the Roman capital to submit themselves to—or, more literally, order themselves under—the governing authorities (13:1).[95] While Paul claims that the governing authorities will praise good behavior and serve God for the good of their people—including, we may suppose, Jesus followers—it is unclear whether he meant this as a universal and timeless statement (13:3–4). What happens, for example, when the government does not reward good behavior but evil? When it does not serve the good of *all* people? Paul certainly is aware of times when the governing authorities praised bad behavior and caused evil, suffering, and death, especially for those following the Messiah, who himself was crucified by the Roman state.[96] In light of this reality, Paul exhorts believers to consider goodness and love (rather than the transitory will of the governing authorities) to be their standard of behavior (12:9, 21). Thus, even when the governing authorities persecute Jesus's followers, Paul seems to direct Christians to resist any attempt at violently overthrowing their rule, since—in Paul's view—the non-violent Messiah would soon set all things right upon his return.[97] Then, after reminding the Christians in Rome that the fullness of

---

94. Tonstad states, "For Paul, debt-free living is possible in all respects except one. Love is the debt owed to all, for Paul a debt the paying of which necessitates his mission to the Gentiles (Rom. 1.14; 1 Cor 9.16)" (Tonstad, *Letter to the Romans*, 325).

95. Douglas Harink interprets ὑποτασσέσθω as literally and simply meaning that Jesus's followers order themselves under those who are "over" them (ὑπερεξούσαις). He resists those interpretations of Rom 13:1–7 that would lead Christians to give blind obedience to those with power over them, stating: "*Hypotassō* simply cannot mean 'obey' in this context; Paul had another word for that (*hypakouō*), and it is owed to Messiah alone. It cannot mean 'trust' or 'allegiance'; Paul has another word for that (*pistis*, aka 'faith'), and it is owed to Messiah alone. It cannot mean 'offer your bodies in public service' (i.e., be good citizens); Paul has other words for that (*thusia zōsa* ['living sacrifice'], *logikē latreia* ['reasonable public service'], Rom 12:1), and these are owed to God, to the social body of the Messiah, and in self-giving service, hospitality, kindness, and blessing to strangers and enemies" (Harink, "Messianic Anarchy," 207).

96. For an illuminating exposition of Rom 13, see Tonstad, *Letter to the Romans*, 309–33.

97. Tonstad provides an interesting and nuanced discussion of Rom 13 and suggests similar lines of interpretation as given here (Tonstad, *Letter to the Romans*, 309–22).

God's salvation is near (13:11), Paul instructs them to resist the demands of fleshly passions (which could lead them into "reveling and drunkenness," among other excesses; 13:13).

The apostle then urges the diverse congregations in Rome to welcome one another as they attempt to love genuinely (14:1; 12:9). This welcome redresses concrete and practical problems in Rome. For, within these congregations, a potentially divisive and destructive problem was brewing. The problem concerned the food God's people would eat together at their communal meals, during which they celebrated the Lord's Supper.[98]

From our best scholarly reckoning, it seems the Jesus followers throughout the Mediterranean gathered with their local Christian siblings for a meal on a regular, frequent basis. These gatherings probably mimicked the structure of a Roman banquet in which participants ate a full evening meal, the *deipnon*, and then transitioned to the *symposion*, in which they read Scripture, sang, shared prophetic utterances, prayed, and learned from one another.[99] It was perhaps between these two segments of the gathering that the worshipping community gave thanks for the bread and wine and shared them in honor and remembrance of Jesus, the crucified and risen Christ. By drinking and eating in honor of their Lord Jesus, the Christians may have simultaneously refrained from offering the libations in honor of the emperor, the Roman gods, or others who were typically honored during banquets.

In addition to eating in honor of a crucified and risen Lord, Christians acting in accordance with the gospel organized their gatherings in more egalitarian, diverse, and inclusive ways than was typical in Roman society. In contrast to Roman banquets, which tended to organize attendees in accordance with socio-economic hierarchies and typically included only those with shared ethnic and religious identities,[100] the Christian gatherings

---

98. Jewett, *Romans*, 834–35; Barclay, "Faith and Self-Detachment," 193.

99. Recent scholarship demonstrates that the early Jesus followers gathered around meals. In many ways these meals mirrored Roman banquets, which "usually lasted three to four hours and were divided into two major components: 1) a full course evening meal (*deipnon*) and 2) the symposium (*symposion*), a prolonged period of leisurely drinking that included entertainment in one form or another. The two segments were joined by lifting and pouring out of a cup of mixed wine known as a libation in honor of the emperor, household, guild, national deities, or a benefactor" (Streett, *Subversive Meals*, 10).

100. Roman banquets often brought together people of similar socio-economic status or people who were clearly the patrons and others who were clearly the clients. The seating arrangements were organized according to status so that "[w]here and with whom one ate conveyed the sense that certain people were more important and powerful than others within a society" (Streett, *Subversive Meals*, 15, 17). Typically, only free men

almost necessarily brought together people who held different social statuses and/or religious heritages. Paul expected the Jesus followers in Rome to offer a radical welcome to one another (Rom 14:1; 15:7),[101] carving out an alternative religious, socio-economic, and political space in the midst of the capital, where Jews and gentiles ate common food in honor of one common Lord. People from all walks of life, religious backgrounds, socio-economic statuses, and sexes were to be included in the meal and the worship service.[102] We find confirmation of Paul's guiding ethic in 1 Cor 11:21–22, where Paul insists that all who participate in the Christian meal have access to the same foods simultaneously. This form of distribution stood in stark contrast to the Roman practice of serving the best, most costly foods to the wealthy and honorable but giving the least desirable food to lower ranking participants. Thus, unlike the typical Roman banquet that solidified social hierarchies, the Christian "love feast" (when functioning properly) gathered diverse people as equal recipients of God's grace and the creation's gifts of nourishment.

Yet, from what we can surmise from Paul's instructions in Rom 14–15, the five to ten congregations in Rome did not gather according to the Pauline ideal. The congregations did not gather in a charitable fashion, all because of a religious dividing line: food.[103] Or, when they gathered, they argued with one another and some likely denigrated others with the name "weak." While the exact identities of the derogatorily-named "weak"

---

reclined together on a *triclinium* while eating. During the first century, it was not typical for women and children to recline at the meal table with the husbands and fathers but to sit on the outskirts of the banquet. Slaves—if they got a chance to eat—also sat on the outskirts (15).

101. Jewett highlights the countercultural value of welcoming those who, according to Roman estimations, were considered "weak," shamed, or dishonorable. He states, "To welcome the 'weak' into the love feast was to treat them as brothers and sisters in Christ, as equal beneficiaries of God's grace, as the formerly shamed who are now equally honored by the blood of Christ" (Jewett, *Romans*, 836). Paul's argument in Rom 14 "intended to reverse the shameful status of the 'weak'" (836).

102. Typically, reputable women did not attend the *symposion* of a Roman banquet, and if they did they would not speak (Streett, *Subversive Meals*, 15). On this matter, too, the Christian gatherings appear to differ radically from the wider culture.

103. We might also add the religious observance of sacred times and the consumption of certain drinks as religious dividing lines (Rom 14:5–6, 21).

and "strong" remain uncertain,[104] Paul's ethical advice in this complex and divisive situation emanates clearly: Jesus's followers must eat in ways that not only maintain the diversity of the body of Christ (12:4–8; 15:1–13) but also (1) rightly express gratitude to God, (2) honor the Lord Jesus, and (3) avoid injuring or destroying others for whom Christ died (14:15).

The contention over what to eat was not simply a matter of interpretation and faith. At its core, it was also a relational matter that concerned the relationships between law-observant and less law-observant people, between people and their God, and between people and nonhuman creation. It seems that the one group of people—castigated as the "weak"—considered proper behavior to be specified by the Law. Consequently, they only ate meat from approved animals that were slaughtered according to Jewish regulations.[105] Practically, this would have meant they sometimes refrained from eating meat entirely, particularly when they lived in foreign lands.[106] A different faction of Christ followers—the "strong" or "empowered"—apparently considered themselves to be free from the dietary restrictions of the Mosaic Law, believing that "in the Lord Jesus . . . nothing is unclean in itself" (14:14 NRSV).[107] These Christians regarded eating meat from ani-

104. I agree with Jewett that Paul did not create these categories but employs them for rhetorical purposes. It is likely that some of the gentile Christians followed the prejudicial patterns of Roman society by using the pejorative term "weak" to describe people they deemed to be inferior, in particular, those who followed ascetic eating practices (Jewett, *Romans*, 834–35).

105. Barclay, "Faith and Self-Detachment," 192–93. Paul's term "weak" may have functioned as a derogatory label that the group itself would likely have rejected (Jewett, *Romans*, 834–35; Tonstad, *Letter to the Romans*, 344). Perhaps Paul employed this label for rhetorical purposes but did not necessarily consider it to represent people accurately or to be edifying.

106. The specific identity of those who eat only vegetables is debated, but many scholars agree that these Christ followers refrain from eating meat in order to follow Torah. They are followers of Jesus who may be of either Jewish or gentile ancestry. Their diet may be practically motivated since kosher meats would be difficult to obtain, but it could also be motivated by devotional goals. As Gary Shogren illustrates, important Jewish heroes (for example, Daniel [Dan 1:8–13], Tobit [Tob 1:10–11]; Judith [Jdt 10:5; 12:1–4, 17–19]; and Esther [Add Esth 14:17]) refrained from eating meat and wine in foreign lands especially when those foods were associated with imperial regimes and idolatrous activities (Shogren, "Is the Kingdom of God about Eating," 249).

107. In describing the two factions, however, Paul exaggerates their positions by suggesting some eat only green leafy plants while others eat anything and everything. Neither of these extremes provides a realistic portrait of first-century food cultures. Paul likely employs these two extremes to include the wide spectrum of possibilities (Jewett, *Romans*, 837–38).

mals that were not Law-approved or had not been slaughtered according to Jewish custom as an expression of their Christian liberty.[108] Bringing these two factions together for a common meal would prove challenging, to say the least. The vegetarians might judge (and implicitly condemn) those who lived in apparent disrespect of God's Laws (14:3b).[109] The omnivores, in turn, might despise the vegetarians (14:3a).[110]

Paul's response to this conflict is complex. Fundamentally—and perhaps surprisingly to many Christians today—Paul affirmed that both factions were motivated by a desire to honor the Lord and to act in gratitude toward the Creator and Sustainer of life.[111] He states, "those who eat, eat in honor of the Lord, since they give thanks to God; while those who abstain, abstain in honor of the Lord and give thanks to God" (14:6 NRSV). Both groups, then, fulfill at least two of the three ethical tenets Paul presents in 14:15. They honor the Lord and express gratitude to the Creator God. Gratitude is a quality Paul commends to everyone, whether they are feasting or fasting.[112] For, offering thanks to God for the food one eats conforms to the pattern of Christ, who "took a loaf of bread, and when he had given thanks, he broke it and said, 'This is my body that is for you. Do this in remembrance of me'" (1 Cor 11:23–24 NRSV). Gratitude that receives the fruit of the earth as gift recognizes the ways in which the creation that God established both represents and facilitates God's ongoing effort to make alive.

In addition to rendering thanks to God for life-supporting nourishment, Paul exhorts the Jesus followers in Rome to live their new lives in honor of the Lord, for they do not live to themselves but to the Lord (Rom 14:7).[113] Thus, they must live in ways that do not undercut the Lord's

108. Jewett notes that the cheapest and most accessible meat for Rome's poor masses was pork, a decidedly "unclean" animal according to Jewish Law (Jewett, *Romans*, 868).

109. Jewett, *Romans*, 839.

110. Jewett, *Romans*, 838–39.

111. Jewett explains, "That those who refrain from eating do so in relation to the same Lord while offering thanks to God is articulated in v. 6c with the same terminology used in v. 6b, placing the religious devotion of both sides on precisely the same level . . . If each group can acknowledge the devotion of the other, directed to the same Lord Jesus Christ, and giving thanks to the same God, they will be able to share their meals with each other without insisting on uniformity" (Jewett, *Romans*, 847).

112. Not only Jews but also pagan gentiles often gave thanks for food (Jewett, *Romans*, 846; cf., Plato, *Symposium* 176a; Epictetus, *Dissertationes* 2.23.5).

113. All the congregants live for the same Lord because, as Jewett explains, they all share the same group identity, that of having "died to sin and the old self" through baptism into Christ; they now live to the Lord (Rom 6:8–11; Jewett, *Romans*, 847). Honoring

life-saving work. This is because "Christ died and lived, in order that he might rule the dead and the living" (14:9). The lordship and rule of Messiah Jesus orients his followers in such a way that their very living and dying find their bearing in him.[114] This applies even to such mundane matters as eating. Thus, Paul exhorts the Christians in Rome who eat meat to take thought for how their actions affect those around them, since the choices they make could "destroy one for whom Christ died" (14:15). Paul's concern here is that the empowered who eat meat might put pressure on those who refrain from eating meat (14:20–21; 15:1).[115] This might, then, lead the "weak" to stumble in their undivided devotion to the Lord, so that they act against their conscience by eating unlawful meat or walk away from the "Lord's Supper" entirely. The danger is that their faithful orientation to Christ and their honoring of the Lord would be set adrift and even destroyed.[116]

Paul admonishes the Christians in Rome to prevent such destruction, by exhorting them to mimic Jesus Christ's self-restraining love. Because "Christ did not please himself" (15:3 NRSV) neither should the empowered Roman Christians please their palates by demanding that meat be served and eaten during communal meals.[117] For, such a demand could result in

---

the Lord Jesus is a practical expression of their obedience, an obedience Paul understands himself to be advancing in and among all the nations (Rom 1:5; 15:18). Honoring Jesus as Lord and obeying God/Jesus with fidelity stood at cross purposes with imperial aims, as Neil Elliott illustrates (Elliott, *Arrogance of the Nations*, 24–57). Elliott identifies this form of honoring and obeying as encapsulating a core purpose of Romans: "The letter is directed toward a clear end. However courteous Paul's tone, he speaks as the duly commissioned representative of a lord who is to be obeyed, and he writes to secure 'faithful obedience among the nations' to that lord" (45).

114. Keck, *Romans*, 340–41.

115. Barclay, "Faith and Self-Detachment," 201.

116. Paul explains: "But those who have doubts are condemned if they eat, because they do not act from faith; for whatever does not proceed from faith is sin" (14:23). The person's eating "for the Lord" is undone in the process of eating for inclusion or for the approval of others.

117. In commenting on Rom 14:21 ("it is good not to eat meat or drink wine or do anything that makes your brother or sister stumble," NRSV), Jewett understands Paul's choice of the aorist infinitives (rather than *present tense* infinitives) "to eat" and "to drink" to indicate that the restriction on eating meat or drinking wine would *not* be an ongoing, indefinite form of accomodation. The strong Christians' restriction of their dietary liberties was only necessary when "weak" siblings in Christ joined in worship with them. For, Jewett explains, "Given the restricted circumstances of space and resources available to early Christian love feasts, some of which met in the poorest slums of Rome, there was no possibility of envisioning the permanent joining of groups of weak and strong churches. Nevertheless, when a member of an abstaining group was invited, the host group is here

a brother or sister "being injured by what you eat," and this would indicate that the meat-eaters "are no longer walking in love" (14:15a NRSV). To this possibility Paul exclaims: "Do not, by your eating, destroy that one for whom Christ died" (14:15b). Destroying one for whom Christ died is antithetical to love since God's love works to save, reconcile, and glorify those who are vulnerable, hostile, or susceptible to destruction (5:6–10; 14:15).[118] In other words, God's mission is to make alive, and no one should disrupt that mission.

Paul's practical advice, then, is for the Roman Christians to walk in love and exercise self-restraint so that others may flourish—or at least not be destroyed.[119] Those with the religious ability to choose what they eat express their gratitude to God by restraining their own freedoms when in the gathered community so that their eating practices support the flourishing and faith—rather than the destruction and infidelity—of others.[120] This is especially the case, according to Paul, since the kingdom of God is not focused on the enjoyment of food and drink. "By contrast, love, righteousness,

---

encouraged to view their" own temporary abstention from offensive food items as "good" and, therefore, "matching the high standards of the Christian ethic (12:2; 16:16)" (Jewett, *Romans*, 867–68).

118. Love is a primary guiding principle for Paul, as Eberhart articulates: "Above all, what matters according to Paul, is that we remain in loving relationship with one another. As such, although it may be 'lawful' to eat all foods—'for the earth and its fullness are the Lord's' (1 Cor 10:26)—in certain circumstances, it may be necessary to refrain out of consideration for another. Whatever the situation, 'do not seek your own advantage,' he says, 'but that of the other' (10:24), for the holiness of God is present not in any particular food or drink per se, but within the 'righteousness and peace and joy in the Holy Spirit' (Rom 14:17). In the gathering together that occurs in the Holy Communion meal, the holiness of God is present in and through the relational ties that bind diverse elements and participants together in love" (Eberhart, *Rooted and Grounded in Love*, 78).

119. Paul presents self-restraint and self-giving as shaping the Christian's behavior especially because of Jesus Christ's own self-giving and self-restraint. Paul exhorts the Jesus followers in Rome: "Each of us must please our neighbor for the good purpose of building up the neighbor. For Christ did not please himself" (Rom 15:2–3 NRSV). Like Christ, God's children (especially the empowered) are to pursue the edification of others more than their own gratification or glorification; and, therefore, they must exercise self-restraint (see Jewett, *Romans*, 878–80).

120. Barclay argues, "This is not a compromise of the good news but precisely its necessary expression: only so can they act in love (14,15) which is the central characteristic and core product of the Christ-event (5,5.8; 8,39; 13,8–10). Like Christ, and because of Christ, their priority is to work for the good of their neighbour (15,1–3), such that their strength is expressed not in getting their own way, but in 'bearing the weaknesses of the powerless' (15,1; cf. Gal 6,2)" (Barclay, "Faith and Self-Detachment," 204).

peace and joy in the Holy Spirit *are* of ultimate value" (14:15, 17).[121] Living according to these virtues helps God's people avoid destroying one for whom Christ died.

Although, in the immediate context of Rom 14:15, the phrase "the one for whom Christ died" clearly refers to a brother or sister in Christ, the creation-wide scope of God's salvation broadens its potential application. Since God intends to liberate the nonhuman creation from its slavery to destruction and since this liberation depends upon Jesus Christ's salvation of humanity (8:19–21; 5:12–21), "the one for whom Christ died" can be said to encompass the whole of creation. Walking in love so as not to destroy "one for whom Christ died" means that Christians take thought for how procuring and eating food (as one of many human acts) might bring inordinate amounts of destruction to God's creation.[122] As God's people become increasingly aware of how their eating unnecessarily destroys not only human and nonhuman life but also soil, water, and air quality, they are encouraged by Rom 14–15 to exercise self-restraint in their eating choices because they are motivated by Christlike love. Such self-restraint may, consequently, lead them to exercise significant caution (and even abstention) when they suspect that their actions cause grief, pain, or destruction for others (Rom 14:15).[123]

By taking on the practices of self-restraint and other-regard for creational well-being, however, God's people do not perceive themselves as liberators or saviors. They do not consider themselves as bringing about God's New Creation by their own efforts. Instead, they walk and live by the indwelling Spirit's life-giving power that enables them to act in correspondence with God's gracious and, as yet, future creational liberation.

---

121. Barclay, "Faith and Self-Detachment," 199.

122. Perhaps the ethical principles drawn from Romans ultimately lead Christians toward eating only humanely raised and slaughtered animals or becoming vegetarian or vegan. While vegetarianism still involves killing living things, plants as well as insects, it does not lead to the destruction of vertebrates—birds, fish, and mammals—to nearly the same degree as meat eating. Veganism attempts to avoid all destructive and oppressive treatments of animals by cutting out dairy and egg consumption. Especially because the production of meat releases so many greenhouse gasses and exacerbates global warming, John Barclay exhorts Christians today to reduce or even eliminate their consumption of meat on the basis of Paul's ethical logic in Rom 14–15 (Barclay, "Food, Christian Identity and Global Warming"). It is important to recognize that all eating entails the death of other living things, as Wirzba discusses in detail in *Food and Faith*, 110–43.

123. Horrell, Hunt, and Southgate also emphasize other-regard in their interpretation of Romans (*Greening Paul*, 189–220).

Jesus's followers, therefore, actively wait for the apocalypse of the children of God when God will complete their redemption and will finally liberate creation from its slavery to destruction (8:19, 21). Yet, even as they wait, they remain motivated by gratitude and Christlike, self-restraining love so that their feasting might be transformed in light of who God the Creator is, what Jesus the Christ has accomplished, and how the Spirit of life vivifies.

From a bird's eye view, this section exhorts those who have died to sin and have been raised to serve God to devote themselves to a new form of worshipful service and to live into the liberty of glorification (6:11, 22; 8:2, 21–23; 12:1). This liberation entails freedom from the fear of death, whether death at the hands of human enemies or as the result of natural or supernatural forces (8:35–39). The hope of eternal life with God even empowers those enlivened with the Spirit to go far beyond the empire's *frumentationes* by giving their daily bread to their enemies (Rom 12:20); to forego eating foods that destroy the life or faith of others (14:15, 20); to pursue justice, peace, and joy rather than the gratification of alimentary cravings (14:17); to live at peace with all (12:16, 18); and to live into their glorious liberation as the children of God, a liberation that the nonhuman creation too is meant to enjoy (8:21).

3.3 Paul's Eco-Ethical Vision

While a chief concern of Romans is to establish ecclesial health, this theologically rich letter also offers ways in which people in the twenty-first century can support ecological health. Of course, Paul did not have our modern ecological problems in view as he wrote his instructions to the congregations in Rome. Therefore, we need to exercise discernment as we attend to this letter and to the witness of creation (including its forms of suffering) so that we may understand how freedom from our slaveries to sin and death and Christlike gratitude, self-restraining love, and other-regard can lead us to live now in congruence with God's future liberation. The contributions of natural and ecological sciences prove indispensible in such discernment. Thankfully, our hermeneutical lens shaped by these sciences reveals some of the ways in which human activity causes destruction throughout creation and how, instead, people might live within the constraints of their ecosystems. Pursuing such discernment requires courage, patience, and solidarity as we come face to face with the suffering of creation. At the same time, by employing our theological/scriptural lens, we keep in view God's ultimate desire to liberate creation from its slavery to destruction. This God's eye perspective provides the moral and spiritual guidance we need in order to embody Christlike servant leadership and to exercise the self-restraint, self-giving, and justice/righteousness necessary for creation's (preliminary) liberation.[124]

As Jesus's followers intentionally become conformed to his glorious image, they will be inclined to take on the forms of servant leadership that God intends for humanity (Rom 8:29; Gen 1:26–28). In this way, their leadership and way of life will align with God's efforts of making right and making alive. Thus, in conformity with Christ, God's people will "reign in life" (5:17) as they nourish the vitality, diversity, and flourishing of God's creation. Yet, conformity to Christ does not magically or passively happen without the individual's and the community's cooperation. *Intentionality* is key. Communal *accountability* and *support* are necessary. Yet, what facilitates all of this is God's gracious and liberative relationship with creation, which is most poignantly articulated and demonstrated in the ecclesial practice of Eucharist (for more discussion, see conclusion).[125] By regularly remembering God's story of salvation and reincorporating themselves into it through the practice of Eucharist, Jesus's followers participate in body, mind, and heart in his resurrection life and become fitted for "reigning in life."

The rectified human-nonhuman relationships made possible in Christ may appear to build upon a hierarchical view of the created world in which humans "reign" over the nonhuman creation. As people living in the twenty-first century, we may recoil at such a hierarchical form of theology, for we can see how conceptions of human dominion (especially as they have been empowered by the industrial revolution) have often led to horrific forms of ecological and social destruction.[126] Yet, we may nevertheless recognize with many ecologists that a particular form of human "dominion"—which I call "servant leadership" but scientists may term "active management"—may now help the ecosphere regain its vitality. Ellen Davis notes:

---

124. Human activity prior to their resurrection provides only partial liberation since humans cannot deliver the creation from every form of destruction. For a study on how it often takes more than just knowledge to implement ecologically-friendly practices, see Biviano, *Inspired Sustainability*.

125. Especially in light of Rom 6, the formative and transformative practice of baptism is also important.

126. See Merchant, *Columbia Guide*, 34; Bauckham, *Bible and Ecology*, 1–12; White, "Historical Roots."

> A Stanford team of terrestrial ecologists concludes its survey of grievous and even disastrous conditions with the paradoxical statement that precisely because our activities are causing "rapid, novel, and substantial changes" in ecosystems, "maintaining the diversity of 'wild' species and the functioning of 'wild' ecosystems will require *increasing human involvement*."[127]

Such involvement may be considered a form of servant leadership that always must be attended by humility, care, and discernment. And truly Christlike servant leadership takes its place within God's story of creational salvation, which aims at liberation from destruction.

As God's people "reign in life" and serve the creation's well-being as self-conscious leaders, we find ourselves back to the creation accounts of Gen 1–2 and our explorations in chapter 1. Thinking back to chapter 1, we find that Paul's story of creation in Romans nicely converges with the Tanakh's depictions of human relationships with creation. Yet, Paul extends creation's story by proclaiming that the promised Messiah and Spirit have indeed come. The Messiah brings atonement and justification, and the Spirit is filling God's people with life. Paul also democratizes the story in interesting ways. He correlates creation's liberation with the glorification of all God's people, not solely with the leadership of the Messiah. Thus, in light of this overview of Romans, we might amend the eco-theological principles we developed from the Tanakh in chapter 1. The amendments, which will be further substantiated in chapters 4 and 5, are indicated with italics:

1. God cooperated with land and water to create living things; commissioned the creation to be diverse and interdependent so that all living things would have adequate access to food, and God instructed the covenant people to share land and food justly and equitably, even with *human enemies and* other creatures.

2. God created humans to be creation's servant leaders but also gave them freedom to disobey and sin; *they did and do sin and have become enslaved to sin's influence.*

3. God created a world in which human activity necessarily affects the vitality, flourishing, and well-being of human and nonhuman creation; *but because of human sin and the consequent reign of sin and death in the world, God is at work making things right (justification) and making things alive (zōopoiēsis).*

---

127. Davis, *Scripture, Culture, and Agriculture*, 54–55. Emphasis added.

4. *In the old age, God provided God's people with the means to atone for impurities and minor sins and promised to cleanse the people and land fully in the new age.*

5. God *sent the* promised Messiah—*God's Son, Jesus Christ*—to make things right (justification); *Messiah Jesus, as the foremost servant leader, has thus provided unending and boundless atonement by his life, death, and resurrection; this atonement liberates human and nonhuman creation from the oppressive effects of sin and reconciles them to one another and God.*

6. God *sent the* promised Spirit to make things alive (*zōopoiēsis*); *God, the Spirit, therefore liberated Messiah Jesus from death through resurrection, is liberating all who walk in the Spirit into new life now and resurrection life in the future, and, ultimately, will liberate the whole creation from its subjection to frustration and slavery to destruction and will usher it into a form of glorification, the New Creation.*

7. *Prior to the resurrection and New Creation, those in Christ embody their justification and zōopoiēsis by pursuing and maintaining right/just relationships with God, people, and nonhuman creation; they thereby grow into a style of servant leadership that supports the vitality, flourishing, and well-being of creation; meanwhile, the nonhuman creation eagerly supports and cooperates with the resurrecting God.*

These theological perspectives, along with Paul's specific ethical exhortations in Romans 12–15, expand into at least seven eco-ethical principles by which Christians might relate to God and God's creation in more life-supporting ways. Through the hermeneutical lenses of theology/Scripture, science, and politics, we may perceive a Pauline vision of creation that encourages God's people to:[128]

1. Attend to creation's story by recognizing the ways in which God's creation not only reveals the Creator God but also exposes its own condition on account of the complex, interdependent relationships between and among nonhuman and human participants.

---

128. I am grateful for the ground-breaking work of David Horrell, Cherryl Hunt, and Christopher Southgate in identifying "other-regard and corporate solidarity" as key "moral norms" in Romans and Colossians (*Greening Paul*, 189–220). The principles I offer here expand upon their insights.

2. Express gratitude to the Creator God for the gifts of creation, sharing the gifts of food and water with God's creatures.

3. Cooperate in the divine work of justification, making right/just, by supporting and protecting the well-being of human and nonhuman members of God's creation, especially the "weak"/disempowered/vulnerable.[129]

4. Cooperate in the divine work of *zōopoiēsis*, making alive, by promoting and maintaining the biodiversity, fertility, and flourishing of entire ecosystems and the biosphere.[130]

5. Honor the Lord Jesus Christ by avoiding activites that would subject creation to frustration, enslave it to destruction, or would injure or destroy those for whom Christ died.

6. Stand in solidarity with the sufferings and hopes of creation by exercising servant leadership, in conformity with Jesus, in ways that serve and maintain the health, flourishing, fertility, and diversity of creation.

7. Exercise appropriate self-restraint in order equitably to share the gifts of creation and support the vitality and fidelity of other members of God's creation.

These theological and ethical principles, along with the holistic message of Romans, orient us as we delve more deeply into Paul's explicit story of creation in 8:19–22. They will also serve as guideposts as we navigate

---

129. See discussion of the "weak" in Rom 14–15. The world's "most vulnerable" includes individuals as well as entire species. Caring for the vulnerable is an eco-ethical principle that attempts to undo some of the destruction humans have caused to entire species, in which human activity threatens their existence and leaves them vulnerable to decline and extinction. Yet, this principle may go even further in its commitment to life by helping individuals that could not otherwise feed and care for themselves to survive. Thus, it is a principle that is not always displayed in nature. Unlike the eco-ethical principles of maintaining fertility and biodiversity, which not only mirror nature but also Christian Scripture, supporting the vulnerable often counters natural processes. The biological principle of natural selection for fitness often mandates that the lame, deformed, sick, and otherwise vulnerable individuals and communities receive fewer resources and less support than more powerful and capable counterparts. Thus, the vulnerable are left to die. When people intentionally care for the vulnerable, however, they draw upon a specifically moral (rather than natural) commitment that corresponds with divine revelation in Scripture and in the person of Jesus Christ. As with all actions, however, wise, informed, communal discernment must attend such interventions.

130. Of course, a difficult and complicating limitation of this principle concerns deadly diseases that are caused by living organisms.

Creation's Slavery and Liberation

the complex terrain of modern industrial agriculture. Paul's statements about creation in Rom 8:19–22 reveal the depth of the problems facing human and nonhuman creation and the magnitude of God's solutions. The next two chapters, therefore, examine the problem—creation's slavery and subjection (chapter 4)—and the solution—creation's liberation (chapter 5). Ultimately, these chapters suggest an ethic in which Jesus's followers pursue liberation and flourishing for all, "[f]or the creation expectantly awaits the apocalypse of the sons of God . . . in hope that the creation itself will be liberated from the slavery of destruction into the liberation of the glory of God's children" (Rom 8:19, 20b, 21).

CHAPTER 4

Creation's Slavery and Subjection

The Story of Human Sin in Romans

As an inheritor and engaged interpreter of Israel's scriptural heritage, the apostle Paul receives inspiration from its creation accounts, divine covenants, laws, and prophecies of hope and restoration. Such an observation is supported by his epistle to the Jesus followers in Rome, in which Paul engages in detailed reinterpretations of this heritage, especially in chapters 3–5 and 9–11. Paul's reinterpretation stresses the ways in which God is (and has been) at work making right and making alive.[1] Perhaps less obvious is the way in which Paul also adopts and assumes creational themes found throughout the Tanakh, such as the perspective that humanity and creation are interdependent (with the result that their destinies intertwine) and that human activity necessarily affects the rest of creation. In the heart of this epistle, stands Paul's famous reflections on creation where he indicates that creation's subjected state as well as its future liberation are intricately associated with human activities and conditions (Rom 8:19–22). Thus, like the sacred writings that inspire him, Paul portrays sinful and selfish human activity as negatively affecting the rest of God's creation but divine and human glory as remediating these destructive consequences. Especially in verses 20 and 21, Paul considers creation's dire situation and describes it as entailing subjection to frustration (or, "futility" in 8:20 NRSV) and slavery to destruction (or, "bondage to decay" in 8:21 NRSV).[2]

---

1. For more discussion of these overarching themes in Romans, see 3.2.

2. All English Scripture citations are the author's own in this chapter unless otherwise noted.

Creation's Slavery and Liberation

Although Paul outlines both the negative and positive aspects of creation's situation in Rom 8:19-22, the current chapter focuses primarily upon creation's "problem," its subjection to frustration and slavery to destruction (8:20-21). The next chapter considers God's liberating solution for creation (8:19, 21, 22). While these chapters follow the logic of problem and then solution, they also trace a narrative logic of past, present, and future.[3] They present a story of creation.

Before turning to the solution, the present chapter first argues that Paul primarily refers to nonhuman creation in 8:19-22 by his use of the term κτίσις.[4] Section two explains that creation's "bondage to decay" (8:21 NRSV), or more accurately "slavery to destruction," refers not simply to its susceptibility to death and decay but to its experience of inordinate amounts of destruction. Creation's slavery of destruction mirrors humanity's own slavery to sin and death that came about, according to Rom 5:12-21, because of Adam's disobedience (Gen 3-6). In light of this underlying scriptural matrix, "slavery of destruction" results, in part, from human sin while creation's liberation is linked to human righteousness and glory. The third section then turns back to Rom 8:20 to consider its complex depiction of creation's predicament, particularly the way in which "creation was subjected to frustration" "by the one subjecting it in hope" (8:20). These references to subjection expand the theological narrative limned in Rom 5 to include not only Gen 3 but now also Gen 1. Paul's two descriptions of creation's "subjection" point towards God's primary responsibility in placing creation under the servant leadership of humanity and to humanity's secondary culpability in exercising that power in ways that render creation's attempts at flourishing ineffective or frustrated. These exegetical claims suggest that Paul perceives human sin as having damaging effects not only on humanity but nonhuman creation as well.

---

3. I am indebted to the work of David Horrell, Cherryl Hunt, and Christopher Southgate for making the narrative logic undergirding this passage clear. After highlighting past, present, and future tense verbs occurring in Rom 8:19-21, the authors contend: "Since the account of our subject not only has a beginning, a middle, and an end, but also entails a transformation, this allows us to construct the outlines of a narrative trajectory, while the employment of γάρ and ὅτι indicates causal links between the elements, thus constituting a plot"; moreover, the passage "implies that it depends on a shared narrative basis" (*Greening Paul*, 71).

4. This term overlaps with the Tanakh's nomenclature of "land" but is more expansive and inclusive, referring to the entire earth. Paul's κτίσις, moreover, shares much of the semantic domain of the Roman category "nature."

Creation's Slavery and Subjection

4.1 "Creation" in Romans

While Paul's focus in this letter is undoubtedly upon human beings, at key points he explicitly directs his attention to the creation, κτίσις (Rom 1:20, 25; 8:19, 20, 21, 22, 39). But when Paul invokes that term in Rom 8:19-22, just who or what does it include? A precise answer is not immediately obvious since in its most literal meaning κτίσις refers to all-that-is-not-God, and, yet, depending upon context, κτίσις may include or exclude angels, humans, nonhuman living things, and/or nonliving matter.[5] Considered in context, and particularly in light of the way that he contrasts κτίσις with other actors, the term most clearly refers to nonhuman creation in Rom 8.

A clue to the meaning of κτίσις comes in its contrast with the "sons of God" (8:19) and the "children of God" (8:21). Determining the identity of this group can help us understand what Paul intends κτίσις to include in this context. Although some might suggest "sons of God" denotes angelic beings, the immediate context instead suggests God's sons and children refer to a group of *human beings* who ultimately enjoy God's gift of glory (8:17, 18, 21, 30).[6] Earlier in this chapter, Paul refers to people led by the Spirit as "sons" (υἱοί, 8:14) and then repeatedly refers to the Roman Christians and himself as "children" (τέκνα, 8:16, 17). He also identifies the Roman Christians as those adopted into God's family (υἱοθεσίας, 8:15) and as those who—along with Paul and others having the first fruits of the Spirit—groan with creation as they await full adoption, the redemption of the body (στενάζομεν υἱοθεσίαν ἀπεκδεχόμενοι, τὴν ἀπολύτρωσιν τοῦ σώματος ἡμῶν 8:23). Since Paul indicates that these children will experience "redemption of the body" (8:23), will be revealed in the future (8:19), and will be glorified (8:17, 18, 21), their identity is distinguished from angelic beings but nevertheless carries an eschatological dimension. Because of

---

5. C. E. B. Cranfield lays out the range of possible referents as eight interpretive options: "the whole creation, including mankind [sic] both believing and unbelieving and also the angels; all mankind; unbelieving mankind only; believers only; the angels only; sub-human nature together with the angels; sub-human nature together with mankind in general; sub-human nature only" (Cranfield, *Critical and Exegetical Commentary*, 411).

6. However, the argument has been made (in light of ideas found in 1 Thess 4:15; 3:13; 2 Thess 1:7; see also *4 Ezra* 7:28; *2 Bar.* 39:7; *1 En.* 38:1) that "sons of God" "refers to the angels of the Last Judgment, who will arrive to free the earth from oppression" (Christoffersson, *Earnest Expectation*, 121). Although tantalizing, this interpretation makes little sense within the immediate context of Romans. It is instead most natural and convincing to understand "sons of God" as another way in which Paul refers to God's redeemed, human children in this chapter.

these textual details, "the sons of God" (8:19) and "children of God" (8:21) seem to refer to all those who will be incorporated into the body of Christ, the eschatological people of God. Taken this way, the sons/children of God encompass not only the "we" of Paul's original audience but all those whom God will deem "saints" (8:27), "children" (8:21), and "beloved" (11:28) at the end of the age.

At several points in 8:19-23, Paul clearly differentiates this eschatological group of people from κτίσις. According to verse 19, it is the apocalypse of the sons of God for which κτίσις eagerly awaits. Then, in the eschaton, "even the creation itself" (καὶ αὐτὴ ἡ κτίσις)—as distinguished from the children of God—will move into the glorious experience of redeemed humanity, receiving by extension the liberation and glory that God intends the children to inhabit (8:21). Paul further distinguishes the adopted children of God from κτίσις with his emphatic statement in 8:23, "And not only [creation], but also those having the first fruits of the Spirit, we and they groan in ourselves while awaiting adoption, the redemption of our body."[7] Paul stresses that he and his audience ("we") groan along with all those who have experienced the Spirit's adoptive and liberating power (8:2, 14-16; 9:4), since this group of people continues to wait for the consummation of God's redemptive work through resurrection (8:11, 23). *People* who have experienced the enlivening power of the Spirit, then, await the personal experience of resurrection; in contrast, κτίσις awaits the completion of *those persons'* redemption, when resurrected human beings will be revealed (8:19, 23).

In addition to distinguishing κτίσις from redeemed humanity, Paul also differentiates κτίσις from those who do not participate in the eschatological people of God, in other words, disobedient humans.[8] This

---

7. This translation follows the Greek more literally than does the NRSV, which reads "and not only the creation, but we ourselves, who have the first fruits of the Spirit, groan inwardly while we wait for adoption, the redemption of our bodies" (8:23). Instead of collapsing Paul's reference to "those with the first fruits of the Spirit" into the group called "we," my translation recognizes the possibility that Paul distinguished "we" from a much more universal group: those not living in Rome or writing this letter with Paul. My translation of "we and they" maintains Paul's wording, reminding us that those who experience the Spirit include those whom "we" have never met and who may have already died.

8. Some interpreters suggest that since Paul indicates κτίσις was subjected to futility "not of its own will" (8:20 NRSV) it necessarily excludes disobedient humans (see Cranfield, *Critical and Exegetical Commentary*, 411). This is because Paul supposedly portrays humans as willfully sinning and being made "futile in their thinking" (1:21 NRSV). Responding to this interpretive perspective, Susan Eastman points out that although

differentiation appears most clearly in light of the broader theological anthropology articulated in this letter. From early on, Paul portrays disobedient human beings as those who refuse to glorify and thank God (1:21) and who turn their eyes and hearts away when the created world, κτίσεως κόσμου, fulfills its God-given purpose by communicating aspects of God's being and existence to them (1:18–21).[9] He later goes so far as to employ the phrase "enemies of God" to refer to all people (including "us") before they are reconciled to God (5:10). Such people, who remain disobedient to the Messiah (1:5; 15:18), seem peculiarly unlikely to join with κτίσις in anticipating the consummation of God's salvation (8:19) and emulating the Spirit in its groaning (8:22, 26). Thus, disobedient humans often stand in contrast with κτίσις—and particularly so in 8:19–22—as the latter rightly aligns itself with God's purposes and desires.[10] In keeping with this theology of creation and the theological anthropology it assumes, κτίσις thus appears distinguished from both obedient and disobedient human beings and seems specifically to refer to *nonhuman creation*.

Yet even as κτίσις and human beings refer to distinct members of God's created world in Romans, the current experiences and future salvation of the nonhuman creation and that of the eschatological people of God are nevertheless interdependent. Before the eschaton, they share similar—though not identical—experiences of slavery; ultimately, they will share a final destiny of liberation. Their interconnectedness is so strong that κτίσις eagerly anticipates the moment when God's resurrected and glorified children will appear and thus lead creation into liberation.

---

these humans willfully sinned, they did not will the negative consequences of their sin, which includes subjection to futility (Eastman, "Whose Apocalypse?," 274–75). Accordingly, she argues that disobedient humans could be included in κτίσις, since they may be described as *being subjected* unwillingly. If we consider 8:20 alone, we find insufficient data for defining κτίσις with precision. We therefore must consider other features in the epistolary context, as done in the body of this chapter.

9. Just before he indicates that unjust humans (1:18) knew God and eventually became futile in their thinking because they did not glorify God (1:21), Paul describes the "created world" (κτίσεως κόσμου) and the "things made" (τοῖς ποιήμασιν) as manifesting something of the invisible God to people (1:20). He explains, "For God's invisible character, namely, his eternal power and divinity, is observed from the creation of the world, being understood in the things made" (1:20). It would appear that the "things made" exist or act in some contrast to unjust humanity.

10. Admittedly however, Paul acknowledges in 8:38–39 that some "other" created thing (τις κτίσις ἑτέρα) could resist God and even war against God's children.

4.2 Romans 8:21: Creation's Slavery

In Rom 8:21, Paul claims that creation exists in a state of slavery he associates with "ruin," "decay," "destruction" (τῆς δουλείας τῆς φθορᾶς). Yet, humanity too is enslaved, as he indicated earlier in chapters 5 and 6. All humans are enslaved to sin (τοῦ δουλεύειν ἡμᾶς τῇ ἁμαρτίᾳ 6:6; see also 6:17, 20) and ruled by death (ἐβασίλευσεν ὁ θάνατος; 5:14) because God's first human creature, Adam, disobeyed, and all his descendants follow suit (5:12–14). When these two sets of slaveries are taken together, we find that nonhuman and human members of creation share a common bond as they experience slavery in this time before the eschaton. But does Paul go further to suggest that their enslaved conditions both rise out of Adam's transgression? Although Paul is explicit when describing the human predicament, he is not so forthcoming when he claims that creation too is enslaved; he does not explicitly indicate who or what caused creation's slavery to destruction (8:21). However, his use of thematic words and his contrast between creation's current slavery and its future liberation with God's children together provide subtle indications that creation's enslaved condition results, at least in part, from human sin.

At notable points in Romans, Paul refers to the concept of slavery with the Greek word group δουλεία ("slavery," 8:15, 21), δοῦλος ("slave," 1:1; 6:16, 17, 19, 20), δουλεύω ("to serve as a slave," 6:6; 7:6, 25; 9:12; 12:11; 14:18; 16:18), and δουλόω ("to enslave," 6:18, 22). The Greek noun δουλεία, which Paul uses in 8:21, refers to a "state or condition of being held as chattel by another" or a "state or condition of being subservient."[11] Although these definitions often carry negative connotations,[12] Paul uses the word group to describe not only negative but also positive situations. In his opening description of himself, Paul states that he is a slave (δοῦλος) of Christ Jesus (1:1). He later exhorts followers of Jesus to recognize their new identity as those enslaved (ἐδουλώθητε) to righteousness, enslaved (δουλωθέντες) to God, and serving (δουλεύων) Christ for the edification of others (6:18, 22;

---

11. BDAG, 259.

12. Rengstorf explains that, according to a Greek worldview, "the Greek can only reject and scorn the type of service which in inner or outer structure bears even the slightest resemblance to that of the slave" (Rengstorf, "Δοῦλος," *TDNT* 2:262). Accordingly, the δουλ- word group originally was not used in the context of religious devotion but eventually devotees of eastern religious traditions, such as Judaism, applied it to religious service (2:264–65). The word group repeatedly appears in the LXX to describe both service to God and slavery to other humans. Thus, in agreement with his biblical heritage, Paul employs the word group in both positive and negative ways.

14:18).¹³ These examples of δουλεύω indicate that Paul does not consider δουλεύω to be an inherently negative condition. In such cases, the English "to serve" rather than "be a slave" best captures this positive connotation (so long as the thing to which one is bound is God or is a truly just and life-giving servant leader who aligns with God's purposes of making right and making alive).¹⁴

Despite these positive uses of the δουλ- word group, Paul more often refers to negative forms of slavery that permeate the human and even nonhuman experience. In many circumstances δουλεία results from oppressive relationships and leads to devastating consequences, and in these contexts the English term "slavery" rather than "bondage" or "servitude" most poignantly conveys the negative valence of unwilled service and a debased condition of servility that Paul sometimes describes in Romans.¹⁵ It is with this negative valence of δουλεία that Paul describes nonhuman creation's predicament in Rom 8. As we shall see, Paul goes further than simply describing the oppressive dynamics at work in the world; he also traces the origins of this common condition to humanity's first father, Adam.¹⁶

---

13. On the basis of Gen 1:28, we might envision humanity's "dominion" in creation as entailing *servant* leadership. Perhaps in a related way, creation's subjection, as Paul seems to describe it in Rom 8:20, is a subjection to humanity's servant leadership that may yield positive, flourishing results for all involved when carried out properly.

14. To be sure, we humans must always exercise caution when we want to claim that we are aligned with God, especially since we may misperceive the intentions and effects of our actions. This is all the more the case when we consider the topic of slavery. Even though Paul appropriates slavery terminology for positive purposes and does not explicitly or clearly oppose the institution of human slavery in his letters, it may be appropriate for Christians not only to reject all forms of human slavery but also critically to reconceive of and perhaps rename other forms of "servitude" (such as "slavery to God" and even creation's service to the "dominion" of humanity) in our theologies.

15. Therefore, I prefer to translate the δουλ- word group with slave, slavery, and to enslave as opposed to the NRSV and NIV's "bondage" when used negatively.

16. Even as Paul portrays human beings as participating in Adam's legacy, however, this portrayal in fact rises out of a more fundamental Christological and theological focus. As E. P. Sanders suggests, Paul introduces Adam into his discussion of universal sin because he already understands God's solution in a particular way: as bringing universal rectification through Jesus Christ (Sanders, *Paul and Palestinian Judaism*, 442–47). "[Paul] did not begin with the sin and transgression of man, but with the opportunity for salvation offered by God . . . man's plight does not seem to be primarily what Paul preached *about*" (446; see also Legarreta-Castillo, *Figure of Adam*, 14). Paul's underlying assumption in his comparison of Adam and Christ is that Adam brought about the universal experience of sin. Susan Eastman observes: "Paul's logic throughout this section [5:12—7:7] depends on connections between all human beings over space and

Creation's Slavery and Liberation

4.2.1 The Genesis of Slavery

In Rom 5, Paul claims all people stand in solidarity with one another because they share a common physical and spiritual ancestry.[17] Making this claim, Paul is following the creation narrative of Gen 2–3, which suggests Adam is the progenitor of the human race. Like Adam, all people disobey and sin, as Paul asserts at Rom 5:12: "just as sin entered the world through one human and death came along through sin, thus also death came upon all humans because all sinned." Later, Paul explains, "through the disobedience of the one human, the many were made sinners" (5:19). Such a correlation between the one and the many parallels the perspectives of other Jewish thinkers, such as the authors of *Life of Adam and Eve*, *4 Ezra*, and *2 Baruch*.[18] Like them, Paul perceives that all human beings sin just as their ancestor Adam sinned.[19] The basic anthropological point here is that human beings are physical and spiritual kin as they stand together "in Adam."[20]

Not only do Adam's descendants resemble their forefather's disobedient behavior, they appear to be trapped in it, for those in Adam are "slaves

---

time, in a thoroughly participatory and interconnected web of relation. It is cosmically anthropological, in that both Adam and Christ are agents whose actions have universal consequences for all human agents" (Eastman, *Paul and the Person*, 111). From a slightly different perspective, Robert Jewett explains, "Paul depicts Adam's act as decisively determining the behavior of his descendants. A social theory of sin appears to be implied here in which the actions of forebears determine those of their descendants" (Jewett, *Romans*, 375).

17. Legarreta-Castillo, *Figure of Adam*, 161–62. In a discussion of how Paul employs an Adam–Christ typology, Ryan Jackson explains, "In continuity with the first century Jewish understanding of the unity of humanity in Adam, Paul saw Adam as representative of the entire human race" (*New Creation in Paul's Letters*, 140).

18. Legarreta-Castillo, *Figure of Adam*, 155. The knotty question I am sidestepping is whether humans sin and are found guilty by their own free choice or are constrained to sin and deemed guilty because of someone else's sinful choice (or because of an external power, called "Sin"). I am inclined to interpret Paul, in the words of Robert Jewett, as "advancing a paradoxical combination of fateful influence from Adam and individual responsibility for sins" (Jewett, *Romans*, 376). To this I would add that "Sin" as a cosmic power also seems to be in play in Romans and Paul's letters more broadly (see Gaventa, "Cosmic Power of Sin").

19. Legarreta-Castillo, *Figure of Adam*, 155; see also Perkins, "Adam and Christ," 145.

20. Admittedly, Paul does not use the phrase "in Adam" in Romans to describe this solidarity. However, he does use the phrase ἐν τῷ Ἀδάμ in 1 Cor 15:22 to indicate the analogy between participation in Adam, with the result of death, and participation in Christ, with the result of life. He states, "for as all die in Adam, so all will be made alive in Christ" (NRSV).

Creation's Slavery and Subjection

of sin" (6:17). In the legacy of Adam, "sin ruled [ἐβασίλευσεν] in death" (5:21). Describing death as entering the human experience through Adam's sin (5:12), Paul implies that he considered death (at least for humanity) to be an undesirable, unoriginal phenomenon. This phenomenon most likely entails something more than the cessation of physical life, consisting also of what opposes God's life and life-giving purposes in the world.[21] As a result, now "death is everywhere, the logic and reality of death felt throughout the created order," as Paul will make plain in 8:19–22.[22]

However, "the Spirit of life in Christ Jesus" liberates all who relinquish their participation in Adam by dying with Christ (8:2; 6:3, 18). These participants must nevertheless not "let sin rule [βασιλευέτω] in" their "dying body" before the eschatological moment when they are ultimately freed from sin and death and are glorified (6:12). Paul's use of βασιλεύω here suggests that sin's rule functions as a near synonym to "slavery" (when it is negatively construed), for sin rules people in a domineering way as a master would rule a slave.[23] Because of Adam's legacy, sin acts as a ruling power that attempts to enlist and enslave human beings to do its bidding (6:12–13). Those who have been liberated from sin's oppressive rule, however, must vigilantly and intentionally resist sin's continuing presence and power so as not to fall in line with their old master, sin (6:12–13).

Since Paul's account in chapters 5–6 functions as a universalizing explanation of sin's pervasive presence in the world, perhaps we might categorize all the evils that Paul mentions in Romans as taking place "in Adam" and under sin's enslaving influence. As we do this, we find slavery to sin results in a host of deadly and destructive social consequences. For example, in chapter 1, the speaker depicts impious human beings as "filled with every kind of wickedness, evil, covetousness, malice. Full of envy, murder, strife, deceit, craftiness" (Rom 1:29 NRSV). Later in the letter, Paul describes people as "self-seeking" (2:8 NRSV). They often lack the empathy that is so essential for human societies, as Paul grieves in chapter 3: "there is no one who shows kindness, there is not even one ... Their feet are swift to shed blood; ruin and misery are in their paths, and the way of peace they have not known" (Rom 3:12b, 15–17 NRSV). These impulses

---

21. Tonstad describes this phenomenon as "death-in-life" (*Letter to the Romans*, 160).

22. Tonstad, *Letter to the Romans*, 294.

23. Linguistically, "kingly rule" (βασιλεία) does not inherently mean that the king had slaves; however, many of those who ruled (βασιλεύω) in the ancient world often benefitted from and even depended upon slavery.

toward unkindness and selfishness may lead even followers of Christ to exclude others who think and practice differently than themselves, as it appears some congregants in Rome were tempted to do, according to Rom 14. Taken together, these tendencies toward selfishness, prejudice, violence, and even murder exact heavy tolls on social well-being and result from sin's reign in Adam.

But Adam's sin leads not simply to the destruction of human persons and societies; it also engenders the degradation and destruction of the nonhuman creation. The creation narrative of Gen 2–3 upon which Paul draws in Rom 5 makes it clear that Adam's transgression brings negative consequences on the earth (see 1.2.1). However, other than his oblique reference to sin and death entering the world (κόσμον) at 5:12, Paul does not allude to a curse of the land or other negative consequences affecting nonhuman creation in this chapter. When he later directs his attention to creation in chapter 8, Paul simply indicates that creation experiences slavery to destruction in ways that echo his depiction of humanity earlier in chapter 5.

Yet, by way of linguistic threads (especially the use of δουλεία and its word group), Paul ties creation's negative condition to the demise of humanity. He thereby places creation within the narrative tapestry he wove in Rom 5, which in turn reflects Gen 3. He describes creation's predicament with the same word group (δουλεία, "slavery") by which he narrates humanity's own predicament. This narrative thread stretches from Rom 5–6 into chapter 8, where Paul delights in God's liberation of the Roman Christians from "the law of sin and death" (8:2) and from a "spirit of slavery [δουλείας] to fear" (8:15). It is within this context of considering the liberation of humanity that Paul weaves a portrait of nonhuman creation's own liberation from slavery. Consequently, he identifies creation too as existing in a state of slavery from which God will liberate it.[24] Rather than being marked by sin and death, however, creation's slavery is linked to the word φθορᾶς, "destruction," "ruin," or "decay" (NRSV).

---

24. Joseph Fitzmyer also argues that in Rom 8:19–22 "Paul alludes to Gen 3:17–19 and 5:29, where the earth has been cursed because of Adam's sinful transgression.... He realizes that through Adam came not only sin and death (5:12–14), but 'bondage to decay' and the 'slavery of corruption,' which affect all *material* creation, even apart from humanity (8:19–23)" (Fitzmyer, *Romans*, 505).

Creation's Slavery and Subjection

4.2.2 The Nature of Destruction

The genitive construction, τῆς δουλείας τῆς φθορᾶς, is commonly rendered simply as "bondage *to* decay" (NRSV, NIV) or "bondage *of* corruption" (KJV). Both prepositions—"to" and "of"—express the ambiguity inherent in the phrase. Thus, I regularly translate this phrase as "slavery of" or "slavery to" τῆς φθορᾶς and understand from this phrase that φθορᾶς attends creation's enslaved condition. Yet, greater semantic nuance emerges from this genitive construction as we consider the precise relationship between the nouns δουλείας and φθορᾶς. Because genitive constructions in Greek lend themselves to a variety of interpretations in English, it is helpful to identify, as much as possible, the syntactical relationship that exists between the two genitives in the phrase τῆς δουλείας τῆς φθορᾶς.

While at least five types of relationships may obtain between τῆς δουλείας and τῆς φθορᾶς, only two present themselves as likely candidates in this context. A first option understands φθορᾶς as a descriptive genitive,[25] which would be translated as, "creation will be liberated from the slavery *characterized by* decay/ruin/destruction." This translation simply indicates that decay/ruin/destruction attends or marks creation's enslaved existence. Slavery and decay/ruin/destruction are correlated, but why or how this is the case is not the focus of concern when φθορᾶς is understood as a descriptive genitive.

A second option identifies φθορᾶς as a genitive of product[26] and renders the clause: "creation will be liberated from the slavery that *produces* decay/ruin/destruction." In this translation, it is clear that slavery gives

---

25. Wallace, *Greek Grammar Beyond the Basics*, 79. This is the relationship preferred in *TDNT* (Harder, "Φθείρω Κτλ.," 104).

26. Wallace, *Greek Grammar Beyond the Basics*, 106–7. At least three other syntactical relationships may exist between the genitives: 1) φθορᾶς may stand as a genitive of production (104–6) with the implication that it brings about δουλείας ("the slavery produced by destruction"). In his commentary on Romans, Douglas Moo adopts this interpretation (but calls it a subjective genitive) and translates it as "the state of slavery that comes from decay" (Moo, *Epistle to the Romans*, 517). However, it seems unlikely that Paul portrays destruction as bringing about slavery, since he has been at pains throughout Romans to describe the ways in which Adam's sin led to slavery and how, in turn, this slavery brings about negative effects. 2) φθορᾶς may function as an attributive genitive (see Wallace, *Greek Grammar Beyond the Basics*, 86–88), which specifies the quality or character of the noun δουλείας ("destructive slavery"). 3) φθορᾶς may serve as a genitive of apposition and would specify the type of δουλείας Paul has in view ("slavery that is destruction") (95–100). Options two and three appear plausible but far less convincing than the genitive of product and descriptive genitive discussed in the main text.

Creation's Slavery and Liberation

rise to and engenders destruction. In other words, creation's subjection to an enslaving overlord or force results in destruction. With this meaning, Rom 8:21 may imply that, in the future, creation will be liberated from its *slavery* and not only its experience of destruction. The meaning expressed by this genitive of product relationship, though not the only viable syntactical option at work here, aligns well with the narrative of *creation–subjection–liberation–glorification* the letter to Rome arguably sketches (for more discussion, see 1.0 and 3.2). Nevertheless, while the genitive of product is a reasonable option, I often render the phrase with the ambiguous translation "slavery to/of φθορᾶς" since it is best not to press the syntax too hard.

When we attempt to further define the noun φθορά, we discover it connotes three slightly different ideas, two of which are literal and one is metaphorical in meaning. The Greek word φθορά may refer literally to (1) actions or processes that cause death/harm/ruin/destruction or (2) to natural processes of chemical decomposition/decay.[27] It also metaphorically denotes (3) moral corruption. The noun thus ranges in meaning from "inward depravity" to a natural "breakdown of organic matter" to a more active "destruction of an entity."[28]

While φθορά denotes three different concepts at once, no English term adequately does the same. The common translations, "decay" and "corruption," connote moral contamination and chemical decomposition but do not clearly signify physical harm, ruin, death, or destruction. While not precise, the term "destruction" can refer to the action or process that causes a cessation of life or function as well as to the chemical decomposition that follows. "Ruination" suggests ideas of both moral ruin and the demise of life or function and, thus, of physical harm; however, "ruination" sounds rather archaic.

Because the Tanakh portrays moral sins as contaminating the "land," moral corruption likely figures as one aspect of creation's slavery to φθορᾶς (see Hos 9:9 LXX; Ezek 16:52 LXX). At the same time, Paul's Scriptures also repeatedly demonstrate that human activity can cause physical destruction, ruin, harm, and untimely death in God's nonhuman creation (see Gen 6:11–13 LXX). As in the case of Gen 6:11–13 and Isa 24:1–5, moral corruption brought on by human transgression is attended by physical harm and

---

27. In Greek usage φθορά fundamentally means "destruction" or "death" (Harder, "Φθείρω Κτλ.," 94). Harder notes that in Aristotle's "description of nature φθορά means 'death'" (95).

28. BDAG, 1054–55.

destruction. In ways similar to Gen 6 and Isa 24, Paul places emphasis on human sin and its negative effects in Romans. In Rom 8:21, the meaning of φθορά almost certainly includes ideas of moral corruption *and* physical harm or destruction.[29]

Yet, what of the additional connotation involving natural processes of chemical decomposition? Does φθορᾶς in Rom 8:21 connote passive, natural processes of decomposition as well? Considering the ways in which Paul uses this word group elsewhere in his letters, it becomes clear he understands this term as describing the ability to die and, as a result, decompose.[30] When Paul discusses the resurrection in 1 Cor 15:42, he employs the term φθορᾷ to describe the mortal body as perishable, as able to die and decay. The resurrected body, conversely, is imperishable (ἀφθαρσίᾳ).[31] In his letter to the Romans, Paul similarly employs the related adjective φθαρτός to describe the possibility of physical death and decomposition. Romans 1:23 explains people "exchanged the glory of the indestructible God (ἀφθάρτου θεοῦ) for a poor copy of an image of a destructible (φθαρτοῦ) human and of birds, four-legged animals, and reptiles." The NRSV and NIV translate these occurrences of the word group φθαρτός as "immortal" and "mortal" to capture the idea that God is incapable of death and physical decomposition whereas humans do die and decompose.

Yet φθορά and its cognates also refer to the more active nuances of death and destruction in the Pauline Epistles. Paul unambiguously employs the verb with an active connotation only at 1 Cor 3:17. He warns of the active destruction of things and people when he announces that God will destroy (φθείρει) those people who destroy (φθείρει) God's temple. Here,

---

29. The creation's moral corruption, however, does not result from its own action in light of Paul's narration in Rom 5. Instead, Paul places the blame on the human, Adam and not the serpent (or, interestingly, Eve). When Paul discusses creation in Romans, he consistently portrays it as magnifying God's existence (1:20), eagerly waiting for God to consummate the redemptive plan (8:19–22), and, consequently, as aligned with God. Thus any moral corruption contaminating creation results from human sin.

30. Although Paul presumes decay and death are negative aspects of the world now, he probably identifies untimely destruction and death as particularly against God's purposes. Despite this differentiation, his critical perspective on decay and death stands in stark contrast with science. The importance of decay for the recycling of nutrients cannot be underestimated for the earth's proper functioning and for the ongoing flourishing of life.

31. Here, Paul reflects a common Greco-Roman antithesis between the real and ideal, the perishable and imperishable, the mortal and immortal (Harder, "Φθείρω Κτλ.," 94–95, 104). See Wis 2:23 for another example of ἀφθαρσίᾳ, the English translation of which is: "for God created us for incorruption, and made us in the image of his own eternity" (NRSV).

Paul employs the verb to refer to acts of destruction (whether physical or spiritual) rather than to natural processes of decay.

Decomposition and natural death, then, are not the only connotations of φθορά in Paul's letters. In fact, when we consider human mortality in light of death's intrusion into the world (Rom 5:12), the threat of decomposition alone is not death's most potent weapon, according to the logic of Romans. Instead, the constant threat of active and untimely destruction powerfully enslaves the minds, hearts, and bodies of human beings. Thus, by translating φθαρτοῦ in 1:23 as "destructible," we capture the sense that death, destruction, and decomposition constantly haunt humanity. Similarly, in 8:21, "slavery to destruction" portrays creation's complex experience, which entails not only decomposition but also untimely destruction. It is from these dreadful conditions that Jesus Christ's life, death, and resurrection liberates human and nonhuman creation.

In concert with this more precise rendering of φθαρτός in Rom 1:23 and 8:21, the Greek translation of Gen 6 also suggests that this word group directs the reader's attention to ideas of destruction more than decay.[32] As explained in 1.2, the cognate verb φθείρω describes the ways in which violent human and animal behaviors had ruined or destroyed the earth and how God would consequently destroy all flesh with a flood of water (Gen 6:5, 11–12).[33] The biblical tradition, thus, recognizes the fact that God's

---

32. Sylvia Keesmaat also perceives an intertextual link between Rom 8:21 and Gen 6. While maintaining the NRSV's language of "corruption" in Gen 6, she nevertheless finds human action to stand behind the earth's degraded condition. She explains, "In the flood narrative, the corruption of the earth is expressly linked to the corruption of human beings: it is because of human beings that the earth is filled with violence and so God determines to destroy them along with the earth (Gen. 6.13). We have here the connection made between the corruption of creation and the actions of human beings . . . The flood story makes it clear that human beings are the ones who subjected creation to futility" (Keesmaat, *Paul and His Story*, 119–20).

33. I would suggest, then, that Paul uses the word group similarly to prominent passages of the Greek translation of the Tanakh, which refer to physical destruction and killing as opposed to natural deterioration. As discussed in 1.2, in Gen 6 God plans to *destroy* (καταφθείρω, 6:13) all living things on the earth because the earth was *destroyed* (ἐφθάρη, 6:11) and all flesh had *destroyed* (κατέφθειρεν, 6:12) its way on the earth. The first instance refers to the active killing experienced by living creatures, and the second likely portrays a situation in which the earth's plants, animals, and natural resources had been destroyed or damaged by living things. The third use more abstractly refers to the destruction of a way of life. Similarly, Isa 24 explains that God will destroy (καταφθείρει, 24:1) the world because its inhabitants had sinned (Isa 24:1, 3, 4–6; see 1.3). These passages depict God and humans killing life on earth and employ the term φθείρω and its cognates in ways that denote active destruction.

creation undergoes violent, untimely, active destruction not simply passive processes of decay.

Reconsidering Rom 8:21 with this in mind, we find "decay" does not adequately capture the semantic range of φθορᾶς. Decay in English connotes physical decomposition, but it does not bring to mind active killing or destroying. Furthermore, the translation "bondage to decay" (NRSV) functions as a statement of ontology; it describes a form of being in which living, dead, and nonliving things simply undergo natural processes of decomposition.[34] Some interpreters understand 8:21 in this sense, suggesting that creation is bound by the natural processes of death in a world governed by evolution.[35] Accordingly, creation's slavery of decay is a condition that the Creator God alone can alleviate and remedy; humans consequently bear minimal guilt for creation's ongoing bondage to decay and hold no power for changing the situation. From a scientific perspective, this scenario makes sense since death is a natural process in the world. However, it bears little resemblance to the Jewish cosmology described in chapter 1. What is more, since the English term "decay" does not convey the full semantic weight of Paul's underlying Greek terminology, it mistakenly collapses the wider narrative arc about creation. Thus, the NRSV and NIV's "decay" is misleading and incomplete.

The English word "destruction," however, invokes both the sense of physical harm as well as the natural processes of chemical decomposition, since decomposition naturally takes place after a living thing is destroyed or dies. Less clearly in view is the idea of moral contamination. However, because physical destruction often follows moral corruption in the Tanakh, the damaging, degrading effects of human sin attend the idea of destruction. With these factors in view, "slavery of destruction" appears as a strong translational option since it not only presupposes that creation is subject to death and decay, but it also highlights a dimension of relational interplay that "slavery of decay" does not. "Slavery of destruction" conjures images of someone or something acting in ways that destroy another. Taken this way τῆς δουλείας τῆς φθορᾶς functions as a relational statement in which the nonhuman creation is under the constant threat of being destroyed by

---

34. Harder understands φθορᾶς in this sense and translates it as "corruptibility," but he also recognizes that it likely alludes to something far more expansive, such as "eternal destruction," when it is considered in relation to Gal 6:8 (Harder, "Φθείρω Κτλ.," 104).

35. See, for example, Horrell, Hunt, and Southgate, *Greening Paul*, 74–75.

humanity's moral corruption and harmful actions, even while it is subject to natural processes of decomposition.[36]

Because Paul has connected humanity's own slavery to sin to Adam's disobedience in chapters 5–6 and since ongoing sinful human activity is destructive in a variety of ways, understanding τῆς δουλείας τῆς φθορᾶς as "the slavery of destruction" suggests that creation's experience of destruction may in fact result from human sinfulness, at least in part. This inference finds confirmation in what Paul goes on to state in 8:21b: "the creation itself will be liberated from the slavery of destruction into the liberation produced by the glory that is possessed by God's children" (see 4.2 for more details).[37] In other words, creation will be liberated when God glorifies humans and ultimately frees them from the effects of sin. Because creation's release from bondage rests upon God's work of rectifying and glorifying humanity, it is reasonable to conclude that creation's bondage itself results from human sin, violence, and wrongdoing. This is even more clearly the case when Paul's earlier references to Adam and the creation narrative of Gen 2–3 are kept in view. Consequently, τῆς δουλείας τῆς φθορᾶς not only alludes to creation's susceptibility to death and decay but also to humanity's exploitative and destructive relationship with the nonhuman creation.[38]

4.3 Romans 8:20: Creation's Subjection

While the current relationship between humanity and creation often leads to destruction, it is clear from the creation narratives that undergird Paul's story of creation that God did not originally create humans to enslave

---

36. Perhaps also in view is the idea that natural forces, such as storms and earthquakes, may also enslave creation to destruction.

37. When we consider the theological arc that Paul has developed from chapter 1 to 8, we find humanity exchanging the indestructible image of God for a destructible one (1:23). Perhaps it is from such a destructible, death-prone, and sin-prone image that God liberates people so that they might be conformed to the resurrected, indestructible image of the Son (8:29). So too, as humans are thus glorified, the nonhuman creation is liberated from its destructible, death-prone condition, into a form of glory.

38. Jonathan Moo suggests a similar and corroborating perspective, noting "the sense that creation is prey to 'ruin' and enslaved to the effects of human immorality comports well with what Paul has likely meant by its subjection to ματαιότης" (Moo, "Romans 8.19–22," 82). In more abstract terms, Cranfield contends that φθορά refers to "moral corruption resulting from idolatry" and that "the bondage of decay" denotes "creation's bondage to man's corrupt abuse of it" (Cranfield, *Critical and Exegetical Commentary*, 413).

creation to destruction. Nevertheless, as both Genesis and Paul suggest, God created the world in such a way that this distortion was a possibility. While God commissioned humans to exercise "dominion" over much of the rest of the nonhuman creation (Gen 1:26–28; see 1.1) and thereby subjected nonhuman creation to humanity's "servant leadership" (as I call it), God intended their "servant leadership" to have a life-supporting rather than destructive character. This primordial relationship of subjection, nevertheless, opened the door to the unintended experience of frustration or "futility" (8:20 NRSV) as well as the more pernicious condition of slavery that results in destruction (8:21).

Paul's story of creation in Rom 8:20–21, therefore, leads us back to the creation accounts of Gen 1–3 and their portrait of creation under the "dominion" of humanity. Yet, Paul's retelling of creation's story in 8:20 brings with it interpretive complexity. Two opaque forms of the verb ὑποτάσσω in 8:20 confront us in his statement: "For the creation was subjected to frustration, not willingly but on account of the one subjecting it in hope." The first instance stands as the passive verb ὑπετάγη ("it was subjected"), and the second is an active participle ὑποτάξαντα ("the one subjecting").[39] Neither occurrence of ὑποτάσσω specifies the agent acting behind the verb. By itself, this verse leaves open questions about how creation came into this relationship of subjection and its attending condition of frustration.

As we have already seen, the epistolary and scriptural contexts surrounding and undergirding this passage offer two interconnected answers. In light of Rom 5 and Gen 1–3, it appears that Paul perceives two interrelated agents at work behind creation's subjection: first, God subjected creation to human oversight and, second, sinful human beings subjected creation to frustrated attempts at fulfilling God's commission to flourish. In other words, God stands as the ultimate actor working in and through creation, but humanity is the proximate cause of creation's subjection to frustration.

4.3.1 Primary and Secondary Causes of Subjection

The clearest indication that God is an agent behind at least one aspect of creation's subjection appears in 8:20b: creation was subjected "because of

---

39. An active form of the verb ὑποτάσσω conveys a meaning of "subject, subordinate, place under" (Bergmeier, "Ὑποτάσσω," *EDNT* 3:408). A passive form of the verb means "be subjected to, be placed under" (1042).

the one that subjected [it] *in hope*."⁴⁰ The short prepositional phrase ἐφ' ἐλπίδι, "in hope," indicates the manner in which the agent subjected creation. Thus, "the one that subjected" creation (τὸν ὑποτάξαντα, an aorist active participle that functions as a verbal noun) did so with a hopeful purpose, perhaps even with the commanding presence that God alone could muster. This phrase "in hope" provides evidence that Paul here refers to God as the one who subjected creation, since mere humans (or angelic beings) could not both subject creation and also do so with a confident hope of its future liberation (8:21).⁴¹ Thus, at least in this second occurrence of the word group ὑποτάσσω (8:20b), Paul's wording portrays God as the actor who subjected creation.

As the creation accounts in Gen 1–3 that Paul draws upon in Rom 5 make plain (for more discussion see 1.1—1.2.1 and 3.2.2), God subjected creation to human rule and the possibility of *sinful* human dominion.⁴² Thus, although God subjected creation to human servant leadership with the hope of its ultimate good, God did not also directly subject it to futility (8:20a). Instead, defunct human oversight led to creation's subjection to frustration.⁴³ The intertextual influences at work in and behind Paul's description of creation suggest that the passive verb in the statement "for the creation was not willingly subjected to frustration" (τῇ γὰρ ματαιότητι ἡ κτίσις ὑπετάγη οὐχ ἑκοῦσα) points more directly to sinful human activity than to God.⁴⁴

40. Emphasis added.

41. Cranfield, *Critical and Exegetical Commentary*, 414.

42. Admittedly, the Genesis text does not use the term "creation" but instead indicates that humanity has dominion over nonhuman living creatures. The linguistic concept of "creation" captured by the Hebrew *berîāh* and Greek κτίσις is rarely used in the Tanakh, occurring only at Num 16:30 (Bernhardt, "BāRā," *TDOT* 2:246).

43. Some interpreters, Cranfield for example, do not see human action implicated in creation's subjection. Yet, if Paul truly relies on Gen 1–3 for his cosmology, as many commentators—and even Cranfield himself—assume, we must consider the full implications of humanity's God-given dominion over creation and its power to influence the experience and character of that creation. While we may question the plausibility of humanity's creation-wide influence from a practical and scientific perspective, we would have good reason to consider it a biblical perspective on account of the unfolding narrative of creation in Gen 1–6 and Rom 5–8. Attempting to follow the trajectory of Paul's discourse, then, my reading suggests that two sets of actors stand behind the verbs "subject." Humanity subjects creation to frustration, but God subjects creation to humanity with the resolute hope of its future liberation.

44. In relation to Paul's discussion of subjection in Rom 8:20, James Dunn suggests, "Paul was attempting to convey too briefly a quite complicated point: that God subjected

When we read 8:20 in light of Rom 5–6, we find that human sin stands as the proximate cause of creation's subjection to frustration. The cosmic alterations Paul sees attending Adam's sin—including sin and death's entrance into the cosmos and their consequent domination of the human species (5:12, 14, 21)—impact the whole of creation according to the biblical story of creation, especially Gen 3–9. Thus, although Paul does not explicitly indicate that human deeds negatively affect(ed) the rest of creation, the conceptual and narrative links he establishes with Genesis lead toward the conclusion that sinful human action subjects creation to ματαιότητι because of God's prior decision to subject creation to human "dominion," or, servant leadership. With this in mind, the precise nature of this negative condition termed ματαιότητι needs fleshing out.

4.3.2 The Condition of Frustration

By explaining that creation was subjected τῇ ματαιότητι—to "futility" (NRSV) or frustration—in Rom 8:20, Paul indicates that creation entered a condition that hindered its purpose and progress. The noun's typical semantic range includes "emptiness, futility, purposelessness, transitoriness" and gives the reader the impression that the situation is not what it should be.[45] Depending on the context and the philosophical perspective of the author, ματαιότης may fall into one of three overlapping semantic categories: moral, temporal, or material.[46] If we interpret it with reference to the world of ideas and religious beliefs—that is, in a moral sense—ματαιότης connotes vanity, deceptiveness, emptiness, and futility (e.g., Ps 4:3 LXX; 143:8 LXX; Eccl 2:15; Eph 4:17). Along these lines, when the related noun, μάταιος, occurs as a substantive it often refers to the objects of pagan worship (i.e., idols) as vain or futile things since they do not provide the truth

---

all things to Adam, and that included subjecting creation to fallen Adam, to share in his fallenness" (Dunn, *Romans: 1–8*, 471). While this general sentiment is what I argue above, I would disagree with Dunn's focus on "*fallen* humanity" (emphasis added). Rather, I would contend the biblical tradition portrays God subjecting creation to *good* human beings, who nevertheless have the freedom to transgress.

45. BDAG, 621. Bauernfeind contrasts μάταιος with κενός and concludes that with μάταιος "there is always the implication of what is against the norm, unexpected, offending what ought to be," whereas κενός "means worthless" (Bauernfeind, "Μάταιος," *TDNT* 4:519).

46. These three semantic categories are my own, but they draw upon Bauernfeind's descriptions of μάταιος and its related words (Bauernfeind, "Μάταιος," *TDNT* 4:519-24).

or security that Israel's God provides (e.g., Lev 17:7; 1 Kgs 16:13; Jonah 2:9 LXX; Isa 2:20; 44:9; see also Acts 14:15).[47] In addition to this moral and religious sense, ματαιότης may carry a temporal meaning, referring to things or events that are transitory and fleeting (e.g., Ps 38:6 LXX; 77:33 LXX; Eccl 3:19; 6:12). Finally, if we understand ματαιότης with reference to causation and the material world, its meaning is captured best by terms such as ineffectiveness, fruitlessness, and frustration (e.g., Eccl 2:11; 4:8; 6:2).

When we consider what τῇ ματαιότητι means in Rom 8:20, each of these connotations makes sense within the context: creation may have been subjected to the "deceptiveness" of misdirected moral and religious devotion—in other words, idolatry; to "transitory" existence in a world of death and decay; and to the "ineffectiveness" of material limitations and interruptions. Some interpreters find the moral sense of τῇ ματαιότητι to be in play, and a few even interpret it as a substantive. As such, the clause could be rendered as either "creation was subjected to vain humanity" or "creation was subjected to an empty idol or celestial powers" (c.f., Gal 4:9).[48] Because Paul employs the cognate verb in Rom 1:21 to describe humans as those who "became futile" (ἐματαιώθησαν) when they abandoned proper thankfulness to the Creator God (1:21), it is likely the noun in Rom 8:20 alludes to "man's idolatry which exploits the sub-human creation for its own purposes."[49] Idolatry, in such a construction, is not an abstract form of religious devotion. For, as the Tanakh repeatedly illustrates, the idolatries practiced by Israel, Judah, and the nations are "overwhelmingly linked to an abuse of the land."[50] In other words, when τῇ ματαιότητι carries a religious or moral sense, it suggests that creation is/was subjected to idolatrous people, purposes, and uses.

While this religious connotation provides an instructive interpretation of Rom 8:20, the temporal and causal meanings add further depth

---

47. Bauernfeind indicates that biblical writers often used this word group to refer derogatively to "the pseudo-divine powers to which man cleaves and by which he seeks to avoid the μάταιον" (Bauernfeind, "Μάταιος," *TDNT* 4:522). Both biblical writers and many Greek philosophers considered God/the gods to be humanity's only buffer from the futility of embodied life. In the LXX, "[t]he gods of the ἔθνη are primarily μάταια, i.e., the very gods who in the Greek world are supposed in some way to be the guarantors of that which escapes the μάταιον. Only the one God is the living God" (4:521–22).

48. Cranfield, *Critical and Exegetical Commentary*, 413.

49. Cranfield, *Critical and Exegetical Commentary*, 413. Jonathan Moo also understands this phrase in relation to human idolatry and the emptiness and sinfulness that idolatry entails (Moo, "Romans 8.19–22," 81).

50. Keesmaat, "Land, Idolatry, and Justice," 97.

Creation's Slavery and Subjection

and complexity in accord with Paul's emphases in the immediate context. Throughout Romans and especially in chapter 8, Paul emphasizes the negative effects of destructibility and death. Just as humans experience death, the lives of God's nonhuman creatures and plants are *fleeting* in a temporal sense.[51] The life-creating and life-restoring work of God corrects this problem for humanity especially through resurrection (4:17; 8:11), and the Spirit groans with the groaning and laboring creation as God works to liberate the nonhuman creation from its slavery to destruction (8:22, 26).

Yet, temporality is not the only problem facing humanity and nonhuman creation. Instead, the fundamental problem facing *sinful humans* is their incapacity to do what God calls them to do, as Paul makes plain with his penetrating analysis of human ineffectiveness in the face of sin in chapters 3, 5, and 7. If we interpret creation's subjection τῇ ματαιότητι along these lines, we find that creation is inhibited from "attain[ing] its goal"[52] or "achiev[ing] its purpose."[53] Just as humans attempt to fulfill God's life-promoting commands but are often prevented from doing so because of sin (7:14–19), so too are the efforts of nonhuman creation frustrated and sometimes rendered *ineffective* as it seeks to flourish.

We find this causal or material interpretation strengthened as we read 8:20 in light of the creation narratives of Genesis upon which Paul builds in chapters 5–6, when he explains that sin and death entered the world on account of human sin.[54] According to Gen 1, God commands the marine, avian, and land creatures to be fruitful and multiply, and God also commissions plants to produce edible foods for *all* living creatures (Gen 1:11–12, 22, 24–25, 28; 30; see also 8:17). However, according to Gen 3, human disobedience brings a curse upon the fertile ground, and this led it to produce thorns and thistles rather than edible plants (Gen 3:17–18;

---

51. The *EDNT* interprets τῇ ματαιότητι along temporal lines, stating, "According to Rom 8:20 the creation has been subjected by God to *nothingness/transitoriness* . . . because of the sin of humankind. Paul's hope is that this situation of transitoriness, with its (historical) beginning, will also have an (historical) end in the liberation of creation to the freedom awaited by the children of God" (Balz, "Μάταιος," *EDNT* 396–97).

52. Cranfield, *Critical and Exegetical Commentary*, 413.

53. Horrell, Hunt, and Southgate, *Greening Paul*, 77. Unlike the interpretation I offer here, Horrell, Hunt, and Southgate reject the creation narratives as the most likely scriptural background to Rom 8:19–22, arguing that the so-called "Fall" story of Adam (Gen 1–3) and creation's subjection to futility are evolutionarily impossible (75–77). While this is the case scientifically, I am attempting to follow Paul's theological perspective at this point.

54. For a discussion of the narratives in Genesis, see 1.1—1.2.1.

see 1.2.1). The life-giving, life-sustaining network for God's creatures is frustrated and rendered less effective after the sin of Adam. In a sense, the biological diversity and fertility that God initially created were threatened because of human transgression. Read in light of this narrative trajectory τῇ ματαιότητι refers to creation's frustrated and ineffective attempts at carrying out God's commission to flourish in a world dominated by the powers of sin and death. With creation subjected to the oversight of human beings who are themselves enslaved to sin, it is no wonder that Paul describes creation's subjection as "futile," "ineffective," or "frustrated," since sinful humans cannot execute their servant leadership in accordance with God's glorious purposes.

This larger narrative arc and linguistic multivalence suggests we paraphrase Rom 8:20 (and especially Paul's ambiguous uses of ὑποτάσσω) as: "sinful humans subjected an unwilling creation to frustrated attempts at flourishing on account of God's prior subjection of creation to human servant leadership." This interpretation reflects the ancient worldview that claims humans exercise immense power over the rest of creation by God's creative design. This is so much the case that human sin effectively subjects the creation to an existence that is less than God's fullest intentions for diversity, flourishing, and life. Put simply, human transgression is the proximate cause of creation's subjection to ineffectiveness. Yet, at the same time, God stands as the ultimate, indirect, and nonculpatory cause behind this subjection, for God's decisive power subjected creation to humanity's "dominion" and, by implication, to the unintended effects of human sin.

Paul's story of creation in Rom 8:20–21—embedded as it is in a wider scriptural matrix (especially Gen 1–9)—offers the Christians in Rome an account of creation that contrasts strikingly with the imperial accounts of a renewed Golden Age. For, the nonhuman creation currently suffers in slavery and subjection in ways that lead to untimely destruction and inhibited forms of flourishing. And human greed, injustice, idolatry—or, more broadly, "sin"—stand as chief causes. Accordingly, Paul quite logically perceives that creation waits desperately for the coming appearance of *glorified* humanity (8:19). For only then will the nonhuman creation finally be liberated from its slavery to destruction and subjection to frustration (8:20–21).

CHAPTER 5

Creation's Expectation and Liberation

The Story of Human Glory in Romans

SINCE HUMANS WERE ENSLAVED to sin and death on account of Adam's primordial disobedience, their distorted way of being, in turn, enslaves nonhuman creation to destruction, as explained in 4.2. Therefore, human beings stand in need of liberation, rectification, and glorification for their own sakes but also for the sake of nonhuman creation so that it too can be liberated from its bondage. As Paul implies in 8:19–21, creation's deliverance will take place when God resurrects all of God's children. This future is secure because God's Son, the Messiah Jesus, has faithfully lived, died, and risen again on behalf of all (3:21–30; 5:12–21). And since God created a world in which the destinies of human and nonhuman creation interdepend, nonhuman creation's liberation is secure. While Jesus's righteousness and fidelity first and foremost rectifies humans, it also necessarily delivers the whole creation. For, the re-established righteousness, fidelity, and glory of human beings will transform their dominion of God's creation from one of destruction to a servant leadership marked by life and flourishing (8:21; 5:17). In other words, creation will experience its own form of liberation when God ultimately liberates God's children from the influences of sin and the forces of death at the resurrection. It is for this resurrection that creation so eagerly waits (8:19; section 1) and on which its destiny of liberation depends (8:21; section 2).

Yet, creation's dependence on the ultimate rectification and glorification of humanity stands as only one side of the interdependent relationship that God established. The nonhuman creation's cooperation with God in creating and nurturing life also affects the well-being of God's human creatures. Rom 8:22 hints at this often-muted dynamic in a surprising way by portraying creation as a female who is groaning and laboring in childbirth. In light of intertextual traditions that portray nonhuman creation as laboring and delivering forth humanity *to* God and *with* God for judgment and resurrection, Paul's image in 8:22 suggests that creation cooperates with God in the miraculous work of resurrection (section 3). In order to perceive creation's positive and productive role in God's work of glorification as well as its dependence upon humanity, we must consider the meaning and implications of creation's expectation (8:19; section 1), liberation (8:21; section 2), and collective groaning and laboring (8:22; section 3).

5.1 Romans 8:19: Creation's Expectation

The interconnection between human and nonhuman destinies first appears in 8:19 where Paul employs the term γάρ, "for," to link future human glory (8:18) with creation's expectations of an apocalypse (8:19). As he explains in verse 18, the temporary personal and communal sufferings (παθήματα) that Paul and his fellow Christians now endure cannot compare with the glory of the liberation that is to come. Paul can be confident that the "coming glory to be revealed in us" (8:18) is incomparable to present sufferings, "*[f]or* the eager expectation of the creation awaits the apocalypse of the sons of God" (8:19, emphasis added).[1] By turning his attention to the rest of creation and thereby widening his gaze beyond human resurrection (8:11, 13, 17), Paul illustrates the incomparable glory of the future to come. The apocalypse of Jesus's siblings will usher in a transformation of the whole creation: the glory to come not only will alleviate human suffering but, most remarkably and perhaps surprisingly, it will liberate the rest of creation from its own forms of suffering (8:21). In 8:19–22, then, we encounter Paul's reflections on the wider narrative of creation, a story in which the future consummation of God's salvation will indeed exceed Christians' wildest dreams as well as transcend their most horrific sufferings (see, for example, 8:35–36). At its core, Rom 8:19–22 declares that the creation will be liberated from its present captivity to frustration and destruction as it steps into the glorified existence of God's children. But until then, creation anticipates that future.

---

1. All English Scripture citations are the author's own in this chapter unless otherwise noted.

Creation's Expectation and Liberation

Although creation functions in 8:19 as supporting evidence for Paul's anthropological point in 8:18 (as indicated by the causal connection "for"), it also acts as an agent and participant in the drama of salvation. The nonhuman creation, in fact, is a participant (perhaps even a covenantal partner) with *expectations*. The literal translation of verse 19 quoted above reflects the way in which Paul places "expectation" as the subject of the verb "await" (ἀποκαραδοκία τῆς κτίσεως . . . ἀπεκδέχεται). Most translators smooth out the wording by making κτίσις the subject of the action; for example, the NRSV renders the phrase, "the creation waits with eager longing." Yet, it is rather mundane to indicate that creation "waits." What Paul actually expresses startles his readers by announcing that creation has expectations. He proclaims, "Creation's expectation awaits . . ." The head noun ἀποκαραδοκία, often translated as "eager expectation," combines "head" (κάρα) with "think, imagine" (δοκέω)[2] and may point toward the imaginative capacity that characterizes nonhuman creation as it anticipates God's future. Additionally, ἀποκαραδοκία often connotes a sense of confidence, implying that creation's *confident* expectation awaits the apocalypse of God's sons. Sigve Tonstad perceptively suggests that creation's confident expectation relies upon and grows out of God's prior commitment to bless creation (Gen 1:22, 28). He contends, "'[t]he eager longing' of non-human creation, therefore, has a blessing and a promise stored in the memory bank."[3] With a posture of trust in God's faithfulness to restore creation to the conditions of blessing (see Isa 11; 65), creation expects and waits for the next phase of God's work of liberation.

5.1.1 Apocalypse and the Coming Glory

By awaiting the apocalypse of the sons of God, what specifically does creation anticipate? One option, according to Robert Jewett, interprets this revelation as referring to the ongoing conversion of persons to Jesus Christ. In Jewett's reading, Paul holds that human conversion is "the avenue of divine action" by which God "will begin to restore a rightful balance to the creation once again, overcoming the Adamic legacy of corruption and disorder that fell as a calamitous curse upon the ground (Gen 3:17–19)."[4]

---

2. This term occurs only twice in the New Testament (Rom 8:19 and Phil 1:20) and does not occur in the LXX (BDAG, 112).

3. Tonstad, *Letter to the Romans*, 245.

4. Jewett, *Romans*, 512.

Accordingly, in this view, Paul "assumes that the renewed mind of such groups will be able to discern what God wills for the ecosystem. So the eager longing of the creation awaits the appearance of such transformed persons, knowing that the sources of ecological disorder will be addressed by them in due season."[5] In other words, creation waits for more and more people to live according to God's design.

Although there is much to commend Jewett's ethical impulse, his understanding of "apocalypse" in this context overlooks important elements of Paul's eschatology and misconstrues key indicators about the identity of the sons of God. Strikingly, Jewett makes no mention of the term ἀποκάλυψις ("apocalypse"), nor does he allow this word to shine its appropriate eschatological light upon this section of his commentary. To be sure, Jewett argues that those who convert to Christ do experience a new form of life and liberty now. Yet, according to Paul's thought in Romans, sin's power continues to threaten Christ-followers' lives and the world.[6] In light of this trajectory, it seems more likely that what creation looks forward to in this section is qualitatively different from the ordinary and ongoing appearances of new converts to Christ. Instead, creation anticipates the ultimate revelation and perfection of the resurrected children of God (8:17, 18, and 23).

Several details in the immediate context confirm Paul has a much more holistic transformation in mind than conversion to Christ. First, the wording of the preceding verse ("the coming glory to be apocalypsed in us," 8:18) already shapes the way in which we ought to interpret the apocalypse of the sons of God in 8:19. It is an event of the future, since the "glory to be revealed" is as yet "coming" (μέλλουσαν; 8:18). This glory, moreover, will characterize the future liberated state of the children of God, as 8:21 demonstrates (see section 2 below).

Secondly, the theological and eschatological connotations of "glory" provide important reasons for interpreting Rom 8:19-22 in an eschatological vein. Δόξα, "glory," often carries not only a connotation of God's magnificence and "God's full presence"[7] in the Christian Scriptures but also

---

5. Jewett, *Romans*, 512.

6. Reflecting on Jewett's optimistic anthropology, Tonstad similarly concludes: "To believe that the forces of exploitation and oppression will at last be tamed by the action of 'the children of God' in the sense that 'their altered lifestyle and revised ethics begin to restore the ecological system' seems to overestimate their impact whether in light of biblical or historical evidence" (Tonstad, *Letter to the Romans*, 248).

7. Beker, "Vision of Hope," 29. For a few examples in the Tanakh, see Exod 15:11;

alludes to God's transformative power at work in human and nonhuman creation in Romans. In the Greek translation of the Tanakh, δόξα conveys a specifically theological nuance, since it often translates the Hebrew kābôd. In the Tanakh, the "glory of God" is often associated with "a theme of religious hope" and is "an established part of eschatological expectation" for when God's "claim to rule the world" would be fully accomplished.[8] Consequently, "when the NT refers to the eschatological participation of believers in δόξα," it points toward "the connexion [sic.] and parallelism between the resurrection of Christ and the resurrection and new aeon of believers."[9] A prime example of the transformative nature of glory comes in Rom 6. While exhorting his audience to live in line with their new baptismal identities, Paul nonetheless points toward the ultimate experience of resurrection that comes about through God's glory. He exclaims, "Christ was raised from the dead through the Father's glory," so too will those who participate in Jesus's death undergo resurrection (6:4–5). Paul returns to this profound truth in chapter 8, where he indicates that those who suffer with Christ will be glorified *with* Christ (συνδοξασθῶμεν, 8:17). He then locates this glory as being revealed εἰς ἡμᾶς ("in, to, for us") in verse 18. By the phrase εἰς ἡμᾶς, Paul identifies glory as acting on behalf of and within God's people.[10] They are transformed by this glory and are not mere bystanders who behold the apocalypse. Glory begins to transform people now while they nevertheless wait for its full effects to be revealed (8:23).

40:34; Deut 5:24; 2 Chr 7:1–3; Ps 28:1–3 (LXX); 101:16 (LXX); Isa 2:10, 19, 21; 6:3; 40:5; Ezek 3:12, 23; 11:23; 44:4.

8. Von Rad, "Kābôd in the OT," *TDNT* 2:241–42. Kittel notes that "the NT use of δόξα follows the LXX rather than Greek usage. With the senses of 'reputation' and 'power' already mentioned [and typical in Greek usage], the word is also used strictly in the NT to express the 'divine mode of being'" (Kittel, "Δοκέω," *TDNT* 2:247).

9. Kittel, "Δοκέω," *TDNT* 2:250.

10. In contrast with the NRSV, NIV, NET, and KJV, I understand ἀποκαλυφθῆναι εἰς ἡμᾶς of 8:18 to express the idea that glory will be revealed *in* rather than *to* God's people. The eschatological people of God are not mere spectators but participants in God's work of glorification. Verse 23 alludes to this process of glorification as it will result in the ultimate redemption of the body, and 8:30 even more directly indicates that God's people shall be glorified. Cranfield understands εἰς ἡμᾶς as not simply "for us" or "to us"; rather, the terms together "are naturally understood as indicating where the revelation of the glory is to occur, the persons whose condition will be transformed by it" (Cranfield, *Critical and Exegetical Commentary*, 410). He also states, "the revelation of the glory will be, not something merely internal to us nor something brought about by our own activity, but something outwardly manifest as well as affecting our inward life, done to us by the decisive action of God" (410).

A third reason the apocalypse of God's children points toward a future event is specified in 8:23. After explaining that the whole creation collectively groans and labors, Paul indicates that "we" groan while eagerly awaiting "adoption, the redemption [ἀπολύτρωσιν] of our body" (8:23). Although Jesus Christ has already provided redemption (ἀπολυτρώσεως, Rom 3:24) and, thereby, liberation from slavery to sin and death for the faithful, an aspect of this redemption remains to be experienced. Redemption of the body involves a future corporate resurrection, a detail that Jewett also acknowledges.[11] Redemption, in the words of Leander Keck, involves "not release *from* the body but the transformation *of* the body by resurrection,"[12] a resurrection brought about—we may assume—by "the Father's glory" (6:4). It is this resurrection to which the "coming glory" (8:18), the "apocalypse of the sons of God" (8:19), and "the liberation of the glory of God's children" (8:21) refer. When we understand the apocalypse of the sons of God as an eschatological event, it becomes clear that the group Paul calls the "sons of God" in 8:19 and the "children of God" in 8:21 consists of all those who will enter God's eternal kingdom at the end of time.[13]

The apocalyptic and eschatological event in which God endows dead or dying human beings with glory not only extends indestructible life to humanity but also enacts liberation for the whole creation, as seen in 8:21 (as we will discuss below). Glorification of humanity entails and necessarily

---

11. Jewett, *Romans*, 519.

12. Keck, *Romans*, 212–13. Emphasis original. Jewett also stresses that Paul does not depict this as redemption *from* the body (Jewett, *Romans*, 519). In stark contrast, Origen interpreted Paul through a Platonic lens and considered redemption necessarily to involve the soul's escape from material existence (Tonstad, *Letter to the Romans*, 25–26).

13. This eschatological group, then, includes those who as yet do not display an obedience of faith but at some point will (1:5; 16:26). Because Paul indicates at 9:4 that the adoption (υἱοθεσία) and glory belong to the descendants of Israel and because "sons of God" repeatedly refers to the descendants of Israel in the Tanakh (including passages Paul cites in Romans, such as Hos 2:1 LXX; Deut 32:21 and 32:43), it may be the "sons of God" in Rom 8:19 includes all Jews (Eastman, "Whose Apocalypse?," 266–67). While the constituents included in the group "sons of God" cannot be defined with certainty, it is almost certain this group includes females and not just males. Since Paul employs the more inclusive nomenclature "children of God" in 8:21 perhaps his initial use of "sons of God" in 8:19 is done for rhetorical cohesion. The masculine noun υἱῶν, "*sons* of God," not only calls to mind God's covenant people, Israel, but also God's specially designated "Son" (1:4). It also maintains the theme of adoption (υἱοθεσία) and inheritance in Rom 8. Thus, "sons of God" highlights the linguistic connection between the children of God (whether male or female) and Jesus, the *Son* of God. Meanwhile, perhaps Paul's turn to the phrase "children of God" makes it absolutely clear to his audience that these redeemed persons are not only males.

brings with it the liberation of nonhuman creation, which illustrates that the destiny of humanity affects the destiny of the nonhuman creation. Since these destinies also depend upon the work of God, however, they will come in the form of an apocalypse, a *revelation* originating in and from God.[14] Thus, in 8:19–22, as Frank Matera explains, Paul "portrays the created world as consciously waiting for the general resurrection of the dead, when believers—finally raised from the dead—will be revealed for who they truly are: God's sons and daughters."[15] Contrary to Jewett's interpretation, then, the eschatological character of 8:19–22 and its immediate context suggests that the apocalypse of the sons of God refers primarily to the glorification and resurrection of humanity and only secondarily to the ongoing conversion of individuals, which precedes and prefigures that ultimate eschatological event.

Nevertheless, "conversion" remains important since glorification flows from liberation, justification, and the enduring processes of sanctification, in which God's people no longer succumb to the dominion of sin and death (5:1–2, 17, 21; 8:30). The experience of God's liberative glory not only effects resurrection life in the future, but transforms life now. This is so much the case that Paul can claim Jesus's siblings already are "glorified" in some sense (8:30). Their glorification in Christ would appear to restore the glory that had been lost through their dishonoring of God and dismissal of creation's testimony about the Creator (1:19–23). With this additional facet of glory in view, we begin to see that the process of glorification reestablishes proper relationships between human and nonhuman creation. For, "the glory of the children of God is the nurturing role which human beings were to have over the earth (Gen. 1.28; 2.15)."[16] Yet, even though God's justifying and liberating grace has broken into the human experience, sin continues to wield destructive power. It is no wonder, then, that

---

14. John Collins indicates that "apocalyptic eschatology" may not always refer to an end of history. "All the apocalypses, however, involve a transcendent eschatology that looks for retribution beyond the bounds of history"; thus, some judgment is involved (Collins, *Apocalyptic Imagination*, 9). While Rom 8:18–39 refers only obliquely to an "end" of history, it explicitly describes the future judgment of those in Christ in 8:33–39 with the conclusion that the Judge is the suffering Messiah who intercedes for his brothers and sisters. In light of these factors, it is clear that Romans presents a form of apocalyptic eschatology, or as Collins suggests, it shares affinities with apocalyptic eschatology (9).

15. Matera, *Romans*, 200.

16. Keesmaat, *Paul and His Story*, 100–101.

creation looks forward to the time when humanity's propensity towards sin will ultimately be healed through their glorification.

In this time of waiting, Paul expects followers of Christ continually to resist the enslaving influence of sin and the impulses to live in ways that frustrate and even destroy God's creation (Rom 6:1–23). More positively, Paul believes Christians will "exercise dominion in life" (5:17 NRSV), which replaces the "slavery of destruction" that human sin so often imposes upon the creation (8:21). Rather than carrying out their dominion over creation in ways that bring curse, hostility, and destruction, they exercise servant leadership in a way that "heals rather than destroys."[17]

Paul's subsequent reflections on creation in 8:20–22 further illustrate and confirm the interdependent relationship between humanity's salvation and creation's liberation. Their common experiences of oppression and destruction open into common and interdependent destinies of liberation. Creation awaits the appearance and revealing of the transformed, glorified, resurrected sons of God because only then will it too be liberated from its subjection to frustration and its slavery to destruction.[18]

5.2 Romans 8:21: Creation's Liberation

Although creation is currently "subjected to frustration" and enslaved to "destruction" (8:20–21, see 4.2–3), Paul claims that God nevertheless intends a very different future for it. Paul most clearly describes this future in 8:21, exclaiming, "the creation itself will be liberated from the slavery of destruction into the liberation of the glory of God's children." While the majority of Paul's letter to this point has explained the ways in which God liberates humanity, he here declares that nonhuman creation too is destined for liberation. In fact, Paul's assertion in 8:21 suggests that creation's liberation depends upon the culmination of God's liberation of humanity by way of their glorification. The practical implication of this creation-wide, divine right making is that human righteousness and glory establish the context in which creation might experience its own form of liberation. In other words, creation's liberation goes hand in hand with liberated, righteous human

---

17. Jewett, *Romans*, 519.

18. Paul connects his statement in 8:19 about creation's expectation to his explanation in 8:20 about creation's subjection with the word "for," indicating that creation's subjection to frustration is the reason why creation now eagerly anticipates the apocalypse of the sons of God.

identity and activity that reflects God's own glory. In order to understand these dynamics at work in Rom 8:21, we will examine the meaning and function of "will be liberated" (ἐλευθερωθήσεται) and its cognate noun "liberation" (ἐλευθερίαν), the meaning of δόξης, and the relationships between these concepts as they occur together in the phrase "into the liberation of the glory of God's children" (εἰς τὴν ἐλευθερίαν τῆς δόξης τῶν τέκνων τοῦ θεοῦ, 8:21).

In Rom 8:21, Paul employs the verb ἐλευθερόω (to liberate, to cause "someone to be freed from domination") and the noun ἐλευθερία (liberty, "the state of being free").[19] By using the future passive ἐλευθερωθήσεται, Paul likely points to God and/or Jesus Christ as the agent(s) who enact(s) this liberation.[20] Paul's earlier depiction of God's gracious salvation of humans as a form of liberation from sin and death (6:18, 22) suggests that the passive in 8:21 is a divine passive. With the verb pointing toward God's action in the context of Romans, the condition of ἐλευθερία likely depends upon God's work of liberation. Consequently, the noun here does not refer to an unchanging, ontological condition (in other words, liberty/freedom). Instead, it points toward a new condition that comes from God's emancipation of human beings ("liberation"). On account of this connotation, I often use the term "liberation" ("the state of being liberated")[21] rather than "liberty" to call attention to this newfound condition that God's human and nonhuman creation enjoy.[22]

While Paul directs the reader's attention to liberation, he nevertheless describes the negative condition *from which* creation will be delivered: it "will be liberated from the slavery of destruction" (ἐλευθερωθήσεται ἀπὸ τῆς δουλείας τῆς φθορᾶς). As discussed in 4.2, the slavery that produces destruction likely results—at least in part—from human dominion that has been deployed in violent, sinful, destructive ways. It is from this enslaved condition that God intends to free creation, and the prepositional phrase (εἰς τὴν ἐλευθερίαν τῆς δόξης τῶν τέκνων τοῦ θεοῦ) describes the positive

---

19. BDAG, 316.

20. We find support for understanding ἐλευθερωθήσεται as a divine passive, in part, in chapters 6–8 where Paul repeatedly uses the verb ἐλευθερόω and its cognates to describe the positive effects that result from God's gracious salvation. Through Jesus Christ, God has liberated people from sin and death so that they might grow in holiness and experience eternal life (6:18, 22; 8:2). See 3.2.2 for more discussion.

21. "Liberation."

22. In consultation with LSJ and BDAG, it appears no Greek equivalent exists for the English, "liberation." The noun ἐλευθερία is the primary term at Paul's disposal.

consequences of and conditions for creation's liberation. Yet even more nuance might be gleaned from this long prepositional phrase.

5.2.1 Liberation Produced by Glory

Earlier in the letter, Paul describes the liberation that humans enjoy through Jesus Christ as a process of regaining access to and participating in God's glory, the glory they had exchanged for a poor image of a destructible human, etc. (1:23; 5:2). For human creatures, liberation attends their experience of God's glory. When Paul considers the nonhuman creation in 8:21 he suggests that its liberation too is closely associated with glory, for nonhuman creation will be liberated εἰς τὴν ἐλευθερίαν τῆς δόξης τῶν τέκνων τοῦ θεοῦ.[23] This prepositional phrase contains three sets of genitive nouns, all of which can be interpreted in a variety of ways. Since the genitive construction in Greek is more multivalent than in English, it is worthwhile clarifying each set of genitive relationships in this phrase. The context of the letter suggests that the most probable syntactical relationships are as follows: 1) τοῦ θεοῦ functions as a possessive genitive in relation to τῶν τέκνων and is best rendered, "God's children";[24] 2) τῶν τέκνων relates directly to τῆς δόξης (rather than to τὴν ἐλευθερίαν) as a genitive of possession and could be translated "children's glory";[25] and 3) τῆς δόξης relates to τὴν ἐλευθερίαν

---

23. In 8:21a, Paul also employs a genitive construction to describe creation's slavery ("the slavery characterized by destruction"/"the slavery that brings about destruction"), as we considered in 4.2.2.

24. This is the most straightforward genitive relationship since the genitive τοῦ θεοῦ is quite clearly possessive, indicating that "the children" are possessed by or defined in relation to God.

25. Some argue, however, that "children" modifies *liberation* instead of *glory*. For this to be the case, however, δόξης would function as an attributive genitive to ἐλευθερίαν ("glorious liberty") so that τῶν τέκνων could modify the distal head noun, ἐλευθερίαν, rather than the more proximate noun, δόξης. In other words, this interpretation depends upon the chain of genitives being interrupted so that the phrase would be rendered, "glorious *liberty* of God's children." This is the option followed by Daniel Wallace (Wallace, *Greek Grammar Beyond the Basics*, 87-88).

However, the most common approach in interpreting this set of relationships is to take τῶν τέκνων as modifying δόξης and τῆς δόξης as modifying τὴν ἐλευθερίαν. Cranfield assumes as much when he claims, "τῶν τέκνων τοῦ θεοῦ is dependent on τῆς δόξης, not directly on τὴν ἐλευθερίαν" (*Critical and Exegetical Commentary*, 416n1). In other words, "of the children of God" modifies "glory" rather than "liberation" so that the translation would read: "the liberation of the glory of God's children." This interpretation follows the traditional Greek grammatical principle that in a chain of genitive nouns "each successive

as a genitive of production, which gives rise to the translation: "the glory that produces liberation."[26] On the basis of these syntactical relationships, εἰς τὴν ἐλευθερίαν τῆς δόξης τῶν τέκνων τοῦ θεοῦ means that creation will enter the liberation *produced by* the glory that God's children will *possess* or experience.

According to this reading, "glory" represents a powerful divine force from outside the human and nonhuman sphere that brings about liberation from slavery to death (for humans) and liberation from slavery to destruction (for creation). We find this interpretation supported elsewhere in Romans, especially when Paul explains that Christ was raised from the dead by the *glory* of the Father (6:4). "Glory" here functions as a life giving, divine quality or power. Paul furthermore explains that those who are in Christ may participate in this life-transforming glory of God, so much so that the children of God—as co-heirs of Christ—suffer with Christ and may be *glorified* with him (5:2; 8:17). And this glory is about to be revealed "in us" (8:18). It is this revelation of glory in and among humans for which the creation waits (8:19). These references to glory also indicate that glory is something God and Jesus Christ share with humanity. Glory will be possessed—but not produced—by God's children on account of God's gracious desire to share it with them.[27] The divine glory God shares with creation

---

[genitive] modifies the one that precedes it" (Wallace, *Greek Grammar Beyond the Basics*, 87. See also, Blass and Debrunner, *Greek Grammar*, 93). Because of this principle and Paul's wider use of the term glory, I interpret τῶν τέκνων as directly associated with δόξης and not ἐλευθερίαν.

26. As a genitive of production, δόξης brings about ἐλευθερίαν ("the liberation produced by glory") (see Wallace, *Greek Grammar Beyond the Basics*, 104–6). It should be noted, however, that δόξης may stand in at least four other types of relationships with ἐλευθερίαν according to Greek syntax. (1) If considered a genitive of product, δόξης would be produced by ἐλευθερίαν ("the liberation that produces glory") (see Wallace, *Greek Grammar Beyond the Basics*, 106–7). (2) Δόξης could function as an attributive genitive, specifying the quality or character of ἐλευθερίαν ("glorious liberation") (86–88). Wallace and NET choose this syntactical function with the translation, "glorious freedom." (3) Δόξης could be a genitive of apposition so that it identifies the type of ἐλευθερίαν Paul has in mind ("liberation that is glory") (see 95–100). Or, (4) δόξης may function as a possessive genitive ("glory's liberation" or "the liberation belonging to glory") (see 81–82). Along these lines, Douglas Moo understands τῆς δόξης to function "loosely" as a possessive (Moo, *Epistle to the Romans*, 517n48). Interpreters often slip between these various interpretations. For the reasons explained in the main text, the genitive of production appears to be the most convincing interpretation of τὴν ἐλευθερίαν τῆς δόξης.

27. By interpreting this passage in ways that exclusively focus on the glorification and resurrection of human beings, I do not deny the possibility that Christians may also understand it to be pointing towards the resurrection of nonhuman living things. John

appears to be a primary means by which God accomplishes the divine work of making alive (*zōopoiēsis*).

With glory exercising such gravitational force in Paul's story of creation, this eschatological glory is the likeliest source of liberation foretold in 8:21. God's glory, in other words, powerfully transforms the human situation so that *glory* produces liberation (most especially liberation from the reign of death, 5:14). This liberation, in turn, extends from God's people to the whole creation.[28] Glory, then, is not a mere attribute of creation's liberation (as would be captured by the translation "glorious liberation")[29] but liberation's source. The glorification of humanity provides the context in which nonhuman creation can experience liberation from the slavery to destruction. Thus, although God subjected creation to humanity (Gen 1:26–28), God did so "in hope that the creation itself will be liberated from the slavery of destruction into the liberation *produced by* the glory that is *possessed by* God's children" (8:20b–21).

The interpretation of creation's liberation as being brought about by glory—in particular the eschatological glory God's people will receive as they experience bodily resurrection (as suggested by 8:18 and 8:23)—follows the path laid out by Paul's story of creation. This narrative logic recognizes not only that God is the true source of glory and goodness but also that God has placed humanity in a position of power and responsibility over the nonhuman creation. Although people currently sin and bring about frustration and destruction upon the creation, God through Jesus Christ liberates humanity from sin and death. Then, by the Spirit, God will ultimately glorify humanity in the *zōopoietical* process of resurrection. As a result of humanity's liberation and glorification, the nonhuman creation at last will be liberated from its slavery to destruction.[30] Nonhuman creation

---

Wesley seems to have had this hope, as his sermon "The General Deliverance" indicates. For more discussion, see Burroughs, "Wesleyan Ecological Hermeneutic," 41.

28. Glorification with Christ is further fleshed out in 8:29–30, where Paul proclaims that those whom God foreknew, God predestined to be conformed to the Son's image in order that he would be the firstborn among many siblings. Equally striking as being conformed to Christ is Paul's declaration that those whom God justified God also *glorified* (8:30). By using the aorist tense of δοξάζω, Paul demonstrates supreme confidence in God's faithfulness to complete the work of New Creation. From this context, then, "the liberation of the glory of the children of God" appears to involve the resurrected, or glorified, existence that God's children, Jesus's siblings, will fully enjoy in the eschaton.

29. "Glorious liberty" is the translational choice of the New English Translation (NET).

30. Keesmaat indicates that glorification reverses the "loss of glory that results from

will be liberated *into* the liberation that comes from God's glorification of human beings. Since the condition and well-being of humanity affects the condition and well-being of the nonhuman creation, the liberation into which creation will be liberated is the liberation marked by and even produced by God's glorification of human beings. Until that moment of ultimate liberation and glorification, however, the whole nonhuman creation collectively groans and labors.

5.3 Romans 8:22: Creation's Co-Groaning and Co-Laboring

After delighting in the glorious prospect of the creation being liberated from destructive forms of bondage (8:21), Paul offers evidence for this optimistic conclusion by directing his audience's attention to phenomena in creation, declaring: "For we know that the whole creation is collectively groaning and laboring even till now" (8:22).[31] By his use of the verb "we know" (οἴδαμεν), Paul suggests that there is something about the story of creation or the human experience that causes followers of Christ to know of creation's collective groaning and laboring together. Yet, what does this metaphor of parturition mean? It can be variously interpreted as expressing either a negative or positive situation.

Interpreters frequently understand creation's groaning and laboring as a negative experience, as referring to creation's suffering, perhaps even its pointless suffering. According to this common interpretation, collective groaning and laboring is just one more way in which Paul indicates that creation suffers, maybe even on account of human sin.[32] In their ecologically-informed treatment of Rom 8:19–23, David Horrell, Cherryl Hunt, and Christopher Southgate summarize two dominant interpretations of creation's laboring, both of which are negative. Laboring is either another way Paul describes creation's "suffering of decay and death," or it indicates creation's "frustration at being unable to fulfill its purpose in God's plans."[33]

---

idolatry in Rom 1:23" ("Land, Idolatry, and Justice, 102). This "loss of 'glory' and its restoration," in turn, "has very tangible effects on the land," as Paul's Scriptures testify (102).

31. At 8:22, Paul indicates that it is "all" or the "whole," πᾶσα, creation that is the topic of conversation. It is unclear whether Paul uses πᾶσα here for emphasis or to distinguish the constituents of "creation" (8:19–21) from the "whole creation." I am inclined to understand πᾶσα as emphatic.

32. Moo, "Romans 8.19–22," 83–85.

33. Horrell, Hunt, and Southgate, *Greening Paul*, 77. Nevertheless, the authors recognize the ways in which hope permeates Rom 8. They explain, "Despite the suffering that

Beverly Gaventa arrives at a similarly negative view when interrogating creation's role in the birth of the New Creation. She asserts that the creation births "[e]xactly nothing, because creation itself is captive to nothingness, to 'futility.'"[34] Gaventa highlights the fact that the "offspring" for which creation labors is actually an adopted people, the redeemed corporate body, resurrected humanity (Rom 8:23). She goes on to point out that "[i]t seems odd to imagine a woman in labor who cries out with longing for adoption."[35]

These perspectives resist any interpretation that would understand Paul's image of creation groaning and laboring as positive and productive.[36] The image of laboring, in this view, merely captures the paradox with which Paul wrestles in this chapter, namely hope in the midst of suffering. Creation waits for God to intervene, to stop its suffering, and to do something entirely new; creation "longs for . . . God's action, not its own."[37] Creation's groaning and laboring signifies its pain, not its productivity, as creation stands by as a spectator of the divine drama. In this dependent position, creation would still seem "*to be sold* into slavery, *despite* the resurrection of Jesus Christ and the new life of believers."[38] Creation, in this view, is ontologically incapable of laboring in a positive and productive fashion alongside God. It's collective groaning and laboring stands as a metaphor for the agonies of the present time, in which a cosmic battle takes place.[39]

This understanding of Rom 8:22, however, does not take full account of several textual features or the rhetorical point of the passage. While encapsulating creation's real suffering, Paul's imagery of childbirth also depicts this suffering as temporary and productive, even if metaphorically so. Unfortunately, predominant modern English translations obscure the precise meaning of the underlying Greek text by using perfect tense instead

---

is the current and inevitable experience of those who are in Christ (8:17), the hope and certainty of their salvation cannot be shaken—and it is in the context of this declaration of hope that Paul locates the experience of the Christians in Rome within the wider story of the whole creation" (64–65).

34. Gaventa, "Birthing of Creation," 57.

35. Gaventa, "Birthing of Creation," 57.

36. In some contrast, Tonstad suggests creation's laboring here is presented as a "productive" or at least "hopeful" form of pain (Tonstad, *Letter to the Romans*, 238). However, Tonstad insufficiently identifies the ways in which creation's groaning and laboring might be productive.

37. Gaventa, "Birthing of Creation," 57.

38. Gaventa, "Birthing of Creation," 60. Emphasis added.

39. Gaventa, "Birthing of Creation," 61.

of present tense verbs and giving undue weight to groaning and the *pains* involved in laboring. Thus, although the Greek states, οἴδαμεν γάρ ὅτι πᾶσα ἡ κτίσις συστενάζει καὶ συνωδίνει ἄχρι τοῦ νῦν, the NRSV translates it as: "[w]e know that the whole creation *has been* groaning in labor *pains* until now" (8:22, emphasis added). However, the meaning and function of the present tense verbs συστενάζει ("groans together") and συνωδίνει ("labors together") and the phrase ἄχρι τοῦ νῦν ("until now") suggest that Paul's metaphor of parturition describes not only creation's current experience of intense anguish but also a positive and productive situation. Thus, the verse's specific wording, syntax, and scriptural motifs suggest it should be understood in a positive light so that creation's collective groans and labor pains stand not as signs of death but as harbingers of new life.[40]

5.3.1 Co-Groaning

Paul's compound verb for co-groaning, συστενάζει, occurs only here in the biblical canon. It combines the preposition σύν and the verb στενάζω, the latter of which is derived from the root verb στένω.[41] While στένω simply means "to moan, sigh, groan," στενάζω connotes an intensified state of affairs: "to sigh often, sigh deeply."[42] The prefix σύν adds the concept "with" or "together" so that the compound verb means "to lament with" or "to groan together with."[43]

Groaning in both Greek and English can have either negative or neutral connotations. Understood in a negative light, στενάζω refers to an expression of mourning or lament. Taken more neutrally and literally, it describes the sounds expressed during physical work and pain.[44] As with

---

40. Harry Alan Hahne holds this perspective and asserts: "Although a sensitive person could perceive the suffering of nature, only the eyes of faith in light of divine revelation can see that the suffering of creation is the travail of birth, not the agony of death" (Hahne, *Corruption and Redemption of Creation*, 200).

41. LSJ, 744; BDAG, 942, 78–79.

42. LSJ, 744.

43. BDAG, 978.

44. BDAG illustrates the two nuances by providing two entries for στενάζω, the first with the definition "to express oneself involuntarily in the face of an undesirable circumstance" and the second with the definition "to express discontent" as a "figurative extension of 1" (BDAG, 942). Lamenting intentionally expresses one's discontent with current circumstances so that the sounds of groaning often voice metaphorical, emotional, or physical pain, communicating one's wish to have painful circumstances removed. Taken

all language, the context determines the specific connotation in any given situation. When the context denotes experiences of grief, στενάζω most appropriately means, "to complain,"[45] lament, or groan because of negative circumstances, often in the hope of changing them. This is by far the most common meaning in the Greek translations of the Tanakh.[46] It occurs in Exod 2:23–24, for example, to describe the groaning of the Hebrew slaves in Egypt. But when στενάζω occurs alongside depictions of childbearing—whether literal or metaphorical—it connotes "groaning," a verbal expression of pain and distress and the verbalized exhalations involved in the physical work of laboring (in other words, "grunting"; see Jer 4:31). With this wide range of meaning, the verb συστενάζω as it occurs in Rom 8:22 (as well as the verb στενάζομεν in 8:24 and the noun στεναγμοῖς in 8:26)

---

more neutrally and literally, groaning implies that the actor is experiencing literal or physical pain or exertion and thus grunts or groans.

45. BDAG, 942.

46. The lexeme στενάζω occurs in several noteworthy texts of the Greek translation of the Tanakh. The first such occurrence, however, comes in the context of childbirth and occurs at Gen 3:16 LXX where God declares that God will increase woman's pain and groaning (στεναγμόν) in the bearing of children (τέξῃ τέκνα) because Eve transgressed God's command by eating the forbidden fruit. The term does not occur again until Exodus, when God hears the groaning (στεναγμόν) of the Hebrews whom the Egyptians enslaved (Exod 2:23–24; 6:5). God then remembers the covenant with Abraham and delivers the people from their bondage. Similarly, at Judg 2:18, we learn that God sends a judge to deliver the people whenever they groaned under various forms of oppression. Again, Ps 11:6 LXX depicts God rising up to save those people who groan under various forms of oppression, proclaiming, "'Due to the wretchedness of the poor and due to the groaning [στεναγμοῦ] of the needy, I will now rise up,' says the Lord" (NETS). In addition to the term "groaning," the Greek translation of Ps 11:6 employs νῦν, "now," and the verb ἀνίστημι, "I rise" to describe God's quick response to the oppression of the poor. It is interesting that this Psalm makes it appear as though God dwells in the same conditions as the poor and day-laborers. It is as though God experiences their oppression and ultimately decides to rise from it. The Judean exiles, bereaved of their homeland, likewise undergo oppression but, as Isa 35:10 and 51:11 herald, when God brings the Judeans back to Zion they will rejoice and no longer groan (στεναγμός).

The Greek translation of the Tanakh infrequently identifies a nonhuman member of creation as groaning, but one example is Job 31:38. Job declares: "'"if at any time the land groaned over [ἐστέναξεν] me and if too its furrows wept with one accord and if too I ate its strength alone, without payment, and if too I, in throwing it away, grieved the soul of the land's owner, then may nettles come forth to me instead of wheat, and a bramble instead of barley" (31:38–40 NETS). Job here reckons that the land can indeed groan or lament and, in terms reminiscent of Gen 3, that a just punishment for human crimes against the land and its human owners and workers would entail inedible weeds growing in place of edible grains.

can thereby signify either the intentional activity of lamenting or the less consciously controlled activity of groaning in pain and physical activity.

In light of Paul's overall optimism in this pericope (for example, his strong conviction that creation eagerly anticipates the apocalypse), it seems unlikely that συστενάζει carries a thoroughly pessimistic tone. In its appearance with ὠδίνω ("to labor"), it connotes groaning in painful and difficult work and does not primarily refer to lamenting (for more discussion, see 5.3.2).[47] Any overtones of lament in creation's groaning rise out of distorted human–nonhuman relationships, which themselves result from human injustice and violence.[48] Because humans resist God's purposes for creation-wide life and flourishing, creation endures a subjected and enslaved condition from which God's work of making right and making alive will liberate it. Thus, through its co-groaning with believers and with the Spirit (8:23, 26), creation is not mourning as if the end of life has come, for it eagerly anticipates the resurrection of God's children and the liberation that this resurrection will bring. Creation may indeed collectively groan in agony under experiences of pain. Yet, like a woman in the midst of childbearing, the immediate context softens this agony with an overriding hope. The successful "birth" of God's resurrected children and the consequent "delivery" of the nonhuman creation into their liberation are certain, for Jesus the firstborn has already opened the passage leading from death to

---

47. Some recent ecological interpretations of Rom 8:22 argue that Paul intends to connote *lamentation* by his use of συστενάζει. Drawing upon the foundational work of Sylvia Keesmaat (Keesmaat, *Paul and His Story*, 106–10, 124–33), Laurie Braaten claims: "Paul employed a well known biblical concept in Romans 8:22—the entire creation is groaning in lament because of a history of ongoing human sin and an accompanying divine judgment" (Braaten, "All Creation Groans," 152–53). While Braaten admits that the Tanakh rarely uses the verb στενάζω to describe the earth as lamenting (instead, the verb πενθέω is used), he insists Rom 8:22 refers primarily to creation's lamentation. However, because Paul pairs the verb συστενάζω with συνωδίνω, this collocation narrows the semantic range of συστενάζει from groaning/lamenting/mourning to groaning/grunting. If Paul had wanted clearly to convey the meaning of "lament," he could have used the verb πενθέω, which has a narrow semantic range (specifically referring to expressions of grief). BDAG gives two definitions for the verb πενθέω, the intransitive "to experience sadness as the result of some condition or circumstance" and the transitive "to engage in mourning for one who is dead" (BDAG, 795).

48. Although I disagree with Keesmaat's conclusion that συστενάζει refers first and foremost to creation's groaning in lament, I agree that creation's condition of suffering results from "human sin" ("Land, Idolatry, and Justice," 98). I also agree with Keesmaat that "sin" should not be understood individualistically, since creation's suffering was due, in large measure during Paul's day, to "the exploitative economic practices and violent militarism of Roman imperial rule" (98).

resurrection life (8:29). Thus, it may be that for creation, as any midwife would confirm, co-groaning during labor and delivery is in fact positive and productive; groaning helps to move the process along even when it expresses intense pain and agony.[49]

But creation is not alone in its groaning. Paul uses this same root word to describe the *groaning* of redeemed humanity and the Spirit (8:22, 23, 26). He thereby groups these diverse actors into a common activity and cause.[50] Just as a midwife or partner might groan with a laboring woman (as a means of coaching, of sympathy, and as a verbal expression of the hard work involved in assisting childbirth), humans and the Spirit groan with the laboring creation toward the resurrection ("the redemption of our body," 8:23). Groaning does not itself fully relieve the intense pain, but it does provide an outlet for the pain and expresses to others that the moments of painful, yet productive, contractions have come.

5.3.2 Co-Laboring

In English "to labor" can denote any kind of work, but the Greek term ὠδίνω refers specifically to the process of childbirth, whether literal or metaphorical. It typically occurs in the Greek translations of the Tanakh and Greek New Testament as an intransitive verb and refers to the *process of laboring* rather than the *result of delivery*.[51] Whether it has a metaphorical or literal connotation, ὠδίνω rarely appears with a direct object, that is, without an

---

49. For example, see Gaskin, *Spiritual Midwifery*; Simkin, *Birth Partner*. My emphasis on creation's hopeful outlook does not diminish the fact that hopelessness, fear, and a lack of confidence can also attend the birthing process.

50. In a similar vein, Barbara Rossing states: "We and the whole creation participate in this birth together. God co-groans and co-labors with us and with creation (Rom 8:22), the apostle Paul writes, using the Greek prefix *syn* to underscore solidarity" (Rossing, "Reimagining Eschatology," 330). Although Rossing indicates that God "co-labors" with creation, the text only indicates that creation labors, whereas God's Spirit and people groan along with creation.

51. J. Louis Martyn gets this partially right when he explains in his commentary on Galatians that "in its *metaphorical* use the verb [ὠδίνω] usually lacks the direct object, providing only a picture of suffering comparable to that of a woman in labor, and thus useful even to refer to anguish experienced by a man," or, in the case of Rom 8:22, nonhuman creation (Martyn, *Galatians*, 427. Emphasis added). This is only partially correct because, as I go on to demonstrate in the main text, ὠδίνω seldom takes a direct object even when it is used literally, unless it occurs with a transitive verb, such as τίκτω.

intervening transitive verb such as τίκτω, "give birth (to), bear."⁵² When the semantic focus is upon the result of laboring—the delivery of a literal or metaphorical offspring—the verb τίκτω most often is used and is accompanied by a direct object.⁵³ Yet, this is not the case in 8:22. Instead, Paul's use of the verb ὠδίνω occurs without a direct object and is therefore in keeping with the verb's typical usage. His focus appears to be upon creation's collective laboring *process* rather than its delivery of explicitly named offspring.

Although the thought of nonhuman creation as *laboring in childbirth* may appear novel, this image does occur in another passage in the Christian Scriptures. In the Greek translation of Isa 66:8, γῆ (land, earth) and Zion occur as the subjects of the verb ὠδίνω. Verging on the miraculous, Isa 66:8–10 LXX personifies the earth and Zion as women who give birth to a whole people suddenly, apart from the typical signs of labor and delivery. This passage functions to inspire its readers with hope as they undergo suffering and devastation. With provocative questions, the Lord asks defeated and exiled Israel:

> Can earth labor in one day (ἦ ὤδινεν γῆ ἐν μιᾷ ἡμέρᾳ), or can a nation be born (ἐτέχθη ἔθνος) at once, that Zion labored and delivered

---

52. BDAG, 1004. The few instances in which ὠδίνω occurs in the Greek translation of the Tanakh with its own direct object include: Ps 7:15 (metaphorical); Song 8:5 (literal); and Isa 51:2 (literal). More often, the metaphorical use of ὠδίνω appears with no direct object: Hab 3:10; Isa 26:18; Mic 4:10; Isa 45:10; Jer 30:16 (LXX). Literal uses of ὠδίνω also appear more often without than with a direct object: Isa 26:17; 54:1; 66:7, 8; Jer 4:31. In Isa 23:4 ὠδίνω occurs as one of the verbs in a compound predicate that takes a direct object; however, τίκτω appears between ὠδίνω and the direct object.

In the New Testament, ὠδίνω and its compounds occur only at Rom 8:22; Gal 4:19, 27; and Rev 12:2. Only Gal 4:19 provides a direct object for the verb, which, as Martyn indicates, functions metaphorically. Gal 4:27 and Rev 12:2 use ὠδίνω in literal ways without direct objects and Rom 8:22 uses the verb either metaphorically or literally without a direct object. However, τίκτω often appears with a direct object: Matt 1:21, 23, 25; Luke 1:31; 2:7, 11; Heb 6:7; James 1:15 (metaphorical use); Rev 12:4, 5, 13. Τίκτω may also occur without a direct object: Luke 1:57; John 16:21; Gal 4:27; Rev 12:2.

53. Too many examples of a direct object occurring with the verb τίκτω appear in the Greek translation of the Tanakh to be listed here in full, especially since this construction appears in many stories that read almost like genealogies and in which the mothers are mentioned (see especially, Gen 30; 36; 1 Chr 1; 2; 7). Other examples in which a direct object occurs with literal instances of τίκτω include: Gen 3:16; 4:1, 2, 17, 20, 22, 25; 16:11, 15, 16; 17:19; Exod 2:2, 22; Lev 12:2, 5; Deut 28:57; Judg 8:31; Ruth 4:15, 17; 1 Sam 1:20; 2 Sam 11:27; 1 Kgs 13:2; Hos 1:3, 6, 8; Isa 7:14, 66:7; Jer 15:10. Even when used metaphorically, τίκτω often occurs with a direct object (e.g., Num 11:12; Ps 7:15; Prov 10:23; Isa 59:4; 66:8; Ezek 23:4). Yet, it can also occur without a direct object (e.g., Isa 13:8; 26:18). The text of Heb 6:7 is noteworthy since it has land (γῆ) giving birth (τίκτουσα) to grass.

her children (ὤδινεν καὶ ἔτεκεν Σιων τὰ παιδία αὐτῆς)?... Consider, do I not make both the one who begets and the infertile woman, says God? Rejoice, Jerusalem! Make a feast-day in Jerusalem all those who love her![54]

This passage in Third Isaiah, the Greek translation of which uniquely portrays the earth as laboring, occurs in a context that explains the Lord shall: (1) gather all the nations so that they behold God's glory (Isa 66:18–19); (2) receive the Israelite exiles from the nations as though they were priests (66:20–21); and (3) make a New Heaven and New Earth that remains ever before God just as the descendants of Israel shall remain (66:22).[55] It is as if the land itself and the city of Zion have suddenly given birth to God's people.

These metaphorical uses of ὠδίνω highlight the miraculous nature of Israel's anticipated return from exile even as they depict nonhuman elements (i.e., the land) and a geographical location (i.e., Zion) as laboring and

---

54. Isaiah 66:8–10 LXX, author's translation. Since the apostle Paul and the early Christians would have been most familiar with the Greek translations of Isaiah, I mostly rely on these versions as opposed to the Masoretic text. The Greek translation of Isa 66:8 differs from the Hebrew wording in a startling way. The Hebrew *Vorlage* employs a passive verb, reading, "Shall earth be born in one day?" In contrast, the Greek presents "earth" as the subject of the active verb "labor" (ὤδινεν). Several interesting textual variants exist for the Greek text of Isa 66:8. The most interesting is the text attributed to Symmachus (as found in Origen's Hexapla). Whereas the Göttingen text reads εἰ ὤδινε γῆ ἐν μιᾷ ἡμέρᾳ, "if earth labors in one day," Symmachus reads ἄρα ὠδινήσει γῆ ἐν μιᾷ ἡμέρᾳ, "then will earth labor in one day?" (Ziegler, *Isaias*, 14:366). This early witness of the Greek translation of the Tanakh places the verb in the future tense but retains the active voice of the Greek tradition (as opposed to the Masoretic text of the Hebrew Bible). Another textual difference that occurs as a correction in the text of the Codex Sinaiticus of Isa 66:8 is the replacement of γῆ with γυνή. The corrector, it may be presumed, found it disconcerting or abnormal to consider the land as "laboring" (14:366).

55. In his commentary on Isa 40–66, John Oswalt explains, "Gone will be the days when [Jerusalem] was stripped and barren, when its children were slaughtered, and when it seemed impossible that it could ever give birth again. Now its children will spring to life effortlessly, and a future of fecundity and laughter stretches endlessly ahead" (*Book of Isaiah*, 674). Despite the language expressing instantaneous birth or salvation in the text, Oswalt suggests understanding this passage as pointing towards any possible "number of events in redemption history"; for example, "[t]he day will come when Christ, Isaiah's Servant/Messiah, will break through the skies, and in a single moment Zion will give birth to a brand-new people, a people forever set free from the curse of sin" (675). Depending primarily on the Hebrew text in this interpretation, Oswalt highlights the way in which the passage depicts the surreal image of a land (or, more generally, "earth") being born. The Greek translation provides an even bolder portrait of nonhuman activity in which the land actually labors.

then delivering live human offspring.⁵⁶ With this scriptural background, Paul's portrayal of the whole creation as collectively laboring (συνωδίνει) in Rom 8:22 appears less peculiar. Moreover, it implies that creation's activity of collective laboring is not a negative, purposeless experience. Laboring looks forward to a future birth of innumerable children of God.

5.3.3 Co-Groaning and Co-Laboring Until Now

When we consider συστενάζει and συνωδίνει in connection with the prepositional phrase ἄχρι τοῦ νῦν ("until now") Paul's depiction of creation's activity takes on temporal significance. However, since no other New Testament text coordinates a present tense verb with the phrase ἄχρι τοῦ νῦν, the construction is ambiguous. We are left to infer its meaning from slightly analogous uses of the preposition and adverb.

Several New Testament texts coordinate present tense verbs with the term "until" (ἄχρι) but without the additional word "now." These uses may be interpreted in one of two ways. The first interpretation understands "until" to refer to the end point at which an activity ceases.⁵⁷ Read in this way, Rom 8:22 would suggest that creation collectively groans and labors up to this present time, but *now* it has stopped. The second option interprets "until" not as noting an end point but as an indication of the ongoing and

---

56. Noting Paul's reference to labor in Gal 4:19 and his quotation of Isa 54:1 in Gal 4:27, Eastman examines two texts in Isaiah (54:1 and 66:7–9) that describe the miraculous situation in which a woman bears a child but does not endure the pains of labor to do so. She concludes: "these texts develop the motif of the barren mother who miraculously becomes the mother of a multitude . . . [they] use the metaphor of miraculous birth to emphasize God's power and faithfulness over against human weakness" (Eastman, *Recovering Paul's Mother Tongue*, 115–16). Eastman goes on to explain that while Paul labors so that Christ might be formed in the Galatian Christians, God also is at work in and through Paul's labor (120–21). Thus, "Paul's 'labor' represents God's 'labor,' both as intense anguish on behalf of God's people and as creative power bringing the new creation to birth" (120–21). Because Isa 66:20 arguably stands behind Paul's commitment to take up a collection from among the nations in honor of God and on behalf of God's people in Jerusalem (Rom 15:16) (Jewett, *Romans*, 907; Elliott, *Arrogance of the Nations*, 47), Isaiah's earlier imagery of earth and Zion laboring in 66:8–10 may have also shaped his imagination so that he could conceive of creation as laboring even as God miraculously works to deliver forth the children of God through it.

57. For example, Gal 4:2 states, "but they *remain* under guardians and trustees *until* the date set by the father," (NRSV, emphasis added). The "date set by the father" refers to a future event that will bring the existence under guardians and trustees to an end.

lingering nature of the present action.⁵⁸ This would lead us to translate the verse as follows: "the whole creation is [and continues] groaning and laboring together even until now."

This second option takes seriously Paul's use of present tense verbs as well as his unique wording of "until now." It also best captures the sense of Rom 8:22 in its epistolary context. According to Romans, something important has happened in the "now." Paul's understanding of "now" is informed by a recent event—the apocalyptic life, death, and resurrection of Jesus Christ (Rom 1:16-17; 3:21-26).⁵⁹ By employing the term "now" throughout Romans, Paul indicates that the salvation wrought in and through Christ has concrete effects on the present lives of the faithful.⁶⁰

---

58. For example, 1 Cor 4:11 explains, "To [or, until] the present hour we are hungry and thirsty, we are poorly clothed and beaten and homeless" (NRSV). Here, Paul describes his conditions of suffering in ministry that continue even into the present time (and, apparently, began relatively recently, sometime after Paul became a follower of Jesus, ἄχρι τῆς ἄρτι ὥρας). A similar usage occurs in Acts 2:29. 2 Cor 3:14 also indicates that a certain condition continues into the present: "Indeed, to this very day [ἄχρι γὰρ τῆς σήμερον ἡμέρας], when they hear the reading of the old covenant, that same veil is still there, since only in Christ is it set aside" (NRSV). Although Phil 1:5 does not have a present tense verb occurring near ἄχρι, the verse does contain the same phrase as Rom 8:22, namely, ἄχρι τοῦ νῦν. There, Paul delights that the Philippians have been "sharing in the gospel from the first day until now" (Phil 1:5 NRSV). Clearly, the Philippians continue to share in the gospel into the present, into the "now," of Paul's writing this letter.

59. Although they do not develop an apocalyptic reading of Rom 8:19-22 to the same degree as I do, Horrell, Hunt, and Southgate also recognize the decisive moment in which Paul wrote: "This story is not simply linear, or steadily progressive: it is punctuated by key moments of which the coming of Christ is *the* definitive, climactic moment, which shows that the story is in its final chapter" (*Greening Paul*, 53. Emphasis original.).

60. Throughout the letter, Paul emphasizes the present consequences of salvation in Christ by his use of "now," νῦν and νυνί. In the Pauline present, the righteousness of God has *now* been revealed apart from law and through the faithfulness of Jesus Christ (Rom 3:21-22). Since those in Christ have been justified, they are *now* certain to be saved from God's wrath (5:9). And those in Christ *now* have a reconciled relationship with God through Christ and, so, can rejoice (5:11). Because the Roman Christians have been freed from sin, they must *now* give their bodies as slaves to righteousness for growth in sanctification (6:19). And since the Roman Christians have *now* been freed from sin and enslaved to God, they bear fruit towards sanctification and ultimately eternal life (6:22). Having died to what bound them, Paul and the Roman Christians are *now* "discharged" from the law (7:6). And the infamous "I" of Rom 7 *now* sins because sin dwells in him/her, committing sin instead of doing the good s/he truly desires to do (7:16-24). But since Jesus Christ rescues people from their body of death (7:25), there is *now* no condemnation for people in Christ Jesus (8:1). And, yet, those in Christ suffer in the *now* time, even though these sufferings do not hold water compared to the glory ahead (8:18). Despite creation's subjection to decay, the creation will indeed be liberated since

Creation's Expectation and Liberation

He recognizes, however, that all is not well; God's kingdom of peace and wholeness has not yet healed a warring and broken creation. All creation still awaits the consummation of God's liberative work that will take place at the resurrection of human beings. Even still, Paul's confidence in Jesus's own resurrection assures him that creation's liberation (8:21) and humanity's resurrection (8:18, 19, 21, 23) are sure to come. Consequently, all creation continues to groan and labor together in a particular time, "until now," a time that has been decisively shaped by redemption in Jesus.

The combined meaning of συστενάζει, συνωδίνει, and ἄχρι τοῦ νῦν shines a positive light on Paul's metaphor of creation's groaning and laboring together.[61] Even greater positive light comes from the immediate context. Verse 20 indicates that although creation was subjected to frustration, God subjected it *in hope* of its future liberation. This liberation will come at the full glorification of humanity (8:21) so that the hope for the future gives such present sufferings a positive cast (8:24–25, 18). This passage begins and ends with hope, endowing the metaphor of parturition with a decidedly constructive connotation. It is a picture of a healthy mother laboring productively—though painfully—to bring her offspring into the world. In the day of Christ (as Paul calls it at 1 Cor 1:8; Phil 1:6, 10; 2:16), creation

---

we know that it is groaning and laboring together even till *now* (8:21–22). As God kept a remnant of faithful people alive during the days of Elijah, so even in the *now* time God has a remnant in Israel (11:5). The gentile Christians in Rome were once disobedient to God but *now* have mercy because of Israel's disobedience (11:30). Thus, the people of Israel are *now* disobedient so that the gentiles might receive mercy and also so that they themselves will receive mercy (11:31). In consequence of their deliverance in Christ, the Roman Christians are to live lovingly towards all people since it is already the hour to wake from sleep, for *now* their salvation is nearer than when they first believed (13:9–11). And, finally, Paul commits the Roman Christians to the God who has *now* revealed the mystery of the gospel to the nations (Rom 16:25–26).

Harrison adds another interpretive dimension to the discussion of "now" that pertains to our overview of Roman imperial ideology set forth in chapter 2. The phrases "in the now time" (Rom 3:26; 11:5), "of the now time" (8:18), and "knowing the time" (13:11) "point to the eschatological fulfillment experienced in the present soteriological age, viewed from the perspective of the old covenant (3:26; 11:5) or the coming eschatological glory (8:18; 13:11). In either case, the imperial theology of the cycle of ages is decisively pinpricked" (*Paul and the Imperial Authorities*, 117).

61. My interpretation, then, differs from that of Horrell, Hunt, and Southgate who, although they recognize creation has "reached a crucial moment of eschatological expectation," suggest creation's groaning and laboring has been ongoing and a "forward-looking anguish" (*Greening Paul*, 78). Jonathan Moo also interprets creation's groaning and laboring as a form of suffering but stresses that it is caused by sinful human action ("Romans 8.19–22," 83–85).

Creation's Slavery and Liberation

will be relieved of its groaning and laboring when God delivers up resurrected humanity.

Although Rom 8:22 does not describe an actual birth but only the laboring process, the immediate context does refer to one who was birthed through resurrection. As Paul explains in 8:29, Jesus is the firstborn, πρωτότοκον. Combining πρῶτος and the nominal derivative of τίκτω, πρωτότοκος literally refers to the child who is the firstborn of a mother's womb. It symbolically signifies the "special status enjoyed by a firstborn son as heir apparent in Israel."[62] As it appears in Rom 8:29, πρωτότοκος alludes to Jesus's resurrection as the first birth of the New Creation. Jesus stands as the "firstborn of the dead ones"—even the "firstborn of all creation"—to quote Col 1:18 and 1:15, respectively. Thus, Jesus is "the firstborn of a new humanity which is to be glorified."[63] In the context of Rom 8, Jesus's inaugural birth from among the dead assures Paul and the rest of creation that God's future work of resurrection is certain.

Overcoming death through resurrection, this first resurrection of God's Son, Jesus, necessarily leads to the future birth into resurrection glory of all God's children. Such a theological concept has a corollary in the natural world, for in the literal delivery of multiples an intermission takes place between births. Theologically, we might understand that although the firstborn has been delivered from the realm of the dead, the birth of his many siblings is yet to occur. An intermission stands between the resurrection of the firstborn, Messiah Jesus, and that of the siblings. Thus, while creation has presented the firstborn of the dead, it is still groaning and laboring until the rest of Jesus's siblings are born into resurrection glory. In this reading, then, the creation's collective groaning and laboring communicate to God's people that God is about to act decisively to liberate them and all creation from opposing and oppressive forces (cf. Rom 8:31–39) by completing the New Creation begun in Jesus's own inaugurating birth into resurrection glory.[64]

---

62. BDAG, 894.

63. BDAG, 894.

64. Keesmaat insightfully interprets these opposing and oppressive forces in concrete terms, stating: "When Paul describes the suffering of the Roman believers in Rom 8:35, he includes both poverty (oppression, distress, famine, and nakedness are all economically rooted in the LXX) and political persecution (persecution, peril, and the sword). Paul's language of the groaning of believers in v. 23, therefore, is not just a theological formulation of the suffering that precedes the inauguration of the new age, but has a specific face on the ground in this place, in this community. It looks like poverty and abuse" ("Land, Idolatry, and Justice," 98).

CREATION'S EXPECTATION AND LIBERATION

5.3.4 Creation as Tomb and Womb

Interpreting creation's collective groaning and laboring as a positive and purposeful activity rather than an experience of futile suffering reminds us of God's imminent, miraculous work of making alive, particularly God's certain liberation of creation. Creation's present laboring and its collective groaning with God's children and the Spirit will not end in defeat and death but liberation and new life. The time of waiting is filled with agonizing pain, to be sure; but might it also be filled with fruitful labor?

Romans 8:19–22 stands within a stream of traditions and texts that depict the earth as a mother that labors to bring forth living children. The confluence of these interpretive traditions provides ground to extend our understanding of Rom 8:19–22 a step further: Creation cooperates with God in delivering up resurrected humanity. We cannot be sure of Paul's intentions, but his wording at 8:22—as it stands within a context of mother earth imagery—gestures towards this reading. Without diminishing God's ultimate life-giving power that will be manifest in the eschatological resurrection of humanity, the birthing imagery in Rom 8:22 implies that the nonhuman creation is a central participant and a laboring actor in God's work of New Creation. This cooperation between Creator and creation mirrors the account in Gen 1, which portrays the water and land as creative actors (see 1.1). In addition to bringing forth life initially, creation participates in the Spirit's work of ζωοποίησις, "making alive," through its laboring (8:11, 22); for, creation labors toward the resurrection.

Several Jewish texts, including the Gospel of Matthew, may gesture towards creation's participation in God's work of resurrection. According to Matthew, the earth quaked when Jesus died, and this quaking apparently opened tombs (27:50–52). Consequently, with the passageway opened "many bodies of the saints who had fallen asleep were raised . . . and appeared to many" (27:52, 53). Later, in conjunction with the angel who rolled away the stone that blocked Jesus's tomb, the earth quaked and exposed where Jesus had been laid (28:2). In these instances, the creation—the land in particular—functions not as a mere spectator of the resurrection but an important participant in it.[65]

---

65. Outside Jewish and Christian literature stand Greco-Roman texts that portray the earth as a woman who labors and bears children and provides for humans as would a mother. Courtney Friesen reviews this interpretive tradition (and its variations), highlighting the contributions, among others, of Hesiod (in *Theogony*), Euripides, Pliny the Elder, and Heraclitus ("Birthing the Children of God.").

Creation's Slavery and Liberation

While Matthew's references to earthquakes in the context of tombs opening and bodies being resurrected is unique among the gospels, two Jewish pseudepigraphical works provide additional attestation to the idea that the land holds and bears forth the dead. A chapter of the Similtudes in *1 Enoch* (likely composed during the first century CE) explains, "Sheol will return all the deposits [the dead] which she had received" (51:1).[66] Another first century text, *4 Ezra*, refers to the earth giving forth the dead at the end of time, declaring, "And the earth shall give up those who are asleep in it; and the chambers shall give up the souls which have been committed to them" (7:32).[67] In a later chapter, this text establishes an analogy between a woman who bears forth a son and the earth that also bears forth children (10:10, 14).[68]

It is impossible to determine whether Paul knew of *1 Enoch* or if his later interpreters read *1 Enoch* and *4 Ezra*, yet their existence and the content of their texts provide evidence of a relevant Jewish witness to the idea that creation may deliver up the dead to God for judgment and resurrection. Further evidence of this trope lies in the Greek alterations of Isa 66:8, as discussed above, in which the *land* is said to labor in one day so that Zion labored and delivered children. In an analogous though more muted way, Isa 26 portrays the earth as ultimately uncovering the dead (Isa 26:17, 21 LXX). In this context, the prophet explains that God's people labored and gave birth (ὠδινήσαμεν καὶ ετέκομεν) to the "breath of your salvation in the land" (26:18). Then, the text gives testimony to belief in a resurrection of the dead, explaining that the dead will rise (ἀναστήσονται οἱ νεκροί, 26:19). Moreover, as the Lord brings judgment on the inhabitants of the earth, the earth itself "will disclose [ἀνακαλύψει] its blood and will not cover [οὐ κατακαλύψει] the ones having been killed" (Isa 26:21). Thus, in this text, the earth participates in God's work of making right and making alive by presenting the remains of violence and murder to the Lord; it offers up the dead to God. We discover, then, that several instances of Jewish eschatological literature portray the earth serving not just as a tomb but as a womb,

---

66. Isaac, *1 Enoch*, 1:7, 36.

67. Metzger, *4 Ezra*, 1:538. See also Horrell, Hunt, and Southgate, *Greening Paul*, 80.

68. The text reads: "And from the beginning all have been born of her, and others will come; and behold, almost all go to perdition, and a multitude of them are destined for destruction" (10:10); "As you brought forth in sorrow, so the earth also has from the beginning give her fruit, that is, man, to him who made her" (10:14) (Metzger, *4 Ezra*, 1:546).

not only as a keeper of the dead but a bearer of those who would soon be resurrected.[69]

This Jewish trope of the land releasing the dead sheds light on Paul's depiction of creation collectively groaning and laboring, especially when this light is not filtered to remove the apocalyptic hues of Paul's eschatology. Creation's collective groaning and laboring "until now" happen during a particular moment—the moment soon after the resurrection of Jesus and soon before (according to Paul) the resurrection of the rest of humanity when God would fully establish God's Kingdom on earth. Such a perspective takes Paul's pregnant phrase at face value: the nonhuman creation collectively groans and labors toward the resurrection of humanity so that its role of gestating the dead until the eschaton functions alongside God's fundamental work of raising humanity into glory and establishing the New Creation.[70]

By attending to the birthing imagery set forth in Rom 8:22 in these ways, creation's "groaning and laboring together" casts a positive and productive light. Yet, even as we interpret this phrase positively, we can nevertheless recognize that creation's groaning may signal its suffering. It continues to suffer in agonizing ways in its subjection to sinful humanity even as it groans, labors, and waits for its final deliverance. At that eschatological moment, Paul expects God to remedy the entire situation that allows creation to experience destruction and frustration, in other words, the situation of human sin. Thus, according to this interpretation, creation's groaning is not *directly* caused by human violence but results *indirectly* from the human need for rectification and resurrection. Creation's groaning, then, arises from its painful yet productive laboring in cooperation with God's future deliverance, the glorious work of resurrection.

5.4 Conclusion

Creation's eager anticipation of humanity's resurrection (8:19), its future participation in the liberation produced by the glory that God's children will possess (8:21), and its groaning and laboring together until now (8:22)

---

69. Ezekiel 37:12–13 also testifies to a hope of resurrection. God will open the tombs of the dead and bring forth the dead into new and resurrected life in the land. The following verse then promises that God will give God's Spirit to the people (37:14).

70. Consequently, I would contend that Paul envisions a liberated and restored creation, not a creation that has been evacuated, such as in a so-called "rapture" to heaven.

all illustrate the ways in which nonhuman and human destinies intertwine. Only when humanity experiences its complete liberation from sin and death through resurrection will the nonhuman creation also experience its liberation from slavery to destruction. This, in turn, indicates that creation depends upon a righteous, glorious condition of humanity for its liberation, which (from a Pauline anthropological perspective) implies that creation fundamentally relies upon a miraculous, eschatological act of God rather than feeble human attempts at liberation, even though followers of Christ ought to walk in step with the Spirit and sin no more (6:12–19; 8:12–14; see 3.2.2).

Paul further indicates that humans, along with the Spirit, participate in the nonhuman creation's groaning, and he thereby expects followers of Christ to stand in compassionate solidarity with it. Consequently, they ought to live into their liberation by becoming servants of righteousness and God (6:18, 22). This service will, in turn, support creation's ability to fulfill God's commission effectively (without being subjected to frustration) and to flourish (rather than undergoing destruction).[71] Understood in these ways, Rom 8:19–22 suggests that the health and well-being of human and nonhuman creation go hand in hand and that God intends to liberate human as well as nonhuman creation.

While Paul's story of creation—a story of *creation–subjection–liberation–glorification*—shines brightly through his letter to Rome, especially in 8:19–22, its message is all the more luminous when set in contrast with Roman imperial claims and practices. In contrast to imperial claims, the creation's liberation and revitalization do not rest on the Roman Emperor and his subjection of the world (see 2.1), but on the faithful and just servant leadership of Jesus Christ (15:9–12; 1:1–6) and his siblings (5:17; 8:17, 21, 32, 37; see 3.2).[72] Only by way of God's making right (justification) and making alive (*zōopoiēsis*) will human and nonhuman creation experience

---

71. Jonathan Moo hints at a similar dynamic, suggesting: "if Rom 8.19–22 is to be read in light of Paul's possible use of Isaiah 24–27, the *effects* of creation's subjection may not have entailed for Paul a once-for-all ontological change in the created order, or a 'fall of nature' in the traditional sense. Paul's possible use of Isaiah 24 would suggest instead that the creation's slavery to 'ruin' is a contingent slavery, such that it remains at the mercy of the effects of ongoing human sin and divine judgment" ("Romans 8.19–22," 89).

72. Keesmaat also recognizes the anti-imperial subtext of Paul's creational story. She contends, in Rom 8, "Paul tells a different story: rather than Caesar being the one who brings restoration, abundance, and peace to creation, it is the restored people of God who bring such restoration as part of their creaturely calling" ("Land, Idolatry, and Justice," 102).

Creation's Expectation and Liberation

true flourishing, peace, and vitality. The Roman Empire, while successful in making this happen for some, failed in doing this for the human and nonhuman creation as a whole.

In light of creation's story, it's *creation–subjection–liberation–glorification*, and the role that humanity plays in this story, as Paul expresses it in Rom 8:19–22 and the rest of the letter, we may confirm the eco-ethical principles laid out in 3.3. Paul expects people to:

1. Attend to creation's story by recognizing the ways in which God's creation not only reveals the Creator God but also exposes its own condition on account of the complex, interdependent relationships between and among nonhuman and human participants.

2. Express gratitude to the Creator God for the gifts of creation, sharing the gifts of food and water with God's creatures.

3. Cooperate in the divine work of justification, making right/just, by supporting and protecting the well-being of human and nonhuman members of God's creation, especially the "weak"/disempowered/vulnerable.[73]

4. Cooperate in the divine work of *zōopoiēsis*, making alive, by promoting and maintaining the biodiversity, fertility, and flourishing of entire ecosystems and the biosphere.

5. Honor the Lord Jesus Christ by avoiding activites that would subject creation to frustration, enslave it to destruction, or would injure or destroy those for whom Christ died.

6. Stand in solidarity with the sufferings and hopes of creation by exercising servant leadership, in conformity with Jesus, in ways that serve and maintain the health, flourishing, fertility, and diversity of creation.

7. Exercise appropriate self-restraint in order equitably to share the gifts of creation and support the vitality and fidelity of other members of God's creation.

---

73. Another way in which we might articulate this supporting and protecting is with the language of solidarity. God's people identify themselves with the suffering of creation and, therefore, do not engage in "violent rule over creation" (Keesmaat, "Land, Idolatry, and Justice," 102; see also Horrell, Hunt, and Southgate, *Greening Paul*, 189–220).

However, as is so often the case, people (and perhaps Jesus's followers especially, as history has shamefully revealed) fail to embody true justice/righteousness and to facilitate the flourishing of all life.

Romans 8:19–22 and its attendant story of creation, as we might expect, also shine a critical light on current human relationships with the nonhuman creation. Because modern industrial agricultural regimes (as one of many social processes) do not support the flourishing, vitality, and well-being of human and nonhuman creation but instead inflict significant injuries upon our human brothers and sisters and our nonhuman neighbors, we shall follow Paul's gaze in the next chapter to perceive more accurately creation's present slavery to destruction. By considering the rhetoric and practices of the US grain trade, we shall discover that it is nearly impossible for us *not* to injure and even destroy one for whom Christ died when we eat today. The industrial food system fails to embody true justice and fails to promote holistic vitality, flourishing, and well-being. Nevertheless, hope remains. As we alert ourselves to the realities of our global food economy and adjust our agricultural and eating practices to support the health and well-being of all creation, Jesus's followers may more fully inhabit and make manifest God's creation-wide work of justification and *zōopoiēsis*.

CHAPTER 6

Creation's Destruction

Industrial Agriculture in Action

THE STORY OF CREATION's slavery to destruction is no less true today than it was when Paul wrote his letter to Rome and ministered in the vast expanses of the Roman Empire. In fact, the deterioration of biodiversity, habitats, and nonhuman health and well-being is far more extreme in the world today than ever before in recorded history. Although many forces collude to make this the case, industrial approaches to agriculture and the drive to feed the world's growing human population are among the most potent.[1]

Industrial agriculture, however, did not set out to degrade ecosystems and harm living things. Instead, industrial agriculture promised farmers and consumers it would provide the world with abundant, safe, and inexpensive food through its technologies—tractor power, synthetic chemicals, and specialized and genetically modified seeds. Especially by presenting synthetic chemicals (such as fertilizers and pesticides) and "improved" seeds as the solution to declining soil fertility rates, increasing pests and weeds, and the world's hunger problems, industrial agriculture heralded itself as a kind of savior. We may, therefore, perceive striking commonalities (despite categorical differences) between the claims of industrial agriculture and those of the Roman Empire.

---

1. I am grateful to Dr. Wes Jackson for reading and commending an earlier version of this chapter. I also appreciate the patience and care with which my students at Wake Forest University School of Divinity read and provided feedback on portions of this chapter. Their insights and criticisms propelled me to improve the content, though I am sure the final product does not match the wisdom contained in their suggestions.

Creation's Slavery and Liberation

Although on national and global levels governments and consumers continue to promote and support industrial agriculture, some people have begun raising concerns about its safety. They recognize its shortcomings but see few alternatives that will feed a growing human population. Consequently, they (perhaps I should say "we") participate in it as a necessary evil, thinking it is the best option for supporting the common good. However, when viewed from the perspectives of soil, air, water, nonhuman communities, farmworkers, and even the world's consumers, the combined amount of industrial agriculture's ills reveal the costs to be far too high. The system needs replacing. As creation's servant leaders and as those commanded not to destroy those for whom Christ died by their eating (Gen 1:26–28; Rom 14:15), Christians must take the bold and courageous step forward to advocate for creation's well-being, to toil for its liberation.

In theological terms, since human beings are commissioned to serve and maintain their garden homes (Gen 2:15) and are integral participants in creation's liberation from slavery to destruction (Rom 8:21), it is vital that they as collective communities know how creation's ecosystems work most healthfully and sustainably. Simulateously, they must be willing to admit when ecosystems are not working healthfully and sustainably. It is the contention of this chapter that we are in a particularly destructive moment of agricultural history, in which the methods and assumptions of industrial agriculture force farmers and consumers to undermine the flourishing, biodiversity, and healthy interdependence that God commissioned creation—both human and nonhuman—to sustain. Industrial agriculture demands that God's image bearers no longer exercise servant leadership in ways that serve the soil and maintain the diversity and abundance of God's plants and creatures (Gen 1:11–12, 20–22, 24–30). It entangles them in a food system that leads them away from honoring the Lord through their eating and instead binds them to processes that destroy those for whom Christ died (Rom 14:6, 15).

As people who consume food at least a few times a day, those who confess Jesus as Lord have the privilege and responsibility to know how their food is grown, processed, and distributed and what effects these processes have on the human and nonhuman creation. Because they follow the Creator God, Paul would call them to attend to creation's witness, its witness not only to the creating and life-giving God but also to the life-destroying activities of human beings. He would also invite them to live into the liberation that Jesus Christ offers by employing their bodies as instruments of justice and by transforming their minds to discern God's work in the world (6:13; 12:1–2). He would direct them to recognize how they are a people bound together in ecclesial, ecological, and economic communities and that their eating may cause harm and possibly destruction to others (12:4–8; 14:15, 20; 8:21).

Perhaps Paul would encourage Christians to assess whether their food system is just and life-supporting, whether it avoids enslaving creation to destruction and does not frustrate its vitality, flourishing, diversity, and goodness. This chapter assists in this process by appraising one piece of industrial agriculture—the growing of wheat. The hope is that readers may more accurately discern whether food-growing regimes enable farmers, farmworkers, food processors, grocers, and consumers to fulfill the eco-ethical principles laid out in 5.4 and broadened below. Because some of the people involved in the US food system do not confess Jesus as Lord (and because this book certainly does not support a Christian establishment in which people are expected or forced to do so), I here reconfigure the seven Pauline eco-ethical principles in less confessional ways for this chapter. In conversation with scientists and sociologists, I also begin to flesh out what it might mean (in, admittedly, limited ways) for a food system to embody these principles. As we consider the US grain trade throughout this chapter, therefore, we will consider whether industrial agriculture and its attendant food system empowers people to:

1. Attend to Earth's story by recognizing the limits, climates, and living members that comprise local ecosystems in order to support healthy, interdependent relationships between and among nonhuman and human participants.

    a. In so doing, all people along the food chain (producers, processors, and consumers) dispose of food waste in ways that feed and enrich soils and, thereby, reconnect nutrient cycles.

2. Express gratitude for the gifts of Earth by sharing the gifts of food and water with other living things in ways that

    a. Ensure all people have access to affordable, available, culturally relevant, and healthy foods;[2] and

---

2. An organization established in 2010 called Just Food defines food justice as "communities exercising their right to grow, sell, and eat [food that is] fresh, nutritious, affordable, culturally appropriate, and grown locally with care for the well-being of the land, workers, and animals" (Alkon and Agyeman, "Introduction," 5).

b. Justly compensate those who grow food.³

3. Work for justice, by supporting and protecting the well-being of "weak"/disempowered/vulnerable human and nonhuman members of the ecosphere, which requires

   a. Companies and individuals that process, distribute, and sell food to pay their employees fair wages and receive reasonable wages or profits themselves; and
   b. Governments or governing bodies (such as certification boards) to regulate all aspects of the food system to reward its just components and prosecute unjust ones.

4. Become agents of life, by promoting and maintaining the biodiversity, fertility, and flourishing of entire ecosystems and the biosphere so that

   a. nonhuman creatures have access to species-appropriate food and water resources, allowing them to reproduce and thrive in balanced ecosystems.⁴

5. Avoid, as much as possible, activites that would undercut Earth's fertility and diversity or would injure or destroy living things, making it imperative that

   a. Companies implement practices and use resources that do not harm ecosystems and instead achieve net-zero carbon emissions; and

---

3. It has become increasingly evident that cash-crop farms sometimes dominate arable land so that local people, including farmworkers, have little access to food staples or land on which to grow those staples. These factors intensify the risk that local people succumb to malnutrition (see 6.2.4). This is the case outside the US as well. Andrew Kimbrell explains, "In Africa, where severe famines have occurred in the past decade, industrialized agriculture has not produced foods for the people, but rather record crops of cotton and sugarcane" (Kimbrell, *Fatal Harvest*, 9).

4. In his theological assessment of agriculture in conversation with Christian communion, Timothy Eberhart beautifully explains: "In a holistic economy aligned with the holiness of God's love: *The earth is a commons accessible to all. The exchange of goods fosters social and ecological health. Productive activities are integrated into nature. Neighborly partnerships are localized in cooperative communities. And people are free to enjoy directly the fruit of their labors*" (Eberhart, *Rooted and Grounded in Love*, 6. Emphasis original.).

    b. Companies and individuals protect, as much as possible, workers and human and nonhuman community members from injury and harm.[5]

6. Stand in solidarity with the sufferings of Earth and its communities by leading in ways that serve and maintain Earth's health, flourishing, fertility, and diversity.

    a. In so doing, people advocate at all levels of society for a just and life-supporting food system.

7. Exercise appropriate self-restraint in order equitably to share the Earth (especially access to land, water, and food) and to support the vitality of self and others,[6] which implies that

    a. Nations, companies, and individuals acquire access to land in just ways and make reparations for past injustices;[7] and
    b. Individuals, communities, corporations, and nations reduce and limit their consumption of Earth's goods.

---

5. Although this book does not address the meat, dairy, poultry, or seafood industries, principle 5 certainly applies to these aspects of the food system and our human relationship with animals. It has become increasingly clear that industrial meat, dairy, poultry, and seafood ventures treat animals inhumanely, inflict unnecessary amounts of suffering on them, and greatly inhibit their flourishing during life. Tonstad describes some of the horrors embedded within the industrial meat complex, explaining that many of the "animals have been genetically manipulated in order to reduce the time from artificial insemination to slaughter and from slaughter to the consumer's table; they have been deprived of the opportunity to live out their instincts of mating and nesting; they are largely immobilized in order to reduce caloric waste; and they are tightly confined in buildings that, were the fans that circulate air to ensure survival turned off even for a short time, the animals would suffocate" (Tonstad, *Letter to the Romans*, 305).

6. In stark contrast to this principle, hegemonic regimes (from imperial to colonial to global capital economies) often inhibit God's creatures from having just access to land and water. Eberhart elucidates this reality and contends, "Seen in the light of God's holiness, an economy based in the ongoing severance of people from direct access to the earth is operating opposite the inclusive nature of God's gracious love" (Eberhart, *Rooted and Grounded in Love*, 63).

7. Before unfarmed lands are acquired and prepared, people must consider how the ecosystem and its inhabitants would be affected by farming and adjust farming endeavors in order to fit the ecosystem and make as little impact ecologically as possible.

With these seven eco-ethical goals in mind, we may perceive, describe, and assess Earth's current condition, particularly as it serves the demands of wheat agriculture in the Great Plains.[8]

6.1 Industrial Agriculture's Claims: Abundant, Safe, and Affordable Food

Reminiscent of Rome's emperors, leaders of the United States have promoted and promised abundant wheat harvests throughout the twentieth and twenty-first centuries. Because European-descended settlers occupied the Great Plains and engine-powered machinery became accessible in the late 1800s, agriculture in the early 1900s became an attractive and profitable venture there during a period known as the Golden Age of American Agriculture.[9] Another so-called golden age, the Golden Age of Synthetic Pesticides,[10] began in the mid-1900s when scientists encouraged farmers to employ synthetic chemical fertilizers and pesticides on their fields and crops. Engine-powered machinery, together with synthetic chemicals, provided the key ingredients for industrial agriculture and the industrial food system. Industrial methods and processes, according to its early promoters, would give "consumers the promise of purity, consistency, and a low cost that they could rely on."[11] Because industrial approaches did increase yields and since so many farmers adopted industrial methods in the US, these innovations quickly transformed the Great Plains into the breadbasket of the United States (and, at times, the world).[12] Wheat agriculture, then, seemed effortless and endlessly fruitful. For decades, the US appeared to enter a golden age of abundance.

---

8. The chapter attempts this task by attending to systemic problems in somewhat detailed ways. Of course, many details and factors are overlooked due to space constraints.

9. In the early 1900s US agriculture became a stable, if not profitable, sector of the economy so that some refer to 1909 to 1914 as the "Golden Age of American Agriculture." For several decades economists compared crop prices to that golden age period (Bean and Bollinger, "Base Period," 253; Hurt, *American Agriculture*, 263).

10. Mart, *Pesticides*, 11. Douglas Hurt also explains that by the 1950s, American farmers "applied newly developed pesticides, such as DDT," so that "most farmers believed the postwar chemical industry had created a 'golden age'" (Hurt, *American Agriculture*, 300).

11. Bentley and Hobart, "Food in Recent U.S. History," 167.

12. President John F. Kennedy's secretary of agriculture, Orville Freeman, called the US "the 'greatest agricultural production plant on earth'" (Kroese, "War against Nature," 95).

Creation's Destruction

Underwriting and perhaps accelerating America's adoption of industrial agricultural methods is a mindset that has misshaped American relationships with land since colonial times. With a misappropriation of Gen 1, many early colonists and settlers of the Americas perceived themselves as those commissioned by God, pope, or king to subdue new lands and pagan peoples.[13] All along the eastern seaboard, the European settlers exercised "dominion" and subdued the land as they progressively made their way westward. They perceived themselves as those who transformed a cursed wilderness into a blessed and cultivated garden.[14]

This mindset of dominion and the goal of subduing nature took on increasingly militaristic tones as Americans viewed themselves to be engaged in a war against pests and weeds and as fighting for dominion and abundance. By the end of World War II, chemical companies that had developed chemical weapons and tools for fighting a human war redirected their chemical merchandise towards nonhuman "enemies" of abundance and ease. With great fervor, chemical companies embarked on an advertising campaign with "scores of agro-chemical ads featuring themes of warfare, machismo, or mayhem."[15] The ads contended farmers could, and now *should*, annihilate pests and weeds, attempting to convince farmers to take up agribusiness's new weapon: pesticides, including herbicides. Not only corporate ads but also journalists assumed a warfare mentality. In 1954, a *Saturday Evening Post* article described for its readers the "advances" in agriculture that would feed the world for generations:

---

13. Illustrating such a perspective, *Dum Diversas*—the Papal bull of 1452—commissioned "the King of Portugal 'to invade, search out, capture, vanquish, and subdue all ... pagans whatsoever ... wheresoever placed, and the kingdoms' ... possessions'" (Myers, *Watershed Discipleship*, 5).

14. Carolyn Merchant explains that the early colonists in New England believed "[t]he wilderness [wa]s the antithesis of the garden, or of paradise. The biblical story says that Adam and Eve were driven out of the Garden of Eden into the wilderness, a desert. They had to labor in the earth to change it into a garden, just as the colonists had to change the New England wilderness into a cultivated garden" (Merchant, *Columbia Guide*, 34).

15. Kroese, "War against Nature," 92. Kroese goes on to explain: "By 1945, as the eventual outcome of the war was becoming clear, administration plans to encourage reduced [crop] production in order to maintain high commodity prices after the war were scuttled as it became obvious that food from the United States—the only major power to survive the conflict with its farm production capacity fully intact—was going to be needed more than ever. By 1946, the message to farmers in farm magazines was: don't let up, 'the war isn't over for the farmer,' the battle for full production must continue, and thanks to the war, we have some new weapons for you" (96).

> Airplanes swooping over a field leaving a trail of vapor or dust, are engaged in chemical warfare against crop-destroying insects, or, they may be spreading a new type of nitrogen fertilizer which can be absorbed directly by the plant's leaves. Giant-sized sprinklers are a sign of the farmer's efforts to beat the weather by making artificial rain at just the right time to assure maximum yields. You'll also see spray machines squirting selective chemicals which kill weeds but don't harm the crops.[16]

Because it appeared that new agricultural technologies brought plenty whether in wartime or peace, some believed during the Korean War that "'[s]hort of atomic disaster, it is hard to see how Americans can be seriously threatened by hunger.'"[17] American farmers and the government that protected and supported them seemed to produce unending plenty, with no negative consequences in sight. The earth had been subdued. Its wealth was in hand.

Industrial agriculture has indeed provided many of the world's people with abundant food at affordable prices. And with the advent of certain biotechnologies, industrial agriculture occasionally has done this in ways that decrease certain environmental risks. As one agribusiness advertisement claimed in the late 1990s, genetic engineering technologies would soon liberate the world from hunger, soil erosion, and—supposedly—dependence on increasing amounts of agricultural chemicals. The advertisement claimed:

> Worrying about starving future generations won't feed them. Food biotechnology will. The world's population is growing rapidly, adding the equivalent of a China to the globe every ten years. To feed these billion more mouths, we can try extending our farming land or squeezing greater harvests out of existing cultivation. With the planet set to double in numbers around 2030, this heavy dependency on land can only become heavier. Soil erosion and mineral depletion will exhaust the ground. Lands such as rainforests will be forced into cultivation. Fertilizer, insecticide, and herbicide use will increase globally. *At Monsanto, we now believe food biotechnology is a better way forward.*[18]

---

16. Bird, "Will Your Grandchildren Go Hungry?," 103. See also Mart, *Pesticides*, 14.
17. Mart, *Pesticides*, 14.
18. Shiva, *Stolen Harvest*, 12. Emphasis added.

CREATION'S DESTRUCTION

A better way forward—with less soil exhaustion, fewer toxic chemicals, and fewer forests cut down—sounded positive and promising to many governments, farmers, and consumers. With such alluring prospects, it was only natural that many of the world's farmers and consumers fell right in step with biotechnology's relentless march "forward."

However, when we—like the apostle Paul in his day—read creation's story and discern its actual condition, we perceive a startling reality. Gazing steadily at the effects of biotechnology on the whole of creation, we find significant, holistic problems within the current food system. With the clarity of hindsight, we can see a path of destruction behind us. The path of biotechnology allowed for and even exacerbated the environmental ills that Monsanto's advertisement portended would come if farmers and consumers did *not* follow its leadership.[19] Recent documentaries and books unmask this ugly truth, especially in relation to genetically modified soybean and corn monocultures (e.g., *Food, Inc.*), so that people have become increasingly aware of the environmental and health dangers involved in a food system heavily reliant on genetically modified (GM) and chemically dependent soy and corn.

Less well known, however, are the ways in which industrial approaches to growing non-GM crops may be similarly dangerous to human, animal, and ecological health. As this chapter details, industrial methods of growing non-genetically-modified wheat also involves concerning amounts of ecological and biological deterioration. Thus, industrial wheat agriculture in the United States has become marked by destruction more than liberation, not only for the nonhuman creation but also humans. Some may even say that the production of wheat in the US stands "as one long war on nature and indigenous people."[20] Those attuned to American history will recognize the obvious forms of destruction involved in the United States' confiscation of the Great Plains from the native peoples who once lived there and the decimation of millions of bison so that Americans could upend native peoples and grow wheat. Perhaps less obvious are the deleterious consequences of the plow, engine power, synthetic chemicals, market forces that drive up prices for consumers but drive down income for farmers, and inequitable forms of food distribution. While conventional industrial

---

19. Bayer merged with Monsanto in June of 2018 and now prefers to use the name "Bayer" (Domonoske, "Monsanto No More."). For clarity, I refer to the current conglomerate with the nomenclature "Bayer-Monsanto." But I use "Monsanto" when I refer to its activities prior to the merger.

20. Kroese, "War against Nature," 95.

agriculture throughout the Great Plains has certainly fed millions of people as the breadbasket of the US, it has done so inequitably and at the expense of soils, water, nonhuman lives, and human liberty, well-being, and health.

What is more, industrial agriculture has failed to deliver on its promises. It has failed to produce *safe* food. Scientists, farmers, and consumers have become increasingly aware that these industrial approaches to agriculture are not sustainable or healthy for humans or nonhumans. In fact, the daily bread that so many Americans enjoy and depend upon each day is not only corrupted by a legacy of land confiscation and soil degradation but now, increasingly, with residues from destructive chemicals. In tandem with industrial approaches to growing food is an unjust food system that fails to offer all people *affordable* food. As the decades have passed and agricultural technologies have continued to evolve, millions of Americans continue to face hunger, despite the conventional food system's glowing promises. Injustices abound in this food system.

Keeping in mind the seven expanded Pauline eco-ethical principles outlined above, we now turn to evaluating industrial wheat agriculture step by step. This next section examines the ways in which farmers, governments, and businesses have acquired and prepared land in the Great Plains and have cultivated, collected, transported, processed, and distributed wheat throughout the twentieth and twenty-first centuries. Environmental history and scientific research together facilitate this overview of the industrial food system and reveal that current approaches to securing our "daily bread" unnecessarily enslave creation to destruction; decrease biodiversity, fertility, and flourishing; place undo strain on vulnerable members of creation; exacerbate inequitable forms of food distribution; and disconnect consumers from appropriate forms of gratitude to Earth and God. They make it clear that more liberative agricultural options must be found.

6.2 Environmental History's Report: Degradation of Soil, Water, Air, and Life

6.2.1 Land Preparation

America's significant production of wheat from the late 1800s on has depended first and foremost on its fertile and expansive prairies in the heart of the country. Perhaps from one perspective, the transformation of the Great Plains' wild prairies into cultivated wheat fields may look like progress. One might laud this progress in the Great Plains by explaining, "[a] hostile environment . . . was gradually brought under control and transformed into a garden, making the Great Plains a Garden of the World."[21] The transformation of wilderness into "garden" took place as American settlers subdued the Great Plains with the help of at least six technological breakthroughs: Colt six-shooters, barbed wire, windmills, John Deere steel plows, railroads, and harvesters.[22] These tools enabled settlers to subdue native populations, rid the Plains of bison, and plow up around 70 percent of the eastern Great Plains.

Although the North American Great Plains has an erratic climate—including drying winds, freezing cold spells, and elongated droughts—its soils are remarkably fertile and its features enable plants, and their human and nonhuman dependents, to survive and even thrive there.[23] The Great Plains consists of "tall grass prairies in the east and the short grass prairies in the west,"[24] both of which include a symbiotic balance of plants: "warm-season grasses, cool-season grasses, legumes, and composites."[25] Because precipitation varies dramatically from season to season and year to year, perennial prairie grasses have thick, deep roots to access water and nutrients far underground. And since many of the native plant species are perennial, they can concentrate most of their seasonal efforts on growing above ground and do not expend as much energy as annuals in creating new roots. Their root systems keep precious topsoil in place and pull water and nutrients from deep underground to the surface, where annual plants may also access them. The diversity of plants that naturally occur in the prairies work together symbiotically, with legumes replenishing nitrogen levels in the soil.[26] Moreover, the Great Plains has deep, naturally fertile soils because geological events deposited necessary minerals on the surface.[27]

21. Merchant, *Columbia Guide*, 89.
22. Merchant, *Columbia Guide*, 93–94.
23. Merchant, *Columbia Guide*, 15.
24. The dividing line between the tall and short grass plains is "around the 100th meridian. Westward of that meridian, the rainfall is less than 20 inches and tapers off further toward the western deserts. The 100th meridian is generally thought of as the 20-inch rainfall line. Agriculture is fairly reliable east of that line, but westward it becomes increasingly problematic, hence the Plains Indians were primarily nomadic" (Merchant, *Columbia Guide*, 15).
25. Jackson, "Farming in Nature's Image," 73.
26. Jackson, *Consulting the Genius of the Place*, 162.
27. As glaciers moved across Canada, scraping off helpful nutrients and placing them

Creation's Slavery and Liberation

For millennia, Native American tribes made their homes quite sustainably with the animals and plants of the Great Plains. While it is unclear how many people lived in the Great Plains before Europeans first set foot there, it is equally certain that the native inhabitants' lives, livelihoods, and landscapes were greatly disrupted and sometimes destroyed by the newcomers.[28] American military personnel and settlers subdued and contained the Plains Indians by various means, but eliminating their access to food—especially by nearly extinguishing the bison population and their access to sacred and fertile lands—was chief among them.[29] It is startling to consider the degree to which—from the perspective of the Tanakh—native lands became desecrated and contaminated by moral impurity, by murder (see 1.2.3).

Once the tribal peoples were horrifically and unjustly subdued, settlers had to find a way to subdue the prairie land itself. In a time before strong farming implements and powerful tractors, tough prairie lands limited the amount of acreage wheat farmers might be able to plant in a season. Moreover, harvest time required extensive human labor in a very small window of time and, therefore, also restricted the number of acres farmers could reasonably sow and harvest. It was not until the development of a more effective and affordable plow by John Deere in the 1830s, a seed planter ("grain drill") by Moses and Samuel Pennock in 1841, and a reaper

---

in the middle of America, they made the US "the richest agricultural country of the world" (Jackson, *Consulting the Genius of the Place*, 68).

28. Eventually, the Great Plains received not only new American settlers but also thousands of displaced Native American peoples from the east whom the US government relocated on reservations. Thus, the vegetation and wildlife on which the Plains Indians depended for livelihood now had to be shared with others (Hurt, *Indian Frontier*, 189). Diseases, against which native peoples were not immune, traveled into the Great Plains and killed many of the human population (Merchant, *Columbia Guide*, 17).

29. A particularly sinister way in which the US government allowed, if not planned, to subdue and decimate the Plains Indians was through the intentional eradication of the bison. During the 1860s–1870s, the "U.S. government" apparently encouraged a "policy of ridding the Plains of both Indians and buffalo" (Merchant, *Columbia Guide*, 19). In support of this effort, General Phil Sheridan purportedly told his troops to "'kill, skin, and sell, until the buffalo is exterminated'" as "'the only way to bring a lasting peace and allow civilization to advance'" (19–20). While some scholars doubt whether the General said this and whether the sentiment reflected official US policy, the near extermination of the bison did in fact take place, especially at the hands of white poachers. "In 1876, some 3 to 4 million buffalo killed on the Plains supplied hides and bones for robes and fertilizers . . . In a space of 10 to 15 years, buffalo were removed from the Plains and the remaining Plains tribes relocated to reservations" (20).

by Obed Hussey in the 1830s that a farmer could greatly expand wheat production by means of horsepower.[30]

Eventually, the self-propelled tractor replaced horses on the farm. In contrast to horses, tractors could work day or night without fuss. However, distinct disadvantages also attended tractor use. Due to their weight, tractors compacted the soil. The steel plows that tractors could now pull through the tough prairies to break up their plants' strong roots unwittingly left soil vulnerable to erosion. And because they could plow so many acres in little time, tractors drastically increased the amount of land exposed to soil erosion during unfavorable weather conditions.[31] Plowing the soil and killing its vegetative cover unfortunately began the process of decreasing the land's fertility.[32]

Economically, tractor power was a mixed bag. The increased production that tractors facilitated benefited many farmers in times of war (since demand and prices were high) but harmed farmers' economic situation in times of peace and surplus (when supply was high and prices low).[33] The advent of tractors also displaced many farm laborers from necessary income and at the same time yoked farm owners to heavy debts. Meanwhile, as the decades pressed on, the ecological problems of air pollution and global climate change, stemming, in part, from petroleum-based agriculture, would become increasingly apparent. Expensive tractor power and their crop-specific implements also induced many farmers to specialize by planting one type of crop (called a monoculture). Thus, the tractor

> became the key to the mechanization of the farm; it also helped cause the industrialization of agriculture and the technological revolution that led to the modern agribusiness industry . . . When a farmer purchased a tractor and equipment specially designed to meet the draft capabilities of this new implement, he often borrowed from the bank . . . The diversified farms of the past required a greater variety of implements than one-crop agriculture, but tractors and accompanying implements required a larger capital investment. Consequently, farmers who bought tractors increasingly concentrated on the production of one or two crops such as wheat, corn, sorghum grains.[34]

30. Hurt, *American Agriculture*, 136–43.
31. Hurt, *American Agriculture*, 358.
32. Montgomery, *Growing a Revolution*, 19–26.
33. Hurt, *American Agriculture*, 358.
34. Hurt, *American Agriculture*, 357.

These pros and cons of tractor farming and plowing make these technological breakthroughs an ambivalent, if not unsustainable, means of human survival.[35]

Without fully appreciating the fragility of the Plains as a semi-arid to arid ecosystem, farmers plowed up the native grasses that resiliently weathered the storms of prairie life. The native grasses, with their tough and deep root systems intact throughout the year, protect the soil from wind and water erosion. Removing the perennial grasses results in long-term declines in fertility, since erosion carries essential nutrients out of the soil.[36] This occurs not only because plowing destroys the roots of grasses but also "reduces soil microbial biomass and disrupts mycorrhizal hyphae that help deliver phosphorus to plants."[37] In fact, studies show that from 1900–1950, when settlers first plowed up prairie grasses, the soil's natural carbon and N_2O stores decreased significantly, and large amounts of these components were emitted into the atmosphere as greenhouse gases.[38] Without attention to "place" but with the pride and power of the plow, farmers turned up the rich but fragile soil of the Plains and began a process of degrading their richness.[39] Eventually, prairie farmers plowed up 60–70 percent of the eastern and nearly 30 percent of the western Great Plains.[40]

Because soil fertility declined once the natural polyculture was plowed up, farmers occasionally amended their soils with manure and other natural resources. By the 1940s, however, new chemical fertilizers came on the

---

35. As discussed briefly in the introductory chapter of this book, the effects of modern agriculture, especially as it depends on tractor power, are devastating for the ecosphere. To make our extravagant use of fossil fuels apparent, Jackson provides an illustration: in 2010, a person who was 22 years old would have "lived through over half of all the oil ever burned" (*Consulting the Genius of the Place*, 6). In addition to the negative effects listed here are the ecological costs involved in making tractors and their implements.

36. Jackson, *Consulting the Genius of the Place*, 28.

37. Montgomery, *Growing a Revolution*, 68.

38. Hartman et al., "Impact of Historical Land-Use Changes," 1117.

39. Wes Jackson describes some of the ways in which the American government ignored ecosystem limits as it made decisions about the distribution and cultivation of the Great Plains. Jackson refers to the efforts of John Wesley Powell, who studied the Great Plains and provided the nation with prescient yet unobserved advice about the Plains. Powell argued the region should be divided in plots of about 2,560 acres because of the region's fragility (*Consulting the Genius of the Place*, 43). However, Congress ignored his wisdom and established unsustainable plots of 160 acres per family in the Homestead Act of 1889 (Hurt, *American Agriculture*, 181).

40. Hartman et al., "Impact of Historical Land-Use Changes," 1106.

market and could be sprayed onto fields, usually once seeds were sown. The process that initially made highly destructive nitrogen-based bombs for war now empowered farmers to supplement the soil's fertility by artificial means.[41] This high-energy procedure, called the Haber-Bosch process, empowered chemical companies to combine unreactive atmospheric nitrogen with hydrogen, making ammonia (NH_3). This process "consumes more energy than any other aspect of the agricultural process. It takes the energy from burning 2,200 pounds of coal to produce 5.5 pounds of usable nitrogen."[42] The ammonia produced during this energy-hungry process functions as the chemical feedstock for making a wide variety of chemical fertilizers and other products, such as nylon.[43] Cheap coal and war-time chemical factories made nitrogen fertilizer quickly available, and "[w]orld fertilizer use climbed from 14 million tons in 1950 to 177 million tons in 2010, helping to boost the world grain harvest nearly fourfold."[44]

Yet, the use of nitrogenous fertilizers involves the release of potent and significant amounts of greenhouse gases into the atmosphere. Of serious concern is the emission of N_2O (nitrous oxide) that takes place after synthetic fertilizers are applied to the soil and go through a process called denitrification.[45] Since N_2O is "about three hundred times more powerful

---

41. Jackson, *Consulting the Genius of the Place*, 79.

42. McKenney, "Artificial Fertility," 127.

43. Smil, *Enriching the Earth*, 134.

44. Brown, *Full Planet, Empty Plates*, 77. To its credit, the US uses less fertilizer than does China. Nevertheless, the US has higher yields because US farmers plant soybeans—nitrogen fixers—in rotation with grain crops so that they reduce the need for artificial fertilizers (*Full Planet, Empty Plates*, 77–78). Typical chemical fertilizers used for wheat cultivation include "nitrogen fertilizer (N), phosphorous fertilizer (P_2O_5), potassium fertilizer (K_2O), limestone fertilizer ($CaCO_3$)" (O'Donnell et al., "Relative Contribution of Transportation," 488).

45. Sanders and Webber, "Comparative Analysis," 7; Meisterling, Samaras, and Schweizer, "Decisions to Reduce Greenhouse Gases," 225. Another important factor in determining the amount of greenhouse gases released during agriculture is the role of carbon sequestration in the soil. Different soil types hold varying amounts of carbon, and different tilling practices stimulate the release of CO_2 at different rates. Scientists who study these complex factors, sometimes find themselves confused. For example, one study noted, "the variability and disagreement in studies of wheat's potential to sequester carbon cannot be understated. The magnitude of variance is substantial, with studies reporting up to 1440 kg CO_2 eq/ha sequestered, down to 1404 kg CO_2 eq/ha emitted for conventional tillage wheat cultivation" (O'Donnell et al., "Relative Contribution of Transportation," 491). With further study, however, it is hoped more accurate data and comprehension will become available.

than carbon dioxide in creating climate warming" and because it "accounts for about 60 percent of total agriculture-produced emissions in the United States," according to the EPA, conventional industrial agriculture's heavy dependence on nitrogenous fertilizers is of significant moral and global concern.[46] To put this matter in concrete terms, simply making the nitrogenous fertilizer to nourish the grain that goes into a 1 kg loaf of bread requires 42 grams CO_2 equivalent to be released into the atmosphere during the Haber-Bosch process.[47] This figure does not even include the 96 grams (CO_2 equivalent) of N_2O that is then emitted from the fertilized soil. Overall, in 2010, land preparation and cultivation of wheat on US farms released about 18 billion kg CO_2 equivalent into the atmosphere.

What is particularly ironic about this industrial solution to decreased fertility is that nitrogen fertilizers increase agricultural yields only for a time.[48] In the long-term, synthetic nitrogen fertilizers undermine the health of soils and pollute ecosystems. Whereas healthy soils have an inherent capacity to replenish the nutrients depleted during growing seasons, nitrogen fertilizers interrupt this process. They instead initiate

> the destruction of soil biodiversity by diminishing the role of nitrogen-fixing bacteria and amplifying the role of everything that feeds on nitrogen. These feeders then speed up the decomposition of organic matter and humus. As organic matter decreases [and CO_2 is released into the air], the physical structure of soils changes. With less pore space and loss of their sponge-like qualities, soils are less efficient at retaining moisture and air.[49]

These factors decrease the soil's life-sustaining capacities. Consequently, what appears to be an easy short cut to fertility in fact accelerates soil degradation. Overall, dependence on synthetic fertilizers threatens the entire foundation on which productive agriculture rests: healthy soils.

46. The global agricultural sector emits over 7,000,000 tons of N_2O each year (Miller, *Farming and the Food Supply*, 80–81). While it is true that organically based and manure-based fertilizers also release nitrous oxide, "the majority of agricultural nitrous oxide emissions are the result of the synthetic nitrogen fertilizers used in great quantities by industrial farms" (80).

47. Meisterling, Samaras, and Schweizer, "Decisions to Reduce Greenhouse Gases," 228. A 1 kg loaf of bread requires about 0.67 kg of wheat.

48. Montgomery, *Growing a Revolution*, 11. It is important to note that synthetic fertilizers only help soils that are already nutrient-depleted. Montgomery explains, "fertilizers could boost crop yields on degraded, nutrient-poor soils, but they don't help that much on already fertile land."

49. McKenney, "Artificial Fertility," 125.

Creation's Destruction

In addition to negatively affecting soil structure and composition, synthetic fertilizers degrade and even destroy the health of ecosystems, for they find their way into streams, rivers, lakes, and oceans, and thereby create hypoxic (low oxygen) dead zones.[50] Dead zones have become an all-too-common example of anthropogenic destruction. The dead zone in the Gulf of Mexico—the second largest hypoxic area in the world's waters—is an area with high concentrations of fertilizer run-off that make algae grow at fast rates.[51] But when the algae die, oxygen is used in the process of decomposition. This process, then, takes the limited amounts of oxygen from the water that fish and other animals need for life and causes them to suffocate. "Every summer for more than 30 years high nitrogen levels at the Mississippi River Delta have caused a dead zone where the water empties into the Gulf of Mexico. This dead zone, in which oxygen levels are too low for animals to survive, covered more than 8000 square miles (more than 20,000 km^2) of ocean in 2001" and 8776 square miles in 2017.[52] Because farmers apply nitrogen fertilizers so heavily in the mid-west and Great Plains, the Gulf's dead zone has become a vast area in which God's swarming creatures cannot survive (Gen 1:20–21).

The negative effects on soil, air, water, and aquatic health speak strongly against synthetic fertilizers. And, what is more, since as much as "50% of the [nitrogen] applied to agricultural land [is] not taken up by the crop,"[53] this approach to fertility is highly inefficient. It is also unsustainable for the longhaul. Synthetic nitrogenous fertilizers demand inordinate amounts of energy for their production, alter soil microbial life, change soil structure, disrupt and destroy aquatic communities, and cause global warming. Synthetic nitrogen fertilizers, therefore, fail to measure up to our eco-ethical principles and standards for a just food system.

Although we cannot alter the ways in which the United States acquired land in the past (though we may offer reparations for its injustices against Native Americans), we may begin the difficult process of liberating creation from its slavery to destruction by, first, seeing our acquisition and

---

50. Jackson, *Consulting the Genius of the Place*, 79.

51. NOAA, "Dead Zone."

52. NESTA, "Fertilizing the Earth with Nitrogen"; NOAA, "Smaller-Than-Expected." Dead zones are all over the world, in fact, "[t]here are about 150 dead zones in the world's oceans. Almost all of them are located at the mouths of rivers where fertilizers and other nutrient sources like sewage and livestock waste are added to the seawater" (NESTA, "Fertilizing the Earth with Nitrogen"). See the introduction for more discussion.

53. Jia and Shevliakova, "Land-Climate Interactions," 5.

preparation of land for what it is and, second, transitioning to regenerative forms of agriculture (for more discussion, see 7.1–2). The inordinate amounts of suffering and, at times, the degradation of the long-term health of ecosystems and communities that industrial forms of agriculture in the Great Plains have prompted illustrate that our current approach to farming in the Great Plains initiates local and global forms of destruction even before seeds are sown.

6.2.2 Cultivation

With the land acquired and prepared, farmers cultivate the land by sowing seeds and managing weeds and pests until harvest. The seeds of choice in the Great Plains are typically varieties of wheat since wheat grows in semi-arid conditions, and this area receives limited amounts of rainfall. In the north, farmers often plant spring wheat (planted in the spring) and, in the south, winter wheat (planted in the fall).[54] Because of the harsher conditions in the northern Great Plains, farmers often sow hard winter wheat, which was brought from Siberia and now functions as the core ingredient in America's bread flour because of its high protein content.[55]

Until a few decades ago farmers plowed their fields in order to kill unwanted plants, and, then, they would sow wheat seeds. However, since the development of herbicides, many farmers now spray their fields with a glyphosate-based herbicide (GBH) to kill non-crop plants.[56] They then

---

54. Hartman et al., "Impact of Historical Land-Use Changes," 1106.

55. In 1898, Mark Alfred Carleton traveled throughout Eurasia in search of wheat strains adapted for harsh conditions. Having already encountered a promising option among Russian Mennonites living in the Great Plains, Carleton sought "a variety that would ripen despite extreme weather conditions—wheat that was not only frost resistant but ice-storm resistant" (Kaufman, *Bet the Farm*, 229). In returning to the US, Carleton introduced "twenty-three new cereals" to the agricultural community (230). After testing the new varieties against standard varieties, he found that hard winter wheat from Siberia best endured the intense weather conditions of the northern Plains. Kaufman explains: "By 1914, half of the U.S. annual yield of winter wheat was Carleton's variety, more than eighty million bushels" (230). Carleton's pursuit demonstrates humanity's dire need to preserve earth's biodiversity, especially its seed bank.

56. The way glyphosate works is by interrupting a plant's production of essential amino acids, which are necessary for growth and function. At the same time that it works against "weeds," glyphosate similarly affects any bacteria, fungi, and plants it touches that are not tolerant of this chemical. More specifically, Myers et al. explain, "the primary mode of glyphosate herbicidal activity is the inhibition of a key plant enzyme, namely 5-enolpyruvylshikimate-3-phosphate synthase (EPSPS). This enzyme is part of

CREATION'S DESTRUCTION

use a seed drill to place wheat seeds into the soil. This process is called no-till or low-till agriculture and achieves the important goal of reducing soil erosion. Farmers growing crops other than wheat also spray GBHs to prepare for sowing.[57] After seeds are sown, farmers then face the vagaries of weather; the difficult challenges of providing water to their crops in particularly dry seasons;[58] and keeping weeds, diseases, or unwelcome insects and animals at bay.

---

the shikimic acid pathway and is essential for the synthesis of aromatic amino acids that govern multiple, essential metabolic processes in plants, fungi, and some bacteria. Since this EPSPS-driven pathway does not exist in vertebrate cells, some scientists and most regulators assumed that glyphosate would pose minimal risks to mammals. However, several studies . . . now show that GBHs can adversely affect mammalian biology via multiple mechanisms" (Myers et al., "Concerns over Use," 2). The initial belief that animals, including humans, would remain unscathed by glyphosate spray or residue has had alarming staying power. Despite the findings of many researchers throughout the world deeming glyphosate dangerous and promoting certain forms of cancer, the EPA has maintained its initial designation of glyphosate as a category IV chemical, which is considered "least toxic," and its 1993 categorization of "this compound into class E, which means that it is probably not carcinogenic to humans" (Bai and Ogbourne, "Glyphosate," 18988; George et al., "Studies on Glyphosate-Induced Carcinogenicity," 951).

57. The use of glyphosate-based herbicides (GBHs) dominates industrial agriculture. For an explanation on its origins and its relationship to genetic modification, see the Appendix.

58. Even though unjust and unsustainable forms of water use (especially from rivers and aquifers) plague much of American agriculture, it does not typically characterize wheat agriculture. Most US wheat is not irrigated on a regular basis, but other primary crops are heavily irrigated and quickly draw down freshwater resources (Meisterling, Samaras, and Schweizer, "Decisions to Reduce Greenhouse Gases," 225). Whether the water hydrates wheat or some other crop, much of the irrigation water in the Plains comes from a deep, underground aquifer called the Ogallala. By using the water from the aquifer at rates that far exceed its replenishment rates, current agricultural practices endanger the long-term well-being of the Great Plains and its human societies. By 2010, irrigation of the Ogallala aquifer had depleted its ancient stores of water by 22 percent. Scientists project that, if current practices continue, 55 percent of the aquifer's water will be gone by 2060, and only 27 percent of its water will remain in 2120 (Steward et al., "Tapping Unsustainable Groundwater," 3479). Once the aquifer is empty, it will take an estimated 500–1300 years for its water levels to be restored (3478). Because farms and cities have drawn down aquifer levels so drastically and quickly, millions of acres of farmland that were once irrigated can no longer grow traditional crops because equipment is unable to pump water from the aquifer's increasing depths. At the same time, glacial and snow fed rivers are running dry because of climate change and because urban centers are increasing their demands for water (both from rivers and aquifers) (Brown, *Full Planet, Empty Plates*, 66). And although some farmers have decreased their dependence on irrigation by attempting to maintain the soil's moisture content through low-till and no-till agriculture, even these practices, when allied with herbicides, come with devastating consequences. An additional negative consequence, salinization, attends

After wheat plants (and other cereal grains) have sufficiently developed, some farmers engage in a new practice called green burndown or grain drying. With this approach, they spray their crop with GBHs in order to hasten the plant's death and drying process. With glyphosate's role at the beginning and end of the production process for wheat (which, for now, remains a non-genetically modified crop product) and its season-long uses in the production of genetically modified crops, glyphosate dominates the agricultural scene.[59]

Yet the agricultural gains in ease and yield that agribusinesses promised from the application of glyphosate-based herbicides have been relatively short-lived and accompanied by several unintended and deleterious consequences. While corporations selling Roundup Ready seeds (crop seeds that have been genetically modified to be herbicide tolerant) and their accessory glyphosate-based herbicides (GBHs) promised two outcomes for their clientele, "better yields and less chemical use,"[60] the need for more, different, and stronger herbicides has yearly confronted farmers using GBHs. Because weeds are living things with the ability to adapt to changing conditions, including poisons, weeds resistant to glyphosate have evolved. Thus, farmers have had to rely on increasing amounts and varieties of herbicides to maintain crop yields.[61] For example, in 1993 the average Kansas wheat

---

irrigation. Irrigation increases the amount of salt that resides in soil, making it more difficult—if not impossible—for crops to grow and thrive. It is likely that "[s]ome 55-60 million acres (about 10 percent of all U.S. cropped land) have been degraded by salinization" (Warshall, "Tilth and Technology," 171). As ancient Mesopotamian history tells us, salinization of soils has repeatedly been a root cause of empire collapse (171). Since agriculture typically requires a great deal of water, "70 percent of world water use is for irrigation," shortages in water shall lead to food shortages (Brown, *Full Planet, Empty Plates*, 57). Water use, especially in growing food, is a clear social and ethical concern.

59. Genetically modified wheat strains have been developed, but, as of 2022, farmers had not yet adopted them for use with Roundup®. However, the use of genetically modified, Roundup Ready crop varieties (including soybeans, maize, cotton, alfalfa, and sugar beets) has become extraordinarily popular throughout the world. Because glyphosate tolerance allows for greater use of GBHs (even during the growing season), the agricultural sector uses the majority of glyphosate produced, with agriculture consuming 90 percent in the US in 2010 (Benbrook, "Trends in Glyphosate Herbicide Use," 5).

60. Mart, *Pesticides*, 194; Myers et al., "Concerns over Use," 3.

61. In a study that examined genetically modified (GM) agriculture from 1996 to 2013 (therefore, non-wheat crops), increases in weed resistance to one of the most common herbicides, glyphosate, developed. Applications of herbicides "put tremendous selection pressure on weeds and as a result contributed to the evolution of weed populations predominated by resistant individual weeds" (Brookes and Barfoot, "Environmental Impacts of Genetically Modified," 105). Consequently, farmers have had to apply more and different herbicides to their fields (105). It should be noted, however, that

farmer applied 0.33 kg/hectare of glyphosate in a one-time pass in order to rid fields of weeds before planting wheat. By 2012, however, the farmer had to apply 0.95 kg/hectare for glyphosate to be effective, an almost three-fold increase.[62] Farmers and scientists have found the "severity of the weed control challenges posed, worldwide, by the emergence and spread of glyphosate-resistant weeds is unprecedented."[63] From a theological perspective, we may recognize that the plants we call "weeds" have a God-given biological drive to thrive and reproduce. As a result, their genetic capacity to adapt to and survive in the presence of poisons has thwarted our human attempts to increase yield, decrease labor, and maintain safety.

In response to the problem of ever-evolving "superweeds," Bayer-Monsanto and other GBH manufacturers[64] have developed new and improved GBHs. Commercial formulations—such as Roundup® 400, Roundup® 450, and Roundup® WeatherMAX—contain co-formulants, including surfactants that "facilitate penetration of the active ingredient [glyphosate] and increase efficacy"[65] and adjuvants that promote glyphosate's destructive work. However, "[t]he identity of the co-formulants (declared as inert) is generally

---

conventional farmers who planted non-GM strains of these crops also had to increase their applications of herbicides; thus, non-GM conventional farmers outpaced farmers growing herbicide tolerant crops in their applications of GBHs (105–6). See also Blatt, *America's Environmental Report Card*, 121–22.

62. Benbrook, "Trends in Glyphosate Herbicide Use," 9. Benbrook explains, "For a few years post–1996, one, or at most two applications of glyphosate proved highly effective and economical on nearly all cropland planted to GE-HT [genetically engineered-herbicide tolerant] seeds. As a result, the land area treated with glyphosate rose rapidly. Over time this triggered the emergence of weed phenotypes less sensitive or resistant to glyphosate. In response, farmers increased both the rate of glyphosate application as well as the number of applications. Many farmers also integrated additional herbicides into spray programs" (12).

63. Myers et al., "Concerns over Use," 3–4. On account of these factors, farmers have made "major changes in tillage and cropping patterns" and have endured "large increases in . . . costs and the diversity and volume of herbicides" that they must use (4).

64. Monsanto's patent for glyphosate expired in 2000, which allowed many other companies to create glyphosate-based products. Benbrook et al. explain that Bayer-Monsanto "has typically not competed directly or solely on price, and instead has been successful in holding or expanding market share by bundling purchase of higher-price, Monsanto brand, Roundup herbicides with the purchase of Monsanto herbicide-tolerant seeds. Especially in the U.S., this bundling strategy has been augmented by various volume incentives and discounts, especially financing, rebates for purchase of other herbicides working through a mode of action other than glyphosate's (to delay the spread of resistant weeds), and other non-price benefits tailored to appeal to large volume customers" (Benbrook, "Trends in Glyphosate Herbicide Use," 10).

65. Bai and Ogbourne, "Glyphosate," 18992.

kept confidential."⁶⁶ The negative effects of these additional chemicals have not yet been adequately studied and taken into account by the US Department of Agriculture (USDA) and the Environmental Protection Agency (EPA). In the 1970s and 80s, when US government agencies initially considered the safety of glyphosate, they studied only the effects of pure glyphosate rather than the commercial formulations of glyphosate-based herbicides.⁶⁷ Even to this day, regulatory and oversight agencies commissioned to protect consumers have arguably accepted outdated information regarding GBHs and do not truly regulate current formulations of these herbicides.⁶⁸

With the EPA's limited focus when approving "glyphosate," corporations are free to develop, improve, and offer farmers glyphosate-based herbicide formulations that contain undisclosed ingredients. However, many studies have shown that glyphosate is much more destructive to human and nonhuman health when it is paired with such "inert" co-formulants.⁶⁹ In addition to the problems with commercial formulations, scientists have found that glyphosate itself, along with its metabolites (chemicals into which glyphosate breaks down, the most prominent of which is aminomethylphosphonic acid [AMPA]) are more destructive than once believed. Before we consider scientific findings about how glyphosate-based herbicides are harmful to soil microbes, soil macrobes, insects, animals, and humans that encounter or ingest them, we will first unmask Bayer-Monsanto's

---

66. Defarge et al., "Co-Formulants in Glyphosate-Based Herbicides," 1.

67. Defarge et al., "Co-Formulants in Glyphosate-Based Herbicides," 1. Although "most GBH use has occurred in the last 10 years, . . . most studies considered by regulatory agencies for the assessment of GBHs focused just on the active ingredient, and were conducted in the 1970s through mid–1980s. Since the late 1980s, only a few studies relevant to identifying and quantifying human health risks have been submitted to the U.S. EPA and incorporated in the agency's GBH human-health risk assessment" (Myers et al., "Concerns over Use," 4).

68. See, for example, the Interim Registration Review Decision of January 2020 in which glyphosate alone, not its commercial formulations, is considered (Reaves, "Interim Registration Review Decision").

69. For example, a study illustrated that "neat glyphosate had the least toxicity (~2 g L-1) in vitro, whereas Roundup® 400 and 450 had the highest toxicity (~0.001 g L-1)" (Bai and Ogbourne, "Glyphosate," 18992). Gasnier et al. explain: "The mixtures in formulations in this work are always the most toxic in comparison to G [glyphosate] alone . . . We confirm that the nature of the adjuvants changes the toxicity more than G itself, not only in embryonic or neonate cells . . . but also in human cell lines . . . from young or adult" (Gasnier et al., "Glyphosate Based Herbicides Are Toxic," 189).

role in silencing these findings and pushing governmental agencies to continue to approve the use of glyphosate and GBHs.[70]

6.2.2.1 Glyphosate, Agribusinesses, and Governmental Oversight

Recent lawsuits against Bayer-Monsanto condemn this agribusiness behemoth for unclearly warning users about Roundup®'s possible carcinogenic effects. By 2019, approximately 11,000 lawsuits had come against Bayer-Monsanto for its role in obfuscating Roundup®'s health risks, particularly its correlation with non-Hodgkin Lymphoma.[71] On account of these lawsuits and the documents Bayer-Monsanto has been forced to reveal, investigators have found that Monsanto employees ghostwrote portions of scholarly articles that confound scientific data. These ghostwritten articles attempt to subvert the findings by other scientists and the conclusion that glyphosate causes or promotes cancer. Monsanto scientists also covertly presented data at conferences arguing that glyphosate was not carcinogenic, and they tampered with the conclusions of several peer reviewed journal articles.[72]

In addition to surreptitiously influencing scientific inquiry, Monsanto also unduly influenced the US Environmental Protection Agency (EPA) to maintain its loose regulation of glyphosate-based herbicides (GBHs). After the International Agency for Research on Cancer (IARC) had concluded in 2015 that glyphosate was a probable carcinogen, US agencies once again reviewed scientific evidence for and against its safety. Documents disclosed during recent lawsuits against Bayer-Monsanto "reveal that Monsanto worked very closely with at least three EPA officials to derail a review of glyphosate by the Agency for Toxic Substances and Disease Registry (ATSDR) that was underway in 2015." During this time, Eric Sachs of Monsanto wrote to an EPA employee, "We're trying to do everything we can to keep from having a domestic IARC."[73] In other words, Monsanto was working

---

70. Myers et al., "Concerns over Use," 3.

71. Fang, "Emails Show Monsanto." The number of lawsuits was at 3,500 in 2017 (Krimsky and Gillam, "Roundup Litigation Discovery Documents," 3).

72. Krimsky and Gillam, "Roundup Litigation Discovery Documents," 3. Two articles that were revealed to be ghostwritten by Monsanto employees include: Williams, Kroes, and Munro, "Safety Evaluation and Risk Assessment"; Williams et al., "Review of the Carcinogenic Potential." Scientist Gilles-Eric Seralini similarly criticizes Pablo Steinberg for misrepresenting data and presenting misleading conclusions (Seralini, "Update on Long-Term Toxicity").

73. Krimsky and Gillam, "Roundup Litigation Discovery Documents," 5.

to prevent US agencies from concluding that glyphosate was a probable carcinogen. Ultimately, the EPA disagreed with IARC and declared in 2016 that glyphosate was "not likely" to be carcinogenic, citing articles ghostwritten by Monsanto employees.[74]

While the "EPA continues to find that there are no risks of concern to human health when glyphosate is used in accordance with its current label," it has simultaneously set limits on how much glyphosate residue may safely be on food crops.[75] Over time, the EPA has typically relaxed these limits, permitting increasingly higher amounts of glyphosate residue to exist on food products. For example, the EPA established 0.1 parts per million (ppm) of glyphosate as the residue tolerance allowed on field corn grain in 1993, but it raised this tolerance to 5 ppm in 2015 and maintained this level in 2021. The tolerances for oats and wheat grains went from 0.1 in 1993 to a startling 30 ppm glyphosate in 2015 and 2021 in correlation with green burndown practices. And most striking of all, dry alfalfa hay tolerance of glyphosate residues went from 0.2 in 1993 to 400 ppm in 2015 and 2021 because genetically engineered herbicide-tolerant (GE-HT) alfalfa appeared on the market (and because the hay would feed animals rather than humans directly).[76]

These large increases in tolerance levels are motivated by at least three factors. First, since weeds have evolved herbicide resistance, farmers require higher concentrations and sometimes more varieties of GBHs to

74. Krimsky and Gillam, "Roundup Litigation Discovery Documents," 3. Krimsky and Gillam explain: "The review concluded that IARC's classification of glyphosate as a probable human carcinogen was inaccurate and that glyphosate was 'unlikely to pose a carcinogenic risk to humans.' The internal emails obtained through discovery show that a key goal of the publication of the papers was to influence the European Chemicals Agency (ECHA)" (3). Krimsky and Gillam go on to explain that the "declaration of interests" section of the paper positively denied influence from or even contact with Monsanto employees (4). Yet, "the documents obtained through discovery indicate those statements were not true. The documents demonstrate Monsanto was engaged in organizing, reviewing, and editing the drafts, even arguing with one of the authors and overruling him about language in the manuscript" (4).

75. "Glyphosate."

76. The 1993 and 2015 tolerances are listed in Benbrook, "Trends in Glyphosate Herbicide Use," 9. The tolerances set in 2021 can be found at Electronic Code of Federal Regulations, "Glyphosate; Tolerances for Residues." In slight contrast to the trends described above, the 1993 EPA tolerance of glyphosate residue on soybean seeds was set at 20 ppm (parts per million) but raised to 40 ppm in 2015 and, then, lowered to 20 ppm again in 2021 (Benbrook, "Trends in Glyphosate Herbicide Use," 9; Electronic Code of Federal Regulations, "Glyphosate; Tolerances for Residues.").

maintain desirable effects. Second, because corporations have developed new GM crops that tolerate glyphosate, farmers spray GBHs throughout the growing season on crops that were not previously sprayed directly. Those crops, consequently, require higher tolerance levels in order to be acceptable on the market. Third, because agronomists have introduced green burndown as an agricultural method, farmers now spray non-GM cereal grains (including wheat and oats) with GBHs just before harvest. All these changes have influenced the EPA to increase its residue tolerances. But at the same time that the EPA has increased its tolerances, scientists have disclosed data demonstrating that even the previous, lower tolerances are in some instances toxic to nonhumans and humans.

With all this collusion, obfuscation, and contamination, it becomes difficult at this moment and on this topic to trust governmental agencies as "God's servant for your good" (Rom 13:4 NRSV).[77] Yet, because the EPA has continued to approve glyphosate and has even increased the amounts of allowable glyphosate residue on some crops, it has led farmers and consumers into a false sense of security. The EPA continues to hold the trust of the people. The foregoing and proceeding discussions, however, aim to unsettle this trust in the EPA and agribusinesses, most especially regarding their service of the ecological, biological, and societal good.

6.2.2.2 Glyphosate, Ecological Harm, and Mammalian Disease

Comprehending and evaluating the studies on glyphosate and glyphosate-based herbicides (GBHs) is by no means simple or straightforward.[78]

---

77. In addition to the problems noted above, "FDA officials also were aware that safety testing on the first GE [genetically engineered] food, the Calgene FlavrSavr tomato, had shown that consumption of this product resulted in stomach lesions in laboratory rats. Even more significantly, the FDA had already concluded that genetic engineering was a possible cause for the 37 deaths and 1,500 disabling illnesses caused by consumption of the dietary supplement L-tryptophan. . . . The FDA's response to the potential toxicity problem with GE food was, and continues to be, to ignore it. It has disregarded its own scientists, the clear scientific evidence, and the deaths and illnesses that may have resulted from this problem. The agency refused to require pre-market toxicological testing for GE foods or any toxicity monitoring whatsoever. The FDA made these decisions with no scientific basis and without independent scientific review. The agency's actions can only be seen as a shameful acquiescence to industry pressure and a complete abandonment of its responsibility to assure food safety" (Mendelson, "Untested, Unlabeled," 152–53).

78. The overview I present here certainly does not attempt to be exhaustive or definitive. I am not a medical professional or experimental scientist. However, my basic

However, it is the contention of this section that the use of glyphosate and glyphosate-based herbicides (GBHs) in agriculture leaves consumers vulnerable to unacceptably high personal and ecosystem health risks. It also entangles them in a system of violence that exposes farmworkers to disproportionate amounts of disease and distress. Agricultural uses of glyphosate and GBHs, then, ensnare us in subjecting creation to frustration and destruction (Rom 8:20–21) as we injure others by what we eat (14:15). They fail to meet many of the eco-ethical principles presented in 6.0 above.

Several factors make it very complex for us to comprehend, compare, and assess the scientific literature on glyphosate and GBHs. One set of factors concerns the duration and intensity of exposure to glyphosate and GBHs that test subjects undergo.[79] Scientists often classify their experiments as studying the effects of acute, chronic, or subchronic exposure to glyphosate and/or its commercial formulations.[80] Studies of acute exposures often employ relatively large amounts of glyphosate and/or GBHs that are administered over a short period of time. Since the concentrations and amounts employed in acute studies usually far exceed the concentrations that farmers spray on their fields, these studies mimic accidental or even purposeful large exposures (such as attempted suicide). Such studies are particularly noteworthy for helping us consider the safety of glyphosate and GBHs for those who may be most likely to ingest, touch, or inhale these chemicals at high concentrations or in large quantities, such as farmworkers, factory workers, and landscapers.

In contrast, experiments on chronic or subchronic exposure assess the effects of exposures to glyphosate and/or GBHs taking place over longer periods of time and at relatively lower concentrations. Chronic exposure entails repeated contact with the chemical over a significant portion of the organism's lifetime (about 10 percent or more of its lifetime, or over 90 days in lab animals). Subchronic exposure involves contact with the chemical

---

training in biological sciences at the undergraduate level and my diligent study of scientific journal articles enable me to summarize and, to a limited extent, interpret the scientific findings reviewed here.

79. While this section draws heavily on research that tests laboratory animals so that we might understand the negative effects of glyphosate and GBHs more accurately, I acknowledge the real suffering these animals undergo. Much could be said about the complex topic of laboratory testing and whether it aligns with our eco-ethical principles. For now, however, we will proceed with appreciation for the animals that gave their lives and their well-being for our greater understanding.

80. Bai and Ogbourne, "Glyphosate," 18992.

for a shorter portion of an organism's lifetime, about 30–90 days in lab animals.[81] Chronic and subchronic studies often administer glyphosate and/or GBHs at concentrations that are comparable to or even less than those used in agricultural applications. The results of these studies help us identify the safety of GBHs not only for farmworkers, factory workers, and landscapers but also for community members and consumers who come into contact with low concentrations of glyphosate and/or its commercial formulations over a relatively long period of time.

A second set of complicating factors concerns the fact that experiments examine the effects of varying amounts of glyphosate and a variety of commercial formulations of glyphosate-based herbicides. Scientists have found that it is necessary to study pure glyphosate as well as the wide range of commercially available GBHs since the commercial formulations contain undisclosed ingredients that assist glyphosate in penetrating the interior of plants (and, similarly, exposed animals). As a result of these co-formulants, the commericial formulations often cause harm to test subjects at lower concentrations than does glyphosate alone.

A third factor making interpretation difficult entails the question of how much glyphosate (along with its co-formulants) consumers likely ingest and how this amount compares to the experiments that scientists conduct.[82] One approach to calibrating this comparison is by considering the tolerance levels the EPA has set for how much glyphosate residue can be on common food crops and products.[83] Since farmers must spray their fields in such a way as to stay below these tolerances when their crops and products are harvested, consumers can be relatively confident that the foods they ingest have fewer parts per million (ppm) of glyphosate than the EPA's maximum tolerance levels. The chart below presents the EPA's tolerance levels, as listed in 2021, for a number of popular crops and products (Table 2).[84]

---

81. "Chronic."

82. In 1993, the EPA set the daily reference dose for glyphosate at 2.0 mg/kg/day. Daily reference dose refers to the amount the EPA consideres safe for a human to ingest each day without negative effect (USEPA, "R.E.D. Facts: Glyphosate," 3).

83. Although this section keeps in view the EPA's tolerance levels in order to understand how relevant the research on glyphosate is to consumers, it also recognizes the fact that some chemicals would be removed during food processing. Thus, the wheat bran flakes in one's cereal may not have the (up to) 30 ppm of glyphosate residue that the wheat grains once contained.

84. The EPA explains that the tolerances concern glyphosate and "its metabolites and degradates" that result "from the application of glyphosate, the isopropylamine salt of glyphosate, the ethanolamine salt of glyphosate, the dimethylamine salt of glyphosate,

Table 2. The EPA's Glyphosate Residue Tolerances for Common Food Crops

Crop	Residue Amount (ppm)
Berry and small fruit in group 13–17 (such as, raspberry, blueberry, grape, strawberry)	0.20
Citrus fruit in group 10–10 (such as, grapefruit, lemon, lime, orange)	0.50
Pome fruit in group 11–10 (such as, apple, pear)	0.20
Stone fruit in group 12 (such as, cherry, peach, plum, prune)	0.2
Sweet corn (kernel on cob, no husk)	3.5
Cereal grain for forage, fodder, and straw in group 16 (such as, corn, wheat, and other cereal grains)	100
Cereal grain in group 15 (such as, barley, corn, oats, wheat)[a]	30
Oilseeds in group 20 (such as, cottonseed, flax seed, safflower, sunflower)	40
Canola seed	20
Soybean seed	20

Source: Data adapted from Electronic Code of Federal Regulations, "Glyphosate; Tolerances for Residues"; Electronic Code of Federal Regulations, "Crop Group Tables"

[a] This tolerance applies to group 15, excepting field corn, popcorn, rice, sweet corn, and wild rice.

Of particular interest for the purposes of this chapter is the 30 ppm of glyphosate residue allowed on wheat grain.

---

the ammonium salt of glyphosate, and the potassium salt of glyphosate" (Electronic Code of Federal Regulations, "Glyphosate; Tolerances for Residues.").

While one type of food by itself probably does not deliver harmful levels of glyphosate to the consumer, the combination of foods and water that people ingest day after day may cause dangerous levels of glyphosate to enter people's bodies. This is all the more likely when glyphosate contaminates the core ingredients of the American diet: wheat, soy, and corn.[85] Even those who avoid eating conventional food products are hard pressed to keep glyphosate at bay since this herbicide contaminates many US soils and waters. A study in 2014 showed that "glyphosate . . . [was] detected in" 40 percent "of 3700 soil, water and sediment samples collected from 38 sites in the USA between 2001 and 2010."[86] Although glyphosate does decompose, it does so at different rates depending on the type of soil it contaminates. The half-life of glyphosate is longest in clay soils, halving its concentration within 151 days. Consequently, "[p]rolonged half-life and slow degradation may increase the risk of long-term environmental contamination."[87]

Compared to Canada and Europe, the US EPA has set relatively high tolerance levels for glyphosate residues. When these levels are correlated with the findings from recent scientific studies, as discussed below, we discover that the foods we consume may contain levels of glyphosate or GBHs that have proven to be detrimental to physiological processes. For example, even though the US now allows for up to 30 ppm of glyphosate residue on wheat grains, scientists have found that glyphosate, its metabolites, and its co-formulants cause cell damage and death, interrupt normal endocrine function, alter reproductive capacities, and promote the growth of cancer

---

85. In 2011 the USDA found "residues of glyphosate in 90.3% of 300 soybean samples . . . at concentrations of 1.9 ppm" (Myers et al., "Concerns over Use," 3). Glyphosate's residual presence on food crops raises concerns especially when GM foods already "were found in 70 percent of processed foods in the United States by 2003" (Mart, *Pesticides*, 194). Along with soy, corn has been genetically modified to be herbicide tolerant so that farmers may spray it throughout the growing season with GBHs. Since these ingredients are present "in a high proportion of processed foods, nearly every resident of the United States has consumed foodstuffs containing GMOs or their products" (Kloppenburg, *First the Seed*, 296) and, consequently, have been exposed to glyphosate.

86. Bai and Ogbourne, "Glyphosate," 18999. The authors cite the study by Battaglin et al., "Glyphosate and Its Degradation Product." They explain, "The MCL [maximum contaminant level] for glyphosate before posing a risk to human health is considered to be 700 μg L-1 in the USA (EPA, 2015) and 1000 μg L-1 in Australia" (Bai and Ogbourne, "Glyphosate," 18992).

87. Bai and Ogbourne, "Glyphosate," 18989. Of course, glyphosate and its co-formulants alone are not the only dangerous agricultural chemicals that contaminate conventional foods since insecticides are also sprayed on and around food grains and seeds before harvest and *during* storage (González-Curbelo et al., "Dissipation Kinetics.").

cells beginning at 0.5 ppm.[88] These findings—and those discussed below—underscore the importance of taking full account of the potential negative effects of glyphosate and its commercial formulations on a wide variety of organisms, bodily systems, and even food webs.

Soil microbes, such as bacteria, are important members of the agricultural community yet the effects of glyphosate on this community are difficult to ascertain.[89] Nevertheless, at least one study indicates that glyphosate changes the demographics, so to speak, of the bacterial community over time.[90] Such a shift decreases diversity and may be harmful. Moreover, bacterial metabolism changes once glyphosate is applied, causing bacteria in the rhizosphere of plants to acquire less iron, ammonia, and phosphate but more potassium.[91] This may be due to the fact that glyphosate is a chelator

88. Many consumers have no idea that the EPA has increased its tolerance of glyphosate residues on food and feed so dramatically in the past few decades, and they certainly are not aware of the new dangers that grain drying poses. Unfortunately, the safety testing of grain drying does not adequately assess the present-day glyphosate formulations used on the field. In 1994, a study determined that wheat treated with glyphosate right before harvest contained "less than 5 mg kg-1" and, therefore, was deemed safe (Gélinas, Gagnon, and McKinnon, "Wheat Preharvest Herbicide Application," 1597). More recent formulations of glyphosate used for grain drying, however, contain "different adjuvants or surfactants" than those tested in previous decades (1597). The new formulations are more effective in killing plants and more disruptive to animal physiology. A study in Canada—where the residue tolerance on cereal grains stands at 5 ppm (as opposed to the US's 30 ppm)—found that "wheat harvested after application of a recent Roundup® commercial formulation had 6 to 11 mg glyphosate kg-1 [or, ppm], which is higher" than Canadian tolerances allowed in 2017 (1600).

89. Since soil types and the particular species of microbes present in soils vary so greatly across the US and world, the study of glyphosate's effects on bacteria is incredibly complex. An additional complicating factor is the amount and frequency of glyphosate applied to fields. Thus, it is unclear from scientific studies the degree to which glyphosate negatively effects the microbial community in soils. A recent study indicates, however, "glyphosate has reduced the rate of photosynthesis in Euglena, has decreased the radial growth of mycorrhizal fungal species and is also reducing the profusion of certain bacteria present in rhizospheric microbial communities" (Gill et al., "Glyphosate Toxicity for Animals," 401). A different article suggests that simply measuring "microbial biomass and activity" (which is often the approach) does not determine whether the diversity and health of the microbial community has gone unharmed by glyphosate and its associated chemicals (Bai and Ogbourne, "Glyphosate," 18991).

90. Newman et al., "Changes in Rhizosphere," 33. The authors state: "long-term glyphosate use can affect rhizosphere bacterial activities and potentially shift bacterial community composition favoring more glyphosate-tolerant bacteria."

91. The presence of glyphosate in the soil causes bacteria to adjust the ways in which their RNA (ribonucleic acid) functions, for instance (Newman et al., "Changes in Rhizosphere," 39). The authors explain: "Reduced expression of an iron acquisition transcript

and therefore "binds macro- and micronutrients, essential for many plant processes and pathogen resistance. GBH treatment may thus impede uptake and availability of macro- and micronutrients in plants,"[92] as well as bacteria, resulting in decreased health. These findings indicate that glyphosate alters nutrient uptake in bacteria, which consequently may adversely affect the health not only of bacteria but also the plants that depend upon them. Consequently, the nutritious food that farmers aim to grow for people and animals is diminished at the soil level by the presence of glyphosate.

Other members of the soil community also face deleterious effects when glyphosate is applied. Soil macrobes, such as earthworms, are essential for soil and plant health especially since they decompose dead plants and animals and make their nutrients available to plants. Although a study demonstrated that earthworms are not killed by contact with glyphosate, they show "a steady and considerable decrease in [their] mean body weight" and do not produce "cocoons or juveniles" in the presence of GBHs.[93] These key participants in healthy topsoil thus find their growth foiled and reproductive efforts frustrated by glyphosate.

Scientists have observed that glyphosate and its commercial formulations alter ecosystem communities and negatively affect physiology and behavior in above ground species as well. As we will discuss below, GBHs diminish the survival fitness of insects, fish, amphibians, reptiles, and birds and, therefore, err in relation to principle 5.[94] Put more theologically, GBHs threaten and deteriorate the diversity and vitality that God commissioned for creation (Gen 1).

Sometimes glyphosate interrupts the physiology of living things but other times it eliminates the food sources on which animals depend. For example, glyphosate rids fields in the US Midwest of milkweed (which happens to be the Monarch Butterfly's selected plant on which to lay its eggs, the leaves of which the hatched larvae eat). Consequently, the extensive use of

---

suggests reduced abundance or availability of iron in the rhizosphere of glyphosate-treated crops . . . decreases in the expression of nitrogen and phosphorus metabolism transcripts would suggest decreased availability of these nutrients in the rhizosphere following glyphosate exposure" (39).

92. Mertens et al., "Glyphosate, a Chelating Agent," 5298.

93. Gill et al., "Glyphosate Toxicity for Animals," 406.

94. Glyphosate not only decreases the availability of plant and insect food sources for birds but sometimes also interrupts their reproductive capacities. See, Oliveira et al., "Effects of the Herbicide Roundup"; Gill et al., "Glyphosate Toxicity for Animals."

glyphosate has been linked to declines in Monarch butterfly populations.[95] Our efforts to grow food easily for ourselves ends up removing food from other species. By this means, we[96] do not promote and maintain Earth's biodiversity because we fail to share species-appropriate food with other members of the biotic community (principle 4; see Gen 1:29–30).

Glyphosate and GBHs also interrupt important aspects of the food web by decreasing the population(s) of key predators and prey. For example, damselfly larvae function as "both predators of small invertebrates and prey for large invertebrates and fish" and thereby "occupy an important position in aquatic food webs."[97] However, surface waters become contaminated with GBHs when these herbicides are sprayed near bodies of water, and the chemicals found in GBHs have proven to interfere with damselfly populations.[98] In this polluted environment, damselfly larvae, which hatch and develop in aquatic environments and later live on land as adults, experience "increased mortality" rates and "sublethal effects on life history, behaviour and physiology."[99] While this is a point of concern for the damselfly population itself, it also threatens ecosystem balance. Glyphosate-based herbicides, it would appear, cause negative ripple effects in and beyond the insect population.[100]

95. Pleasants and Oberhauser, "Milkweed Loss."

96. I use the pronoun "we" to refer to the industrial agricultural system most, if not all, of us are caught in, even though I expect most readers of this book are not themselves farmers. What is more, because many Americans follow the typical pattern of having "pristine" grass lawns with few if any native species, even those of us who are not farmers likely participate in a system that removes natural food sources from our fellow creatures.

97. Janssens and Stoks, "Stronger Effects of Roundup," 211. Along with glyphosate, pesticides in general are destructive to aquatic wildlife. Because the heart of American farmland drains into the Mississippi river basin, a watershed covering 1.2 million square miles (McKenney, "Artificial Fertility," 126), the water flowing into the Gulf of Mexico contains significant and deadly quantities of fertilizers and pesticides. Other river basins also have problems because of agriculture. These chemicals kill aquatic life; for example, "[b]etween 1977 and 1984, half of all the fish kills off the coast of South Carolina were attributed to pesticide contamination" (Kimbrell, *Fatal Harvest*, 30).

98. After GBHs are sprayed, natural surface waters often contain a concentration of glyphosate between 0.1 and 5.2 mg/L (or even 7.6 mg/L) (Janssens and Stoks, "Stronger Effects of Roundup," 211).

99. Janssens and Stoks, "Stronger Effects of Roundup," 213. The scientists examined the effects of pure glyphosate as well as its formulation in Roundup® (which includes polyethoxylated tallow amine [POEA]) and determined that the Roundup® mixture was more toxic than its pure "active ingredient," glyphosate.

100. Because researchers have found that glyphosate significantly reduces insect populations, Germany has developed a plan to "phase out all use of glyphosate, the

In addition to these studies on invertebrates, a multitude of studies on mammals, including human cells, have found disturbing results. Although many studies are performed on rats or mice, their results offer insights into how human physiology may be affected by glyphosate and GBHs as well. Recent studies on mammals warrant our attention, especially since US corporations and governing bodies have not yet adequately considered them in their assessment of glyphosate's safety.

Acute forms of exposure to glyphosate and GBHs rarely take place, but their effects are significant. In experiments administering high doses of glyphosate or GBHs—that is, doses that far exceed the residue tolerances in human foods—scientists have found that glyphosate and/or GBHs negatively affect reproductive capacity and functioning[101] and functions as a neurotoxin and disrupts neurotransmitter production.[102]

Alongside the conclusions from these acute studies are experiments interrogating the effects of moderate to relatively small doses of glyphosate and/or GBHs. At moderate doses, over a sub-chronic time period, scientists have found that Roundup® decreases neural cell viability,[103] interrupts proper neural development, and causes damage to neural function

---

world's most common weed killer, by December 2023" ("Germany Acts to Protect Insects," 1063).

101. In a study of adult male rats receiving acute exposure to a GBH (specifically, Roundup® Grand Travaux Plus with 450 g/L of glyphosate), the number and mobility of sperm was not affected. However, the sperm did not develop or function properly. Consequently, affected sperm were unlikely to fertilize an oocyte; or, even if a sperm was successful, scientists expected the fertilized egg would not implant properly (Cassault-Meyer et al., "Acute Exposure," 138).

102. Scientists Martínez et al. demonstrate that glyphosate causes neurotoxic effects in mammals. At doses greater than 35 mg/kg of body weight, glyphosate caused "a significant decrease in the 5-HT [serotonin], DA [dopamine] and NE [norepinephrine] contents in the brain regions studied (striatum, hippocampus, prefrontal cortex, hypothalamus, hypothalamus and midbrain), which indicated that glyphosate transfer[s] across the blood-brain barrier, enters the brain, probably accumulates in significant quantity, and exerts neurotoxicity altering the serotonergic, dopaminergic and noradrenergic systems" (Martínez et al. "Neurotransmitter Changes," 217). They also state: "glyphosate significantly altered central nervous system (CNS) monoaminergic neurotransmitters in a brain regional- and dose-related manner, effects that may contribute to the overall spectrum of neurotoxicity caused by this herbicide" (212).

103. In their 2014 study, Cattani et al. applied 0.01 percent (=0.036 g/L or 36 ppm) Roundup® to "hippocampal slices from immature rats" and found that Roundup® "decreased cell viability" in the brain cells. They highlight the fact that the concentrations of Roundup® used in agricultural applications "ranges from 1% to 2%, concentrations 10,000–20,000 times larger than those used in our experimental protocols" (41).

in gestating and young rats, which in turn negatively affect rat activity in adulthood.[104] Because GBH toxins can cross the placenta, rats whose mothers had received GBHs during pregnancy grew up to express depressive-like behaviors in adulthood.[105] The scientists conducting this study conclude, "subchronic exposure to GBH might result in outcomes ranging from oxidative damage to impairment of brain function, which may account for depressive-like behavior later in life."[106] Such findings raise concerns over the possible deleterious effects of GBHs on brain development and functionality in fetuses and offspring even though these negative effects were not apparent in the pregnant mothers.

Because bacteria play a major role in the digestive tract, altering the microbiome in animal guts can lead to physiological problems as well. A recent study explored the effects of glyphosate in rat guts and found that moderate amounts of glyphosate causes their small intenstines to become inflamed and prevents them from absorbing normal amounts of iron and magnesium.[107] In tandem with these results, the scientists also observed that glyphosate's presence alters the microbial community in the guts in deleterious ways.[108] Since some of the changes they observed have been

104. Cattani et al. explain: "In our previously [sic] work regarding maternal exposure to GBH we demonstrated that exposure during pre and postnatal periods leads to calcium overload and glutamate excitotoxicity in immature offspring hippocampus (Cattani et al., 2014). The mechanism underlying such effects involves the calcium influx by activating N-methyl-D-aspartate (NMDA) glutamate receptors and voltage-dependent calcium channels, which leads to oxidative stress and neural cell death in immature rat hippocampus (PND15)" ("Developmental Exposure," 68).

105. Along similar lines, a study of malformed piglets (whose mothers had eaten soybeans containing GBH residues) contained glyphosate in their tissues, suggesting that glyphosate may cause "congenital malformations" (Myers et al., "Concerns over Use," 3; Krüger et al., "Detection of Glyphosate"). Another study of swine showed that glyphosate and its co-formulants "have caused detrimental effects on the cardiovascular system" (Gill et al., "Glyphosate Toxicity for Animals," 417).

106. Cattani et al., "Developmental Exposure," 78. They even queried whether such observations in adult rats might help to explain the high suicide rates among farmers in recent decades (78). In a different study, scientists demonstrated that since glyphosate disrupts the microbial community in the guts of mice, it also disrupts the body's production of neurotransmitters. With fewer neurotransmitters, mice have difficulty concentrating and are prone to increased behaviors indicating anxiety and depression (Aitbali et al., "Glyphosate Based Herbicide Exposure").

107. Tang et al., "Glyphosate Exposure," 6.

108. Glyphosate promotes the increase of pernicious and pathogenic bacterial communities (such as bacteria in the phyla Spirochaetia and Fusobacteria) and simultaneously decreases the presence of some beneficial bacteria (such as bacteria in the genus *Lactobacillus* and in the phylum Firmicutes) (Tang et al., "Glyphosate Exposure," 7–8).

linked to inflammatory bowel disease, Alzheimer's disease, type II diabetes, major depressive disorder, and Parkinson's disease, glyphosate's possible role in altering the intestinal bacterial community in humans and potentially accelerating the development of these diseases is of significant social and moral concern.[109]

Moderate concentrations (greater than 36 ppm) of glyphosate have also been observed to cause cell death (necrosis) in human cells.[110] In a study on human adipose (fat) stem cells—which may differentiate into fat, connective, or bone cells in order to support the ongoing vitality of a human[111]—scientists found that at a level "below agricultural concentrations" Roundup® Original "induced a decrease in cell viability."[112] They concluded that the "glyphosate-based commercial formulation causes mild toxic effects in human adipose-derived stem cells concerning cell viability, differentiation, and alkaline phosphatase activity."[113] In other words, Roundup® causes decline in at least some human cells.

With the liver as the first organ to remove toxins from the blood, its response to the presence of glyphosate and GBHs is of significant concern. Some scientists have studied the effects of relatively low doses of glyphosate and its formulations on human liver cells and found that GBHs disrupt endocrine function at a concentration of 0.5 ppm and bring about toxic effects at 5 ppm.[114] This study reveals that at "doses far below agricultural dilutions and toxic levels," GBHs may cause endocrine disruption and negatively affect "mitochondrial activities and membrane integrity" in human cells.[115]

Beyond these laboratory studies, several cases of early-onset Parkinson's disease have been reviewed by scientists and determined to be

109. Tang et al., "Glyphosate Exposure," 8.

110. Scientists Melo et al. indicate that "[a]fter 24 h of [Roundup® Original] exposure, cell viability was observed only in concentrations equal to or less than 90 μg mL−1. Differently, for higher time exposure—48 and 72 h—cell viability was only seen in the concentration of 36 μg mL−1" ("Glyphosate-Based Herbicide Induces Toxic Effects," 4).

111. Melo et al. explain that the broad family of adipose stem cells, called "mesenchymal stem cells," "are important for maintenance of a plethora of body physiological functions" ("Glyphosate-Based Herbicide Induces Toxic Effects," 7).

112. Melo et al., "Glyphosate-Based Herbicide Induces Toxic Effects," 2, 9.

113. Melo et al., "Glyphosate-Based Herbicide Induces Toxic Effects," 11.

114. They reported that they "noticed the first toxic effects at 5 ppm [parts per million], and the first endocrine disrupting actions at 0.5 ppm, which is 800 times lower than the level authorized in some food or feed (400 ppm, US EPA, 1998)" (Gasnier et al., "Glyphosate Based Herbicides Are Toxic," 189).

115. Gasnier et al., "Glyphosate Based Herbicides Are Toxic," 189.

associated with sub-lethal levels of glyphosate exposure. After working in an herbicide factory, a 44 year-old woman "presented with rigidity, slowness and resting tremor in all four limbs with no impairment of short-term memory after sustaining long term chemical exposure to glyphosate for 3 years as a worker in a chemical factory."[116] In another case, a 38 year-old man "developed parkinsonism 4 years after ingesting glyphosate," which further suggests that "glyphosate exposure might be related to the onset of [Parkinson's disease]."[117] The woman's chronic exposure to GBHs raises particular concerns about the welfare of factory workers, farmworkers, and landscapers who come into regular contact with these chemicals. The production and use of glyphosate, then, diminishes our collective ability to protect, as much as possible, workers from injury and harm (principle 5).

In addition to Parkinson's disease, several scientific articles propose that glyphosate promotes the development of non-Hodgkin lymphoma (NHL) in humans. A 2019 study concluded that, while "the underlying mechanisms remain unknown, mechanistic studies of glyphosate-induced immunosuppression/inflammation, endocrine disruption, genetic alterations, and oxidative stress suggest plausible links between GBH exposure and NHL development."[118] Along similar lines, the National Cancer Institute has indicated that farmers using industrial herbicides are six times more likely to develop non-Hodgkin lymphoma than those who do not use them.[119] We discover, therefore, that those who grow our food endure unnecessarily high risks of suffering and disease.

And beyond those who work closely with glyphosate and GBHs on a regular basis, consumers too stand at risk, given the fact that GBHs are so ubiquitously used in the production of food and since negative health effects have been shown to result from moderate to low doses. Thus, even though the US EPA has maintained its decision to approve the use of glyphosate, this approval should not lull us into a sense of security. Given the fact that Bayer-Monsanto has inappropriately tampered with scientific studies and has pressed the EPA to continue to permit GBHs, we as consumers, farmers, and concerned citizens ought to proceed with caution.

When we consider the deleterious effects of glyphosate and GBHs in a holistic fashion, recognizing how they negatively impact organisms living

---

116. Wang et al., "Parkinsonism," 486.
117. Eriguchi et al., "Parkinsonism," 1.
118. Zhang et al., "Exposure to Glyphosate-Based Herbicides," 204.
119. Kimbrell, *Fatal Harvest*, 11.

in soil, water, and on land, we may begin to see that through our eating in such an agricultural system, we fail to uphold the eco-ethical principles proposed in this book. Instead, we are enslaving the creation to destruction (Rom 8:21) and are destroying those for whom Christ died (14:15). Such stark realities make it all the more important for consumers, society members, and followers of Christ to consider how they might more healthfully produce and procure their daily bread.

6.2.3 Collection

The amount of wheat a farmer collects during harvest depends in large measure on the number of acres sown during the cultivation phase. Thus, the distinction between a "cultivation" phase and "collection" phase breaks down when we consider farming as an economic endeavor. Farmers necessarily concentrate on how much they hope to harvest when they decide what crops to cultivate and how many acres to plant. All the while, farmers keep in view the economic realities of supply and demand.

As this section outlines, supply and demand strongly affect a farmer's activities. Sometimes when market prices are high—therefore, promising lucrative dividends—farmers might expand their cultivation into more ecologically fragile lands. This expansion into fragile territory may also occur, however, when market prices are low and farmers feel the need to produce more crops in order to sell more in the hopes of receiving more income. There are many times when market forces press farmers to take on increasing debt, usually in the form of loans for equipment, land, seeds, or chemicals. All of these economically and ecologically fraught activities happen in the midst of a food system that is regulated by the government to greater or lesser extents, depending on the prevailing political winds of the time. These and many other economic and political factors shape the process of collecting wheat and, thereby, farmers' economic conditions and the ecological health of their local ecosystems.

The forces of supply and demand changed drastically for the American farmer during World War I. For, during this war, low supplies in Europe and high demand for food pushed America's farmers onto the global stage. Consequently, US farmers in the Midwest and Great Plains significantly expanded their food production efforts to send food to Allied troops and civilians. They focused their efforts especially on growing more wheat. Since labor was scarce and demand and prices for wheat were high during the war, WWI catalyzed and funded America's costly transition from horse-powered harvesters and threshers to gasoline-powered combine farming. Under these global pressures and with these practical changes, farmers could be as productive and efficient as possible in their sowing, harvesting, and threshing of wheat.[120]

The fact that war in one place intensifies agriculture elsewhere is nicely illustrated by a cartoon on the front page of the May 16, 1918 edition of *Farm Implement News* (fig. 4).[121]

Competent Threshing Here Will Hasten the Thrashing Over There

Figure 3. "Competent Threshing Here Will Hasten the Thrashing Over There"

120. Hurt, *American Agriculture*, 251.
121. Thanks to R. Douglas Hurt for providing this image from his personal library.

The caption under the cartoon—"Competent Threshing Here Will Hasten the Thrashing Over There"—expresses the American belief that efficient and abundant food production in the US would significantly improve Allied attempts at winning the war against Germany. Farming as productively as possible became an honored expression of patriotism.

Even once World War I ended, America's leaders continued to press farmers to meet the ongoing food needs in Europe.[122] It was understood that "'Peace will bring added responsibilities to America as *the food source of the world* . . . Now we must feed hundreds of millions'" even "'hungry Germans.'"[123] Practically, this meant that from 1909 to 1929, "[n]ew technology, war, and depressed prices stimulated Great Plains farmers to break 32 million acres of sod . . . for new wheat lands."[124] While this benevolent sense of international responsibility looked after the well-being of hungry people—even former enemies (Rom 12:20)—across the globe, it did so (and continues to do so) at the expense of soil fertility, biodiversity, and the health of the ecosphere. Such a situation highlights the real and perplexing challenge of providing for human needs without sacrificing ecological health. And with so many people affected by American agriculture, the stakes of participating in the global market were, and continue to be, extremely high.

After World War I agricultural products met decreasing demands, decreasing prices, but high supplies since farmers had so effectively increased their acreage and output of wheat during WWI. Crop prices therefore dropped markedly after the war. In response, farmers continued expanding wheat production by plowing still more lands in an effort to increase sales and income.[125]

Meanwhile, ecological forces further aggravated the situation. "When drought struck the region during the early 1930s, it caused crop failure and encouraged farmers to abandon land unprotected by vegetative cover. The

---

122. President Wilson encouraged high productivity through US Food Administration posters that read: "Hunger does not breed reform; it breeds madness and all the ugly distemper that makes an ordered life impossible. The future belongs to those who prove themselves the true friends of mankind," in other words, those who grow enough food to feed the world (Eighmey, "'Food Will Win the War,'" 285).

123. This statement was made by Professor A. D. Wilson, the director of the University of Minnesota's agricultural extension division (Eighmey, "'Food Will Win the War,'" 285. Emphasis added.).

124. Hurt, *American Agriculture*, 235.

125. Hurt, *American Agriculture*, 234.

prevailing winds, averaging 10 to 12 miles per hour throughout the region, increased evaporation, weathered the soil, and brought dust storms to the southern Great Plains in January 1932."[126] Having not anticipated the region's natural cycle between dry and water abundant years, promoters of intensified agriculture in the Great Plains catalyzed the horrific events of the Dust Bowl, when "a towering three-mile-high cloud of dust blocked out the sun from Texas to the Dakotas to Ohio" and "[t]welve million tons of dirt rained down on Chicago."[127]

During this time, governmental leaders recognized that farmers needed federal aid to weather this storm. Under Franklin Delano Roosevelt, the federal government began regulating agriculture and its related economy more extensively than ever before. In 1933 the Agricultural Adjustment Act aimed to help farmers in their desperate circumstances by paying them *not* to produce "wheat, cotton, corn, hogs, rice, tobacco, and dairy products."[128] This act decreased the supply of crops so that prices to farmers might increase.[129] Although this maneuver helped farmers to some degree, complex economic factors left many Americans without access to enough income and food. The "perplexing 'paradox of want in the midst of plenty,'" of having too much produce in the fields and livestock yards while many in the US went penniless and hungry, haunted American society.[130]

Another approach the US government developed for helping farmers navigate these ecological and economic challenges involved financial incentives in support of conservation practices. Through special loan programs, the US Department of Agriculture (USDA) provided financial support to farmers for "soil-conservation practices such as terracing, reseeding native grasses, and contour plowing."[131] The government also paid farmers to replace cash crops with plants that would build up soil and it "provided crop

---

126. Hurt, *American Agriculture*, 235.

127. Montgomery, *Growing a Revolution*, 72.

128. Hurt, *American Agriculture*, 288.

129. "By paying farmers to reduce acreage and production in these basic commodities, the federal government hoped to reduce the surpluses and increase prices to the levels based on prices for the period 1909–1914" (Hurt, *American Agriculture*, 288). To reduce the number of hogs on the market, the government also encouraged farmers to kill piglets.

130. Hurt, *American Agriculture*, 290.

131. This took place through the Soil Conservation Service (Hurt, *American Agriculture*, 292).

insurance, marketing controls, and price-supporting loans."[132] In all these ways, the US government of the 1930s laid "the foundation for American agricultural policy on price-support and acreage-reduction programs" that would shape the agricultural landscape of the future.[133]

Over time, however, legislators, lobbyists, agribusinesses, and voters have pushed the US government to decrease its oversight of agriculture. While farmers often desire greater freedom from governmental regulation, they at the same time recognize the clear economic and security advantages of governmental subsidies, price supports, and other forms of aid.[134] Even as farmers have found they need better prices for their goods or more income support from the government, consumers have vied for lower food costs. Several congressional acts during the 80s and 90s attempted to solve the problem of too much supply and too low prices, but "[b]y the early 1990s . . . [the Food, Agriculture, Conservation, and Trade Act] had not solved the problems of an imbalance of supply and demand, an inadequate income for family farmers, or an escalating national debt."[135] Farmers con-

---

132. The Soil Conservation and Domestic Allotment Act, part of the Agricultural Adjustment Act (AAA) of 1938, provided conservation supporting payments (Hurt, *American Agriculture*, 291).

133. Hurt, *American Agriculture*, 291. After the terrible drought conditions of the 1930s ended, World War II ramped up demands and prices for wheat. Great Plains wheat farmers responded by cultivating more acres, including those recently protected by native grasses (303). Hurt notes that during World War II, "[f]armers recognized that expanded production would enable them to reap large profits from wartime prices and that tractors provided the means to cultivate more acreage. With the aid of tractors, farmers increased corn and wheat production by more than 9 and 2 million acres, respectively, during the war years. By 1945 30.5 percent of the farmers in the United States used tractors" (317). Eventually farmers also increased crop production by using "hybrid seeds, pesticides, insecticides, fertilizer, and mechanization" (321). Since electricity, gasoline-powered engines, and other technologies were available to pump water efficiently from underground aquifers, such as the Ogallala, farmers could irrigate their fields when rain levels were too low (321). Consequently, the drought in the Great Plains during the early and mid-1950s did not bring economic disaster to farmers, as had the Dust Bowl of the 30s, even though the drought of the 50s was more expansive (339). These new technologies increased yield despite the fact that the soil's inherent fertility was exhausted. Thus, during the mid-1900s, some could exclaim: "'it is hard to see how Americans can be seriously threatened by hunger'" (Mart, *Pesticides*, 14).

134. Hurt, *American Agriculture*, 375. Admittedly, much more could be said regarding the positive and negative effects of government subsidies and price supports in the agricultural system. For a recent analysis and explanation, see Miller, *Truth about Industrial Agriculture*.

135. Hurt, *American Agriculture*, 356.

sistently found, and continue to find, that their input costs exceed their income from crops. For example, in 1990, for every $1.50 received for farm products, the farmer spent $1.71 in farming costs.[136] This national state of affairs has led many farmers to "increase production to lower unit costs" and to follow the motto, "[g]et bigger, get better, or get out."[137] Yet the higher productivity made available through technologies and high-cost inputs simply intensifies the problem of over production and ecological degradation. For all these reasons, by the end of the twentieth century, farming had become an economically unsustainable endeavor for many small-scale agriculturalists. Most of those who have stayed in the business either supplement their income with outside employment or grow their farming enterprises to massive proportions.[138]

The economic viability of industrial farming is so perilous, in part, because it requires expensive inputs—specialized seeds bought from seed companies rather than saved; synthetic fertilizers and pesticides; expensive machinery; and fossil fuels. The high output costs lead farmers to see fewer and fewer profits from their sales.[139] This stems, for the most part, from the fact that agribusinesses are controlling food production in ever increasing ways. Since the mid-twentieth century, food manufacturers and those involved in agribusiness have attempted to increase profit by processing and packaging their products in ever-changing and expanding ways in order to captivate the consumers' palate and money. They have also found it beneficial to buy out smaller, competing companies as well as associated businesses involved along the food chain to increase control and profits. This establishes vertical and horizontal integration, in which one corporation takes "control of the production, processing, marketing, and distribution of some agricultural commodities."[140] Because the processing and manufacturing of foods takes place off the farm, the increased income these foods bring goes into the hands of large business owners and investors rather

---

136. Hurt, *American Agriculture*, 356, 75.

137. Hurt, *American Agriculture*, 374.

138. Hurt, *American Agriculture*, 375. Hurt explains, "the cost-price squeeze became the most important reason for the rapid decline in the number of farms" in the US (375).

139. For example, "[i]n 1990, three-fourths of all farmers earned less than $50,000; after they paid expenses, they averaged a net of about $16,000" in the US (Hurt, *American Agriculture*).

140. Hurt, *American Agriculture*, 388. This has, in turn, created a monopoly situation in which one company owns seeds, farming implements, and chemicals (390).

than farmers.[141] At the same time, farmers lose a great deal of decision-making freedom and incur increasing amounts of debt.[142]

The injustices at work in the food system may be accurately identified as leading to a "stolen harvest," as environmental activist Vandana Shiva explains. "As farmers are transformed from producers into consumers of corporate-patented agricultural products, as markets are destroyed locally and nationally but expanded globally, the myth of 'free trade' and the global economy becomes a means for the rich to rob the poor of their right to food and even their right to life."[143] Andrew Kimbrell also contends: "Advances in industrial agriculture have . . . put millions of the world's farmers in a fatal bind, as they spend ever more in production costs, yet receive ever less income."[144] These economic injustices result because much of the income along the food chain ends up in the hands of a few food processors rather than growers.

In light of these dynamics and the fact that, "[a]lthough farmers received large government subsidies . . . they garnered only 21 cents of each dollar that Americans spent for food by 2000, down from 32 cents in 1990,"

---

141. However, it must be acknowledged that food manufacturing provides employment opportunities to people and, so, provides income to other workers. Moreover, a farmer who signs a contract with an agribusiness acquires a certain measure of security since he or she is guaranteed a specific price for agricultural products and receives the loans necessary to purchase equipment, seed, and chemicals. Even still, Michael Pollan gives an apt example of vertical integration and its power over government: "Though the companies won't say it, it has been estimated that Cargill and ADM together probably buy somewhere near a third of all the corn grown in America. These two companies now guide corn's path at every step of the way: They provide the pesticide and fertilizer to farmers; operate most of America's grain elevators . . . ; broker and ship most of the exports; perform the wet and dry milling; feed the livestock and then slaughter the corn-fattened animals; distill the ethanol; and manufacture the high-fructose corn syrup and the numberless other fractions derived from number 2 field corn. Oh, yes—and help write many of the rules that govern this whole game, for Cargill and ADM exert considerable influence over U.S. agricultural policies . . . Cargill is the biggest privately held corporation in the world" (Pollan, *Omnivore's Dilemma*, 63).

142. Hurt, *American Agriculture*, 388. As a concrete example of the increasing gap between the market price of processed foods and the wholesale price of ingredients, Hurt explains: "Bread averaged 79 cents per loaf in 1995 but 87 cents in 1997, even though the cost of wheat per loaf dropped from 6 cents to 5 cents. The USDA attributed the increase in food prices to escalating labor costs; wages and salaries accounted for 49 percent of the cost of processing and manufacturing food by the late 1990s" (398).

143. Shiva, *Stolen Harvest*, 7.

144. Kimbrell, *Fatal Harvest*, 8.

many farmers in the US and across the world find it impossible to stay solvent.[145] Farmers and their spouses depend heavily on income from part-time and full-time jobs off the farm to supplement their inadequate agricultural income.[146] If this does not succeed, farming families leave their farms and migrate to urban centers for employment. In such a demoralizing and dismal economic situation, some farmers resort to suicide in order to escape their destructive, economic indebtedness.[147] The food system, as it now stands, consequently fails to compensate those who grow our food with just amounts of income (principle 2) and prompts degrading and destructive forms of being (principle 5).

Because an adequate income for farming is hard to come by, market forces understandably drive some farmers to sacrifice a measure of ecological health for economic gain. For example, despite the positive effects of renewed soil conservation efforts in the latter half of the twentieth century, northern Great Plains farmers again began plowing up native grasslands and exposing them to the forces of erosion between 2007–2012.[148] During that time, "nearly 20% of grasslands in the Dakotas were converted to croplands."[149] This is because market forces encouraged farmers to expand production due to "high crop prices"; consequently the "conversion of grasslands to croplands" occurred "at rates not seen since the 1920s and 1930s."[150] However, because soils were again exposed to the elements at precarious times, the Great Plains and Midwest experienced huge dust storms as well as severe water erosion that removed precious topsoils in the years after this surge in production.[151] From this recent occurrence it appears that the conservation practices agronomists and farmers learned

---

145. Hurt, *American Agriculture*, 398. The issue of government subsidies to farmers is a complex and, in certain respects, problematic topic that will not be addressed in this chapter.

146. Hurt, *American Agriculture*, 372–73.

147. Davis explains, "In both the United States and Britain, the suicide rate among farmers is twice that of the general population; in other parts of the world it may be even higher. Rural residents experience significantly higher rates of depression and mental disorder, and studies have shown 'exceptionally large increases' in the incidence of substance abuse and domestic violence" (*Scripture, Culture, and Agriculture*, 105).

148. Wang et al., "Soil Conservation Practice Adoption," 405.

149. Wang et al., "Soil Conservation Practice Adoption," 405.

150. Follett et al., "Great Plains," 262.

151. Turner et al., "Scientific Case Studies," 66–72.

throughout the twentieth century are effective only when economic and political incentives convince farmers to implement them.

The economic and ecological lessons learned in the twentieth and twenty-first centuries from America's expansion of wheat agriculture in the Great Plains highlights the need for at least three large-scale practices: (1) In order for supply and demand to remain in healthy balance—so that farmers receive equitable income for their products and consumers can buy products at affordable prices—large-scale collaboration and coordination is necessary. Typically, the government would be the institution overseeing this coordination so that a just food system is created and maintained (principle 3). (2) Because inclement weather and unforeseen market forces may disrupt a beneficial balance in the market, widespread—usually governmental—supports must be in place to help farmers and consumers meet financial and nutritional needs during ecological or economic crises. In other words, we as a society must anticipate and financially prepare for unfavorable weather conditions (or other crises, such as pandemics), especially in a time of climate change (principles 3, 6, 7). (3) Since farming is not a particularly lucrative or reliable economic venture for many farmers, governments and/or consumers must provide farmers with economic incentives to engage in practices that protect human and ecological health, conserve and buildup soils, protect biodiversity, and prevent pollution of water, air, and soil (principles 2, 3, 4, 6). By advocating for and implementing practices such as these, we can better ensure the ecological health of the land and the economic well-being of the farming neighbors that feed us. We must come to see that we are all in this together.

6.2.4 Transportation, Processing, and Distribution

With the average American consuming 62 kg of wheat per year,[152] the social and ecological effects of wheat's transportation, processing, and distribution in the US are of important consequence. From an ecological perspective, the way in which wheat is currently transported, processed, and distributed demands the release of unsustainable amounts of greenhouse gases and involves unconscientable levels of food waste. In relation to health concerns, food safety continues to remain a pressing issue. Socially, the distribution of wheat-based products—and food generally—in the US entails racial and

---

152. Meisterling, Samaras, and Schweizer, "Decisions to Reduce Greenhouse Gases," 223.

socio-economic factors that are patently unjust.[153] This section considers limited aspects of these complex factors and argues that industrial methods of transporting, processing, and distributing wheat fail to meet the promises of safe and affordable food for all Americans.

The global "safety" of industrial wheat production comes into question when we consider the fact that this industry adds greenhouse gases to such an extent that climate stability is threatened. While many people across North America enjoy chewy, fluffy breads, which are made from the grains of hard red spring wheat, this type of wheat grows best only in the northern Great Plains.[154] Consequently, for many Americans to enjoy their bread, the grain must travel hundreds, if not thousands, of miles from their ideal cultivation grounds to the dinner table.[155] Other varieties of wheat that go into cereals, pastas, cookies, and other food products grow in California and throughout the Midwest and Great Plains. Yet, because all these grains travel from farms to food processing factories to distribution centers and then to grocery stores, the transportation of wheat and wheat products demands the release of about 2.6 billion kg of CO_2 equivalent.[156] Meanwhile, the overall production of wheat and wheat-based products in the US emits a total of about 63 billion kg of CO_2 equivalent each year.[157] Even though emissions during the cultivation of wheat releases the highest percentage

---

153. An unjust feature not discussed in this section but certainly deserving of attention concerns food processing plants. The wages and working conditions for many who process the foods we enjoy are unjust and, at times, destructive. This became especially apparent as a result of the COVID-19 pandemic (Fremstad, Rho, and Brown, "Meatpacking Workers").

154. Hard red spring wheat has high protein content, which enables it to create chewy loaves of bread (Kaufman, *Bet the Farm*, 235).

155. At first, harvested wheat is transported by truck to local grain elevators and distribution centers, usually within 100 km away. From there, wheat must travel by train, truck, or barge to flour mills, processing plants, or other distribution centers in the US and throughout the world (O'Donnell et al., "Relative Contribution of Transportation," 489). All together, the combined distances embedded within the food system have become increasingly concerning since fossil fuel-powered transportation contributes to global warming.

156. This amount is based on data from 2010 (Sanders and Webber, "Comparative Analysis," 4).

157. More precisely, the amount for the year 2010 was 63 ± 7.5 billion kg of CO_2. This staggering figure includes not only carbon dioxide (CO_2) but also nitrous oxide (N_2O) and methane (CH_4), whose warming potential is calculated in order to approximate that of CO_2 (called a CO_2 equivalent, or, CO_2e) (Sanders and Webber, "Comparative Analysis," 7).

of greenhouse gases along the wheat-based food chain, as discussed in section 6.2.1, the processing, packaging, and transportation of wheat-based products contribute even more emissions, when these three categories are calculated together.[158] Thus, not only must farming practices change in order to release fewer greenhouse gases, but food processors and distributors must work to ameliorate the devastating effects of global warming on vulnerable human, animal, and plant communities. By reconfiguring our production and processing of wheat and other cereal grains in ways that are more regional and carbon neutral, we can further reduce greenhouse gas emissions and slow global warming. Such a feat would certainly be daunting, but as a matter of global climate justice, biosphere stability, and care for the weak and vulnerable (Rom 14), it is of essential consequence.

Along with altering our production and distribution of wheat in ways that reduce global warming, our food system faces the dire need to provide food that is safer to individual people's health. Although developments in food processing have enabled our food system to nourish many people well, they have not always lived up to their promises, especially the promise of purity. According to the Center for Disease Control and Prevention (CDC), "between 1970 and 1999, food-borne illnesses increased more than tenfold" in the US.[159] While most of us think of meat, vegetable, and fruit products as potentially carrying food-borne diseases, wheat flour also is occasionally contaminated. For instance, within the US, 21 people from across 9 states

---

158. Meisterling, Samaras, and Schweizer, "Decisions to Reduce Greenhouse Gases," 228. Trains are more efficient and release fewer greenhouse gases than do trucks (O'Donnell et al., "Relative Contribution of Transportation," 491). One of the challenges that wheat growing areas face is transporting grain to central processing and distribution centers in a timely fashion. Farmers haul grain in trucks to the local grain elevator. From there, train cars have traditionally transported the grain to mills and factories or to ports for export. However, train cars quickly fill, and "farmers have categorized rail freight as often unreliable and uneconomical during harvest peaks" (Meisterling, Samaras, and Schweizer, "Decisions to Reduce Greenhouse Gases," 227). It has therefore become increasingly common for tractor-trailers to haul grain to the factories. In fact, "[t]he share of wheat tonnage shipped domestically by rail in the US has declined from 70.4% in 1987 to 45.8% in 2000. Wheat rail freight has shifted to truck transport, which increased its share from 27.1% to 52.7% over the same period (with the remaining small fraction shipped by barge)" (227). However, tractor-trailers release more greenhouse gases than do trains. In order to decrease emissions, grain should travel by train or barge whenever possible to regional processing plants. The authors explain: "Decision-makers interested in reducing GHG [greenhouse gas] emissions should identify methods to maximize utilization of rail freight transport for wheat and other appropriate commodities" (227).

159. Kimbrell, *Fatal Harvest*, 10.

from December 11, 2018 to May 21, 2019 got sick from eating flour that was contaminated by *E. coli* 026.[160] Overall, from all types of food, the CDC "estimates 48 million people get sick, 128,000 are hospitalized, and 3,000 die from foodborne diseases each year in the United States."[161] Arguably, these failures in food safety are endemic to the industrial food system itself.

In addition to food purity concerns is the exorbitant amount of food that is wasted along the path from field to table. In fact:

> [t]hirty to 40 percent of all crops are lost to pests and disease before harvest—despite heavy use of pesticides. And about a quarter of all food produced worldwide gets lost after harvest or wasted between production and consumption. Add those together and half the crops we plant don't end up feeding anyone. The United States alone wastes 133 billion pounds of food each year, more than enough to feed the 50 million Americans who regularly face hunger.[162]

Consumers, processors, and growers have arguably become inured to this waste and fail to see it as an aggregious form of disrespect to the earth that offered these gifts of food in the first place (in contradistinction to principles 1 and 2).[163] Expressions of true gratitude for the gifts of the earth thus become muted and even nullified in such a system.

Food waste not only communicates disrespect for the earth but also for its people who go hungry. Whether on account of wasted food or its inequitable distribution, the current food system leaves billions of people hungry across the world everyday. Globally, "over 2 billion people do not have regular access to safe, nutritious and sufficient food, including 8 percent of the population in Northern America and Europe."[164] In 2018, 29 mil-

---

160. CDC, "Outbreak of *E. Coli* Infections Linked to Flour."

161. *Camphylobacter, Salmonella, Cyclospora*, STEC (caused by *E. coli*), *Vibrio*, and *Yersinia* infections are all increasing as foodborne illnesses in the US. These increases appear in part because more precise technologies enable laboratories to detect them. However, it is also likely that these pathogens are more frequently present in more foods, making the American people sick more often (CDC, "Foodnet 2018 Preliminary Data"). From March 1 to May 1 of 2019, 209 people got sick from eating beef contaminated by *E. coli* O103, at least 29 of them were hospitalized, and two developed hemolytic uremic syndrome. This led two meat-processing plants to recall 166,624 pounds of unsafe raw beef (CDC, "Outbreak of *E. Coli* Infections Linked to Ground Beef").

162. Montgomery, *Growing a Revolution*, 38.

163. In contrast, composting food waste directs organic matter away from landfills so that it might nourish earth's soils.

164. FAO, "State of Food Security," xiv.

lion people across the globe faced "acute food insecurity" on account of climate and natural disasters.[165] With more than 2 billion people going hungry and millions more facing hunger because of climate change, it would appear to many that the world's farmers must produce even more crops.

However, according to the Food and Agriculture Organization (FAO) of the United Nations, global agriculture provides enough food for all people. "Every year, enough wheat, rice, and other grains are produced to provide every human with 3,500 daily calories. In fact, enough food is grown worldwide to provide 4.3 pounds of food per person per day, which would include two and a half pounds of grain, beans, and nuts, a pound of fruits and vegetables, and nearly another pound of meat, milk, and eggs."[166] When we consider the United States, we find its farmers grow plenty of food for its inhabitants too, yet 14 percent of its population remains food insecure.[167] By food insecurity, many researchers mean that a person or household has "difficulty at some time during the year providing enough food for all their members due to a lack of resources."[168] Food insecurity, we find, "lies not with the amount of food being produced, but rather with how this food is distributed."[169]

Since enough food is produced to feed the world, including those living in the US, at least three interrelated obstacles prevent people in the US from nourishing themselves and their children: (1) Inadequate and/or inconsistent food provisions within reasonable and accessible distances; (2) Unaffordable food prices; and (3) Racist zoning policies and business practices and deregulated market forces that drive food prices up and prevent food from being accessible. While these and other factors are incredibly complex, we will elevate them for consideration especially since their presence in the food system undermines our eco-ethical principles and testifies to our failure to share creation's food with all people.

While most Americans are food secure, too many people find themselves without the financial means to feed themselves adequately. In 2014, 14 percent of American households—totaling 17.4 million households—were

165. "Global Report on Food Crises," 2.

166. Kimbrell, *Fatal Harvest*, 7. A different study suggests that "providing enough food for the 13% of the world's people who suffer from hunger would require raising world supplies by just 1%" (BirdLife International, "State of the World's Birds," 32).

167. Jurkovich, *Feeding the Hungry*, 5.

168. Green, *U.S. Household Food Security*, 3. In contrast, food security entails: "consistent, dependable access to enough food for active, healthy living" (vii).

169. Kimbrell, *Fatal Harvest*, 33.

food insecure. Among this number, children living with a single parent, "women living alone, and Black- and Hispanic-headed households" existing "near or below the Federal poverty line" experienced "substantially higher" "rates of food insecurity" "than the national average."[170] An astonishing 422,000 children in 2014 went "hungry, skipped a meal, or did not eat for a whole day because there was not enough money for food."[171] These horrifying realities only intensified in the midst of the COVID-19 pandemic when—according to Feeding America—up to 45 million people in the US, including 15 million children, were food insecure.[172]

Food insecurity stems not only from insufficient funds but also from inadequate access to groceries and grocery stores. Racial and economic prejudices lie at the heart of this problem. Pervading the food system is the ugly fact that "race and class play a central role in organizing the production, distribution, and consumption of food."[173] For example, because of zoning restrictions and business practices, fewer full service grocery stores serve non-white communities and low-income communities than serve white and/or higher-income communities.[174] Instead of grocery stores, low-income and non-white communities tend to have "more convenience stores than White and higher-income communities"; and these convenience stores "have lower relative availability of healthier alternatives."[175] Rural versus urban location also plays a role in food access and security. Researchers have found that a higher percentage of rural ("nonmetropolitan") inhabitants experience food insecurity than do those who live in "principal cities of metropolitan areas." As many as 17.1 percent of rural households and 15.7 percent of urban households face inconsistent food resources

---

170. Green, *U.S. Household Food Security*, 4.

171. Green, *U.S. Household Food Security*, 11. Even beyond ethnicity or family composition, "9.4 percent of households with children" in the US face food insecurity for "one or more" of their children (25). The researchers note: "The percentage of households with food-insecure children was higher for female-headed households (18.5 percent); Black, non-Hispanic households (16.1 percent); Hispanic households (14.0 percent); low-income households with incomes below 185 percent of the poverty line (20.1 percent); households within principal cities of metropolitan areas (11.2 percent); households in nonmetropolitan areas (12.0 percent); and households in the South (10.3 percent)."

172. "Impact of the Coronavirus," 1.

173. Alkon and Agyeman, "Introduction," 4.

174. Zenk et al., "Relative and Absolute Availability," 2174.

175. Zenk et al., "Relative and Absolute Availability," 2174.

during the year.[176] The dearth of grocery stores—whether in rural or urban locations—makes healthy food less accessible for many members of society.

What is perhaps less obvious is that the food sold in low-income and non-white communities "is often more expensive than similar purchases in wealthier areas."[177] When healthy food happens to be sold in low-income neighborhoods, many of the residents cannot afford to purchase it because of its elevated price.[178] The price, or affordability, of food is just as significant a factor in addressing food insecurity as access.[179]

The inaffordability of food becomes more apparent when we consider the fact that in 1995 a loaf of bread cost about $0.79.[180] However, by 2010, the price of "1 kg of wheat bread" had jumped to "an average of $4.00 in US cities."[181] This significant hike in bread prices depended, in part, on changes taking place in the stock market and, in particular, commodity indexes.[182] As is so often the case, those on the underside of the economy

---

176. Green, *U.S. Household Food Security*, 22. The researchers also indicate that when food insecurity is examined across the United States, "the prevalence of food insecurity was higher in the South (15.1 percent) than in the Northeast (13.3 percent), Midwest (13.8 percent), or the West (13.1 percent)."

177. Alkon and Agyeman, "Introduction," 4.

178. For illuminating discussions, see Alkon et al., "Foodways of the Urban Poor"; Myers and Sbicca, "Bridging Good Food and Good Jobs."

179. Myers and Caruso, "Towards a Public Food Infrastructure," 31.

180. Hurt, *American Agriculture*, 398.

181. Sanders and Webber, "Comparative Analysis," 4.

182. Although the US government and the Commodity Futures Trading Commission (CFTC) had successfully kept wheat at relatively stable prices in the twentieth century, new governmental and CFTC policies and banking ventures unsettled this stability near the turn of the twenty-first century (Kaufman, *Bet the Farm*, 212–14). In 1991 employees of Goldman Sachs created a new form of investment, the commodity index (210). The employees "selected eighteen commodifiable ingredients and contrived an elixir that included cattle, coffee, cocoa, corn, hogs, and a couple of varieties of wheat. They weighted the investment value of each element, blended and commingled the parts into sums, then reduced what had been a complicated system of speculation and hedging into a mathematical formula that could be expressed as a single manifestation, to be known henceforth as the Goldman Sachs Commodity Index (GSCI)." Although the CFTC initially limited the number of wheat futures contracts that an investment firm could hold to five thousand (in order to prevent speculation and consequent volatile market conditions), by 2001 the CFTC reduced these constraints. It allowed "six commodity index traders" "to hold as many as 130,000 wheat futures contracts at a time" (211). This initiated a significant increase in investment in commodity index funds so that "from 2003 to 2008, the volume of commodity index fund speculation increased by 1,900 percent" (225). In 2008 alone, investment in food commodities went from $55

suffered, for the price of real wheat and real bread shot through the roof while investors reaped the rewards from wheat stocks.[183] "From 2005 to 2008 the worldwide price of food rose 80 percent."[184] This terrifying situation was the case even though "2008 witnessed the greatest wheat crop in human history"; nevertheless, 2008 also beheld "the greatest number of starving people in human history . . . [and] a historic run on the price of hard red spring wheat."[185] People around the globe felt the effects of high food prices, and civil unrest mounted in the Middle East and Africa.[186] What might have appeared to investors as a socially benign but financially profitable growth in commodity indexes turned out to be a deadly cancer for the world's poor.[187] These economic realities and others like them reveal that the industrial food system does not deliver on its promise of affordable food for all people, let alone all Americans. "Too many people are simply too poor to buy the food that is available."[188] With these and other systemic

million to $318 million in a couple months (220). These increases meant more money in the pockets of investors and business owners (226). For example, "Cargill attributed its 86 percent jump in annual profits to commodity trading." From the perspective of investment firms and grain trading corporations, the advent of commodity indexes heralded good news (250). One might think the good news extended to the farmers, with increased grain prices leading to increased income in farmers' pockets. But this is not the case. Just as market prices increased, the cost of all the "ingredients" for grain production (seeds, fertilizer, fuel) also escalated.

183. Kaufman explains, "The index funds may never have held a single bushel of actual wheat, but they were hoarding staggering quantities of wheat futures—billions of promises to buy, not one of them ever to be fulfilled. The dreaded market corner had emerged not from a shortage in the wheat supply but from a much rarer economic occurrence, a shock to the system inspired by the ceaseless call of food indexes for wheat that did not exist and would never need to exist . . . The investment instrument itself—the index—had taken over and created the effects of a traditional corner" (*Bet the Farm*, 243–44).

184. Kaufman, *Bet the Farm*, 226. Kaufman explains, "As $200 billion new dollars plunked into commodities, 250 million new people descended into poverty."

185. Kaufman, *Bet the Farm*, 237.

186. Kaufman, *Bet the Farm*, 227–29, 50–51.

187. And this cancer would return with a vengeance in 2011 (Kaufman, *Bet the Farm*, 248). Kaufman exclaims: "For the second time in three years, food was more expensive than it had ever been in all of human history" (248). The high cost of bread and other foods, caused in large part because of invisible market forces, arguably "helped fuel the Arab Spring" (Brown, *Full Planet, Empty Plates*, 3).

188. Kimbrell, *Fatal Harvest*, 33. Michelle Jurkovich similarly explains that a greater supply of food will not bring down food's price to a level that society's poorest members can afford, while at the same time producers would earn enough profit from selling it.

forces driving up prices, no wonder so many people then and now find it difficult to procure their daily bread.[189]

Whether by its high susceptibility to bacterial contamination; its heavy reliance on fossil-fuel based forms of processing and transportation; its racially, socio-economically, and geographically prejudiced approaches to distribution; or its unjust market structures, the industrial food system is failing to provide safe and affordable food for all (principles 2 and 3). The system as a whole is broken, and it certainly contradicts the visions set forth in Gen 1 and Romans, where all humans and animals may nourish themselves on an earth free from frustration, injury, and destruction. It becomes apparent, then, that the industrial food system needs serious reform, for it entangles consumers—and even producers—in a web of enslaving the creation to destruction (Rom 8:21) and doing wrong to the neighbors who nourish us (13:10).

6.3 Conclusion

With the aid of biotechnologies, industrial agriculture is heralded by many to feed the world with abundant, affordable, and safe crops and even to do so in ways that result in less ecological harm than agriculture did fifty years ago. However, as our examination, limited though it was, of the wheat food system demonstrates, industrial agriculture does not even cause all the *humans* who participate in it to flourish. Many go hungry; many get sick; some die in untimely and painful ways. Thus, even if we assess wheat agriculture from

---

Thus, "The market alone has never been able to solve the hunger problem" (Jurkovich, *Feeding the Hungry*, 5).

189. Although some people creating and investing in commodity index funds may think it an ethically neutral activity, even a corporate official at MGEX (Minneapolis Grain Exchange) admits: "two principles that govern the movement of grain markets [are] 'fear and greed'" (Kaufman, *Bet the Farm*, 231). It would appear that greed has the threatening potential to rear its ugly head in even more vicious ways in the future. Although nations, including the US, have traditionally maintained grain reserves in case of need, "in 1993 the international General Agreement on Tariffs and Trade put an end to grain reserves as a government responsibility. The 1996 farm bill abolished the grain reserve of the United States" (248). By 2003, the US food reserve held only 8 hours worth of soybeans and 5 hours worth of corn; one former USDA administrator told Kaufman: "'Our current reserve is in the hands of multinational grain corporations . . . We are only one disaster away from being in their hands'" (247). Although from 1986 to 2001 the world had 107 days worth of the previous year's grain when the new harvest appeared, global grain stores "averaged only 74 days of consumption, a drop of one third" between 2002 and 2011 (Brown, *Full Planet, Empty Plates*, 5).

an entirely anthropocentric perspective, we find that industrial agriculture does not adequately help humans flourish. Viewing agriculture through an ecological lens, we find the industrial food system also does not support the flourishing, fertility, and biodiversity of nonhuman creation. This system fails and even harms us all. A truly golden age of agriculture has not yet arrived; the creation still expects and awaits its liberation.

In reflecting theologically and eco-ethically upon this alarming national and global situation, the eco-ethical criteria developed in 3.3, 5.4, and 6.0 assist our assessment. Modern agricultural practices, food industries, and unrestrained economic and corporate forces combine their powers over human societies and the nonhuman creation in deleterious and destructive ways. Consequently, America's production and trade of wheat fails our seven Pauline criteria, since the industrial food system:

1. Fails to attend sufficiently to creation's story, especially in regard to ecosystem limits, climates, and living members, and thus undermines healthy, interdependent relationships between and among nonhuman and human participants.

2. Arguably diminishes people's ability to express gratitude for the gifts of Earth by inequitably distributing those gifts, obscuring their origins within long food chains, and necessitating substantial amounts of food waste, processing, and packaging.[190]

3. Does not adequately protect vulnerable and/or endangered species and does not support the well-being of economically or geographically vulnerable people (especially children, women, and those with low incomes, including farmers) since corporate and market forces limit farmers' incomes and some people's access to affordable food.

4. Undermines the health, biodiversity, fertility, and flourishing of soil, water, and land ecosystems.[191]

---

190. In more theological terms, Wirzba contends that, in modern agriculture, "food ceases to speak as the grace of God. Eating ceases to be the occasion through which we experience life as a membership of belonging, responsibility, and gratitude" (Wirzba, *Food and Faith*, xiv).

191. Evidence suggests that "[a]s we turn fertile ground into large-scale, industrial farms growing only a single crop, the variety of plant life in our ecosystems shrinks. Pollution of the air, water, and soil profoundly affects the millions and billions of other creatures with whom humanity shares this planet" (O'Brien, *Ethics of Biodiversity*, 4–5). Also, Jackson, *Consulting the Genius of the Place*, 87, 186.

5. Injures, reduces the reproductive capacity of, and sometimes destroys nonhuman and human creatures through its heavy reliance on synthetic pesticides and herbicides and its excessive greenhouse gas emissions.

6. Inhibits farmers and the food system from serving and maintaining Earth's fertility and diversity, especially because food waste rarely makes it back to the fields and since the industrial food regime hinders people from sharing food and water resources with all other living things.

7. Presses people to buy and consume excessive amounts of food products and does not support them in exercising appropriate self-restraint for the benefit and vitality of themselves and others.[192]

These failures and injustices demand our attention and action. We must implement alternative forms of agriculture that mirror God's ultimate liberation of creation from excessive and untimely destruction. Such alternative forms of agriculture must take the well-being of the whole creation, human and nonhuman, into account.

In light of these realities and creation's real subjection to frustration and slavery to destruction, it behooves Christian communities to take an active role in promoting just, sustainable, and healthy systems of growing, distributing, and storing grain (and other foods), not for abhorrent economic gain at the cost of people's lives or at the expense of ecological health but for the sake of the hungry now and the hungry in the future. In the process, they must resist corruption, fear, and greed and instead work collectively at circumventing the imperialistic effects of global corporate control, commodities investment, and global climate change.[193] Paul's vision of a liberated creation must remain at the center of Christian ethical and practical deliberations as God's people procure their daily bread and submit their minds and bodies to God so that they might be conformed to Jesus Christ rather than the forces of destruction (Rom 12:1–2; 8:21). While it would take hundreds of pages to illustrate some of the ways in which the food system might become more liberative and life supporting, the next chapter briefly provides several suggestions for how this might be done.

---

192. Although marketing and consumerism were not examined in this chapter, they have a role in undermining healthy forms of self-restraint. For some discussion, see Wirzba, *Food and Faith*, 71–109.

193. Perhaps a sobering reminder would curb our greed: "The benefit of wheat is not cash. The benefit of wheat is bread, and the benefit of bread is life" (Kaufman, *Bet the Farm*, 253).

CHAPTER 7

Creation's Preliminary Liberation

Regenerative Agriculture at Work

THE ENTIRE CREATION IS embedded within God's story, a theological story. Within this narrative during the past few millennia, humankind has played a leading role in the drama of creation, as we have altered the entire biosphere. Even still, the nonhuman creation never left the cast of characters and has faithfully played its part despite humanity's proud attempts at surpassing and subduing it. Although we humans tend to neglect it, the nonhuman creation is an essential member of God's story and exercises agency, collaborates with God and humanity, and even holds expectations for the present and future. Because human and nonhuman members of creation enjoy an interdependent—perhaps even covenantal relationship with each other—each member has expectations for the other. Most fundamentally, each member expects that it will be able to play its God-given part well, that it will fulfill God's commission without disruption from the other members. In scene after scene, however, human beings thwart creation's purposes of flourishing and instead bring unnecessary forms of destruction upon it. Accordingly, creation expects with eager anticipation the point at which human beings will fulfill their role of servant leadership rightly. In this theological story of *creation–subjection–liberation–glorification*, all members have integral parts to play and sacred responsibilities to all others involved in the drama. Even the nonhuman creation has sacred duties and, along with these, has expectations that necessarily involve human participation and cooperation.

Arguably encompassed within this theological narrative is an ecological story that tells the day-to-day details of life and death on micro- and macro-level scales. This is the story of evolution and extinction, speciation and fertility, nutrient cycling, changing weather, flourishing, and degradation. In this story, the nonhuman creation also has expectations of its human inhabitants, expectations that agrarians might name "the expectations of the land." "The land," in this case, refers to particular ecosystems, which have their own weather patterns, soil conditions, water availability, flora and fauna, and carrying capacity. These conditions establish the constraints, or perhaps we might say the expectations, of that ecosystem. If human members live within these constraints, they will live sustainably and thereby meet the expectations of the land, the ecosystem. But to do this as they grow food, people must "look at the soils, climate, human and natural communities—the whole environment—of a place and then go to work *with* them to produce food."[1] The consequent agricultural systems (wherever their location) will "act like wild ecosystems" by "build[ing] the health of the soil even as they deliver the seeds (grains), leaves, fruits, meats, and roots that compose a healthy diet."[2] In other words, when agriculture is done with the long-term health of ecosystems in view, people will engage in liberative rather than destructive forms of growing food.

7.1 The Land's Expectations: Regenerative Agriculture

The expectations of the land within ecology's story teach humans to allow an ecosystem's requirements for long-term health to shape human activity—whether we are growing food or developing systems of transportation. According to ecology's story, ecosystems are always changing and evolving, and, yet, they reach points of homeostasis in which energy and nutrient consumption, for example, do not exceed supply and replenishment rates. The ecosystem is sustained for the long haul. According to one notable agrarian, Wes Jackson, ecology's story provides the model for human society, especially our growing of food. Thus, he asserts, "the best agriculture for any region is the one that best mimics the region's natural ecosystems."[3] As humans play their part well in this story, they will adjust their farming methods according to the conditions and needs of the ecosystem, since no one agricultural regime suits all places at all times. Thus, sustainable forms of

---

1. Jackson, Berry, and Colman, *Meeting the Expectations of the Land*, x. Emphasis added.
2. Jackson, Berry, and Colman, *Meeting the Expectations of the Land*, x.
3. Jackson, Berry, and Colman, *Meeting the Expectations of the Land*, 183.

Creation's Slavery and Liberation

agriculture in which we humans meet the expectations of the land resist the universalizing and extractive pretensions of empire (ch. 2) and agribusiness (ch. 6), whose fables of (unsustainable) abundance abound.

Since the ecological story speaks the truth about an ecosystem's conditions, it repeatedly narrates situations in which societies degrade, exploit, and sometimes destroy ecosystems for the sake of their daily bread. As our investigations of Roman and US wheat agriculture in chapters 2 and 6 elucidate, this narrative of degradation is the story of the past and present, but it does not necessarily have to be the dominant narrative of the future. Farmers and researchers throughout the world are developing more sustainable forms of agriculture that meet both the expectations of the land (its drive towards biodiversity, fertility, flourishing, and stability) and the expectations of creation (its longing for just humans who lead and serve in and for life rather than destruction). Such forms of agriculture are labeled many things, including natural systems agriculture, sustainable agriculture, regenerative agriculture, and conservation agriculture.

Farmers and agronomists across the globe have stumbled upon three common themes in their pursuit of agriculture that regenerates (rather than depletes) the soil. While the particulars vary from region to region, the practices that we might place in the general category of "regenerative agriculture"[4] engages in: "(1) minimum disturbance of the soil; (2) growing cover crops and retaining crop residue so that the soil is *always* covered; and (3) use of diverse crop rotations."[5] When these principles are employed consistently and together, they allow farmers to build rather than deplete soils, and they provide equivalent yields to industrial approaches but at a much lower cost.[6] Because principles 1 and 2 require the soil to be as undisturbed as possible and always covered with plants (whether

---

4. Geologist David Montgomery prefers to name this broad category "conservation agriculture," and he explains that it can accommodate a variety of ideological perspectives (Montgomery, *Growing a Revolution*, 66–71). Fundamentally this approach to agriculture attempts to conserve or, more precisely, regenerate the soils on which farming depends. Thus, I prefer the more specific nomenclature, "regenerative agriculture."

5. Montgomery, *Growing a Revolution*, 68.

6. Montgomery, *Growing a Revolution*, 84. Describing the positive results that regenerative farmers encounter, Montgomery explains, "[t]he secret to their success is that they are also maintaining or increasing their yields *and* increasing their profits. The extra money in their pockets comes from spending less on fossil fuels and agrochemicals. They replace these costly inputs with practices that cultivate diverse communities of soil life that efficiently deliver nutrients, minerals, and other compounds that crops need to grow while fending off pests and pathogens" (Montgomery, *Growing a Revolution*, 9–10).

Creation's Preliminary Liberation

dead or living), plowing is frowned upon.[7] This is the case even though industrial agriculture "considers plowing essential to control weeds, that erosion is an unavoidable result of rainfall, that cover crops and crop rotations are optional, and that chemical pest control is a necessity."[8] While some regenerative agriculturalists would support the use of herbicides in no-till agriculture, the evidence against its safety is mounting (see 6.2.2). Thus, truly regenerative agriculture goes against the stream and requires new mindsets, new methods, and ancient or new seed varieties to liberate us from the destructive effects of soil loss and species poisonings.

Although regenerative agriculture is in some ways new to the field, its principles have been taught and practiced for generations.[9] In a time when industrial agriculture was transforming the landscape of American agriculture, especially for those with financial resources to buy machinery and chemicals, George Washington Carver studied, developed, and taught a regenerative—and more economically feasible—approach to living on the land. Born a slave, Carver secretly tended a small garden plot while he was young and enslaved.[10] Despite all obstacles, he deepened his love and knowledge of botany by attending college and graduate school once slavery was abolished in the US.[11] The wisdom he gained by studying plants, nutrient cycles, and agriculture led him to insist on the "value of composting, crop rotation, and diversification."[12] In tandom with Booker T. Washington

---

7. Montgomery notes, "Time and again, at one farming conference after another . . . farmers readily acknowledge the possibility that plowing resulted in long-term damage to the soil" (*Growing a Revolution*, 23).

8. Montgomery, *Growing a Revolution*, 69.

9. A few scientists and agronomists have begun to recognize and announce the deep wisdom indigenous peoples have developed in their traditional agricultural approaches. While much could be discussed about the variety of agricultural techniques employed by Native Americans, for instance, their worldview is especially instructive. Rather than considering themselves as entitled to dominating and subduing the land, many Tribal peoples have recognized their primary responsibility to sustain the long-term health of their earth home. They therefore work to honor the earth and all its gifts. Although many people attuned to ecological realities today may think humans can only function as a blight to the earth's ecosystems, indigenous peoples know from experience that people can nurture and assist ecological health, as Robin Wall Kimmerer beautifully demonstrates in *Braiding Sweetgrass*. Much continues to be learned from the agricultural wisdom of Native Americans and other indigenous peoples around the world and their approaches to growing food, whether past or present.

10. White, *Freedom Farmers*, 39–40.

11. White, *Freedom Farmers*, 40.

12. White, *Freedom Farmers*, 46.

and the Tuskegee Institute, Carver shared these soil-building insights with black farmers of the South, believing "this line of education is the key to unlock the golden door of freedom to our people."[13] Because composting offered an affordable and sustainable way to increase the soil's fertility and "water-holding power," it provided black farmers the means to liberate themselves from utter poverty as they farmed land that had already been depleted of many nutrients.[14] Through his research, writing, and teaching, Carver instructed people to plant "peas, beans, clover, vetches, peanuts" as "absolutely indispensible" components "in a wise crop rotation."[15] Such insights empowered thousands of black farmers to improve their land,[16] personal health, and economic conditions in a time when many white farmers turned to industrial means of agriculture.

Depsite the wisdom offered by Carver and others like him, many people question whether approaches to agriculture that do not depend on frequent plowing and consistent applications of synthetic pesticides and fertilizers can feed the world. Yet, the Rodale Institute has demonstrated that organic regenerative farming systems "are competitive with conventional yields after a 5-year transition period." More specifically, organic regenerative approaches "produce yields up to 40% higher in times of drought"; "earn 3–6x greater profits for farmers"; "leach no toxic chemicals into waterways"; "use 45% less energy"; and "release 40% fewer carbon emissions" than industrial farming systems.[17] With so many advantages and very few disadvantages, organic regenerative agriculture makes it much more feasible for humanity to implement our seven Pauline eco-ethical principles (3.3; 6.0).

7.2 The Land's Hope: Perennial Agriculture

Taking our eco-ethical and regenerative agricultural principles closer to their ideal extent, perennial agriculture offers a peculiarly promising new

---

13. White, *Freedom Farmers*, 41. Here, White quotes part of Carver's response to Booker T. Washington when he accepted a teaching position at Tuskegee Institute.

14. White, *Freedom Farmers*, 47.

15. White, *Freedom Farmers*, 48.

16. White explains that "the value of black-owned land in the South increased more than sevenfold by 1920" and suggests that this increase stemmed, in part, from Tuskegee Institute's educational and financial offerings (White, *Freedom Farmers*, 38).

17. Rodale Institute, "Farming Systems Trial."

approach to growing staple crops.[18] Perennial agriculture attempts to bypass disturbing the soil almost entirely (whether by seasonal plowing or grain drilling) by developing and cultivating perennial varieties of staple crops, which remain in the ground year-round (after they are first sown) and do not need to be re-seeded annually. The need for crop rotations is also circumvented when perennial grains are interspersed with perennial legumes. Perennial agriculture, when done well, leaves behind some plant debris after harvest in order to cover the land and return organic matter to the soil. These practices have been called natural systems agriculture, and they attempt to mimic the perennially based ecosystems that naturally occur in nature. While a natural systems approach to agriculture provides a beneficial way to meet the expectations of the land and creation, its far-reaching implementation stands off in the future since perennial crop varieties are still being developed. Perennial agriculture, as one form of regenerative agriculture and in tandem with permaculture and polyculture farming, offers an opportunity for humans to promote life rather than destroy it even as we feed ourselves.[19]

As a leader in the perennial agricultural movement, Wes Jackson has spent decades collaborating with the land in the hopes of discovering a new model for human food production, a model that takes its shape from ecologically beneficial and productive natural ecosystems. By assuming the status of a learner, Jackson looks to nature for answers. In so doing, he has discovered that a missing link in sustainable agriculture is the development of perennial crops and has worked with countless others across the globe to find and breed perennial varieties of wheat, sorghum, legumes, oilseeds, rice, and corn so that agriculture might be redeemed from the ground up.[20]

Ecologists have found that thriving terrestrial ecosystems depend primarily on a wide variety of perennial rather than annual herbaceous

18. Montgomery explains, "The advantages of developing perennial crops from annual crops is huge. Not plowing to plant each year would be the ultimate in no-till agriculture, since the best way to stop using the plow is to grow crops in fields that never need plowing" (*Growing a Revolution*, 86).

19. Since human societies depend heavily on grains for their daily calories, perennial agriculture provides a more ecologically healthy approach to growing these foods than do industrial approaches to growing annual grains. However, this is not to say that the vision of this section is to replace annual monocultures with perennial monocultures. As much as possible, perennial agriculture in the Great Plains and elsewhere should strive to incorporate legumes as intercrops and to surround fields with ecologically beneficial plants. In other words, perennial agriculture should be a form of polyculture.

20. Jackson, *Consulting the Genius of the Place*, 156–58.

species, and these perennial plants maintain and even build the fertile soil on which they grow. The native prairie ecosystems of the Great Plains, which Jackson studies, are covered in perennial plants with strong and permanent root systems that hold soils in place even during dry windstorms or the deluge of rainstorms. Perennials absorb precious nutrients held deep in the ground and incorporate these nutrients into their tissues, allowing animals and insects near the surface to gain access to their life-supporting nutrients. As Jackson explains:

> essentially all of nature's land-based ecosystems feature perennials. This has to do with the fact that only twenty-some elements represented on the periodic chart in our science classrooms go into all of earth's organisms. And importantly, only four of these building blocks circulate in the atmospheric commons. The rest are in the soil, and they are all water-soluble. Managing these elements and water is accomplished by a diversity of roots below the surface.[21]

Of all their herbaceous relatives, perennial plants most effectively facilitate the natural cycles of nutrient and energy flow on which life depends.

Yet, ever since the birth of agriculture, the primary components of the human diet have come from annual plants. Even now, when Americans consume larger percentages of meat, we directly or indirectly "obtain at least two-thirds of our total calories from grains and oilseed crops, none of them perennial."[22] Much of the wheat and corn on which the US population depends are grown in the Great Plains. This region

> contains the best topsoils in the world, yet a growing body of research demonstrates conclusively that the cultivation of annual crops there is degrading soils, rendering water unfit to drink, rolling back biodiversity, spreading toxic chemicals, and even creating a hypoxic, or "dead," zone hundreds of miles downstream in the Gulf of Mexico.[23]

Such is the case throughout the world where industrial farming practices are employed; in fact, the Millennium Ecosystems Assessment maintains, "agriculture is the 'largest threat to biodiversity and ecosystem function of

---

21. Jackson, *Consulting the Genius of the Place*, 151. Carbon, hydrogen, oxygen, and nitrogen come from the atmosphere; phosphorus, potassium, iodine, sulphur, calcium, iron, manganese, and other nutrients come from the soil (131).

22. Jackson, *Consulting the Genius of the Place*, 154.

23. Jackson, *Consulting the Genius of the Place*, 154.

any single human activity.'"[24] The challenge, then, is to reinvent agriculture so that humans may not only survive on earth but thrive *along with* the rest of God's life-filled creation, in accordance with Paul's vision in Rom 8:19–22.

Jackson and those who work with him at The Land Institute believe that perennial-based agriculture opens new, liberative approaches to feeding ourselves and our animals. If perennial crops are grown, "a farm will no longer have to be an ecological sacrifice zone; rather, it will provide food and at the same time protect soils, water, and biodiversity."[25] This is the case because of five powerful characteristics of perennial plants:

1. They diminish runoff and soil erosion because their strong root systems are not plowed up.

2. Their roots are deeper and can reach nutrients and water that annuals cannot obtain.

3. Their roots create good, granular soil structure at a faster rate than annuals.

4. They grow above ground herbage earlier and faster in the growing season than annuals. They also remain alive and continue to photosynthesize after harvest when their annual counterparts would be dead. This means that perennial plants have a greater capacity for sequestering carbon, a process that has become essential for reducing the amount of greenhouse gases in the atmosphere.

5. They provide a context in which a wider variety of organisms—including nitrogen fixers—may thrive than do annual crops.[26]

Each of these features of perennial plants addresses significant challenges that industrial agriculture faces and even creates. Regenerative, perennial agriculture reduces soil erosion, decreases the need for added fertilizers and irrigation, maintains healthy soil structure, sequesters

---

24. Jackson, *Consulting the Genius of the Place*, 186. Jackson refers to Aldo Leopold, the great early ecologist, who understood that "when we disrupt the diverse integration of species (as we do with farming), the ecosystem will decline—which means that the harvest of contemporary sunlight also will decline, for without the soil-sponsored nutrients, land plants are unable to capture the carbon, hydrogen, oxygen, and nitrogen bound together in water and carbon dioxide afloat in the atmospheric commons and store the sun's energy through photosynthesis" (30).

25. Jackson, *Consulting the Genius of the Place*, 156.

26. Jackson, *Consulting the Genius of the Place*, 162.

carbon more effectively, and establishes a better context for biodiversity and flourishing. In addition to these positive aspects of perennial crop production, at least four other benefits come to mind, especially in light of our foregoing investigation of modern agriculture. The fact that perennial crops do not require annual plowing and planting, as do annuals, prevents thousands of barrels of fuel from being burned. This helpfully addresses the world's escalating global warming crisis caused by fossil fuel use. Since farmers do not replant these crops each year, they are liberated from the annual expense of purchasing seed (often from multinational corporations). Since perennial plants secure and also make available more soil nutrients than do their annual counterparts, they require fewer (or no) additions of fertilizer. This further frees farmers from the heavy financial burdens that industrial farming demands and also decreases N_2O emissions and run-off. Finally, since the grain grown from perennial varieties may exist outside the traditional grain market, consumers are not captive to the market forces driving up conventional food prices.

Since this book has focused on wheat and its production, I will highlight one example of a perennial grain currently being developed by The Land Institute (a *non-profit* organization) and several collaborating universities. The perennial wheat alternative called Kernza® perennial grain is a domesticated intermediate wheatgrass that produces grain that may be used, to a limited extent, in place of wheat.[27] While Kernza® is a trademarked plant strain, it is not patented. Therefore, after farmers purchase their initial seed from "an approved seed source," they "can then save their own seed and replant for subsequent acres."[28] Because Kernza® plants grow year after year—beneficially alleviating the need for annual plowing, it

---

27. Steve Culman of Ohio State University grows Kernza® as part of his research and explained several of its features for me in an email conversation (Culman).

28. In an email clarifying Kernza®'s trademark (TM) status, Tessa Peters explained that the initial purchase "from an approved seed source" "ensure[s] that the seed is of an improved genetic background" (Peters, email correspondence, March 17, 2022). She also explained the rationale behind The Land Institute's efforts in this regard: "We are actively trying to use the trademark to create a 'protected commons' in the sense of Elinor Ostrom's work. We use the TM to create boundaries and specify communal action amongst supply chain stakeholders, working toward increasing their agency in the system by providing increasing mechanisms for licensee input . . . For example, giving licensees a voice in how many acres are approved and what kinds of regulations are required by the Identity Preserved Program (which is how we protect seed rather than patenting)." For more discussion of the Identity Preservation Program of the USDA, see https://www.ams.usda.gov/services/auditing/identity-preservation.

develops incredibly deep, strong roots and, therefore, can access water and nutrients far below the surface and hold precious soils in place. Figure 5 illustrates the vast difference between the roots of a Kernza® perennial grain plant and those of annual wheat.

In certain respects, Kernza® perennial grain's nutritional qualities are "superior to those of annual wheat," making it a strong competitor to reigning annual varieties.[29] Since Kernza® offers "more bran, which means more fiber" and "more minerals and more of some vitamins," Kernza® flour is more nutritious than traditional wheat flour.[30] And because Kernza® is an entirely different species from wheat varieties that are available from traditional seed companies, it does not easily cross-pollinate with annual wheat crops.[31] This allows farmers to avoid the potentially hazardous threat of infringing upon corporations' seed patents. Moreover, farmers who desire to transition slowly to perennial agriculture with Kernza® would not incur heavy losses in sales since it "yields well in the first year or two."[32] In addition to these positive qualities, my family and I have enjoyed the nutty flavor Kernza® adds to our baked goods when blended with wheat flour.[33]

However, Kernza®, as it has been developed thus far, displays several weaknesses. One obstacle to its widespread implementation is that it is still in its research and development phase. Sci-

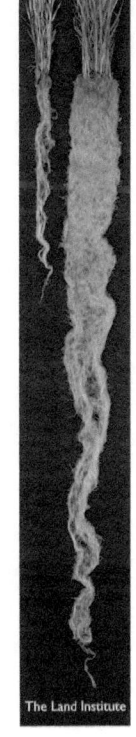

Figure 4. Roots Comparison: A comparison of the roots systems of annual wheat (left) and intermediate wheatgrass, which produces Kernza® perennial grain (right). © The Land Institute. Used by permission.

---

29. Jackson, *Consulting the Genius of the Place*, 156.

30. DeHaan, email correspondence, April 4–8, 2014.

31. DeHaan, email correspondence, April 4–8, 2014. Additionally, farmers can successfully plant Kernza® in fields that have been treated with conventional chemical applications (as long as they would not hurt grass). Kernza® appears to grow well across a wide geographical region, mostly in the north where humidity is lower than in the southeast.

32. DeHaan, email correspondence, April 4–8, 2014. Culman suggests that interested farmers begin with "an acre or so and experiment for a few years before expanding" (email correspondence, June 21, 2017).

33. I have had the best success with taste and texture when I have mixed two parts Kernza® with three parts white wheat flour.

entists at The Land Institute would like to continue improving and testing Kernza® even as they encourage its expanded cultivation and production.[34] In recent years, The Land Institute has collaborated with Patagonia, Cascadian Farms, and local restaurants and breweries to develop Kernza®-based products. Increasingly more farmers in the prairies and cool regions of the US (where Kernza® grows best) have begun to grow and sell Kernza®.[35]

A more challenging weakness of Kernza® is that it does not have the high gluten content that makes hard red spring wheat, in particular, so successful as a bread flour. However, the lead Kernza® scientist at The Land Institute indicates that "[b]reeding to increase gluten quality is planned, but that will take at least a decade. Right now, it can be used in a mix with wheat flour to make bread, or alone to make muffins, pancakes, cookies, etc."[36] From my experience, bread made entirely from Kernza® flour has a rather bitter taste and a crumbly texture whereas a 40/60 blend of Kernza® and white wheat flour is both tasty and chewy.

With these strengths and weaknesses in view, the potential for developing a perennial grain that functions effectively for our daily bread remains open. Kernza® stands as a positive example of how researchers may serve society in ways that promote what are likely to be ecologically beneficial changes to our food system. As scientists, farmers, bakers, and consumers collaborate and keep human and ecological health clearly in view, perhaps we might direct our collective talents towards revolutionizing agriculture. It may even be possible to do so by replacing our staple annual crops with perennial ones. Perhaps creation eagerly awaits the revelation of such crops.

In addition to Kernza®, other perennial crops—such as rice,[37] sorghum,[38] legumes,[39] and oilseeds[40] (which are farther behind in

---

34. In 2014, Dehaan indicated: "We have plenty of farmer interest, but we've had to put off planting on farms until we can be sure that the grains are strong perennials and yield well" (DeHaan). Since that time The Land Institute has allowed for commercial production of Kernza® (The Kernza® Network, "Kernza® Grain").

35. The Kernza® Network, "Kernza® Grain." Consumers can purchase Kernza® grain and flour at Perennial Pantry (https://perennial-pantry.com/collections/frontpage) and elsewhere.

36. DeHaan, email correspondence, April 4–8, 2014.

37. See The Land Institute, "Perennial Rice."

38. See The Land Institute, "Perennial Sorghum."

39. See The Land Institute, "Perennial Legumes."

40. See The Land Institute, "Perennial Oilseeds."

development)—are currently being developed throughout the world. As primary foods in the global south, rice and sorghum crops—if they were bred to function as perennial plants—hold great potential for alleviating anthropogenic forms of ecological degradation and may better withstand climate changes. They would build soils, more efficiently use water and nutrients, and generally support greater biodiversity and the flourishing of life than do the annual varieties used in modern agriculture. As with Kernza®, farmers of perennial rice and sorghum would not need to purchase seed annually or expend the money and energy to plow and sow annually. These crops would likely have greater resistance to drought and insects and provide more reliable harvests in a time of climate change. Therefore, they would provide more sustainable options for addressing the needs of vulnerable societies now and in the future.

Although transitioning to perennial-based staple crops and other regenerative forms of agriculture would likely liberate people and ecosystems from many of the destructive effects of industrial agriculture, its implementation on a global scale may appear to be a daunting, if not impossible, pursuit. Conventional seed and chemical corporations and their many allies in the corporate, political, and financial world have vested interests in maintaining their grip on the profit they receive from farmers, who annually purchase seeds, chemicals, and equipment, and who then produce commodity crops, all to the benefit of agribusinesses.[41] Because of these deep-seated interests in industrial agriculture, few resources and incentives enable farmers to transition to them. Meanwhile, little research money is available for scientists to develop perennial crops or hone regenerative approaches.[42] It consequently takes great courage and determination for farmers to

---

41. Montgomery explains that governments resist transitioning to regenerative agriculture "[b]ecause the solution challenges a century of conventional wisdom and powerful commercial interests, and requires a profound shift in how we think about and treat the least glamorous resource of all—the soil beneath our feet" (*Growing a Revolution*, 17). Even when well-meaning aid organizations have tried to establish better systems of agriculture, they have chosen industrial rather than regenerative approaches. "Funders and aid agencies alike wanted breakthroughs and rapid revolutions, not gradual improvement of the soil. Commercial interests pushed to develop solutions that could be commodified; they wanted agrochemical products, not practices that anyone could adopt for free. No modern, forward-looking foundation or agency wanted to hear about mulching or growing a diversity of crops. Such simple answers did not—and still don't—fit the technophilic narrative of progress" (81).

42. Nevertheless, the University of Minnesota's Forever Green Initiative has received significant funds for such projects ("Forever Green").

implement regenerative agricultural practices "in the face of regulatory disincentives and skeptical corporate and academic crop advisors."[43]

Beyond the financial and systemic barriers that stand in the way of more sustainable, ecologically healthy forms of agriculture is the misinformation about the industrial system that pervades the American consciousness. Full grocery store shelves and enticing commercials misguide Americans into believing that industrial agriculture provides abundant, healthy, and affordable food that is also safe.[44] Agribusinesses and supporters of industrial agriculture inspire this misinformation and purposely veil the true ecological and social costs underlying it. Meanwhile, many Americans see little need for changing industrial agriculture, the food system, or our food choices. Wes Jackson suggests that this inertia and myopia stems, in part, from a condition like Stockholm Syndrome.[45] Although industrial agriculture, as a system, is the world's captor and oppressor, according to Jackson, we have come to identify ourselves with it and align ourselves with its purposes. Under its influence and dominion, we do not seek and cannot see any alternatives. Said a bit differently, we as a society have accepted industrial agriculture's story about ourselves, how we best relate to the nonhuman creation in order to feed ourselves, and how we should perceive technology. By embracing an industrial narrative, we have tied ourselves to the past and cannot envision a different future.[46] It is eerie to consider just how much like sin and death's dominion this situation sounds. If this is truly the case, we need prophets of God and advocates of creation to wake us from our stupor.

Because we are so enamored by agribusiness myths and methods, many Americans and global citizens find it difficult to believe that small, polyculture farms can feed the world. Yet, "[a]ccording to the U.N. Food

43. Montgomery, *Growing a Revolution*, 30.

44. For example, Michael Pollan explains, "Naturalists regard biodiversity as a measure of a landscape's health, and the modern supermarket's devotion to variety and choice would seem to reflect, perhaps even promote, precisely that sort of ecological vigor . . . The great edifice of variety and choice that is an American supermarket turns out to rest on a remarkably narrow biological foundation comprised of a tiny group of plants that is dominated by a single species: *Zea mays*, the giant tropical grass most Americans know as corn" (Pollan, *Omnivore's Dilemma*, 17–18). See also Bahnson and Wirzba, *Making Peace with the Land*, 83–111.

45. Jackson, "Phone Conversation with Wes Jackson."

46. Community builder, Peter Block, argues that communities are often hindered by the stories they tell about their pasts; too often "stories are our limitation" so that we cannot move freely into a different future (Block, *Community*, 15–16).

and Agriculture Organization, family farms produce 80 percent of the world's food, and almost three-quarters (72 percent) of all farms worldwide are smaller than one hectare."[47] What is more, industrial monocultures actually produce less food per hectare even though they can produce a single crop at a cheaper price per bushel than small farms. In fact, "small farms produce more than twice as much food per acre than large farms do."[48] The American consciousness has been held captive by industrial agriculture's alluring promises of cheap, abundant, and safe food. But at what personal, social, and ecological health costs?[49] Taking an honest look at industrial agriculture and considering its alternative in regenerative agriculture may begin to liberate our minds to conceive of more liberative and life-supporting ways of being.

Those who identify themselves as Jesus's followers, may discover in this agricultural transition a holistic means of offering themselves to God as living sacrifices as they more fully inhabit their identities as servant leaders. Their growing, producing, eating, and sharing of regeneratively grown foods will more genuinely honor Christ and engender thanksgiving to God. By promoting biodiversity, ecosystem balance, and soil fertility through their agricultural systems, God's people will more adequately be conformed to the divine image of the Creating and Gardening God and fulfill their commission to be creation's servant leaders (Gen 1:26, 28) while they maintain and nurture the fertility of Earth and its creatures (2:15).

---

47. Montgomery, *Growing a Revolution*, 35.

48. Montgomery, *Growing a Revolution*, 36.

49. An illuminating exposition of these costs is found in Miller, *Truth about Industrial Agriculture*.

CONCLUSION

Cultivating Liberative Relationships
with Human and Nonhuman Creation

WE BEGAN THIS BOOK with an account of creation's current story—a story of habitat destruction and mass extinction caused in large measure by human activity. We continued to read creation's story through the lenses of Scripture/theology, ecology, and politics as we reviewed some of the ways in which the Tanakh portrays the complex set of relationships among the Creator God, Israel, the nations, and nonhuman creation (ch. 1). Directing our attention to the Roman Empire, we then perceived a few ways in which the empire viewed the gods, people, and nature and presented itself and its emperor as renewing nature's fertility; yet we also discovered a variety of ways in which the empire simultaneously exploited and degraded people and ecosystems (ch. 2). With these literary and historical contexts in view, we turned to Paul's letter to the congregations in Rome, straining to understand Paul's story of creation—a story of *creation–subjection–liberation–glorification*—as it was now recast through the life, death, and resurrection of Jesus Christ (chs. 3–5). Finally, we examined Euro-American accounts of and interactions with creation, disclosing some of the ways in which US industrial agriculture has prompted pervasive and pernicious forms of destruction and how, instead, regenerative forms of agriculture provide more ecologically-sound methods for feeding the world (chs. 6–7). In all of this, we considered significant amounts of literary, historical, and scientific data. Arguably, however, data and information alone cannot effectively motivate people and societies to cultivate liberative relationships with the nonhuman creation.¹ Why, then, should we even have concerned ourselves with scientific information, ecological insight, or theological wisdom?

For those with ears to hear and eyes to see, the information we reviewed and continue to receive from creation's story, enables us to perceive the cracks in industrial agriculture's stories about who we are, what the nonhuman creation's purpose and *telos* is, and what effects we humans are having on the entire creation. By piecing disparate forms of information together into a larger narrative framework, we may perceive the past, present, and future in new ways and gain insights into our identities, purposes, and relationships.²

What is more, by viewing this information through a scriptural and theological lens, we are enabled to see the divergence between creation's current moment in the story and where God intends it to be. And this divergence is morally and theologically relevant. Creation's condition—of frustration and excessive destruction in the first century and today—occurs within a

---

1. Jennifer Ayres highlights the fact that although public education over the past few decades in the US has stressed ecological education, especially education around global warming, it has not effectively transformed the country's policies and perspectives so that it prioritizes ecological health and stability (Ayres, *Inhabitance*, 3). She points out that, at least initially, most attempts at ecological education assumed that "knowing facts [would] prompt human repentance and an ecological conversion. This has not proved to be the case" (3). Instead, she insists that "[g]ood ecological learning, the kind that nurtures inhabitance, is learning of the head *and* heart" (3). I concur with Ayres on the importance of holistic forms of education and would argue that "head" matters involving data and scientific information remain important, though not the only important aspect of ecological education and formation. This is because, at least to some extent, institutions, individuals, and societies make decisions on the basis of contextualized information. Such information is helpful, if not necessary, in guiding people as they weigh the immediate financial costs, for example, of an action against its probable effects on long-term personal and ecological health. Yet, when it comes right down to it, once institutions have set out on a course—even a well-researched course—they have a hard time changing directions even when the latest information tells them their current trajectory is off target or harmful. This is arguably the case when it comes to how industrialized societies currently feed themselves. They set out with laudable goals, continue to invest themselves completely in their work, but—when negative effects become apparent—they cannot accept the possibility that their perspectives and practices may need radical revision. Thus, as Ayres indicates, institutions, political bodies, and individuals *also* need something *more* than mere facts to stimulate change.

2. From a Native American perspective, Kimmerer contends: "Stories are among our most potent tools for restoring the land as well as our relationship to land. We need to unearth the old stories that live in a place and begin to create new ones, for we are storymakers, not just storytellers. All stories are connected, new ones woven from the threads of the old" (*Braiding Sweetgrass*, 341).

theological story, in which God, humans, and nonhuman creation are actors and for which God intends a particular *telos*. Since this theological story is a story that moves from slavery to liberation, from destruction to flourishing, justice, and life, it calls into question any activity that undermines this movement. Thus, the Pauline story of creation powerfully opposes forces in ourselves and our polities that would seek to enslave and deform us.

As chapter 6 demonstrated, many of the impulses and actions characterizing industrial agriculture work at cross purposes with God's liberation, justice, and life for all creation. We unfortunately find ourselves caught up in an agricultural regime that attempts to provide abundant, safe, and affordable foods but in the process sacrifices ecological and social health and well-being. Modern industrial agriculture bears significant responsibility for current declines in soil, water, and air qualities; biodiversity; and overall ecosystem health. What is more, through its captivating story of food production, industrial agriculture shapes—or, perhaps, misshapes—our expectations, relationships, identities, and practices. It leads us to expect food to be cheap (no matter the ecological and social costs), always available (no matter the local season), teeming with variety, fast, and edible on the go. It clouds our vision so that we no longer see the vast number of creatures and processes that provide us with food. It blinds us to the complex set of relationships that bind people to animals, to plants, to soils, to air, to water. The food system today even teaches us as a species to hoard (or even destroy) rather than share the earth's gifts of food.

Some of these forms of misshaping result especially because of how we conceive of our relationships with human and nonhuman creation. Industrial agriculture's rather utilitarian and atomistic views of humans, soil, water, insects, animals, and plants influence our own perspectives and actions. On account of this disintegrated view of the world, farmers may find themselves unable to meet their vital and ethical responsibilities to nonhuman and human neighbors and simultaneously become enslaved to market demands and crushing debt. They may then succumb to the pressure of increasing production while decreasing cost and human labor. As producers and consumers, we may all find ourselves accepting the assumption that we can and even should control earth's fertility in fast, synthetic, and fossil-fuel-dependent ways.

Perhaps most startling of all, is the way in which the industrial regime places us in an adversarial relationship with the nonhuman creation. It tells us to wage war on insects we name "pests" and on plants we identify as "weeds."³ As a result, we humans fail to consider ourselves in collaborative, interconnected, interdependent relationships with the nonhuman creation. We find ourselves standing against creation. We consequently forget—or even reject—our unique identity as God's servant leaders who are commissioned to serve and maintain the fertile soil (Gen 2:15).

Our sense of identity may become so mutated that we succumb to the captivating narrative told by Western society, and especially the US, that we are and should be relentless consumers.⁴ While it is true that, as creatures, we necessarily "consume" some of the earth's resources, an unfettered consumerist society distracts us from questioning our means of consumption and how much we consume. It presses us so to identify ourselves as consumers that we find it nearly impossible to be creatures in this world in ways that do not contribute to its degradation and destruction.⁵ Even when we resist such pressures, systemic forces make it difficult for us to extract ourselves from deleterious networks of consumption.

---

3. Wirzba articulates the complex interconnections between narrative, identity, and action, stating, "The way we think about food depends on how we name and narrate the world in which we eat. Food does not simply appear, nor is everything food. It is a chosen and named entity that draws its significance from the wider contexts in which it appears. To appreciate the significance of naming, consider the difference between calling a plant a 'weed,' a 'flower,' or a 'fruit.' Any of these names carries with it a set of dispositions and responses that have widely different effects. So too with the world as a whole. How we name and narrate it will greatly affect how we relate to it" (Wirzba, *Food and Faith*, 5). Certainly this insight into the power of naming critiques the nomenclature of "thorns and thistles" (Gen 3:17–19).

4. Horrell, Hunt, and Southgate contend that "Capitalism's increasingly globalized story . . . describes human beings as customers and producers and increasingly narrates their relationships in market terms; it tends to depict human interaction with the nonhuman world in terms of resources, prices, market value . . ." (*Greening Paul*, 58–59). In somewhat different terms, Fred Bahnson and Norman Wirzba suggest, "[w]e live amid two competing narratives. One is the abundant kingdom Jesus brought, where all receive enough and often there is abundance. The second narrative for most of us, however, is not scarcity but a glamorous and alluring kind of abundance. I call it the *abundant mirage*. Nowhere are these two competing narratives more manifest than in the way we eat" (*Making Peace with the Land*, 85).

5. For an insightful discussion of the effects of a consumer culture on our eating, see Wirzba, *Food and Faith*, 159–60. Vincent Miller illustrates some of the insidious effects of our consumer culture. He argues it influences people to express their identity through belongings so that people become "motivated by the need to form and communicate an identity in a dynamic and competitive social setting" through their consumption of earth's goods (Miller, *Consuming Religion*, 114–15). Our excessive, conspicuous forms of consumption (9) is dangerously correlated with our identities, and all of this exacerbates creation's degradation.

Creation's Slavery and Liberation

Through it all, we may even come to believe humans can do little else than degrade creation.[6]

Yet, Paul's good news breaks through our despair and malaise.[7] It does so by telling us the truth about the Creator God and the nonhuman creation's condition (that it is suffering in large part because of human injustice and exploitation), announcing the truth about ourselves (that we are liberated so that we might cooperate with God's purposes of justice and life), and reminding us of God's liberative intentions for all creation. Thus:

> the Pauline story can be a means to articulate a counter-narrative, a challenge to dominant economic and cultural narratives, a means to envisage communities in which a different story constructs a different sense of identity and undergirds different patterns of practice.[8]

In this book, I summarized the trajectory of Paul's counternarrative as *creation-subjection-liberation-glorification*.

Although the scriptural stories of creation reviewed in this book may be summarized in a variety of ways, we here recall the broad contours of the Pauline story of creation we traced in 3.3:

1. God cooperated with land and water to create living things; commissioned the creation to be diverse and interdependent so that all living things would have adequate access to food; and instructed people to share land and food justly and equitably, even with human enemies and other creatures.

2. God created humans to be creation's servant leaders but also gave them freedom to disobey and sin; they did and do sin and have become enslaved to sin's influence.

---

6. Kimmerer illustrates this point by describing the results of a survey she gives at the beginning of her ecology class. The "third-year students who had selected a career in environmental protection" "confidently" considered "humans and nature to be a bad mix" (*Braiding Sweetgrass*, 6). By and large, the students found it difficult to identify "positive interactions between people and land" so that "they cannot think of any beneficial relationships between people and the environment" (6).

7. The positive witness of some indigenous peoples (both past and present) and other community groups may also dispel the fog, revealing to us cooperative and mutually beneficial ways of living with the nonhuman creation. For examples of such communities, see Kimmerer, *Braiding Sweetgrass*; White, *Freedom Farmers*; Penniman, *Farming While Black*; Bahnson and Wirzba, *Making Peace with the Land*; Ayres, *Good Food*; McMinn, *To the Table*; Pollan, *Omnivore's Dilemma*.

8. Horrell, Hunt, and Southgate, *Greening Paul*, 59.

3. God created a world in which human activity necessarily affects the vitality, flourishing, and well-being of human and nonhuman creation; but because of human sin and the consequent reign of sin and death in the world, God is at work making things right (justification) and making things alive (*zōopoiēsis*).

4. In the old age, God provided God's people with the means to atone for impurities and minor sins and promised to cleanse the people and land fully in the new age.

5. God sent the promised Messiah—God's Son, Jesus Christ—to make things right (justification); Messiah Jesus, as the foremost servant leader, has thus provided unending and boundless atonement by his life, death, and resurrection; this atonement liberates human and nonhuman creation from the oppressive effects of sin and reconciles them to one another and God.

6. God sent the promised Spirit to make things alive (*zōopoiēsis*); God, the Spirit, therefore liberated Messiah Jesus from death through resurrection, is liberating all who walk in the Spirit into new life now and resurrection life in the future, and, ultimately, will liberate the whole creation from its subjection to frustration and slavery to destruction and will usher it into a form of glorification, the New Creation.

7. Prior to the resurrection and New Creation, people in Christ embody their justification and *zōopoiēsis* by pursuing and maintaining right/just relationships with God, people, and nonhuman creation; they thereby grow into a style of servant leadership that supports the vitality, flourishing, and well-being of creation; meanwhile, the nonhuman creation eagerly supports and cooperates with the resurrecting God.

This summary and the fuller accounts of creation on which it depends introduces us to the counternarrative's cast of characters, who have particular identities and purposes: God, nonhuman creation, and humanity.

We encounter God, the Creator, who is the wellspring of life, having established a world of interdependence, diversity, and flourishing. A primary concern of this Creator is that plant life may flourish so that all creatures may feed themselves (for more discussion, see ch. 1). Where human and nonhuman creation fails to achieve God's ideals, God the Son and God the Spirit offer atonement, justice, and restored life.[9]

9. Undoubtedly, some of these forms of rectification come in the eschatological future.

The nonhuman creation, in turn, is a cooperative actor that presses towards life and even absorbs death in ways that nourish more life. In the words of Norman Wirzba:

> Creation is an immense altar upon which the incomprehensible, self-offering love of God is daily made manifest. Here, in the living and dying of creatures, in the seed that dies into the ground, we discover that sacrificial offering is a condition for the possibility of the membership of life we call creation. Creation, understood as God's offering of creatures to each other as food and nurture, reflects a sacrificial power in which life continually moves through death to new life.[10]

As a whole, nonhuman creation cooperates with God and—even in limited ways—reveals God. It is tasked with the self-giving commission to support the flourishing and life of all creatures. Humans, nevertheless, must not perceive it as a mere "natural resource."

While much more could be said about the identities and purposes of the Creator and nonhuman creation, we turn now to propose several ways in which Paul's counternarrative shapes and transforms *human* identities, purposes, and practices. Overall, the Pauline gospel directs humans to worship the living Creator God, honor the Lord Jesus Christ, and live by the enlivening power of the Spirit. Our diverse human identities, moreover, are to conform to the pattern of Jesus Christ, who is the self-giving, self-restraining servant leader and liberator of human and nonhuman creation. To the extent that we allow ourselves to be conformed to Jesus's image and transformed by God's eschatological purposes, Paul's narrative mobilizes us to live into God's liberation already at work in the world around us and in us.

While worship of the Creator God and conformation to the Son offer us a basic blueprint for who we are and what we are to do, the seven Pauline eco-ethical principles developed in 3.3 suggest further detail and specificity. They exhort people to:

1. Attend to creation's story by recognizing the ways in which God's creation not only reveals the Creator God but also exposes its own condition on account of the complex, interdependent relationships between and among nonhuman and human participants.

---

10. Wirzba, *Food and Faith*, 126.

2. Express gratitude to the Creator God for the gifts of creation, sharing the gifts of food with God's creatures.

3. Cooperate in the divine work of justification, making right/just, by supporting and protecting the well-being of the members of God's creation, both human and nonhuman and, especially, the "weak"/disempowered/vulnerable.

4. Cooperate in the divine work of *zōopoiēsis*, making alive, by promoting and supporting the vitality of life: the biodiversity, fertility, and flourishing of entire ecosystems and the biosphere.

5. Honor the Lord Jesus Christ by avoiding activities that would subject creation to frustration, enslave it to destruction, or would injure or destroy those for whom Christ died.

6. Stand in solidarity with the sufferings and hopes of creation by exercising servant leadership, in conformity with Jesus, in ways that serve and maintain the health, flourishing, fertility, and diversity of creation.

7. Exercise appropriate self-restraint in order to share the gifts of creation and support the vitality and fidelity of other members of God's creation.

Practically, these narratively shaped principles inspire us to engage in and restrain ourselves to forms of consumption that alleviate the destruction of creation, promote biodiversity and the flourishing of life, enhance the well-being of creation's vulnerable members, and engender expressions of thanksgiving to God.[11] On the basis of these principles and Paul's theological and ethical logic in Romans more broadly, we may decipher several important facets of our human identities: We are co-recipients, servants, agents of liberation, and priests.

First, we are *co-recipients* of God's life-giving energies. *Along with* the nonhuman creation, we receive from our divine Parent the gift of life and the resources for life. This means human and nonhuman creatures rely on many of the same resources, which requires us to share. As food sharers who respect the needs, dignity, and consciences of others, we exercise self-restraint in our demands, expectations, and actions as we offer ourselves as living sacrifices to God and thereby support God's liberative work in the world (Rom 14–15; 12:1–2; 8:21). Understood concretely, our commission to *share* food, then,

---

11. These purposes are here expressed with explicit focus on how *Christians* relate to nonhuman creation and are not meant to be exhaustive nor are they meant to be imposed on others.

leads us not only to feast together but also to fast as one form of sacrifice for the life and well-being of others. Wirzba insightfully notes:

> If sacrifice is about healing the alienation and violence that destroy membership and about establishing the communion that leads to abundant life, then feasting, understood as the celebration of the good of others and of our membership in a common life, and fasting, understood as the restraining of personal desires that otherwise would seek to possess and consume the world, must be two of its correlative practices. People should feast so they do not forget the grace and the blessing of the world. People should fast so they do not degrade or hoard the good gifts of God.[12]

As co-recipients of God's nourishing gifts, then, we humans intentionally become food sharers, willing to sacrifice some objects of our desire. This may even lead us to expect that some nonhuman creatures will partake in the produce of our farms and gardens. By recognizing this fact and our given identity as co-recipients, we consequently reject industrial agriculture's war on "pests" and "weeds" and instead learn to grow our food in the context of a diverse and flourishing network of living things that depends on natural forms of predation and competition to maintain ecosystem balance.

Not only are we co-recipients of life, we are also *co-recipients* of liberation. Thus, also *along with* the nonhuman creation, human creatures are invited to share in God's gracious liberation. Through the work of Christ and the Spirit, we humans may be liberated from the enslaving forces of sin and death so that we can walk according to the rule of the Spirit of life (Rom 8:2). But God's liberative work does not stop there. God also will liberate the nonhuman creation from its subjection to frustration and slavery to destruction (8:21). Consequently, as those experiencing liberation along with the rest of creation, we are reminded that God's loving, salvific intentions stretch far beyond human beings alone.

An appropriate outgrowth of our status as co-recipients of God's life-giving and liberative presence is a response of gratitude. Expressions of gratitude, in turn, enable us to break free from false narratives and identities, and they instead help us participate more appropriately in God's story of creation.[13] The practice of Eucharist, as we will consider more below,

---

12. Wirzba, *Food and Faith*, 137.

13. People of many different religious traditions recognize the importance of gratitude for orienting us properly towards the sources of life, both divine and creational. For example, the "Thanksgiving Address" of the Onondaga Nation of North America illustrates humanity's profound dependence on a wide range of creational and supernatural

provides a primary means by which we as Jesus's followers may inculcate, enact, and express holistic forms of gratitude.

Second, we are *servant leaders*. In conversation with Gen 1–2, Paul's account implies we are servant leaders who are given the weighty responsibility of serving and maintaining the land's fertility. As servants, we find ourselves to be co-producers rather than mere consumers. What is more, as servants of the Creating and Gardening God, we discover we are "nurturing participants" in this bountiful creation (Gen 2:7–8).[14]

In more Pauline terms, we are servants of righteousness/justice and servants of God; we consequently learn how to "reign" in and for life (Rom 6:18, 22; 5:17). Thus, we are not slaves to our own desires and ambitions (especially as these tend to be manipulated and shaped by a consumerist and even idolatrous culture). Instead, with the nonhuman creation specifically in view, we serve God the Gardener by nurturing—and, as need be, restoring—the fertile earth by collaborating with God and creation in producing life. We are thus servant leaders of God's justification and *zōopoiēsis*.

God's life-giving liberation empowers us, thirdly, to be *agents of liberation*. This is not to say that those who have been liberated by God through Christ and the Spirit are themselves liberators in an ultimate sense of the word. Rather, in light of our unavoidable effects on God's creatures and creation, we intentionally live our lives in ways that liberate the nonhuman creation from frustrated attempts of flourishing and nourishing life; we liberate it, whenever possible, from untimely and excessive forms of death and destruction.

As *agents of liberation*, we accept the responsibility to be advocates and resist thinking of creation or its members as our adversaries.[15] Shining

---

entities. Although Christians would identify the supernatural characters differently, we may nevertheless agree with the Thanksgiving Address's effects: it inspires contentment. Kimmerer suggests the practice of gratitude expressed through the Thanksgiving Address carries culture-transforming ramifications. "In a consumer society, contentment is a radical proposition. Recognizing abundance rather than scarcity undermines an economy that thrives by creating unmet desires. Gratitude cultivates an ethic of fullness, but the economy needs emptiness. The Thanksgiving Address reminds you that you already have everything you need. Gratitude doesn't send you out shopping to find satisfaction; it comes as a gift rather than a commodity, subverting the foundation of the whole economy. That's good medicine for land and people alike" (*Braiding Sweetgrass*, 111).

14. Wirzba, *Food and Faith*, 151.

15. In order to avoid adversarial pressures, we will likely need to reinterpret biblical passages such as Gen 3:17–19 that some may interpret as placing us in antagonistic relationships with the earth.

a light on all forms of anthropogenic destruction and speaking the truth about them, we offer our embodied selves as instruments of righteousness/justice and life in collaboration with God's work of liberation. More specifically, we lift the veil on the destructive perspectives and practices of industrial agriculture, so that we all might see the ways in which our actions are degrading creation's fertility and destroying biodiversity and societal well-being. As creation's advocates and agents of liberation, God's human creatures consequently must hold our polities and governing bodies accountable to being "God's servant" for the good of all (Rom 13:4). In so doing, we meanwhile resist the dominant socio-political narrative that would have us believe industrialized society has created an age of fertility and peace through military and industrial might. We instead proclaim again and again creation's story and the gospel: while humans too often enslave creation to inordinate forms of destruction and frustrate its life-supporting purposes, we are called to walk in line with God's work of justification and *zōopoiēsis*.

Fourth, in close connection with our identities as agents and servant leaders, we are also *priests*, perhaps even creation's priests. Offering our living selves continuously to God (Rom 12:1–2), we offer up prayers and other forms of intercession for creation's flourishing and well-being.[16] As priests, we stand in solidarity with creation's sufferings and its hopes, offering our prayers, services, and selves for its good. We embody the hopeful theological narrative in which God's children serve the whole creation as they cooperate with God's justifying and *zōopoietical* work and groan with the laboring creation as it collectively awaits (and works toward) God's fullest liberation (Rom 8:19–22).

It is likely that many Western Christians have limited liturgical imaginations for our priestly identities, and, so, we fail to see how we can cultivate these identities as both lay and ordained people. Perhaps recalling the ways in which ancient Israelites and Judeans offered creation's fruits to the Creator God and petitioned God for agricultural success, we may be inspired to recover and develop appropriate liturgical practices for churches and families today.[17] As we take seriously the importance of prayer, we might intentionally engage in petitioning God for timely and healthful rains. Yet,

---

16. This is not to say that God does not provide these blessings upon nonhuman creatures/creation apart from human intercession. Yet, God does invite humans to employ their bodily selves in ways that request specific blessings upon creation (see 1.2.3).

17. In conversation with the Jewish agricultural festivals, the Christian liturgical year, and the New Testament, I hope to devote future research to this topic.

even as we begin to intercede for healthful rains, we certainly will encounter our need to repent of and witness against our collective human actions that catalyze hurricanes, floods, droughts, and the disappearance of glaciers. We will find ourselves in need of mutual accountability, forgiveness, and encouragement as we attempt to embody God's liberation every day. Such priestly practices may inculcate within us a primary sense of dependence on the goodness and generosity of creation, God's good purposes for it, and our human effects on creation. Engaging in priestly intercession on behalf of all creation simultaneously may strengthen our resistance to the all-too-common expectation that technology will save us in times of struggle.

While these four identities by no means encapsulate all of who we are, they stand as helpful reminders of God's story with and for creation and God's gracious purposes for all. They also correlate closely with the eco-ethical principles we found pulsing through God's creation-wide activity of making right and making alive. Our identities and the principles inspiring them nevertheless remain abstract until they are instantiated in our daily, communal lives. What is more, they may easily be forgotten and ignored apart from consistent reminders of God's gracious and liberative involvement with and purposes for creation.[18] Thus, we need common, Christian practices to help us recall and enact these principles and cultivate the countercultural identities suggested in Paul's liberative story of creation. One peculiarly poignant and relevant practice presents itself in the pages of Romans: Eucharist.

As a place where theology meets ecology, where Spirit touches B/body, the Eucharist invites ecclesial communities to offer ourselves and the gifts of creation to God with integrity, vitality, and justice. The practice of Eucharist, when done well, reminds us of God's mission of liberating *all* creation, human and nonhuman. It reminds us of our true identities as co-recipients, servants, agents of liberation, and priests. It physically integrates

---

18. I draw inspiration here from Michael Lamb, Jonathan Brant, and Edward Brooks's contribution to the field of character development in "How is Virtue Cultivated?: Seven Strategies for Postgraduate Character Development." They suggest seven approaches to stimulating particular ways of being, identified as virtues. In order to facilitate character formation, participants engage in and inculcate: habituation through practice; reflection on personal experience; engagement with virtuous exemplars; dialogue that increases virtue literacy; awareness of situational variables; moral reminders; and friendships of mutual accountability ("How is Virtue Cultivated?," 84–98).

us with a host of other created beings and elements that make our lives possible.[19] And, of course, Eucharist unifies us with our Lord and Creator.

Partaking of any food, but especially the eucharistic elements, reminds us of our humble status as co-recipients. In the process of receiving the body of Christ during communion, Christians are not only reminded of our dependence on the Savior but also ideally of our interdependence with the whole of God's creation. It is humbling to recognize that

> [t]he eucharistic bread, which is a human offering, is totally dependent on the activity of yeasts, the physical and chemical processes that provide nutrients to the soil, and the unremitting labor of microorganisms that create humus, to name but a few essential contributors. On a purely physical level, the Eucharist is a cosmic celebration on an awe-inspiring scale. We are the ones who literally make the "offering," since offering is a conscious activity. But by analogy, we could see the bread and wine as also being the "offering" of all the creatures involved in their making: of the rocks and plants and bacteria without which there would be no soil, and indeed the cosmic dust of which the earth is composed. Without us, the product of these creatures' activity would not be offered to God in thankfulness; but without them, there would be nothing for us to offer.[20]

When celebrated well, then, Eucharist draws God's people to feel inexpressible gratitude, awe, and dependence on God and God's elaborate creation since the celebration of Eucharist includes all of creation in a cosmic communion. While the eucharistic elements display humanity's ultimate reliance on ecological processes beyond our control, they also reveal the important role humans play in bringing the fruit of the earth to God with intentionality

---

19. Wirzba beautifully captures the power of eucharistic eating: "To transform eating into a practical exercise is to cultivate the practical conditions and habits—attention, conversation, reflection, gratitude, honest accounting—in which food and the world can be perceived to have a face. When we meet and receive the face of creation, personal freedom can be called into question because now we are responsible for what we do, and must give an account as to whether or not we honored the sanctity before us" (Wirzba, *Food and Faith*, 32).

20. Theokritoff, *Living in God's Creation*, 193–94. Similarly, Wirzba declares, "Good, healthy soil is not dead but teeming with life. Death decays into it and reemerges as new life, all because of the astoundingly complex and mostly invisible work of billions of bacteria and microorganisms. Without their work our world would be overwhelmed by the corpses and stench of death. Soil is a marvel and a mystery that we have not yet even begun to comprehend" (Wirzba, *Food and Faith*, 13).

and integrity.[21] Without creation's fertility, biodiversity, and flourishing maintained, the theological story told in the Eucharist would not be proclaimed with integrity nor would the ecological story be one of celebration.

As priests (lay and ordained), we express thanksgiving to God for the gifts of creation through Eucharist. It gives us the opportunity to "offer the firstfruits of God's own creation as a token of our own thankfulness."[22] This process of offering up to God the elements of bread and wine flows out of human intentionality and agency. As a body of believers—farmers, bakers, consumers, priests—we rightly reconceive of ourselves as producers, as cocreators with God's living creation. Thus, the eucharistic elements no longer appear to "passive" church goers as something we *receive* but also as something we as a human community *offer* up to God.[23] This is because, in the Eucharist, we "*offer back* to God his own gifts (since nothing in the world is our own), accompanied by the only thing that is properly ours: our praise, blessing, and *thanksgiving*. In the eucharistic Gifts, our gratitude is given in tangible form. And in return, we receive God's Gift of himself in tangible form."[24] Participation in Eucharist not only is an expression of our Christian identity and integrity but also functions to reintegrate us into God's creational story so that we might do God's work in the world as the body of Christ.

Eucharist, therefore, gives God's people the opportunity to develop our skills of serving and of becoming agents of liberation. Especially when the sacrament of Eucharist occurs within the context of a full meal—as it did in the first Christian communities (see 3.2.4)—it prompts us not only to nourish one another's bodies but to do so with foods that both honor the Lord Jesus and do not destroy those for whom he died (Rom 14:6, 15).

---

21. Timothy Eberhart beautifully portrays the incarnational and ethical dynamic at work in Eucharist. He explains, "God's holiness is offered to us as *enfleshed love*, which we consume in the bread and cup as the nourishment of our earthly life together. Faithful acceptance of God's summons to participate in Holy Communion, then, includes faithfully worshipping the Creator by tending to the bodily well-being of God's creation" (*Rooted and Grounded in Love*, 96).

22. Theokritoff, *Living in God's Creation*, 187.

23. Elizabeth Theokritoff perceptively notes, "In communities divorced from agriculture, where few in the congregation have ever made bread, let alone grown and harvested wheat, it is perhaps not surprising that the Eucharist is regarded less as something we offer than as something we receive" (*Living in God's Creation*, 188–89).

24. Theokritoff, *Living in God's Creation*, 189. In the words of my own liturgical tradition, the United Methodist Church, God makes the bread and wine (or, more commonly, juice) "the body and blood of Christ" in order that God's people "may be for the world the body of Christ, redeemed by his blood" (The United Methodist Book of Worship, 38).

Done with these goals in view, Eucharist-as-meal may powerfully motivate congregations to develop relationships with local and regional farmers and food producers. Different congregations might even collaborate with one another and collectively partner with farmers, millers, and bakers to grow, mill, and bake communion bread and other baked-goods from regeneratively-grown grains. By requesting regeneratively grown products and partnering with farmers as they transition to regenerative forms of agriculture, God's people become agents of liberation, playing a small role in moving creation's story away from destruction and towards health. As the Body of Christ engaged in liberative networks of food production, we may produce, eat, and enjoy our daily "bread" with the knowledge that it did not come from an "ecological sacrifice zone."[25] Our eucharistically-inspired efforts conform us to be more like Jesus the Christ as we support creation's liberation in these tangible ways. And since the ingredients for the Eucharist meal would not require the sacrifice of ecological health for its production, the church's offering of the bread and wine to God in the Eucharist can represent the *one* intended sacrifice: that of Jesus Christ.

We may begin to find the practice of Eucharist invites us to be servants and agents of liberation in all facets of our lives and in all our relationships. In keeping with Paul's concern for the disempowered (the "weak"), those who find themselves empowered (the "strong") may choose to restrain themselves for the well-being, fidelity, and vitality of the disempowered (see 3.2.4). For, as theologian Timothy Eberhart explains, "Because both human and natural history are joined together in the Eucharist meal, in the elements of the field and the dynamics of shared human life, 'full communion' entails a willingness of the Christian community to be immersed in 'life as a whole and to stand where Jesus stands in all walks of life,' especially in intimate and just relationship with the suffering poor and the injured creation."[26] When we courageously acknowledge sin, countenance death and destruction, and turn towards life, which a holistic practice of Eucharist facilitates, we find ourselves becoming agents of liberation and servants of those who are vulnerable. We stand in solidarity with their suffering as well as their hope. In our holistic approaches to working towards equity and justice with those who have been impoverished and by alleviating creation's experiences of destruction, Jesus's followers embody God's marvelous work of justification and *zōopoiēsis* in local, concrete ways. And

---

25. Jackson, *Consulting the Genius of the Place*, 156.
26. Eberhart, *Rooted and Grounded in Love*, 36.

all of this presages the glory to come. "For the creation expectantly awaits the apocalypse of the sons of God" when "the creation itself will be liberated from the slavery of destruction into the liberation of the glory of God's children" (Rom 8:19, 21).[27]

---

27. Author's translation.

APPENDIX

Forgotten Truths

Synthetic Pesticides and Genetic Modification

FARMERS CONSTANTLY FACE THE challenge of restraining pests and weeds so they do not diminish yields. Since insects eat and damage crops and weeds take up precious nutrients and space, their presence makes crops less productive and harvesting more difficult.[1] Thus, in order to harvest more of their delicate crops, farmers toil and sweat daily in their attempts to keep non-crop species at bay. Alongside farmers, scientists have worked to develop new technologies that attempt to overcome these factors that limit yields.

By the late 1930s and early 1940s war efforts stimulated the development of new classes of chemicals that could function as pesticides. Carbon-based organophosphates (for example, parathion) and organochlorines (chlorinated hydrocarbons) killed insects and phenoxy herbicides killed plants.[2] Perfected by the Nazi government, organophosphates served as nerve agents.[3] Meanwhile, the organochlorine DDT (dichlorodiphenyl-trichloroethane) became an important pesticide used against lice during WWII and against a myriad of household, farm, and even forest "pests" thereafter.[4] Soon after the war's end, the USDA's primary chemist in the Bureau of Entomology and Plant Quarantine described the power of these new chemicals in this way: "'War-developed products gave man new and

---

1. Some elements in this appendix first appeared in Burroughs, "Christlike Feasting." I thank Cascade Books for allowing me to reproduce some material here.
2. Mart, *Pesticides*, 21.
3. Mart, *Pesticides*, 20.
4. Mart, *Pesticides*, 19–28.

important weapons in his ageless *war against insects*, but unless we devote less of our energy to killing each other and more of it to *annihilating pests*, the insect may win out in the long run and inherit the earth."[5] Annihilating pests supposedly would empower people to inherit the earth, enabling-farmers to increase their yields—in the short-term—and feed much of the world's human population.

The US considered itself and its farmers to be responsible for feeding the world after World War II. Since the US is a nation with extensive farmland that emerged victorious from WWII, it strove to feed Europeans bereft of crops at the end of WWII and employed industrial agricultural methods—including synthetic chemicals—to do so.[6] To many, the powerful new chemicals on offer rightly empowered them to take control of the earth and its resources more fully: synthetic fertilizers, insecticides, herbicides, and other pesticides dramatically increased crops yields. All of these developments facilitated large-scale changes in US agriculture so that it entered what some call the Golden Age of Synthetic Pesticides.[7] The US, in turn, encouraged and supported these changes across the globe, especially in developing countries, ushering in the so-called Green Revolution.[8]

Despite immediate gains in agricultural yield, by the late 1970s many criticized industrial agriculture's "heavy use of chemical and petrochemical

---

5. Mart, *Pesticides*, 22. Emphasis added. This statement, along with many others of the time, not only reveals the culture's militaristic mentality towards insects but also an anthropocentric and misguided use of Scripture. According to this chemist, it would be a travesty if insects rather than the "meek" inherited the earth (see Matt 5:5). And, in his view, the meek supposedly are those humans who would use deadly poisons against insects to inherit the earth.

6. Mart, *Pesticides*, 85.

7. Mart, *Pesticides*, 11.

8. The birth of the Green Revolution took place in 1941 when "the Rockefeller Foundation sent three scientists to Mexico to study how to improve that nation's production of food" (Mart, *Pesticides*, 84). As these scientists and their US supporters worked alongside the Mexican government to transform agricultural yields, they introduced the "pesticides developed during the war," "hybrid seeds, up-to-date equipment, new methods, and synthetic chemicals" (87). The "development" taking place in Mexico became a model for how the US would assist developing countries across the globe during the Cold War, especially those areas vulnerable to the threats of communism (85). Bentley and Hobart also explain: "Rockefeller Foundation scientists engineered new seeds designed to produce significantly more grain in countries all over the world. Known as the Green Revolution, these developments seemed to work miracles by vastly increasing the amount of food available to developing countries. Yet they also put a severe strain on local economies and endangered subsistence farmers, the environment, and indigenous cultures" (Bentley and Hobart, "Food in Recent U.S. History," 169).

inputs."⁹ Agribusinesses claimed in response that advances in genetic engineering and biotechnology promised a "better way forward."¹⁰ These developments would purportedly reduce the amount of chemicals and fossil fuels needed to maintain—and even increase—crop yields. Thus, new biotechnologies allowed agribusinesses to promote the impression that industrial agriculture was "gradually giving up its dependence on pesticides."¹¹ In order to use fewer synthetic chemicals, biotechnicians had to develop the genetically modified seed.

Scientists expected the new technology of genetic modification (GM), which introduces genetic material from an entirely unrelated species into the crop species, to revolutionize agriculture just as much as engine power and synthetic chemicals had done earlier in the twentieth century. When genetic engineers and plant scientists first began applying genetic modification to new seed development, the possibilities seemed endless and unimaginably fruitful. Plant molecular biologist, Mary-Dell Chilton of Ciba-Geigy Corporation, explained in 1984 that "[t]he solutions are coming very fast now. In three years, we'll be able to do anything [with gene manipulations] that our imaginations will get us to."¹² In 1985 during his presidential address to the American Society of Agronomy, Kenneth Frey imagined near miraculous crop yields that could occur when environmental agronomists worked together with genetic engineers, so that "from this team effort will come an enormity of crop production that may dwarf the accomplishments of the 'Green Revolution.'"¹³ Frey continued his address by giving example after example of inventive ways in which biotechnology might revolutionize agriculture, such as infiltrating crop plants with genes that make their rhizomes able to fix nitrogen or able to tolerate more salt or aluminum in soils.¹⁴

Although the science of agriculture appeared to have "no foreseeable bounds" as it held hands with genetic engineering in 1985, the types of genetic modification applied to large-scale commercial agriculture since that

9. Mart, *Pesticides*, 193. Mart explains: "The increase in pesticide use due to Green Revolution policies was dramatic. By the middle of the 1980s, for example, one-fifth of world pesticides use was found in Asia, and the number of acres sprayed in India went from 15 million in 1960 to 200 million by the mid-1980s."
10. Shiva, *Stolen Harvest*, 12. For more discussion, see 6.1.
11. Moore, "Hidden Dimensions of Damage," 144.
12. Kloppenburg, *First the Seed*, 191.
13. Frey, "Presidential Address," 187.
14. Frey, "Presidential Address," 188.

Appendix

time have been rather limited.[15] On a commercial scale, biotechnology has modified two main traits in crop species in order to address the primary problems of pests and weeds. One type of modification makes the crop pest resistant by transferring qualities that deter pests from one species to a pest-prone crop species. For example, genetic engineers introduce genetic material from the bacterium *Bacillus thuringiensis* (*Bt*), which produces a protein that is harmful to insects, into a crop plant (such as *Bt* corn) so that the plant itself can then produce its own insecticidal protein.[16] With this resistance, the farmer is able to use fewer insecticides (at least until pests further evolve) and still maintain high yields.

Scientists employ a second type of genetic modification in order to make crop species that are able to live in the presence of herbicides. This allows farmers to kill unwanted plants ("weeds") while their crop species survives. Genetic modification makes a crop herbicide tolerant by introducing genetic material from an unrelated species that is able to withstand a specific herbicide into the crop species that would otherwise die when that herbicide is applied. For example, the herbicide glyphosate (*N*-[phosphonomethyl]-glycine, formerly patented as the active ingredient in Roundup®) kills weeds by interrupting their production of essential amino acids; while it does this to weeds, glyphosate also undermines the production of essential amino acids in bacteria and plants that are not tolerant. Since animals do not produce their own amino acids but instead ingest them, they are thought to remain unscathed by glyphosate. It appeared reasonable and harmless, therefore, for scientists at Monsanto genetically to modify crops in order to be "Roundup Ready." Then, farmers could use this "benign" chemical to kill weeds while the crops themselves would withstand the deadly effects of Roundup® because genetic material from the soil bacterium *Agrobacterium tumefaciens* had been incorporated into the crop species.[17]

---

15. Mart, *Pesticides*, 194.

16. For explanations see "Global Insect Resistance Management." For information about the development and safety of a wide variety of GM crops, see CERA, "Welcome to CERA."

17. *Agrobacterium tumefaciens* is able to continue producing essential amino acids even in the presence of the herbicide glyphosate. Consequently, the genetic material from this bacterium introduced into the cells of the GM crop plant enables the plant to survive during glyphosate applications. For more explanation of this process, see CERA, "GM Crop Database".

Genetic modification has become a primary way in which agronomists have attempted to address the problems of weeds and pests. Although genetic modification at first was supposed to reduce farmers' reliance on and use of synthetic chemicals, the use of GM crops only reduced the need for synthetic chemicals for a short time. In the case of herbicide tolerant crops and the extensive use of glyphosate-based herbicides, the weeds that used to be a nuisance to farmers have now evolved into superweeds that require more and different chemicals to kill them (see 6.2.2 for more discussion of glyphosate).

Bibliography

Adams, Edward. *Constructing the World: A Study in Paul's Cosmological Language.* Edinburgh: T. & T. Clark, 2000.

Aitbali, Yassine, et al. "Glyphosate Based-Herbicide Exposure Affects Gut Microbiota, Anxiety and Depression-Like Behaviors in Mice." *Neurotoxicology and Teratology* 67 (2018) 44–49.

"Aldo Leopold." The Aldo Leopold Foundation. https://www.aldoleopold.org/about/aldo-leopold/.

Aldrete, Gregory S. *Floods of the Tiber in Ancient Rome.* Baltimore: The John Hopkins University Press, 2007.

Alkon, Alison Hope, and Julian Agyeman. "Introduction: The Food Movement as Polyculture." In *Cultivating Food Justice: Race, Class, and Sustainability,* edited by Alison Hope Alkon and Julian Agyeman, 1–20. Cambridge, MA: The MIT Press, 2011.

Alkon, Alison Hope, et al. "Foodways of the Urban Poor." *Geoforum* 48 (2013) 126–35.

Allan, Mohammed, et al. "Reconstruction of Atmospheric Lead Pollution During the Roman Period Recorded in Belgian Ombrotrophic Peatlands Cores." *Atmosphere* 9 (2018) nd.

Andersen, Francis I., and David Noel Freedman. *Amos.* AB 24A. New York: Doubleday, 1989.

Armstrong, Gail E. "Sacrificial Iconography: Creating History, Making Myth, and Negotiating Ideology on the Ara Pacis Augustae." *Religion and Theology* 15 (2008) 340–56.

Arsenault, Chris. "Only 60 Years of Farming Left If Soil Degradation Continues." *Scientific American* (2014). https://www.scientificamerican.com/article/only-60-years-of-farming-left-if-soil-degradation-continues/.

Augustus. *Velleius Paterculus and Res Gestae Divi Augusti.* Translated by Frederick W. Shipley. LCL 152. Edited by G. P. Goold. Cambridge, MA: Harvard University Press, 1924.

Ayres, Jennifer R. *Good Food: Grounded Practical Theology.* Waco, TX: Baylor University Press, 2013.

———. *Inhabitance: Ecological Religious Education.* Waco, TX: Baylor University Press, 2019.

Bahnson, Fred, and Norman Wirzba. *Making Peace with the Land: God's Call to Reconcile with Creation.* Downers Grove, IL: InterVarsity, 2012.

Bai, Shahla Hosseini, and Steven M. Ogbourne. "Glyphosate: Environmental Contamination, Toxicity and Potential Risks to Human Health Via Food Contamination." *Environmental Science and Pollution Research* 23 (2016) 18988–19001.

Bibliography

Balz, Horst and Gerhard Schneider, eds. *EDNT*. Grand Rapids: Eerdmans, 1993.
Barclay, John M. G. "Faith and Self-Detachment from Cultural Norms: A Study in Romans 14–15." *Zeitschrift für die neutestamentliche Wissenschaft* 104 (2013) 192–208.
———. "Food, Christian Identity and Global Warming: A Pauline Call for a Christian Food Taboo." *The Expository Times* 121 (2010) 585–93.
———. *Paul and the Gift*. Grand Rapids: Eerdmans, 2015.
———. "Why the Roman Empire Was Insignificant to Paul." In *Pauline Churches and Diaspora Jews*, by John M. G. Barclay, 363–87. Grand Rapids: Eerdmans, 2016.
Battaglin, W., et al. "Glyphosate and Its Degradation Product AMPA Occur Frequently and Widely in US Soils, Surface Water, Groundwater, and Precipitation." *Journal of the American Water Resources Association* 50 (2014) 275–90.
Bauckham, Richard. *The Bible and Ecology: Rediscovering the Community of Creation*. Waco, TX: Baylor University Press, 2010.
Bean, L. H., and P. H. Bollinger. "The Base Period for Parity Prices." *Journal of Farm Economics* 21 (1939) 253–57.
Beard, Mary, John North, and Simon Price. *Religions of Rome: A History*. Vol. 1. Cambridge: Cambridge University Press, 1998.
Beker, J. Christiaan. "Vision of Hope for a Suffering World: Romans 8:17–30." *Princeton Seminary Bulletin* 3 (1994) 26–32.
Benbrook, Charles M. "Trends in Glyphosate Herbicide Use in the United States and Globally." *Environmental Sciences Europe* 28 (2016) 1–15.
Bentley, Amy, and Hiʻilei Hobart. "Food in Recent U.S. History." In *Food in Time and Place: The American Historical Association Companion to Food History*, edited by Paul Freedman, Joyce E. Chaplin and Ken Albala, 165–87. Oakland, CA: University of California Press, 2014.
Bird, John. "Will Your Grandchildren Go Hungry?" *The Saturday Evening Post* 227 (1954) 30, 103.
BirdLife International. "State of the World's Birds: Taking the Pulse of the Planet (2018)." https://www.birdlife.org/papers-reports/state-of-the-worlds-birds/#:~:text=The%20 2018%20State%20of%20the,now%20at%20risk%20of%20extinction.
Blass, Friedrich, and Albert Debrunner. *A Greek Grammar of the New Testament and Other Early Christian Literature*. Translated by Robert W. Funk. Chicago: University of Chicago Press, 1961.
Blatt, Harvey. *America's Environmental Report Card: Are We Making the Grade?* 2nd ed. Cambridge, MA: MIT Press, 2011.
Blenkinsopp, Joseph. *Isaiah 1–39*. AB 19. New York: Doubleday, 2000.
Block, Peter. *Community: The Structure of Belonging*. Oakland, CA: Berrett-Koehler, 2018.
Botterweck, G. Johannes, and Helmer Ringgren, eds. *TDOT*. Translated by John T. Willis. Grand Rapids: Eerdmans, 1975.
Braaten, Laurie J. "All Creation Groans: Romans 8:22 in Light of the Biblical Sources." *Horizons in Biblical Theology* 28 (2006) 131–59.
Brenton, Sir Lancelot. *The Septuagint Version with Apocrypha: Greek and English*. 1851.
Brookes, Graham, and Peter Barfoot. "Environmental Impacts of Genetically Modified (GM) Crop Use 1996–2013: Impacts on Pesticide Use and Carbon Emissions." *GM Crops and Food* 6 (2015) 103–33.
Brown, Francis, S. R. Driver, and Charles A. Briggs. BDB. Peabody, MA: Hendrickson, 1996.
Brown, Lester R. *Full Planet, Empty Plates: The New Geopolitics of Food Scarcity*. New York: W. W. Norton, 2012.

Bibliography

Brueggemann, Walter. *Isaiah 1–39*. Louisville: Westminster John Knox, 1998.
Burer, Michael H., et al. *New Testament: New English Translation, Novum Testamentum Graece*. Dallas: Deutsche Bibelgesellschaft, 2004.
Burroughs, Bradley B. *Christianity, Politics, and the Predicament of Evil: A Constructive Theological Ethic of Soulcraft and Statecraft*. Lanham, MD: Lexington, 2019.
Burroughs, Presian R. "Christlike Feasting: Attentiveness, Solidarity, and Self-Restraint in Romans." In *Practicing with Paul: Reflections on Paul and the Practices of Ministry in Honor of Susan G. Eastman*, edited by Presian R. Burroughs, 157–79. Eugene, OR: Cascade, 2018.
Burroughs, Presian Renee. "In the Image of God and Earth." Unpublished.
———. "Liberation in the Midst of Futility and Destruction: Romans 8:19–22 and the Christian Vocation of Nourishing Life." ThD diss., Duke University, 2014.
———. "Romans." In *Wesley One Volume Commentary*, edited by Kenneth J. Collins and Robert W. Wall, 709–35. Nashville: Abingdon, 2020.
———. "A Wesleyan Ecological Hermeneutic: Interpreting Scripture, Science, and Society Ecologically." *Wesleyan Theological Journal* 56 (2020) 37–56.
Campbell, Douglas A. "Natural Theology in Paul? Reading Romans 1.19–20." *International Journal of Systematic Theology* 1 (1999) 231–52.
———. *The Quest for Paul's Gospel: A Suggested Strategy*. London: T. & T. Clark, 2005.
Campbell, Douglas Atchison. *The Deliverance of God: An Apocalyptic Rereading of Justification in Paul*. Grand Rapids: Eerdmans, 2009.
Cancik, Hubert, and Helmuth Schneider, eds. *Cura Annonae*. Brill's New Pauly: Brill Online, 2012.
Carson, Rachel. *Silent Spring*. Boston: Houghton Mifflin, 1962.
Cassault-Meyer, Estelle, et al. "An Acute Exposure to Glyphosate-Based Herbicide Alters Aromatase Levels in Testis and Sperm Nuclear Quality." *Environmental Toxicology and Pharmacology* 38 (2014) 131–40.
Casson, Lionel. "The Role of the State in Rome's Grain Trade." *Memoirs of the American Academy in Rome* 36 (1980) 21–33.
Castriota, David. *The Ara Pacis Augustae and the Imagery of Abundance in Later Greek and Early Roman Imperial Art*. Princeton: Princeton University Press, 1995.
Cattani, Daiane, et al. "Mechanisms Underlying the Neurotoxicity Induced by Glyphosate-Based Herbicide in Immature Rat Hippocampus: Involvement of Glutamate Excitotoxicity." *Toxicology* 320 (2014) 34–45.
Cattani, Daiane, et al. "Developmental Exposure to Glyphosate-Based Herbicide and Depressive-Like Behavior in Adult Offspring: Implication of Glutamate Excitotoxicity and Oxidative Stress." *Toxicology* 387 (2017) 67–80.
CDC. "Foodnet 2018 Preliminary Data." In *Foodborne Diseases Active Surveillance Network (FoodNet)*, 2019. https://www.cdc.gov/foodnet/reports/prelim-data-intro-2018.html.
———. "Outbreak of *E. Coli* Infections Linked to Flour." 2019. https://www.cdc.gov/ecoli/2019/flour-05-19/index.html#:~:text=WGS%20results%20showed%20that%20the,got%20sick%20from%20eating%20flour.
———. "Outbreak of *E. Coli* Infections Linked to Ground Beef." 2019. https://www.cdc.gov/ecoli/2019/0103-04-19/index.html#:~:text=Restaurants%2C%20retailers%2C%20and%20institutions%20should,products%20on%20April%2024%2C%202019.
CERA. "GM Crop Database: Mon802 (Mon-80200-7)." http://www.cera-gmc.org/GMCropDatabaseEvent/MON802.

Bibliography

———. "Welcome to CERA." http://www.cera-gmc.org/.
Childs, Brevard. *Isaiah*. Louisville: Westminster John Knox, 2001.
Christoffersson, Olle. *The Earnest Expectation of the Creature: The Flood-Tradition as Matrix of Romans 8:18–27*. Stockholm, Sweden: Almquist & Wiksell International, 1990.
"Chronic Exposure." In *EPA: Integrated Risk Information System (IRIS) Glossary*. https://sor.epa.gov/sor_internet/registry/termreg/searchandretrieve/glossariesandkeywordlists/search.do?details=&vocabName=IRIS%20Glossary.
Collins, John J. *The Apocalyptic Imagination: An Introduction to the Jewish Matrix of Christianity*. New York: Crossroad, 1984.
Combs, Eugene. "Has God Cursed the Ground? Perplexity of Interpretation in Genesis 1–5." In *Ascribe to the Lord: Biblical and Other Studies in Memory of Peter C. Craigie*, edited by Lyle Eslinger and Glen Taylor, 265–87. Sheffield: Sheffield Academic, 1988.
Conradie, Ernst. "The Road Towards an Ecological Biblical and Theological Hermeneutics." *Scriptura* 93 (2006) 305–14.
Cranfield, C. E. B. *A Critical and Exegetical Commentary on the Epistle to the Romans*. ICC. Edinburgh: T. & T. Clark, 1975.
Culman, Steve. Email correspondence. June 21, 2017.
Danker, Frederick W., et al., eds. BDAG. 3rd ed. Chicago: University of Chicago Press, 2000.
Davis, Ellen F. *Biblical Prophecy: Perspectives for Christian Theology, Discipleship, and Ministry*. Louisville: Westminster John Knox, 2014.
———. *Getting Involved with God: Rediscovering the Old Testament*. Cambridge, MA: Cowley, 2001.
———. *Scripture, Culture, and Agriculture: An Agrarian Reading of the Bible*. New York: Cambridge University Press, 2009.
Defarge, Nicolas, et al. "Co-Formulants in Glyphosate-Based Herbicides Disrupt Aromatase Activity in Human Cells Below Toxic Levels." *International Journal of Environmental Research and Public Health* 13 (2016) 1–17.
DeHaan, Lee. Email correspondence. April 4–8, 2014.
Delile, Hugo, et al. "Demise of a Harbor: A Geochemical Chronicle from Ephesus." *Journal of Archaeological Science* 53 (2015) 202–13.
Domonoske, Camila. "Monsanto No More: Agri-Chemical Giant's Name Dropped in Bayer Acquisition." *NPR*, June 4, 2018. https://www.npr.org/sections/thetwo-way/2018/06/04/616772911/monsanto-no-more-agri-chemical-giants-name-dropped-in-bayer-acquisition.
Drewnowski, Adam, et al. "Why Whole Grains Should Be Incorporated into Nutrient-Profile Models to Better Capture Nutrient Density." *Advances in Nutrition* 12 (2021) 600–608.
Dunn, James D. G. *Romans: 1–8*. WBC. Dallas: Word, 1988.
Dunstan, William E. *Ancient Rome*. New York: Rowman & Littlefield, 2011.
Eastman, Susan. *Recovering Paul's Mother Tongue: Language and Theology in Galatians*. Grand Rapids: Eerdmans, 2007.
———. "Whose Apocalypse? The Identity of the Sons of God in Romans 8:19." *JBL* 121 (2002) 263–77.
Eastman, Susan Grove. *Paul and the Person: Reframing Paul's Anthropology*. Grand Rapids: Eerdmans, 2017.
Eberhart, Timothy Reinhold. *Rooted and Grounded in Love: Holy Communion for the Whole Creation*. Distinguished Dissertations in Christian Theology. Edited by Alan G. Padgett and Joy J. Moore. Eugene, OR: Pickwick, 2017.

Bibliography

Eighmey, Rae Katherine. "'Food Will Win the War': Minnesota Conservation Efforts, 1917–18." *Minnesota History* 59 (2005) 272–86.

Electronic Code of Federal Regulations. "Crop Group Tables." Office of the Federal Register.

———. "Glyphosate; Tolerances for Residues." Office of the Federal Register, 2021.

Elliger, Kar, William Rudolph, and Adrian Schenker. *Biblia Hebraica Stuttgartensia*. Fourth Edition. Stuttgart: Deutsche Bibelgesellschaft, 1966, 1977, 1983.

Elliott, Neil. *The Arrogance of Nations: Reading Romans in the Shadow of Empire*. Minneapolis: Fortress, 2008.

———. "Paul and the Politics of Empire: Problems and Prospects." In *Paul and Politics: Ekklesia, Israel, Imperium, Interpretation*, edited by Richard A. Horsley, 17–39. Harrisburg, PA: Trinity Press International, 2000.

Elliott, Neil, and Mark Reasoner, eds. *Documents and Images for the Study of Paul*. Minneapolis: Fortress, 2011.

Erdkamp, Paul. *The Grain Market in the Roman Empire: A Social, Political and Economic Study*. Cambridge: Cambridge University Press, 2005.

Eriguchi, Makoto, et al. "Parkinsonism Relating to Intoxication with Glyphosate: A Case Report." *Internal Medicine* 58 (2019) 1–4.

Fang, Lee. "Emails Show Monsanto Orchestrated GOP Effort to Intimidate Cancer Researchers." *The Intercept*, 2019. https://theintercept.com/2019/08/23/monsanto-republicans-cancer-research/

FAO, IFAD, UNICEF, WFP and WHO. "The State of Food Security and Nutrition in the World 2019. Safeguarding against Economic Slowdowns and Downturns." Rome: FAO, 2019.

Faust, Dominik, et al. "High-Resolution Fluvial Record of Late Holocene Geomorphic Change in Northern Tunisia: Climatic or Human Impact?" *Quarternary Science Reviews* 23 (2004) 1757–75.

Fitzmyer, Joseph A. *Romans: A New Translation with Introduction and Commentary*. AB 33. New York: Doubleday, 1993.

Follett, Ronald F., et al. "Great Plains Climate and Land-Use Effects on Soil Organic Carbon." *Soil Science Society of America Journal* 79 (2015) 261–71.

"Forever Green." University of Minnesota. https://www.forevergreen.umn.edu/.

Forster, Piers M., et al. "Current and Future Global Climate Impacts Resulting from COVID-19." *Nature Climate Change* 10 (2020) 913–19.

Fredriksen, Paula. *Paul: The Pagans' Apostle*. New Haven, CT: Yale University Press, 2017.

Fremstad, Shawn, Hye Jin Rho, and Hayley Brown. "Meatpacking Workers are a Diverse Group Who Need Better Protections." Center for Economic and Policy Research. April 29, 2020. https://cepr.net/meatpacking-workers-are-a-diverse-group-who-need-better-protections/.

Fretheim, Terence E. *Genesis*. Edited by Leander E. Keck. NIB 1. Nashville: Abingdon, 1994.

———. *God and World in the Old Testament: A Relational Theology of Creation*. Nashville: Abingdon, 2005.

Frey, Kenneth J. "Presidential Address: The Unifying Force in Agronomy–Biotechnology." *Agronomy Journal* 77 (1985) 187–89.

Friedman, Richard Elliott. *Commentary on the Torah: With a New English Translation and the Hebrew Text*. San Francisco: HarperSanFrancisco, 2003.

Bibliography

Friesen, Courtney. "Birthing the Children of God: Echoes of Theogony in Romans 8:19–23." *NTS* 63 (2017) 246–60.

Galen, Coen van. "Grain Distribution and Gender in the City of Rome." In *Women and the Roman City in the Latin West*, edited by Emily Hemelrijk and Greg Woolf, 331–47. Leiden: Brill, 2013.

Galinsky, Karl. *Augustan Culture: An Interpretive Introduction*. Princeton: Princeton University Press, 1996.

Garnsey, Peter, and Dominic Rathbone. "The Background to the Grain Law of Gaius Gracchus." *The Journal of Roman Studies* 75 (1985) 20–25.

Garr, W. Randall. *In His Own Image and Likeness: Humanity, Divinity, and Monotheism*. Culture and History of the Ancient near East. Leiden: Brill, 2003.

Gaskin, Ina May. *Spiritual Midwifery*. 4th ed. Summertown, TN: Book Publishing Company, 2002.

Gasnier, Céline, et al. "Glyphosate Based Herbicides Are Toxic and Endocrine Disruptors in Human Cell Lines." *Toxicology* 262 (2009) 184–91.

Gaventa, Beverly Roberts. "The Birthing of Creation." In *Our Mother Saint Paul*, 51–62. Louisville: Westminster John Knox, 2007.

———. "The Cosmic Power of Sin in Paul's Letter to the Romans: Toward a Widescreen Edition." *Interpretation* (July 2004) 229–40.

Gélinas, Pierre, Fleur Gagnon, and Carole McKinnon. "Wheat Preharvest Herbicide Application, Whole-Grain Flour Properties, Yeast Activity and the Degradation of Glyphosate in Bread." *International Journal of Food Science and Technology* 53 (2018) 1597–602.

George, Jasmine, et al. "Studies on Glyphosate-Induced Carcinogenicity in Mouse Skin: A Proteomic Approach." *Journal of Proteomics* 73 (2010) 951–64.

"Germany Acts to Protect Insects." *Science* 365 (2019) 1062–63.

Gill, Jatinder Pal Kaur, et al. "Glyphosate Toxicity for Animals." *Environmental Chemistry Letters* 16 (2018) 401–26.

"Global Insect Resistance Management." https://monsanto.com/products/product-stewardship/insect-resistance-management/.

"Global Report on Food Crises: Joint Analysis for Better Decisions." Food Security Information Network, 2019. https://www.ifpri.org/publication/2019-global-report-food-crises-joint-analysis-better-decisions.

"Glyphosate." United States EPA. https://www.epa.gov/ingredients-used-pesticide-products/glyphosate.

González-Curbelo, Miguel Ángel, et al. "Dissipation Kinetics of Organophosphorous Pesticides in Milled Toasted Maize and Wheat Flour (Gofio) During Storage." *Food Chemistry* 229 (2017) 854–59.

Green, Clara, ed. *U.S. Household Food Security: Statistics and Analysis for 2014*. New York: Nova, 2016.

Habel, Norman C. "Geophany: The Earth Story in Genesis 1." In *The Earth Story in Genesis*, edited by Norman C. Habel and Shirley Wurst, 34–48. Sheffield: Sheffield Academic, 2000.

———. "Reading as an Earth Being: Rereading Genesis 2–3—Again." In *Interested Readers: Essays on the Hebrew Bible in Honor of David J. A. Clines*, edited by James K. Aitken et al., 95–104. Atlanta: Society of Biblical Literature, 2013.

Hahne, Harry Alan. *The Corruption and Redemption of Creation: Nature in Romans 8.19–22 and Jewish Apocalyptic Literature*. New York: T. & T. Clark, 2006.

Bibliography

Hardin, Garret. "Human Ecology The Subversive, Conservative Science." *Human Ecology Review* 23 (2017) 101–12.
Harink, Douglas. "Messianic Anarchy: The Liberating Word of Romans 13:1–7." In *Practicing with Paul: Reflections on Paul and the Practices of Ministry in Honor of Susan G. Eastman*, edited by Presian R. Burroughs, 197–210. Eugene, OR: Cascade, 2018.
Harper, Kyle. *The Fate of Rome: Climate, Disease, and the End of an Empire.* Princeton: Princeton University Press, 2017.
Harris, W. V. "Defining and Detecting Mediterranean Deforestation, 800 BCE to 700 CE." In *The Ancient Mediterranean Environment Between Science and History*, edited by W. V. Harris, 173–94. Leiden: Brill, 2013.
Harrison, James R. *Paul and the Imperial Authorities at Thessalonica and Rome: A Study in the Conflict of Ideology.* Tübingen: Mohr Siebeck, 2011.
Hartman, Melannie D., et al. "Impact of Historical Land-Use Changes on Greenhouse Gas Exchange in the U.S. Great Plains, 1883–2003." *Ecological Applications* 21 (2011) 1105–19.
Hays, Richard B. *Echoes of Scripture in the Letters of Paul.* New Haven, CT: Yale University Press, 1989.
———. *The Faith of Jesus Christ: The Narrative Substructure of Galatians 3:1—4:11.* Grand Rapids: Eerdmans, 2002.
———. "Mapping the Field: Approaches to New Testament Ethics." In *Identity, Ethics and Ethos in the New Testament*, edited by Jan G. Van der Watt, 3–22. Berlin: Walter de Gruyter, 2006.
Hong, Sungmin, et al. "Greenland Ice Evidence of Hemispheric Lead Pollution Two Millennia Ago by Greek and Roman Civilizations." *Science* 265 (1994) 1841–43.
Horace. *The Odes.* Translated by J. D. McClatchy. Princeton: Princeton University Press, 2002.
Horden, Peregrine, and Nicholas Purcell. *The Corrupting Sea: A Study of Mediterranean History.* Oxford: Blackwell, 2000.
Horrell, David G., Cherryl Hunt, and Christopher Southgate. *Greening Paul: Rereading the Apostle in a Time of Ecological Crisis.* Waco, TX: Baylor University Press, 2010.
Howard, George. "Faith of Christ." In *ABD*, edited by David Noel Freedman, 758–60. New York: Doubleday, 1992.
Hughes, J. Donald. *Environmental Problems of the Greeks and Romans: Ecology in the Ancient Mediterranean.* 2nd ed. Baltimore: Johns Hopkins University Press, 2014.
Hurt, R. Douglas. *American Agriculture: A Brief History.* West Lafayette, IN: Purdue University Press, 2002.
———. *The Indian Frontier: 1763–1846.* Albuquerque: University of New Mexico Press, 2002.
"The Impact of the Coronavirus on Local Food Insecurity in 2020 & 2021." https://www.feedingamerica.org/research/coronavirus-hunger-research.
Isaac, E., trans. *1 Enoch.* The Old Testament Pseudepigrapha: Apocalyptic Literature and Testaments. Vol. 1. Edited by James H. Charlesworth. Garden City: Doubleday, 1983.
Jackson, T. Ryan. *New Creation in Paul's Letters: A Study of the Historical and Social Setting of a Pauline Concept.* Tübingen: Mohr Siebeck, 2010.
Jackson, Wes. *Consulting the Genius of the Place: An Ecological Approach to a New Agriculture.* Berkeley: Counterpoint, 2010.

Bibliography

———. "Farming in Nature's Image: Natural Systems Agriculture." In *The Fatal Harvest Reader: The Tragedy of Industrial Agriculture*, edited by Andrew Kimbrell, 65–76. Washington: Island, 2002.

———. Phone conversation with Wes Jackson, November 30, 2020.

Jackson, Wes, Wendell Berry, and Bruce Colman, eds. *Meeting the Expectations of the Land: Essays in Sustainable Agriculture and Stewardship*. San Francisco: North Point, 1984.

Janssens, Lizanne, and Robby Stoks. "Stronger Effects of Roundup Than Its Active Ingredient Glyphosate in Damselfly Larvae." *Aquatic Toxicology* 193 (2017) 210–16.

Jewett, Robert. "The Corruption and Redemption of Creation: Reading Rom 8:18–23 within the Imperial Context." In *Paul and the Roman Imperial Order*, edited by Richard A. Horsley, 25–46. New York: Trinity Press International, 2004.

———. *Romans: A Commentary*. Hermeneia. Edited by Eldon Jay Epp. Minneapolis: Fortress, 2007.

Jia, Gensuo, and Elena Shevliakova. "Chapter 2: Land-Climate Interactions." In *Climate Change and Land: An IPCC Special Report on Climate Change, Desertification, Land Degradation, Sustainable Land Management, Food Security, and Greenhouse Gas Fluxes in Terrestrial Ecosystems*, edited by Pierre Bernier et al. 2019. https://www.ipcc.ch/srccl/chapter/chapter-2/.

Jurkovich, Michelle. *Feeding the Hungry: Advocacy and Blame in the Global Fight against Hunger*. Ithaca, NY: Cornell University Press, 2020.

Kachuri, Linda, et al. "Cancer Risks in a Population-Based Study of 70,570 Agricultural Workers: Results from the Canadian Census Health and Environment Cohort (Canchec)." *BMC Cancer* 17 (2017). https://bmccancer.biomedcentral.com/articles/10.1186/s12885-017-3346-x.

Kaufman, David B. "Horrea Romana: Roman Storehouses." *The Classical Weekly* 23 (1929) 49–54.

Kaufman, Frederick. *Bet the Farm: How Food Stopped Being Food*. Hoboken, NJ: John Wiley & Sons, Inc., 2012.

Keck, Leander E. *Romans*. ANTC. Nashville: Abingdon, 2005.

Keesmaat, Sylvia C. "Land, Idolatry, and Justice in Romans." In *Conception, Reception, and the Spirit: Essays in Honor of Andrew T. Lincoln*, edited by J. Gordon McConville and Lloyd K. Pietersen, 90–103. Eugene, OR: Wipf & Stock, 2015.

———. *Paul and his Story: (Re)Interpreting the Exodus Tradition*. JSNTSup 181. London: Bloomsbury, 1999.

Kehoe, Dennis P. *The Economics of Agriculture on Roman Imperial Estates in North Africa*. Göttingen: Vandenhoeck & Ruprecht, 1988.

The Kernza® Network. "Kernza® Grain: From a Wild Perennial Grass to Store Shelves." https://kernza.org/the-kernza-network/?_sft_partner_type=grower.

Kimbrell, Andrew, ed. *Fatal Harvest: The Tragedy of Industrial Agriculture*. Washington: Foundation for Deep Ecology, 2002.

Kimmerer, Robin Wall. *Braiding Sweetgrass: Indigenous Wisdom, Scientific Knowledge, and the Teachings of Plants*. Minneapolis: Milkweed, 2013.

Kittel, Gerhard, and Geoffrey W. Bromiley, eds. *TDNT*. Translated by Geoffrey W. Bromiley. Grand Rapids: Eerdmans, 1964.

Klawans, Jonathan. *Impurity and Sin in Ancient Judaism*. Oxford: Oxford University Press, 2000.

Bibliography

Kleiner, Diana E. E. "Semblance and Storytelling in Augustan Rome." In *The Cambridge Companion to the Age of Augustus*, edited by Karl Galinsky, 197–233. Cambridge: Cambridge University Press, 2005.

Kloppenburg, Jack Ralph, Jr. *First the Seed: The Political Economy of Plant Biotechnology, 1492–2000*. 2nd ed. Madison, WI: The University of Wisconsin Press, 2004.

Knipping, Maria, Marc Müllenhoff, and Helmut Brückner. "Human Induced Landscape Changes around Bafa Gölü (Western Turkey)." *Vegetation History and Archaeobotany* 17 (2008) 365–80.

Kolbert, Elizabeth. *The Sixth Extinction: An Unnatural History*. New York: Henry Holt, 2014.

Kreitzer, Larry J. *Striking New Images: Roman Imperial Coinage and the New Testament World*. Edited by Stanley E. Porter. JSNTSup 134. Sheffield: Sheffield Academic Press, 1996.

Krimsky, Sheldon, and Carey Gillam. "Roundup Litigation Discovery Documents: Implications for Public Health and Journal Ethics." *Journal of Public Health Policy* 39 (2018) 318–26.

Kroese, Ron. "Industrial Agriculture's War against Nature." In *The Fatal Harvest Reader: The Tragedy of Industrial Agriculture*, edited by Andrew Kimbrell, 92–105. Washington: Island, 2002.

Krüger, Monika, et al. "Detection of Glyphosate in Malformed Pigs." *Environmental and Analytical Toxicology* 4 (2014) 1–2.

Laird, Margaret L. "The Emperor in a Roman Town: The Base of the *Augustales* in the Forum at Corinth." In *Corinth in Context: Comparative Studies on Religion and Society*, edited by Steven J. Friesen et al., 64–114. Leiden: Brill, 2010.

Lamb, Michael, Jonathan Brant, and Edward Brooks. "How is Virtue Cultivated?: Seven Strategies for Postgraduate Character Development." *Journal of Character Education* 17 (2021) 81–108.

Lampe, Peter. *From Paul to Valentinus: Christians at Rome in the First Two Centuries*. Translated by Michael Steinhauser. Edited by Marshall D. Johnson. Minneapolis: Fortress, 2003.

The Land Institute. "Kernza® Grain." https://landinstitute.org/our-work/perennial-crops/kernza/.

———. "Perennial Legumes." https://landinstitute.org/our-work/perennial-crops/legumes/.

———. "Perennial Oilseeds." https://landinstitute.org/our-work/perennial-crops/perennial-oilseeds.

———. "Perennial Rice." https://landinstitute.org/our-work/perennial-crops/perennial-rice/.

———. "Perennial Sorghum." https://landinstitute.org/our-work/perennial-crops/perennial-sorghum.

Legarreta-Castillo, Felipe de Jesús. *The Figure of Adam in Romans 5 and 1 Corinthians 15: The New Creation and Its Ethical and Social Reconfiguration*. Minneapolis: Fortress, 2014.

Lenski, Gerhard. *Power and Privilege: A Theory of Social Stratification*. Chapel Hill: The University of North Carolina Press, 1984.

Leopold, Aldo. *A Sand County Almanac And Sketches Here and There*. New York: Oxford University Press, 1949, 2020.

"Liberation." *Merriam-Webster Dictionary*. https://www.merriam-webster.com/dictionary/liberation.

Bibliography

Liddell, Henry George, and Robert Scott. LSJ. Oxford: Clarendon, 1889.

Lindbeck, George A. *The Nature of Doctrine: Religion and Theology in a Postliberal Age*. Philadelphia: Westminster, 1984.

Lopez, Davina C. "Roman Imperial Culture." In *The Oxford Handbook of New Testament, Gender, and Sexuality*, edited by Benjamin H. Dunning, 257–76. Oxford: Oxford University Press, 2019.

"Mapping Past Societies: Formerly, the Digital Atlas of Roman and Medieval Civilizations." https://darmc.harvard.edu/.

Mart, Michelle. *Pesticides, a Love Story*. Lawrence: University Press of Kansas, 2015.

Martínez, María-Aránzazu, et al. "Neurotransmitter Changes in Rat Brain Regions Following Glyphosate Exposure." *Environmental Research* 161 (2018) 212–19.

Martyn, J. Louis. *Galatians: A New Translation with Introduction and Commentary*. AB 33A. New York: Doubleday, 2004.

Mason, Matthew. "Ecology: Examining the Relationships between Living Things." https://www.environmentalscience.org/ecology.

Matera, Frank J. *Romans*. Paideia: Commentaries on the New Testament. Grand Rapids: Baker Academic, 2010.

Mbuwayesango, Dora Rudo. "'The Canaanites Were in the Land': The Book of Genesis as an Anti-Conquest Narrative." *Journal of Commonwealth and Postcolonial Studies* 15 (2008) 84–93.

McCormick, Michael, et al. "Climate Change During and after the Roman Empire: Reconstructing the Past from Scientific and Historical Evidence." *Journal of Interdisciplinary History* 43 (2012) 169–220.

McKenney, Jason. "Artificial Fertility: The Environmental Costs of Industrial Fertilizers." In *The Fatal Harvest Reader: The Tragedy of Industrial Agriculture*, edited by Andrew Kimbrell, 121–29. Washington, DC: Island, 2002.

McMinn, Lisa Graham. *To the Table: A Spirituality of Food, Farming, and Community*. Grand Rapids: Brazos, 2016.

Meisterling, Kyle, Constantine Samaras, and Vanessa Schweizer. "Decisions to Reduce Greenhouse Gases from Agriculture and Product Transport: LCA Case Study of Organic and Coventional Wheat." *Journal of Cleaner Production* 17 (2009) 222–30.

Melo, Mariane Izabella Abreu, et al. "Glyphosate-Based Herbicide Induces Toxic Effects on Human Adipose-Derived Mesenchymal Stem Cells Grown in Human Plasma." *Comparative Clinical Pathology* (2018) 1–12.

Mendelson, Joseph, III. "Untested, Unlabeled, and You're Eating It: The Health and Environmental Hazards of Genetically Engineered Foods." In *The Fatal Harvest Reader: The Tragedy of Industrial Agriculture*, edited by Andrew Kimbrell, 148–60. Washington, DC: Island, 2002.

Merchant, Carolyn. *The Columbia Guide to American Environmental History*. New York: Columbia University Press, 2002.

Mertens, Martha, et al. "Glyphosate, a Chelating Agent–Relevant for Ecological Risk Assessment?" *Environmental Science and Pollution Research* 25 (2018) 5298–317.

Metzger, B. M., trans. *4 Ezra*. The Old Testament Pseudepigrapha: Apocalyptic Literature and Testaments 1. Edited by James H. Charlesworth. Garden City: Doubleday, 1983.

Middleton, J. Richard. *The Liberating Image: The Imago Dei in Genesis 1*. Grand Rapids: Brazos, 2005

―――. *A New Heaven and a New Earth: Reclaiming Biblical Eschatology*. Grand Rapids: Baker Academic, 2014.

Bibliography

Milgrom, Jacob. *Leviticus: A Book of Ritual and Ethics.* Minneapolis: Fortress, 2004.

Miller, Debra A. *Farming and the Food Supply.* Edited by Michael Mann. Confronting Global Warming. Detroit: Greenhaven, 2011.

Miller, Emily M. *The Truth about Industrial Agriculture: A Fragile System Propped up by Myths and Hidden Costs (2021).* https://farmaction.us/wp-content/uploads/2021/07/Truth-Report.pdf.

Miller, Vincent Jude. *Consuming Religion: Christian Faith and Practice in a Consumer Culture.* New York: Continuum, 2004.

Montgomery, David R. *Dirt: The Erosion of Civilizations.* Berkeley: University of California Press, 2008.

———. *Growing a Revolution: Bringing Our Soil Back to Life.* New York: W. W. Norton & Company, 2017.

Moo, Douglas J. *The Epistle to the Romans.* NICNT. Grand Rapids: Eerdmans, 1996.

Moo, Jonathan. "Romans 8.19–22 and Isaiah's Cosmic Covenant." *NTS* 54 (2008) 74–89.

Moore, Monica. "Hidden Dimensions of Damage: Pesticides and Health." In *The Fatal Harvest Reader: The Tragedy of Industrial Agriculture,* edited by Andrew Kimbrell, 130–37. Washington, DC: Island, 2002.

Murray, Robert. *Cosmic Covenant: Biblical Themes of Justice, Peace, and the Integrity of Creation.* Piscataway, NJ: Tigris, 2007.

Myers, Ched, ed. *Watershed Discipleship: Reinhabiting Bioregional Faith and Practice.* Eugene, OR: Cascade, 2016.

Myers, John Peterson, et al. "Concerns over Use of Glyphosate-Based Herbicides and Risks Associated with Exposures: A Consensus Statement." *Environmental Health* 15 (2016) 1–13.

Myers, Justin Sean, and Christine C. Caruso. "Towards a Public Food Infrastructure: Closing the Food Gaps through State-Run Grocery Stores." *Geoforum* 72 (2016) 30–33.

Myers, Justin Sean, and Joshua Sbicca. "Bridging Good Food and Good Jobs: From Secession to Confrontation within Alternative Food Movement Politics." *Geoforum* 61 (2015) 17–26.

National Amphibian Research and Monitoring Initiative. "Stressors." https://armi.usgs.gov/topic.php?topic=Stressors.

NESTA. "Fertilizing the Earth with Nitrogen." http://www.windows2universe.org/earth/climate/nitrogen_fertilizer.html.

Newman, Molli M., et al. "Changes in Rhizosphere Bacterial Gene Expression Following Glyphosate Treatment." *Science of the Total Environment* 553 (2016) 32–41.

NOAA. "'Dead Zone' Is a More Common Term for Hypoxia." http://oceanservice.noaa.gov/facts/deadzone.html.

———. "Global Climate Report–July 2019." https://www.ncdc.noaa.gov/sotc/global/201907.

———. "Global Climate Report–July 2021." https://www.ncdc.noaa.gov/sotc/global/202107.

———. "Smaller-Than-Expected Gulf of Mexico 'Dead Zone' Measured: Hurricane Hanna Mixed Water Column, Reducing Size." https://www.noaa.gov/media-release/smaller-than-expected-gulf-of-mexico-dead-zone-measured.

———. "State of the Climate: Global Climate Report for July 2020." https://www.ncdc.noaa.gov/sotc/global/202007/supplemental/page-1.

Bibliography

Oakes, Peter. "Remapping the Universe: Paul and the Emperor in 1 Thessalonians and Philippians." In *Empire, Economics, and the New Testament*, by Peter Oakes, 121–37. Grand Rapids: Eerdmans, 2020.

O'Brien, Kevin J. *An Ethics of Biodiversity: Christianity, Ecology, and the Variety of Life*. Washington, DC: Georgetown University Press, 2010.

O'Donnell, Brendan, et al. "The Relative Contribution of Transportation to Supply Chain Greenhouse Gas Emissions: A Case Study of American Wheat." *Transportation Research Part D* 14 (2009) 487–92.

Oliveira, A. G., et al. "Effects of the Herbicide Roundup on the Epididymal Region of Drakes *Anas Platyrhynchos*." *Reproductive Toxicology* 23 (2007) 182–91.

O'Reilly, Matt. *Paul and the Resurrected Body: Social Identity and Ethical Practice*. Edited by Vernon K. Robbins and David B. Gowler. Emory Studies in Early Christianity 22. Atlanta: Society of Biblical Literature, 2020.

Oswalt, John N. *The Book of Isaiah: Chapters 40–66*. Edited by Robert L. Hubbard Jr. NICOT. Grand Rapids: Eerdmans, 1998.

Ovid. *Metamorphoses, Volume I: Books 1–8*. Translated by Frank Justus Miller. LCL 42. Cambridge, MA: Harvard University Press, 1921.

Penniman, Leah. *Farming While Black: Soul Fire Farm's Practical Guide to Liberation on the Land*. White River Junction, VT: Chelsea Green, 2018.

Perennial Pantry. https://perennial-pantry.com/collections/frontpage.

Perkins, Pheme. "Adam and Christ in the Pauline Epistles." In *Celebrating Paul: Festschrift in Honor of Jerome Murphy-O'Connor, O.P., and Joseph A. Fitzmyer*, edited by Peter Spitaler. Washington, DC: The Catholic Biblical Association of America, 2011.

Peters, Tessa. Email correspondence. March 17, 2022.

Pietersma, Albert, and Benjamin G. Wright, eds. *A New English Translation of the Septuagint*. Oxford: Oxford University Press, 2007.

Plato. "Critias." Translated by Robert Gregg Bury. In *Timaeus Critias; Cleitophon; Menexenus; Epistles*. LCL 234. Cambridge, MA: Harvard University Press, 2014.

Pleasants, J. M., and K. S. Oberhauser. "Milkweed Loss in Agricultural Fields Because of Herbicide Use: Effect on the Monarch Butterfly Population." *Insect Conservation and Diversity* 6 (2013) 135–44.

Pliny. *Natural History, Volume V: Books 17–19*. Translated by H. Rackham. LCL 371. Cambridge, MA: Harvard University Press, 1950.

Pollan, Michael. *The Omnivore's Dilemma: A Natural History of Four Meals*. New York: Penguin, 2007.

Rahlfs, Alfred, and Robert Hanhart. *Septuaginta*. Stuttgart: Deutsche Bibelgesellschaft, 2006.

Reaves, Elissa. "Interim Registration Review Decision: Case Number 0178." Edited by USEPA. January 2020. https://www.epa.gov/sites/default/files/2020-21/documents/glyphosate-interim-reg-review-decision-case-num-0178.pdf.

Rickman, G. E. "The Grain Trade under the Roman Empire." *Memoirs of the American Academy in Rome* 36 (1980) 261–75.

Rickman, Geoffrey. *The Corn Supply of Ancient Rome*. Oxford: Oxford University Press, 1980.

Rodale Institute. "Farming Systems Trial." https://rodaleinstitute.org/science/farming-systems-trial/.

The Roman Imperial Coinage. Vol. 1. London: Spink and Son, 1984.

Bibliography

Rossing, Barbara R. "Reimagining Eschatology: Toward Healing and Hope for a World at the Eschatos." In *Planetary Solidarity*, edited by Grace Ji-Sun Kim and Hilda P. Koster, 325-47. Minneapolis: Fortress, 2017.
Sánchez-Bayo, Francisco, and Kris A. G. Wyckhuys. "Worldwide Decline of the Entomofauna: A Review of Its Drivers." *Biological Conservation* 232 (2019) 8-27.
Sanders, E. P. *Paul and Palestinian Judaism: A Comparison of Patterns of Religion.* Minneapolis: Fortress, 1977.
Sanders, Kelly Twomey, and Michael E. Webber. "A Comparative Analysis of the Greenhouse Gas Emissions Intensity of Wheat and Beef in the United States." *Environmental Research Letters* 9 (2014) 1-9.
Sarna, Nahum M. *Genesis*. Jewish Publication Society Torah Commentary. Philadelphia: Jewish Publication Society, 1989.
Scott, James C. *Domination and the Arts of Resistance: Hidden Transcripts.* New Haven, CT: Yale University Press, 1990.
Scheid, Daniel P. *The Cosmic Common Good: Religious Grounds for Ecological Ethics.* Oxford: Oxford University Press, 2015.
Scherrer, Peter. "The City of Ephesos: From the Roman Period to Late Antiquity." In *Ephesos Metropolis of Asia: An Interdisciplinary Approach to Its Archaeology, Religion, and Culture*, edited by Helmut Koester, 1-26. Valley Forge, Pennsylvania: Trinity Press International, 1995.
Schmid, H. H. "Creation, Righteousness, and Salvation: 'Creation Theology' as the Broad Horizon of Biblical Theology." In *Creation in the Old Testament*, edited by Bernhard W. Anderson, 102-17. Philadelphia: Fortress, 1984.
Seralini, Gilles-Eric. "Update on Long-Term Toxicity of Agricultural GMOs Tolerant to Roundup." *Environmental Sciences Europe* 32 (2020) 1-7.
Shahar, Meir Ben. "Jewish Views of Gentiles." In *The Jewish Annotated New Testament*, edited by Amy-Jill Levine and Marc Zvi Brettler, 640-45. New York: Oxford University Press, 2011, 2017.
Shiva, Vandana. *Stolen Harvest: The Hijacking of the Global Food Supply.* Cambridge, MA: South End, 2000.
Siculus, Calpurnius. "Eclogue 1." Translated by J. Wight Duff and Arnold M. Duff. In *Minor Latin Poets: With Introductions and English Translations*. Cambridge, MA: Harvard University Press, 1961.
Simkin, Penny. *The Birth Partner*. Beverly, MA: The Harvard Commons, 2013.
Skinner, John. *A Critical and Exegetical Commentary on Genesis*. ICC. Edinburgh: T. & T. Clark, 1930.
Smil, Vaclav. *Enriching the Earth: Fritz Haber, Carl Bosch, and the Transformation of World Food Production.* Cambridge, MA: The MIT Press, 2001.
Smith, Robert Leo. "Ecology." In *Britannica*. https://www.britannica.com/science/ecology.
Steward, David R., et al. "Tapping Unsustainable Groundwater Stores for Agricultural Production in the High Plains Aquifer of Kansas, Projections to 2110." *Proceedings of the National Academy of Sciences of the United States of America* 110 (2013) 3477-86.
Stock, Friederike, et al. "Human Impact on Holocene Sediment Dynamics in the Eastern Mediterranean-the Example of the Roman Harbour of Ephesus." *Earth Surface Processes and Landforms* 41 (2016) 980-96.
Streett, R. Alan. *Subversive Meals: An Analysis of the Lord's Supper under Roman Domination during the First Century.* Cambridge: James Clarke & Co, 2013.
Stuart, Douglas. *Hosea—Jonah*. WBC. Waco, TX: Word, 1987.

Stulac, Daniel J. *History and Hope: The Agrarian Wisdom of Isaiah 28–35*. Siphrut: Literature and Theology of the Hebrew Scriptures, edited by Stephen B. Chapman, Tremper Longman III, and Nathan MacDonald. University Park, PA: Eisenbrauns, 2018.

"Subchronic Exposure." In *EPA: Integrated Risk Information System (IRIS) Glossary*. https://sor.epa.gov/sor_internet/registry/termreg/searchandretrieve/glossariesandkeywordlists/search.do?details=&vocabName=IRIS%20Glossary#formTop.

Sutherland, C. H. V. *Roman History and Coinage 44 BC–AD 69: Fifty Points of Relation from Julius Caesar to Vespasian*. Oxford: Clarendon, 1987.

Tang, Qian, et al. "Glyphosate Exposure Induces Inflammatory Responses in the Small Intestine and Alters Gut Microbial Composition in Rats." *Environmental Pollution* 261 (2020) 1–10.

Theokritoff, Elizabeth. *Living in God's Creation: Orthodox Perspectives on Ecology*. Crestwood, NY: St Vladimir's Seminary Press, 2009.

Tonstad, Sigve K. *The Letter to the Romans: Paul among the Ecologists*. Sheffield: Sheffield Phoenix, 2017.

Turcan, Robert. *The Gods of Ancient Rome: Religion in Everyday Life from Archaic to Imperial Times*. Translated by Antonia Nevill. New York: Routledge, 2000.

Turner, Benjamin L., et al. "Scientific Case Studies in Land-Use Driven Soil Erosion in the Central United States: Why Soil Potential and Risk Concepts Should Be Included in the Principles of Soil Health." *International Soil and Water Conservation Research* 6 (2018) 63–78.

The United Methodist Book of Worship. Nashville: United Methodist Pub. House, 1992.

USEPA. "R.E.D. Facts: Glyphosate." 1993. https://archive.epa.gov/pesticides/reregistration/web/pdf/0178fact.pdf.

USGS. "Pesticides in Groundwater." https://www.usgs.gov/special-topic/water-science-school/science/pesticides-groundwater?qt-science_center_objects=0—qt-science_center_objects.

Virgil. *The Aeneid*. Translated by Robert Fagles. New York: Viking, 2006.

———. *Eclogues*. Translated by Len Krisak. Philadelphia: University of Pennsylvania Press, 2010.

———. *Georgics: A Poem of the Land*. Translated by Kimberly Johnson. London: Penguin Classics, 2009.

von Rad, Gerhard. *Genesis: A Commentary*. OTL. Philadelphia: Westminster, 1972.

Wagner, J. Ross. "The Christ, Servant of Jew and Gentile: A Fresh Perspective to Romans 15:8–9." *JBL* 116 (1997) 473–85.

Wallace, Daniel B. *Greek Grammar Beyond the Basics*. Grand Rapids: Zondervan, 1996.

Wang, Gang, et al. "Parkinsonism after Chronic Occupational Exposure to Glyphosate." *Parkinsonism and Related Disorders* 17 (2010) 486–87.

Wang, Tom, et al. "Soil Conservation Practice Adoption in the Northern Great Plains: Economic Versus Stewardship Motivations." *Journal of Agricultural and Resource Economics* 44 (2019) 404–21.

Warshall, Peter. "Tilth and Technology: The Industrial Redesign of Our Nation's Soils." In *The Fatal Harvest Reader: The Tragedy of Industrial Agriculture*, edited by Andrew Kimbrell, 167–80. Washington, DC: Island, 2002.

Wenham, Gordon J. *Genesis 1–15, Volume 1*. WBC. Waco, TX: Word, 1987.

White Jr., Lynn. "The Historical Roots of Our Ecologic Crisis." *Science* 155 (1967) 1203–7.

Bibliography

White, Monica M. *Freedom Farmers: Agricultural Resistance and the Black Freedom Movement.* Chapel Hill: The University of North Carolina Press, 2018.

Williams, Gary M., et al. "A Review of the Carcinogenic Potential of Glyphosate by Four Independent Expert Panels and Comparison to the IARC Assessment." *Critical Reviews in Toxicology* 46 sup1 (2016) 3–20.

Williams, Gary M., Robert Kroes, and Ian C. Munro. "Safety Evaluation and Risk Assessment of the Herbicide Roundup and Its Active Ingredient, Glyphosate, for Humans." *Regulatory Toxicology and Pharmacology* 31 (2000) 117–65.

Wilson, Andrew. "The Mediterranean Environment in Ancient History: Perspectives and Prospects." In *The Ancient Mediterranean Environment between Science and History*, edited by W. V. Harris, 259–76. Leiden: Brill, 2013.

Wirzba, Norman. *Food and Faith: A Theology of Eating.* Cambridge: Cambridge University Press, 2011.

———. *From Nature to Creation: A Christian Vision for Understanding and Loving Our World.* Edited by James K. A. Smith. The Church and Postmodern Culture. Grand Rapids: Baker Academic, 2015.

———. *The Paradise of God: Renewing Religion in an Ecological Age.* Oxford: Oxford University Press, 2007.

World Wildlife Foundation. "Soil Erosion and Degradation." https://www.worldwildlife.org/threats/soil-erosion-and-degradation.

Zenk, Shannon N., et al. "Relative and Absolute Availability of Healthier Food and Beverage Alternatives across Communities in the United States." *American Journal of Public Health* 104 (2014) 2170–78.

Zhang, Luoping, et al. "Exposure to Glyphosate-Based Herbicides and Risk for Non-Hodgkin Lymphoma: A Meta-Analysis and Supporting Evidence." *Mutation Research* 781 (2019) 186–206.

Ziegler, Joseph. *Isaias.* Septuaginta: Vetus Testamentum Graecum 14. Göttingen: Vandenhoek & Ruprecht, 1939.

Bibliography

White, Monica M. *Freedom Farmers: Agricultural Resistance and the Black Freedom Movement.* Chapel Hill: The University of North Carolina Press, 2018.

Williams, Gary M., et al. "A Review of the Carcinogenic Potential of Glyphosate by Four Independent Expert Panels and Comparison to the IARC Assessment." *Critical Reviews in Toxicology* 46 sup1 (2016) 3–20.

Williams, Gary M., Robert Kroes, and Ian C. Munro. "Safety Evaluation and Risk Assessment of the Herbicide Roundup and Its Active Ingredient, Glyphosate, for Humans." *Regulatory Toxicology and Pharmacology* 31 (2000) 117–65.

Wilson, Andrew. "The Mediterranean Environment in Ancient History: Perspectives and Prospects." In *The Ancient Mediterranean Environment between Science and History*, edited by W. V. Harris, 259–76. Leiden: Brill, 2013.

Wirzba, Norman. *Food and Faith: A Theology of Eating.* Cambridge: Cambridge University Press, 2011.

———. *From Nature to Creation: A Christian Vision for Understanding and Loving Our World.* Edited by James K. A. Smith. The Church and Postmodern Culture. Grand Rapids: Baker Academic, 2015.

———. *The Paradise of God: Renewing Religion in an Ecological Age.* Oxford: Oxford University Press, 2007.

World Wildlife Foundation. "Soil Erosion and Degradation." https://www.worldwildlife.org/threats/soil-erosion-and-degradation.

Zenk, Shannon N., et al. "Relative and Absolute Availability of Healthier Food and Beverage Alternatives across Communities in the United States." *American Journal of Public Health* 104 (2014) 2170–78.

Zhang, Luoping, et al. "Exposure to Glyphosate-Based Herbicides and Risk for Non-Hodgkin Lymphoma: A Meta-Analysis and Supporting Evidence." *Mutation Research* 781 (2019) 186–206.

Ziegler, Joseph. *Isaias.* Septuaginta: Vetus Testamentum Graecum 14. Göttingen: Vandenhoek & Ruprecht, 1939.

Subject Index

abundance, 20, 23, 25, 29, 30, 31, 34, 38, 48, 49, 59, 60, 61, 66, 68, 69, 70, 72, 73, 74, 75, 76, 77, 82, 84, 85, 86, 87, 88, 101, 105, 109, 115, 120, 121, 194, 198, 202, 203, 227, 254, 269, 275

access, to God's glory, 176; to grain mills, 100; to income, 236; to land, 57, 201, 208; to machinery, 202; to nutrients, 207, 258, 261; to ovens, 100; to water, 201, 207, 261; see also food, access

Adam, 2, 38, 39, 40, 42, 43, 104, 114, 118, 120, 126, 128, 146, 150, 151, 152, 153, 154, 155, 157, 160, 163, 165, 166, 167, 169, 203

Abram / Abraham, 22, 28, 31, 41, 45, 46, 67, 112, 113, 118, 119, 128, 182

affordable, plow, 208; products, 241; soil fertilizer, 256

Africa Procunsularis, 88, 91; see also North Africa(n) and Tunisia

age(s), 69, 86, 119; of fertility and peace, 276; new / eschatological age, 55, 63, 130, 142, 148, 189, 190, 271; old age / aeon, 16, 130, 142, 271

agriculture, alternative, 26, 25, 265; industrial, 5, 6, 8, 25, 144, 196, 197, 198, 199, 201, 202, 204, 205, 206, 212, 214, 215, 228, 232, 238, 239, 242, 244, 248, 249, 250, 251, 254, 255, 256, 257, 258, 259, 260, 263, 264, 265, 266, 267, 268, 274, 276, 284; perennial, 26, 256, 257, 258, 259, 260, 261, 262, 263; regenerative, 8, 26, 252, 253, 254, 255, 256, 257, 259, 263, 264, 265, 266, 280

alive / make alive, 7, 8, 11, 13, 23, 24, 33, 68, 103, 109, 110, 111, 112, 119, 121, 122, 123, 127, 129, 130, 135, 137, 140, 141, 142, 143, 145, 151, 152, 178, 183, 189, 191, 192, 194, 195, 259, 271, 273, 277; see also *zōopoiēsis*

allegiance, 17, 18, 87, 131

ancient Near East(ern) / ANE, 30, 31, 32, 37, 38, 39, 45, 46, 61

animal(s), 1, 2, 8, 12, 14, 31, 33, 34, 36, 38, 39, 44, 45, 46, 48, 49, 51, 52, 56, 60, 63, 83, 115, 134, 135, 138, 157, 158, 199, 201, 205, 208, 213, 215, 218, 220, 222, 223, 226, 230, 243

anointed, 55, 63

Antioch, Pisidian, 85, 105; Syrian, 106

apocalypse, 29, 168, 170, 171, 173, 183; of Isaiah, 64; of sons / children of God, 102, 139, 144, 148, 168, 169, 170, 172, 173, 174, 281

apocalyptic, 17, 41, 42, 104, 172, 173, 188, 193

arable, 90, 92

Ara Pacis, 81, 82, 83, 105

archaeology, 23, 103, 104

arid / aridity, 90, 92, 93, 210; semi-arid, 51, 93, 210, 214

artifact(s), 19, 109

Arval Fraternity, 77

Subject Index

ascend / ascension, to power, 77; to the gods, 78, 105
Asia Minor, 74, 98, 103, 106, 285; as Asia, province of Roman Empire, 75
Assyria(n), 30, 62
atmosphere, 2, 3, 95, 210, 211, 212, 258, 259
atonement, 41, 52, 53, 54, 55, 111, 117, 118, 128, 141, 142, 271; Day of Atonement, see festivals
Augustan, 17, 71, 73, 82
Augustus, see emperor
Aventine Hill, 82, 99

barbarian, 71, 81, 126, 127
behavior, animal, 158, 227, 230; human, 9, 48, 53, 115, 116, 122, 130, 131, 134, 137, 152, 158
benefit / beneficial, 5, 9, 26, 37, 39, 42, 51, 58, 79, 89, 93, 100, 118, 153, 209, 217, 230, 241, 251, 257, 260, 262, 263, 270
beneficence, 73, 84, 108
biodiversity, 5, 6, 25, 35, 67, 143, 195, 197, 198, 200, 206, 212, 214, 228, 235, 241, 250, 254, 258, 259, 260, 263, 264, 265, 268, 273, 276, 279
biotic community, 12, 228
blessing, 22, 28, 31, 35, 45, 48, 49, 52, 67, 73, 76, 80, 115, 131, 169, 274, 276, 279
blood, 43, 56, 60, 117, 133, 153, 192, 229, 231, 279
bloodshed, see murder
breadbasket, 25, 91, 202, 206

calorie, 85, 245, 257, 258
capacity, carrying, 14, 253; of creation, 169; of humans, 121, 165, 229, 251; of nonhuman living things, 2, 34, 67, 217, 229, 251, 259; of land / soil, 11, 93, 212; of US agriculture, 203
Carthage, 83, 96, 97
Christianity, 17, 36, 46, 114
church(es), 20, 69, 136, 276, 280; members / attenders, 21, 279

Claudius, see emperor
clean, see pure
cleanse / cleansing, 29, 52, 53, 55, 60, 61, 68, 111, 118, 120, 142, 271
climate, 3, 23, 69, 75, 89, 90, 93, 101, 106, 107, 199, 207, 213, 242, 243, 245, 250, 253
climate change, 2, 3, 92, 101, 107, 209, 212, 215, 241, 245, 251, 263; see also global warming
coin(s) / coinage, 19, 73, 74, 75, 78, 79, 81, 83, 84, 98, 105, 108, 109; coin-makers, 23, 69
collaborate / collaborator / collaboration, 21, 24, 33, 62, 241, 252, 257, 260, 262, 269, 275, 276, 280
colonial / colonization, 25, 69, 74, 83, 201, 203; colonized imaginations, 86
conform / conformation / conformity, 21, 27, 28, 34, 41, 103, 121, 122, 130, 135, 140, 143, 160, 178, 195, 251, 265, 272, 273, 280
congregation(s), 279, 280; in Rome, 17, 82, 132, 133, 139, 266
conserve / conservation, 11, 26, 236, 237, 240, 241, 254
consequence(s), 204, 241, 243; act-consequence, 62; of anthropogenic ecosystem changes, 106; of negative acts, 42, 43, 54, 57, 58, 114, 145, 149, 151, 153, 154, 205, 215, 216; of positive acts, 62, 152, 176, 188, 189
constrain / constraint, 10, 14, 35, 36, 40, 47, 57, 139, 152, 247, 253
consume / consumption / consumptive, 4, 25, 57, 64, 65, 107, 126, 133, 138, 198, 201, 211, 216, 221, 225, 241, 244, 246, 249, 251, 258, 269, 273, 274, 279
consumer(s) / consumerism / consumerist, 86, 100, 197, 198, 199, 201, 202, 205, 206, 218, 223, 225, 226, 232, 233, 237, 238, 239,

306

Subject Index

241, 244, 249, 251, 260, 262, 268, 269, 275, 279
common good, 12, 198
community, 6, 11, 12, 13, 37, 40, 46, 65, 82, 94, 115, 130, 132, 137, 140, 190, 201, 214, 223, 226, 227, 228, 230, 231, 264, 270, 279, 280
communion, 137, 274, 278, 279, 280
cornucopia, 73, 74, 75, 78, 105
cooperate / cooperation / cooperative, 13, 24, 25, 27, 32, 33, 35, 38, 40, 67, 124, 140, 141, 142, 143, 167, 168, 191, 193, 195, 200, 252, 270, 271, 272, 273, 276
corpse, 53, 278
corruption, 41, 44, 71, 126, 128, 154, 155, 156, 157, 158, 159, 160, 169, 251; see also decay and destruction
cosmic, 11, 58, 62, 118, 120, 152, 163, 180, 278
cosmology(ies), 9, 29, 32, 39, 159, 162
cosmos, 9, 33, 37, 61, 81, 128, 163
covenant, 12, 22, 27, 28, 39, 40, 43, 44, 45, 46, 47, 48, 49, 53, 54, 57, 58, 62, 64, 65, 66, 67, 113, 117, 127, 128, 141, 169, 172, 182, 188, 189, 252
create, 4, 9, 17, 20, 25, 27, 29, 30, 31, 33, 37, 38, 39, 40, 41, 46, 52, 56, 62, 65, 67, 75, 77, 84, 90, 113, 114, 115, 116, 134, 140, 141, 149, 153, 157, 160, 161, 166, 167, 173, 194, 202, 217, 238, 241, 242, 247, 248, 259, 260, 267, 270, 271, 276, 278
Creator / Creator God, 13, 27, 32, 34, 35, 38, 42, 46, 49, 50, 54, 58, 109, 110, 113, 114, 115, 116, 119, 125, 126, 128, 129, 130, 135, 139, 142, 143, 159, 164, 173, 191, 195, 198, 266, 270, 271, 272, 273, 278, 279
crop(s), 5, 26, 48, 50, 72, 87, 90, 93, 96, 200, 202, 204, 205, 209, 211, 215, 216, 217, 220, 221, 223, 224, 225, 227, 233, 236, 238, 244, 245, 249, 254, 255, 257, 258, 259, 260, 261, 262, 263, 283, 284, 286, 287

cult / cultic, 15, 19, 49, 76, 77, 83, 114, 117
cultivate / cultivation, fields, 23, 57, 90, 92, 93, 94, 96, 100, 204, 210, 214, 237, 242, 254; crops / food, 43, 89, 91, 211, 212, 233, 242, 258, 262; identities, 276, 277; practices, 278; relationships, 26, 116, 266
curse, 2, 43, 45, 64, 116, 128, 154, 165, 169, 174, 186

David / Davidic, 62, 63, 112, 126
dead, 13, 23, 61, 112, 119, 122, 123, 128, 129, 136, 159, 171, 172, 173, 177, 183, 190, 192, 193, 227, 255, 259, 278
dead zone, 3, 4, 25, 213, 258
death, 2, 71, 77, 78, 84, 85, 88, 131, 138, 139, 146, 156, 157, 159, 164, 181, 183, 190, 191, 194, 216, 221, 225, 230, 231, 252, 278, 280 ; as consequence, 24, 28, 42, 110, 119, 120, 141, 152, 153, 154, 156, 157, 158, 159, 165 ; as destructive of / to life, 2, 3, 5, 115, 116, 142, 152, 154, 156, 157, 158, 160, 164, 165, 179, 275, 279; of Jesus, 53, 111, 112, 118, 119, 120, 121, 122, 125, 142, 153, 163, 171, 178, 188, 266, 271; as means to new life, 2, 120, 121, 122, 272; as cosmic power or force, 16, 17, 19, 20, 21, 24, 28, 68, 110, 111, 115, 116, 119, 123, 124, 125, 126, 127, 130, 139, 141, 150, 153, 154, 158, 159, 160, 163, 166, 167, 172, 173, 175, 177, 178, 188, 264, 271, 274; see also slavery
decay, 24, 145, 146, 150, 154, 155, 156, 157, 158, 159, 160, 164, 179, 188, 278; see also corruption and destruction
decomposition, 13, 42, 156, 157, 158, 159, 160, 212, 213
defile / defilement, 52, 53, 54, 55, 60, 64

Subject Index

deforestation, 90, 92, 93, 95, 97, 98, 105, 106, 107, 108, 109

degrade / degradation, 4, 15, 19, 23, 25, 29, 40, 52, 53, 54, 55, 59, 60, 64, 70, 88, 93, 101, 103, 105, 106, 107, 109, 117, 120, 131, 154, 158, 159, 197, 206, 210, 212, 213, 214, 216, 223, 225, 238, 240, 253, 254, 258, 263, 266, 269, 270, 274, 276

deified / deification, 83, 105

deity, 39, 45, 125

depend / dependence / dependent, 5, 6, 11, 12, 13, 14, 16, 19, 21, 23, 24, 30, 34, 37, 43, 51, 54, 61, 66, 70, 72, 73, 76, 84, 87, 88, 92, 93, 94, 95, 97, 100, 108, 111, 116, 124, 127, 138, 146, 147, 151, 153, 163, 167, 168, 173, 174, 175, 176, 180, 186, 194, 204, 205, 206, 207, 208, 210, 212, 215, 225, 227, 230, 233, 240, 245, 247, 254, 256, 257, 258, 268, 269, 271, 274, 277, 278, 285

deplete / depletion, 40, 92, 100, 105, 204, 212, 215, 254, 256

desertification, 92

destroy / destroyer, 4, 5, 8, 27, 43, 44, 50, 52, 64, 66, 67, 71, 84, 116, 123, 131, 134, 136, 137, 138, 139, 143, 157, 158, 159, 174, 195, 196, 198, 200, 104, 208, 210, 213, 233, 239, 251, 254, 257, 268, 273, 274, 276, 279

destruction, 2, 4, 6, 7, 9, 13, 16, 19, 20, 21, 23, 24, 25, 28, 29, 43, 44, 46, 52, 53, 56, 58, 62, 64, 65, 66, 68, 70, 88, 101, 102, 103, 107, 109, 110, 111, 116, 121, 123, 124, 127, 136, 137, 138, 139, 140, 141, 142, 143, 144, 145, 146, 150, 154, 155, 156, 157, 158, 159, 160, 161, 165, 166, 167, 168, 174, 175, 176, 177, 178, 192, 193, 194, 195, 196, 197, 198, 199, 205, 206, 212, 213, 214, 222, 233, 249, 251, 252, 254, 266, 267, 268, 271, 273, 274, 275, 276, 280, 281; see also corruption and decay

deterioration, 5, 7, 29, 43, 64, 89, 158, 197, 205, 227

deus, 78

discernment, 9, 10, 11, 12, 16, 17, 20, 54, 130, 139, 141, 143, 170, 199, 205

disempower / disempowered, 143, 195, 200, 273, 280

disobedient / disobediently / disobedience, 24, 42, 43, 45, 52, 120, 146, 148, 149, 160, 165, 167, 189

distribution, 23, 25, 72, 82, 84, 87, 88, 91, 97, 99, 100, 133, 198, 200, 205, 206, 210, 238, 241, 242, 243, 244, 245, 246, 249, 250, 251

diverse / diversity / diversified / diversification, 4, 5, 9, 11, 13, 27, 34, 35, 36, 40, 43, 67, 75, 93, 124, 132, 133, 134, 137, 140, 141, 143, 166, 184, 195, 198, 199, 201, 207, 209, 217, 226, 227, 251, 254, 255, 258, 259, 263, 270, 271, 272, 273, 274; see also biodiversity

divine / divinely / divinity / divinized, 2, 10, 24, 27, 30, 31, 33, 34, 36, 37, 39, 40, 41, 42, 44, 45, 46, 52, 53, 56, 59, 61, 62, 65, 67, 73, 75, 77, 78, 79, 80, 82, 84, 104, 111, 112, 113, 114, 115, 116, 117, 118, 119, 120, 124, 127, 128, 129, 130, 143, 145, 149, 164, 169, 171, 174, 175, 177, 178, 180, 181, 183, 194, 195, 265, 273, 274

divus, 77, 78, 79, 125

dominion, 19, 22, 24, 25, 28, 29, 31, 32, 35, 36, 37, 40, 41, 56, 66, 67, 70, 71, 73, 77, 81, 84, 88, 103, 114, 119, 120, 121, 123, 124, 130, 140, 151, 161, 162, 163, 166, 167, 173, 174, 175, 203, 264; see also servant leadership

earthquake, 58, 106, 160, 192

ecclesial, 10, 21, 26, 129, 139, 140, 199, 277

ecology, 11, 12, 14, 253, 266, 270, 277

Subject Index

ecological / ecologically, 4, 9, 10, 11, 12, 14, 18, 19, 20, 21, 22, 23, 24, 34, 37, 64, 68, 69, 70, 88, 89, 91, 93, 94, 95, 96, 100, 101, 104, 105, 109, 115, 123, 131, 139, 140, 170, 179, 183, 199, 200, 201, 205, 209, 210, 221, 233, 235, 236, 238, 240, 241, 249, 250, 251, 252, 254, 255, 257, 259, 262, 263, 264, 265, 266, 267, 268, 278, 279, 280

economy / economics / economic / economically / socio-economic / uneconomical, 3, 6, 34, 47, 56, 57, 58, 73, 84, 90, 91, 92, 93, 100, 104, 107, 115, 116, 117, 123, 125, 132, 133, 183, 190, 196, 199, 200, 201, 202, 209, 217, 233, 236, 237, 238, 239, 240, 241, 242, 243, 246, 247, 248, 249, 250, 251, 255, 256, 270, 275, 284

ecosphere, 8, 13, 140, 200, 210, 235

ecosystem, 6, 8, 10, 11, 14, 25, 26, 139, 141, 143, 170, 195, 197, 198, 199, 200, 201, 210, 212, 213, 214, 222, 227, 228, 233, 250, 253, 254, 255, 257, 258, 259, 263, 265, 266, 268, 273, 274

eco-ethical principles, 23, 25, 103, 195, 199, 202, 206, 213, 222, 233, 245, 256, 272, 277

eco-theological principle(s), 22, 23, 67, 103, 119, 141

eco-theology, 68

Egypt, 6, 23, 46, 47, 48, 58, 69, 87, 88, 89, 90, 91, 97, 182

embody / embodied / embodiment, 9, 28, 67, 82, 116, 119, 121, 122, 126, 140, 142, 164, 196, 199, 271, 276, 277, 280

emission, 3, 25, 200, 211, 212, 242, 243, 251, 256, 260

emperor, 19, 23, 63, 68, 69, 70, 72, 76, 77, 79, 82, 83, 84, 85, 86, 87, 89, 91, 93, 94, 100, 103, 105, 108, 109, 114, 125, 132, 202, 266; Augustus (Octavian), 20, 22, 23, 69, 72, 73, 74, 75, 76, 77, 78, 79, 80, 81, 82, 83, 84, 85, 86, 87, 88, 89, 90, 91, 97, 99, 105, 126; Claudius, 74, 75, 78, 79, 98, 105, 108; Hadrian, 91, 98; Nero, 20, 22, 23, 79, 83, 84, 88, 89, 91, 98, 108, 126; Tiberius, 78, 79, 83, 85, 108; Trajan, 98, 108

empire, 19, 21, 23, 68, 69, 102 106, 115, 216, 254; Roman Empire, 15, 16, 17, 18, 19, 20, 21, 68, 69, 70, 71, 72, 73, 76, 79, 80, 82, 84, 85, 88, 89, 91, 92, 94, 95, 97, 98, 99, 101, 102, 103, 104, 105, 106, 107, 109, 112, 117, 126, 139, 195, 197, 266

empower / empowered, 11, 20, 36, 80, 122, 123, 134, 136, 137, 139, 140, 199, 211, 256, 275, 284

enemy, 30, 35, 48, 52, 63, 119, 131, 139, 141, 149, 203, 235, 270

enslave / enslaving / enslavement, 8, 21, 28, 29, 35, 47, 56, 65, 68, 70, 73, 102, 103, 119, 124, 126, 128, 141, 143, 150, 151, 153, 155, 156, 158, 160, 166, 167, 174, 175, 182, 183, 188, 195, 199, 206, 233, 249, 255, 268, 270, 273, 274, 276; see also slavery

environment / environmental, 4, 11, 14, 19, 21, 70, 95, 103, 104, 105, 106, 107, 109, 204, 205, 207, 218, 219, 225, 228, 239, 253, 270, 284, 285

environmental history, 23, 25, 89, 103, 104, 206

Ephesus, 75, 79, 105, 106, 107

erosion, see soil

eschatology / eschatological, 22, 55, 62, 104, 123, 128, 129, 147, 148, 149, 153, 170, 171, 172, 173, 178, 189, 191, 192, 193, 194, 271, 272

eschaton, 121, 148, 149, 150, 178, 193; see also age

ethic / ethics / ethical / ethicist, 9, 10, 11, 12, 48, 67, 121, 122, 133, 134, 135, 137, 138, 139, 142, 143, 144, 170, 216, 249, 250, 251, 268, 273, 275, 279

eucharist, 26, 114, 140, 274, 277, 278, 279, 280; see also communion

Subject Index

evidence, 6, 15, 17, 19, 86, 93, 94, 95, 103, 104, 105, 106, 113, 123, 162, 170, 179, 192, 219, 221, 250, 255

exile, 54, 66; Babylonian, 31, 182, 185, 186

expect / expectation / expectantly, 10, 13, 14, 18, 19, 24, 28, 29, 32, 36, 37, 39, 40, 47, 51, 60, 65, 67, 68, 75, 90, 102, 103, 113, 115, 117, 121, 122, 124, 126, 127, 128, 130, 131, 133, 144, 167, 168, 169, 171, 174, 193, 194, 195, 199, 229, 250, 252, 253, 254, 257, 268, 273, 274, 277, 281

experiment / experimentation, 222, 223, 229, 261; acute, 222, 229; chronic, 222, 223, 232; sub-chronic, 222, 223, 229, 230

exploit / exploitation / exploitative, 23, 25, 29, 35, 36, 37, 40, 47, 55, 56, 70, 82, 84, 87, 93, 94, 100, 104, 106, 108, 115, 116, 160, 164, 170, 183, 254, 266, 270

extinction, 2, 7, 143, 253, 266

faith / faithful / faithfulness / faithfully, 11, 12, 18, 24, 48, 59, 62, 63, 65, 68, 70, 72, 112, 113, 117, 118, 119, 121, 122, 123, 127, 128, 131, 134, 136, 137, 139, 167, 169, 172, 178, 181, 187, 188, 189, 194, 252, 279; see also fidelity

fail / failure, 28, 41, 50, 52, 53, 57, 65, 75, 91, 113, 114, 116, 195, 196, 206, 213, 222, 228, 233, 235, 240, 242, 244, 245, 249, 250, 251, 269, 271, 276

famine, 30, 59, 60, 190, 200

farmer, 4, 5, 6, 23, 25, 26, 47, 48, 56, 57, 69, 70, 72, 76, 77, 86, 89, 90, 91, 92, 93, 94, 95, 96, 97, 197, 198, 199, 202, 203, 204, 205, 206, 208, 209, 210, 211, 213, 214, 215, 216, 217, 218, 220, 221, 222, 223, 225, 227, 228, 230, 232, 233, 234, 235, 236, 237, 238, 239, 240, 241, 243, 245, 248, 250, 251, 254, 255, 256, 260, 261, 262, 263, 268, 279, 280, 283, 284, 286, 287

farmworker, 5, 6, 39, 198, 199, 200, 222, 223, 232

female, 31, 34, 39, 75, 83, 168, 172, 246

fertility / fertile, 4, 13, 20, 23, 25, 27, 29, 30, 31, 34, 35, 36, 37, 40, 43, 51, 55, 56, 58, 62, 63, 70, 73, 76, 80, 81, 82, 88, 89, 93, 103, 115, 143, 165, 166, 195, 197, 200, 201, 206, 207, 208, 209, 210, 211, 212, 213, 235, 237, 250, 251, 253, 254, 256, 258, 265, 266, 268, 269, 273, 275, 276, 279

fertilizer, 3, 5, 25, 197, 202, 204, 208, 210, 211, 212, 213, 228, 237, 238, 248, 256, 259, 260, 284

festival(s), 19, 40, 49, 50, 51, 84, 109, 276; of Booths, 49, 51; Day of Atonement, 51, 54, 55, 118; of Passover, 50, 118; of Trumpets, 49, 51; of Unleavened Bread, 49, 50

fidelity, 10, 46, 70, 112, 128, 136, 143, 167, 195, 273, 280; see also faith

field, 39, 43, 47, 48, 49, 50, 60, 66, 69, 70, 77, 78, 80, 89, 90, 91, 100, 105, 202, 204, 206, 211, 214, 216, 217, 220, 222, 223, 224, 226, 227, 236, 237, 244, 251, 255, 257, 261, 280; as subject of inquiry, 15, 16, 277; number 2 field corn, 239; of Mars / Campus Martinus, 81, 82, 85

first fruits, 50, 147, 148, 249

flesh / fleshly / enflesh, 41, 43, 44, 46, 60, 127, 128, 132, 158, 279; as cosmic power, 16, 17

flood / flooding, 44, 84, 89, 90, 91, 99, 107, 108, 109, 158, 277

flourish / flourishing, 8, 13, 22, 24, 25, 27, 28, 29, 35, 36, 38, 39, 40, 50, 53, 66, 67, 102, 126, 127, 137, 140, 141, 142, 143, 144, 146, 151, 157, 161, 165, 166, 167, 183, 194, 195, 196, 199, 200, 201, 206, 249, 250, 252, 253, 254, 260, 263, 268, 271, 272, 273, 274, 275, 276, 279

Subject Index

food, 1, 4, 6, 8, 9, 23, 26, 30, 34, 36, 37, 39, 40, 43, 44, 45, 46, 66, 71, 72, 75, 76, 115, 132, 134, 135, 137, 138, 139, 165, 198, 203, 220, 221, 223, 224, 225, 227, 228, 229, 231, 232, 233, 235, 238, 253, 255, 257, 259, 263, 265, 269, 272, 278, 279, 280; access / sharing, 25, 57, 67, 86, 94, 131, 133, 135, 141, 143, 195, 199, 200, 201, 204, 208, 216, 236, 244, 245, 246, 247, 250, 258, 261, 270, 272, 274; affordability, 25, 197, 199, 202, 204, 206, 237, 242, 248, 249, 250, 264, 270; unaffordability, 245, 247, 248, 249, 260; justice / injustice, 199, 200, 206, 213, 241, 270; safety, 25, 197, 242, 244, 249; security / provision, 25, 69, 80, 82, 84, 86, 88, 90, 96, 99; system, 92, 196, 200, 202, 238, 239, 240, 241, 243, 246, 250, 251, 262, 264, 265, 268; waste, 250, 251; web, 5, 226

force, 53, 61, 72, 97, 120, 156, 177, 178, 198

forces, of agriculture, 5, 197, 250; of earth, 32, 84, 160, 235; of the market or society, 107, 170, 190, 205, 233, 240, 241, 245, 248, 249, 260, 268, 269; of cosmos or supernatural, 13, 17, 21, 24, 46, 52, 109, 139, 167, 251, 274; see also slavery

forgive / forgiveness, 29, 60, 61, 72, 110, 117, 118, 277

forum, of Augustus, 82; of Corinth, 83, 105

fossil fuel, 2, 210, 238, 242, 248, 249, 254, 260, 268

fragile, 2, 93, 210, 233

free / freedom / freely, 12, 40, 67, 70, 71, 72, 94, 95, 99, 103, 108, 117, 124, 127, 131, 132, 134, 137, 139, 141, 147, 152, 153, 160, 163, 165, 175, 177, 186, 188, 200, 218, 237, 239, 249, 256, 260, 264, 270, 274, 278; see also liberty

fruit / fruitful / fruitfully / fruitfulness, 1, 8, 9, 34, 42, 46, 48, 52, 55, 59, 60, 64, 66, 70, 72, 77, 83, 96, 120, 135, 164, 165, 182, 188, 191, 192, 200, 202, 224, 243, 245, 253, 269, 276, 278, 285; fruit trees, 1, 49; be fruitful, 32, 35, 44, 60, 165

frumentationes / grain dole / free grain, 63, 82, 84, 85, 86, 87, 99, 100, 139; *plebs frumentaria*, 82, 86, 91

frustrate / frustration, 2, 8, 20, 24, 28, 29, 68, 70, 102, 103, 111, 114, 124, 127, 142, 143, 145, 146, 161, 162, 163, 164, 165, 166, 168, 174, 178, 179, 189, 193, 195, 199, 222, 227, 249, 251, 267, 271, 273, 274, 275, 276

garden, 9, 38, 39, 40, 41, 43, 51, 59, 114, 198, 203, 207, 255, 265, 274, 275; Gardening God, 265, 275

gardener, 39, 275

Gaul, 81, 95

genetically engineered / GE, 217, 220, 221

genetically modified / GM / GMO, 197, 205, 216, 221, 225, 285, 286, 287

generous / generosity, 37, 38, 40, 42, 51, 89, 114, 277

gift / gifted, 34, 48, 49, 50, 86, 113, 115, 121, 133, 135, 143, 147, 195, 199, 244, 250, 255, 268, 273, 274, 275, 277, 279

global warming, 3, 138, 213, 242, 243, 260, 267; see also climate change

glorify / glorification, 7, 10, 13, 20, 24, 27, 28, 29, 42, 111, 121, 124, 125, 126, 127, 137, 139, 141, 142, 147, 149, 153, 156, 160, 166, 167, 168, 171, 172, 173, 174, 177, 178, 179, 189, 190, 194, 195, 252, 266, 270, 271

glory, 2, 7, 13, 19, 22, 24, 102, 114, 115, 121, 122, 124, 125, 127, 144, 145, 146, 147, 148, 157, 160, 167, 168, 170, 171, 172, 173, 174, 175, 176, 177, 178, 179, 186, 188, 189, 190, 193, 281

Subject Index

glyphosate / glyphosate-based herbicide / GBH, 9, 214, 215, 216, 217, 218, 219, 220, 221, 222, 223, 224, 225, 226, 227, 228, 229, 230, 231, 232, 286, 287

golden age, of Agriculture, 202, 250, 276; of Augustus, 20, 23, 69, 70, 71, 73, 77, 78, 82, 86, 88, 103, 104, 105, 109, 117, 128, 166; of Nero, 126; of Pesticides, 202, 284

gospel, of Matthew, 191; of Paul, 6, 7, 16, 17, 18, 68, 83, 102, 110, 118, 120, 128, 129, 132, 188, 189, 272, 276; of Roman Empire, 22, 23, 69, 70, 82, 102, 103, 104, 105, 109, 126

grace, 41, 46, 102, 111, 121, 122, 123, 130, 133, 173, 250, 274

gracious / graciously, 7, 9, 13, 47, 59, 116, 117, 118, 119, 121, 138, 140, 175, 177, 201, 274, 277

grain, 49, 50, 56, 57, 60, 66, 69, 70, 81, 82, 84, 85, 86, 87, 88, 90, 91, 92, 93, 94, 96, 97, 99, 100, 107, 109, 130, 182, 208, 209, 211, 212, 216, 220, 221, 223, 224, 225, 226, 239, 242, 243, 245, 249, 251, 253, 257, 258, 260, 261, 262, 280, 284

grain trade, 22, 89, 91, 97, 98, 100, 196, 199, 248

grape(s), 59, 90, 91, 224

gratitude, 50, 134, 135, 137, 139, 143, 195, 199, 206, 244, 250, 273, 274, 275, 278, 279

Great Plains, 8, 22, 25, 202, 205, 206, 207, 208, 210, 213, 214, 215, 233, 235, 236, 237, 240, 241, 242, 257, 258

greed / greedy, 56, 71, 115, 166, 249, 251

greenhouse gas(es), 2, 3, 25, 138, 210, 211, 241, 242, 243, 251, 259

Hadrian, see emperor
harmony / harmonious / harmoniously, 29, 37, 62, 63, 66, 78, 82, 120
harvest / harvested, 42, 49, 50, 51, 59, 76, 87, 90, 91, 94, 96, 97, 202, 204, 208, 211, 214, 221, 223, 225, 226, 233, 239, 242, 243, 244, 249, 257, 259, 263, 279, 283

heal / healing, 6, 22, 61, 123, 274

health / healthy / healthful, 6, 8, 11, 12, 25, 26, 28, 29, 35, 40, 46, 54, 55, 59, 61, 63, 67, 70, 73, 88, 106, 111, 116, 120, 129, 139, 143, 189, 194, 195, 196, 197, 198, 199, 200, 201, 205, 206, 212, 213, 214, 218, 219, 220, 222, 225, 226, 227, 232, 233, 235, 240, 241, 243, 245, 246, 247, 250, 251, 253, 255, 256, 257, 259, 262, 264, 265, 267, 268, 273, 276, 278, 280

hermeneutical lens, 10, 20, 139, 142

holy / holiness, 50, 52, 53, 54, 57, 66, 77, 120, 128, 129, 130, 137, 175, 200, 279

Holy Spirit, 137, 138

Holiness Code, 49, 55

home, 3, 11, 14, 38, 40, 51, 59, 60, 72, 80, 198, 208, 255; homeland, 54, 182

hope / hopeful, 7, 8, 9, 22, 24, 29, 50, 55, 56, 59, 61, 63, 68, 71, 77, 102, 103, 104, 111, 139, 143, 144, 145, 146, 161, 162, 165, 171 178, 179, 180, 182, 183, 184, 185, 189, 193, 195, 196, 199, 211, 233, 236, 256, 257, 273, 276, 280

hypoxic, see dead zone

identity, 6, 9, 10, 14, 31, 38, 41, 47, 79, 83, 134, 135, 147, 150, 170, 175, 217, 269, 270, 274, 279

ideology, 17, 31, 37, 71, 189

idol, 60, 114, 163, 164

idolatry, 53, 54, 56, 60, 66, 111, 114, 115, 117, 118, 119, 160, 164, 166, 179

image, 25, 36, 61, 65, 73, 83, 101, 118, 157, 159, 160, 168, 176, 180, 185, 186; of Caesar / emperor, 78; of g/ God, 1, 27, 29, 30, 31, 32, 33, 34, 35, 37, 38, 41, 67, 125, 160, 198, 265; of Jesus Christ, 21, 28, 121, 140, 160, 178, 272

imagery, 19, 180, 187, 191, 193

Subject Index

imperial / imperialistic, 8, 9, 15, 16, 17, 18, 19, 20, 21, 22, 23, 38, 56, 57, 69, 70, 73, 75, 76, 78, 79, 81, 82, 83, 84, 85, 86, 87, 88, 89, 90, 91, 92, 93, 94, 95, 96, 98, 101, 102, 103, 104, 105, 106, 108, 109, 112, 114, 115, 125, 126, 128, 134, 136, 166, 183, 189, 194, 201, 251
impiety / impious, 71, 81, 153
impure / impurity, 41, 52, 54, 60, 68, 110, 142, 271; moral contamination, 43, 53, 54, 117, 118, 208; ritual contamination, 52, 53, 61, 118
inedible, 43, 182
infidelity, 66, 137
ingratitude, 114
injustice, 6, 11, 25, 29, 58, 71, 72, 115, 122, 127, 166, 183, 201, 206, 213, 239, 251
inscription, 19, 78, 79, 81, 83, 84, 92
integrity, 11, 55, 66, 231, 277, 279
intercede / intercession, 22, 28, 75, 173, 276, 277
intercessor / intercessory, 51, 67
interdepend / interdependence / interdependent, 11, 12, 13, 22, 25, 27, 29, 42, 46, 67, 68, 125, 141, 142, 145, 149, 167, 174, 195, 198, 199, 250, 252, 269, 270, 271, 272, 278
intertext / intertextual, 17, 24, 62, 64, 158, 162, 168
irrigate / irrigation, 30, 215, 216, 237, 259
Israel / Israelite, 6, 18, 19, 22, 27, 28, 29, 30, 31, 37, 38, 39, 41, 45, 46, 47, 48, 49, 50, 51, 52, 53, 54, 55, 56, 57, 58, 59, 60, 61, 62, 63, 65, 66, 67, 68, 102, 112, 113, 117, 118, 127, 128, 129, 130, 145, 164, 172, 185, 186, 189, 190, 266, 276

Jerusalem, 50, 51, 54, 107, 130, 186, 187
Jesus Christ, 7, 17, 18, 19, 20, 21, 24, 25, 28, 29, 37, 53, 68, 82, 83, 102, 103, 104, 107, 109, 110, 111, 112, 113, 117, 118, 119, 120, 121, 122, 123, 124, 125, 126, 127, 128, 129, 130, 131, 132, 133, 134, 135, 136, 137, 138, 139, 140, 142, 143, 144, 145, 148, 150, 151, 152, 153, 154, 158, 167, 168, 169, 170, 171, 172, 173, 174, 175, 176, 177, 178, 179, 180, 183, 187, 188, 189, 190, 191, 193, 194, 195, 196, 198, 199, 233, 251, 265, 266, 269, 271, 272, 273, 274, 275, 278, 279, 280
Jewish, 15, 16, 17, 18, 19, 41, 47, 51, 52, 61, 104, 112, 113, 117, 118, 126, 128, 129, 130, 134, 135, 152, 159, 191, 192, 193, 276
Josephus, 91, 97
jubilee, 47, 57
Judah, 56, 61, 63, 164
Judaism, 17, 18, 36, 65, 113, 150
Judea / Judean, 17, 48, 49, 50, 51, 106, 116, 127, 182, 276
judge / judgment, 6, 25, 43, 44, 53, 56, 57, 63, 65, 66, 116, 124, 127, 135, 147, 168, 173, 182, 183, 192, 194
Julio-Claudian, 88, 125
Julius Caesar, 71, 72, 78, 79, 85, 108
just / justice, 10, 25, 28, 37, 55, 56, 61, 62, 63, 66, 67, 68, 79, 105, 110, 112, 113, 117, 121, 123, 125, 126, 127, 139, 140, 142, 143, 151, 182, 194, 195, 196, 199, 200, 201, 213, 240, 241, 243, 251, 254, 268, 271, 273, 275, 276, 277, 280
justify / justification / justifier, 7, 10, 18, 20, 23, 24, 26, 61, 110, 111, 112, 113, 117, 118, 119, 121, 123, 126, 127, 129, 141, 142, 143, 173, 178, 188, 194, 195, 196, 271, 273, 275, 276, 280; see also make right

keep / observe / maintain, 39, 40, 43, 46, 48, 51, 67, 119, 193, 207
king, 30, 31, 37, 51, 62, 66, 112, 125, 126, 153, 203
kingdom, 18, 56, 61, 62, 137, 172, 189, 193, 203, 269

Subject Index

labor / laborer, as in childbirth, 25, 102, 165, 168, 172, 179, 180, 181, 182, 183, 184, 185, 186, 187, 188, 189, 190, 191, 192, 193; as in work, 30, 40, 43, 50, 59, 72, 73, 90, 93, 94, 95, 97, 182, 200, 203, 208, 209, 217, 233, 239, 268, 278

land, 1, 2, 3, 4, 5, 6, 8, 9, 11, 12, 14, 25, 27, 31, 32, 33, 34, 35, 36, 38, 40, 41, 42, 43, 44, 45, 46, 47, 48, 49, 51, 52, 53, 54, 55, 56, 57, 58, 59, 60, 61, 64, 65, 66, 67, 68, 69, 70, 71, 72, 87, 88, 90, 91, 92, 93, 94, 95, 98, 100, 106, 109, 111, 116, 117, 128, 134, 141, 142, 146, 154, 156, 164, 165, 179, 182, 185, 186, 191, 192, 193, 199, 200, 201, 203, 204, 206, 209, 212, 213, 214, 215, 216, 217, 228, 233, 235, 241, 244, 250, 253, 254, 256, 257, 258, 267, 270, 271, 275, 284; landscape, 15, 18, 21, 82, 89, 208, 264; landscaper, 222, 223, 232, 237, 255; *adamah*, 42, 43

land ethic, 12

Land Institute, The, 259, 260, 261, 262

Levant, 8, 50, 51, 56, 89

liberate / liberation / liberator / liberty / liberative, 2, 7, 8, 10, 13, 18, 20, 21, 22, 24, 25, 26, 27, 28, 29, 46, 47, 53, 55, 56, 67, 68, 70, 85, 100, 102, 103,109, 110, 111, 118, 119, 121, 122, 123, 124, 125, 126, 127, 128, 135, 136, 138, 139, 140, 141, 142, 144, 145, 146, 148, 149, 150, 153, 154, 155, 156, 158, 160, 162, 165, 166, 167, 168, 169, 170, 172, 173, 174, 175, 176, 177, 178, 179, 183, 188, 189, 190, 191, 193, 194, 195, 198, 204, 205, 206, 213, 250, 251, 252, 253, 255, 256, 259, 260, 263, 265, 266, 268, 270, 271, 272, 274, 275, 276, 277, 279, 280, 281

life-supporting, 9, 22, 25, 28, 121, 123, 135, 142, 161, 199, 201, 258, 276

liturgy / liturgical, 22, 27, 28, 48, 49, 50, 51, 55, 118, 130, 276, 279

living being, 29, 38

make alive, 7, 11, 13, 23, 33, 68, 103, 109, 110, 112, 119, 123, 127, 135, 137, 142, 271; see also *zōopoiēsis*

make right, 7, 11, 13, 23, 68, 103, 109, 110, 119, 123, 127, 142, 271; see also justify

male, 31, 34, 61, 63, 86, 99, 100, 172, 229

Medjerda / *Bagrada* River, 92, 93, 96

mediate / mediation / mediator, 30, 33, 46, 49, 50, 76, 128

Mediterranean, 16, 23, 69, 70, 73, 75, 86, 89, 92, 95, 98, 101, 104, 106, 109, 132

mercy / merciful, 6, 41, 62, 111, 115, 129, 130, 189, 194

Mesopotamia(n), 29, 30, 31, 37, 125, 216

messiah, 17, 18, 20, 21, 28, 29, 37, 55, 62, 63, 68, 110, 111, 120, 121, 122, 126, 127, 128, 131, 136, 141, 142, 149, 167, 173, 186, 190, 271

metallurgy, 95

Midwest, 21, 227, 233, 240, 242, 247

military / militaristic / militarism, 23, 63, 64, 69, 73, 76, 87, 104, 106, 117, 128, 183, 203, 208, 276, 284; martial, 75

misappropriate / misappropriation, 42, 114, 115, 116, 203

misperception, 42, 114, 115, 116, 151

Mississippi River, 3, 213, 228

mission, 7, 20, 24, 40, 103, 129, 131, 137, 277

modii, 85, 87, 91, 94, 97

monarch / monarchy, 55, 61, 63, 66

Monarch butterfly, 227, 228

monument, 79, 81, 83, 84, 85, 105

mortal / mortality, 112, 157, 158, 228

Mosaic, 45, 47, 57, 111, 117, 134

multiply, 32, 35, 36, 44, 60, 119, 122, 165

murder / murderous / murderer, 37, 43, 53, 54, 60, 88, 108, 111, 115, 116, 117, 118, 153, 192, 208

mutate / mutated, 42, 269

mythology / mythological, 31, 70, 71, 82

314

Subject Index

narrative / narratival / narratively, 7, 8, 9, 10, 14, 20, 27, 28, 29, 31, 34, 35, 38, 41, 44, 84, 86, 120, 146, 152, 154, 156, 158, 159, 160, 162, 163, 165, 166, 168, 178, 252, 254, 263, 264, 267, 269, 270, 273, 274, 276; counternarrative, 38, 270, 271, 272
nation / national, 18, 19, 20, 27, 35, 37, 45, 46, 52, 54, 60, 62, 63, 65, 66, 67, 113, 121, 126, 127, 128, 132, 136, 164, 186, 187, 189, 198, 201, 210, 237, 238, 239, 246, 249, 266, 284
Nero, see emperor
neurotoxin / neurotoxic / neurotoxicity, 5, 229, 289, 291
New Creation, 17, 22, 28, 29, 41, 62, 63, 64, 81, 138, 178, 180, 187, 190, 191, 271
Nile, 58, 91
nitrogenous fertilizer, 3, 211, 212, 213
non-genetically modified / non-GMO, 205, 217, 221
nonhuman, 7, 8, 9, 11, 12, 13, 14, 20, 21, 22, 24, 25, 26, 27, 28, 30, 32, 33, 34, 35, 36, 37, 39, 43, 44, 45, 47, 50, 52, 53, 54, 62, 63, 66, 67, 84, 103, 109, 110, 111, 113, 117, 118, 123, 124, 125, 126, 127, 129, 130, 134, 138, 139, 140, 141, 142, 143, 144, 146, 147, 149, 150, 151, 154, 156, 158, 159, 160, 161, 162, 165, 166, 167, 168, 169, 171, 173, 174, 175, 176, 177, 178, 179, 182, 183, 185, 186, 191, 193, 194, 195, 196, 197, 198, 199, 200, 201, 203, 205, 206, 207, 207, 218, 221, 250, 251, 252, 253, 266, 267, 268, 269, 270, 271, 272, 273, 274, 275, 276, 277
non-Hodgkin lymphoma, 6, 216, 232
North Africa(n), 22, 23, 69, 70, 83, 87, 88, 89, 90, 91, 92, 93, 94, 97, 100
nourish / nourishing / nourishment, 2, 4, 8, 34, 40, 42, 48, 49, 65, 116, 133, 140, 212, 243, 244, 245, 249, 272, 274, 275, 279

nurture, 22, 28, 29, 34, 39, 43, 120, 255, 265, 267, 272
nutrient(s), 49, 157, 207, 210, 212, 213, 227, 254, 256, 258, 259, 260, 261, 278, 283
nutrient cycle / cycling, 199, 253

obedient / obedience, 16, 18, 46, 48, 52, 70, 136, 149; of the nations, 20, 128
obligation, see responsibility
oil, 56, 96, 210
oppress / oppression / oppressive / oppressor, 29, 35, 46, 56, 57, 62, 87, 115, 117, 119, 138, 142, 147, 151, 153, 170, 174, 182, 190, 264, 271
organic, 11, 12, 26, 38, 49, 156, 212, 244, 256, 257
Ostia, 82, 98, 108

paradise, 73, 203
Parkinson's disease / parkinsonism, 6, 231, 232
Passover, 47, 50, 118
partner / partnership, 11, 33, 38, 39, 43, 169, 184, 200, 280
pattern, 41, 76, 92, 121, 122, 128, 134, 135, 217, 228, 253, 272
peace / peaceful, 22, 23, 27, 29, 30, 37, 48, 56, 58, 62, 63, 66, 68, 69, 70, 72, 76, 77, 80, 81, 82, 83, 84, 88, 90, 104, 105, 113, 116, 126, 127, 130, 137, 138, 139, 153, 189, 194, 195, 204, 208, 209, 235, 276
Pentecost, 50
perennial, 26, 207, 210, 256, 257, 258, 259, 260, 261, 263
Pesaḥ, see Passover
pesticide, 4, 5, 25, 197, 202, 203, 228, 237, 238, 239, 244, 251, 256, 283, 284, 285; fungicide, 4; insecticide, 4, 5, 204, 225, 237, 284, 286; herbicide, 4, 5, 6, 9, 25, 203, 204, 214, 215, 216, 217, 218, 219, 220, 221, 222, 223, 225, 228, 229, 232, 251, 255, 283, 286, 287

315

Subject Index

pious / piety, 16, 70, 76, 77, 79, 80, 82, 89, 114, 126, 128

plants, 1, 2, 4, 5, 7, 8, 12, 34, 36, 39, 43, 44, 45, 49, 51, 82, 134, 138, 158, 165, 198, 207, 208, 209, 210, 214, 215, 216, 217, 223, 226, 227, 236, 242, 243, 244, 254, 255, 257, 258, 259, 260, 263, 264, 268, 278, 283, 285, 286

plow, 4, 59, 95, 96, 205, 207, 208, 209, 210, 214, 235, 236, 240, 255, 256, 257, 259, 260, 263

pneumatology, 61

polity / politics / political / politically / politicians, 9, 10, 14, 15, 17, 18, 19, 20, 21, 22, 23, 24, 30, 48, 56, 63, 64, 68, 69, 71, 72, 75, 76, 77, 80, 81, 82, 86, 88, 90, 91, 99, 105, 109, 121, 129, 133, 142, 190, 233, 241, 263, 266, 267, 268, 276

poison / poisoning / poisonous, 4, 5, 95, 116, 216, 217, 255, 284

poor / poorest / poorly / poverty, 47, 49, 50, 56, 57, 63, 66, 71, 135, 136, 157, 176, 182, 188, 212, 239, 248, 280

possess / possession / possessive, 35, 47, 48, 79, 88, 160, 176, 177, 178, 193, 203, 274

power(s) / powerful / powerfully, 3, 6, 7, 10, 14, 16, 17, 18, 19, 24, 29, 31, 32, 33, 37, 52, 53, 57, 60, 61, 64, 75, 76, 77, 79, 80, 82, 86, 93, 96, 102, 112, 113, 114, 115, 116, 119, 123, 124, 128, 138, 146, 148, 149, 152, 153, 158, 159, 162, 164, 166, 170, 171, 173, 177, 178, 187, 191, 197, 202, 203, 205, 208, 209, 210, 215, 234, 237, 239, 242, 256, 259, 263, 268, 269, 272, 278, 280, 283, 284, 285

powerless, 100, 137

practice(s), 5, 8, 10, 15, 16, 17, 18, 19, 20, 23, 26, 31, 47, 52, 57, 65, 75, 76, 116, 117, 118, 133, 134, 137, 138, 140, 154, 164, 183, 194, 196, 200, 211, 215, 216, 220, 236, 240, 241, 243, 246, 250, 254, 255, 257, 258, 263, 264, 267, 268, 270, 272, 274, 275, 276, 277, 280

prairie, 25, 206, 207, 208, 209, 210, 258, 262

precipitation, 92, 101, 207

presence, 52, 54, 82, 104, 117, 153, 162, 170, 217, 225, 226, 227, 230, 231, 274, 283, 286

priest / priestly, 23, 30, 39, 54, 55, 130, 186, 273, 276, 277, 279

priesthood, 30, 77

Priestly writer / source / tradition, 33, 35, 49, 52

principles / rules / mores / instructions, 11, 20, 22, 23, 25, 26, 40, 67, 68, 78, 103, 119, 123, 137, 138, 141, 142, 143, 176, 177, 195, 199, 201, 206, 213, 222, 227, 228, 232, 233, 240, 241, 244, 245, 249, 254, 255, 256, 272, 273, 274, 277

processing, 95, 223, 238, 239, 241, 242, 243, 244, 249, 250

produce / product / production / productive / productively / productivity / producer, 6, 22, 23, 25, 33, 36, 39, 42, 43, 48, 49, 52, 57, 59, 60, 63, 64, 65, 69, 78, 87, 89, 90, 91, 92, 95, 96, 137, 138, 155, 156, 160, 165, 168, 175, 177, 178, 180, 181, 184, 189, 193, 197, 199, 202, 203, 204, 205, 206, 209, 211, 212, 213, 214, 216, 217, 220, 221, 223, 225, 227, 230, 232, 233, 234, 235, 236, 237, 238, 239, 240, 241, 242, 243, 244, 245, 246, 248, 249, 250, 253, 256, 257, 260, 261, 262, 263, 265, 268, 269, 274, 275, 278, 279, 280, 283, 284, 285, 286

profit / profitable / profitably, 25, 76, 94, 100, 200, 202, 237, 238, 248, 254, 256, 263

prohibition, 41, 42

promise(d), 22, 25, 45, 59, 60, 65, 68, 78, 105, 118, 121, 127, 141, 142, 169, 193, 197, 202, 206, 216, 243, 248, 265, 271, 285; Promised Land, 31, 47, 52, 55, 66, 128

Subject Index

propaganda, 17, 19, 23, 78, 82, 84, 103, 104
prophet(s), 8, 9, 22, 27, 28, 37, 47, 51, 55, 58, 59, 60, 61, 65, 67, 192, 264
prophetic, 6, 8, 27, 56, 57, 59, 61, 63, 104, 132
prosperity / prosperous, 45, 66, 72, 73, 76, 77, 81, 82, 84, 104
pure / purify / purity, 52, 54, 55, 111, 118, 202, 218, 223, 228, 243, 244
purge / purgation, 52, 54, 55
Puteoli, 97, 98

reap / reaping / reaper, 59, 90, 95, 116, 208, 237, 248
rectify / rectification, 24, 41, 65, 110, 117, 127, 140, 151, 160, 167, 193, 271
recycle / recycling, 13, 157
reign, 13, 19, 22, 37, 62, 63, 69, 72, 74, 81, 83, 85, 88, 89, 97, 98, 99, 108, 120, 121, 122, 123, 124, 126, 140, 141, 154, 178, 261, 271, 275
relationship, 6, 9, 10, 11, 12, 13, 14, 20, 22, 23, 26, 27, 28, 29, 35, 36, 37, 38, 40, 41, 42, 43, 44, 45, 48, 49, 54, 56, 62, 63, 64, 67, 78, 110, 115, 116, 118, 120, 129, 134, 137, 140, 141, 142, 151, 155, 156, 160, 161, 173, 174, 175, 176, 177, 183, 188, 195, 196, 199, 201, 215, 250, 252, 266, 267, 268, 269, 270, 271, 272, 275, 280
renew / renewal / renewed, 11, 22, 23, 40, 55, 59, 66, 69, 70, 71, 73, 77, 78, 80, 103, 105, 118, 119, 125, 130, 166, 170, 240, 266
repent / repentance, 52, 267, 277
represent / representation / representative, 10, 31, 58, 61, 62, 73, 74, 75, 81, 110, 127, 129, 134, 135, 136, 152, 177, 187, 280
Res Gestae, 72, 77, 79, 84, 85, 86, 87, 105, 289
resilient / resiliently / resilience, 7, 13, 210
responsible / responsibility, 11, 12, 13, 14, 24, 36, 37, 39, 41, 49, 52, 61, 67, 76, 102, 113, 122, 125, 146, 152, 178, 198, 221, 235, 249, 250, 252, 255, 268, 275, 278, 284
restore / restoration, 15, 20, 22, 27, 28, 29, 45, 47, 55, 56, 58, 59, 60, 61, 62, 63, 64, 65, 66, 68, 70, 78, 80, 105, 110, 111, 112, 117, 118, 119, 121, 123, 126, 128, 145, 165, 169, 170, 173, 193, 194, 215, 267, 271, 275
resurrect / resurrection, 7, 24, 25, 53, 61, 110, 111, 112, 119, 120, 121, 122, 123, 124, 125, 126, 128, 129, 140, 142, 148, 149, 157, 158, 160, 165, 167, 168, 170, 171, 172, 173, 174, 177, 178, 180, 183, 184, 188, 189, 190, 191, 192, 193, 194, 266, 271
rhetoric / rhetorical, 15, 17, 18, 19, 20, 25, 70, 109, 112, 125, 134, 172, 180, 196
righteous / righteousness, 13, 24, 27, 37, 41, 42, 61, 62, 63, 66, 68, 110, 112, 113, 118, 119, 120, 121, 122, 123, 127, 128, 130, 137, 140, 146, 150, 167, 174, 188, 194, 196, 275, 276
ritual / religious practice, 6, 23, 47, 50, 52, 53, 54, 55, 61, 62, 75, 76, 77, 114, 117, 118
Rome, 8, 17, 19, 20, 21, 22, 23, 63, 68, 69, 70, 72, 73, 76, 79, 80, 81, 82, 83, 84, 85, 86, 87, 88, 90, 91, 94, 96, 97, 98, 99, 100, 102, 103, 104, 105, 107, 108, 109, 112, 125, 127, 128, 129, 130, 131, 132, 133, 135, 136, 137, 139, 145, 148, 154, 156, 166, 180, 189, 194, 197, 202, 266
Roman Climate Optimum / RCO, 89, 90, 93, 107
Roman Empire, 15, 16, 17, 18, 19, 20, 21, 68, 69, 82, 89, 92, 95, 97, 98, 103, 104, 105, 106, 107, 109, 112, 117, 126, 195, 197, 266
Roundup®, 6, 216, 217, 218, 219, 226, 228, 229, 231, 286; see also glyphosate
ruin / ruined, 41, 43, 44, 57, 59, 65, 72, 105, 114, 116, 150, 153, 154, 155, 156, 158, 160, 194

Subject Index

Sabbath, 40, 49, 52, 57
sacred, 42, 50, 53, 54, 62, 77, 83, 85, 133, 145, 208, 252
sacrifice / sacrificial, 49, 53, 55, 77, 117, 118, 129, 130, 131, 235, 240, 259, 265, 268, 272, 273, 274, 280
salvation, 7, 28, 29, 58, 66, 123, 124, 125, 128, 129, 132, 138, 140, 141, 149, 151, 168, 169, 174, 175, 180, 186, 188, 189, 192
sanctuary, 53, 54
Sarah, 46, 119, 128
scarce / scarcity, 30, 84, 100, 233, 269, 275
Second Temple, 41, 42, 47, 104, 113
security, 48, 76, 164, 221, 232, 237, 239
semi-arid, see arid
Septuagint / LXX, 1, 42, 44, 50, 65, 115, 126, 150, 156, 163, 164, 169, 171, 172, 182, 185, 186, 190, 192
servant leadership, 22, 27, 29, 36, 38, 40, 42, 51, 55, 67, 122, 124, 127, 140, 141, 142, 143, 146, 151, 161, 162, 163, 166, 167, 174, 194, 195, 198, 252, 271, 273
service, 19, 37, 39, 46, 49, 50, 55, 69, 79, 97, 114, 128, 130, 131, 133, 139, 150, 151, 194, 221, 246, 276
sex / sexual, 6, 53, 54, 111, 118, 133
shape, see conform
sharecrop / sharecropper, 70, 91, 92, 94, 96, 97
ship / boat, 72, 82, 97, 98, 99, 100, 106, 107, 243
shrine, 55
Sinai, 57
slavery, 2, 6, 7, 8, 9, 13, 16, 20, 24, 26, 46, 47, 48, 57, 65, 102, 109, 110, 111, 118, 124, 125, 127, 138, 139, 140, 142, 144, 145, 146, 149, 150, 151, 153, 154, 155, 156, 158, 159, 160, 161, 165, 166, 172, 174, 175, 176, 177, 178, 180, 194, 196, 197, 198, 213, 251, 255, 268, 271, 274, 281
soil, 4, 8, 12, 14, 25, 26, 38, 39, 40, 43, 49, 60, 72, 90, 91, 93, 95, 96, 98, 100, 138, 197, 198, 199, 204, 205, 206, 207, 209, 210, 211, 212, 213, 215, 216, 218, 225, 226, 227, 233, 235, 236, 237, 240, 241, 244, 250, 253, 254, 255, 256, 257, 258, 259, 260, 261, 263, 265, 268, 269, 278, 285, 286; depletion, 100, 204; exhaustion, 91, 100, 204, 205, 237; salinization, 215, 216; wind erosion, 210; water erosion, 90, 93, 107, 210, 240
sojourner, 49
s/Son(s) of g/God, 18, 19, 20, 77, 78, 79, 102, 105, 112, 114, 123, 125, 126, 128, 144, 147, 148, 168, 169, 170, 172, 173, 174, 281
Spain, 74, 81
Spirit / spirit, 7, 17, 21, 60, 61, 63, 67, 68, 109, 110, 111, 112, 119, 120, 122, 123, 124, 125, 128, 130, 137, 138, 139, 141, 142, 147, 148, 149, 153, 154, 165, 178, 183, 184, 191, 193, 194, 271, 272, 274, 275, 277
spiritual / spiritualize, 16, 43, 116, 140, 152, 158
stable / stability, 12, 14, 56, 69, 81, 89, 90, 202, 242, 243, 247, 254, 267
starving / starvation, 70, 100, 103, 107, 204, 248
story, 2, 4, 5, 6, 7, 8, 9, 11, 13, 14, 16, 21, 22, 23, 24, 25, 26, 27, 28, 29, 30, 33, 35, 38, 39, 41, 43, 47, 68, 72, 81, 102, 111, 116, 120, 121, 123, 126, 129, 140, 141, 142, 143, 145, 146, 158, 160, 161, 163, 165, 166, 167, 168, 178, 179, 180, 185, 188, 194, 195, 196, 197, 199, 203, 205, 250, 252, 253, 254, 264, 266, 267, 268, 269, 270, 272, 274, 276, 277, 279, 280
subdue, 9, 32, 35, 84, 104, 203, 204, 207, 208, 252, 255
subject / subjection, 2, 7, 8, 10, 11, 17, 24, 28, 29, 32, 33, 41, 43, 54, 61, 69, 70, 73, 79, 85, 102, 103, 111, 114, 124, 127, 142, 143, 144, 145, 146, 148, 149, 151, 156, 158, 159, 160, 161, 162, 163, 164, 165, 166, 169,

Subject Index

174, 178, 183, 188, 189, 193, 194, 195, 222, 223, 251, 252, 266, 270, 271, 273, 274
supernatural, 13, 76, 119, 139, 274, 275
sustain / sustainable / sustainably / sustainability, 6, 11, 14, 26, 40, 45, 61, 89, 115, 119, 135, 166, 198, 206, 212, 232, 251, 253, 255, 256, 257, 263, 264
Syria, 98, 103, 106

Tanakh, 7, 8, 17, 21, 22, 27, 32, 37, 40, 41, 42, 52, 53, 56, 65, 67, 68, 70, 103, 110, 111, 114, 117, 118, 121, 129, 130, 141, 145, 146, 156, 158, 159, 162, 164, 170, 171, 172, 182, 183, 184, 185, 186, 208, 266
tax, 69, 87, 91, 92
temple, 19, 30, 53, 54, 75, 79, 80, 82, 83, 85, 130, 157
terrace / terracing, 69, 90, 93, 94, 236
thorn(s) and thistle(s), 42, 43, 165, 269
Tiber River, 82, 84, 90, 97, 98, 107, 108
Tiberius, see emperor
till / tillage / no-till / low-till, 26, 39, 40, 43, 49, 60, 72, 116, 179, 211, 215, 217, 255; see also plow
Torah, 8, 27, 28, 37, 39, 40, 41, 43, 45, 46, 48, 49, 52, 54, 64, 117, 134
toxin / toxic / toxicity, 205, 215, 219, 221, 228, 230, 231, 256, 258; excitotoxicity, 230; see also neurotoxin
tractor, 25, 197, 208, 209, 210, 237, 243
Trajan, see emperor
transform / transformation / transformative, 7, 10, 16, 41, 80, 82, 86, 104, 120, 121, 122, 126, 139, 140, 146, 167, 168, 170, 171, 172, 173, 174, 177, 178, 199, 202, 203, 206, 207, 239, 255, 267, 272, 275, 278, 284
transgress / transgression, 27, 42, 53, 54, 64, 65, 120, 150, 151, 154, 156, 163, 166, 182
transport / transportation, 23, 25, 82, 91, 93, 96, 97, 98, 100, 108, 206, 241, 242, 243, 249, 253

tree / timber / arboreal, 1, 2, 9, 34, 39, 40, 42, 46, 48, 49, 60, 92, 94, 95, 97, 98, 106, 108, 120
tribe / tribal, 25, 54, 56, 208, 255
Tunisia, 87, 91; see also Africa Procunsularis and North Africa(n)

unfaithfulness / unfaithfully / infidelity / faithless, 52, 57, 64, 66, 115, 137
unhealthy / unhealthful, 10, 52
unholy / unholiness, 29
unjust, 58; see also injustice
unrighteous / unrighteousness, 58
unsustainable, 25, 210, 213, 215, 238, 241, 254

vineyard, 57, 59
vital / vitality, 4, 5, 6, 7, 10, 11, 29, 34, 38, 40, 41, 52, 67, 68, 122, 140, 141, 142, 143, 195, 196, 198, 199, 201, 227, 231, 251, 268, 271, 273, 277, 280
violent / violently / violence, 2, 7, 22, 28, 31, 32, 35, 38, 40, 43, 44, 62, 72, 73, 77, 97, 106, 117, 119, 120, 124, 128, 131, 154, 158, 159, 160, 175, 183, 192, 193, 195, 222, 240, 274
virtue, 73, 81, 138, 277
vivify / vivification, 7, 61, 104, 111, 113, 122, 123, 124, 139
vulnerable / vulnerability, 40, 46, 50, 57, 76, 100, 137, 143, 195, 200, 206, 209, 222, 243, 250, 263, 273, 280, 284

water, 2, 3, 4, 5, 12, 13, 27, 32, 34, 35, 36, 40, 50, 51, 58, 60, 61, 67, 89, 90, 92, 93, 95, 97, 99, 101, 108, 116, 138, 141, 143, 158, 188, 191, 195, 198, 199, 200, 201, 206, 207, 210, 213, 215, 216, 225, 228, 233, 236, 237, 240, 241, 250, 251, 253, 256, 258, 259, 261, 263, 270; watershed, 107; floodwaters, 107; acidify / acidification, 3;

Subject Index

aqueduct, 93; aquifer, 25, 215, 237; siltation, 93, 98, 106

weak / weakness, 16, 66, 133, 134, 136, 137, 143, 187, 195, 200, 243, 261, 262, 273, 280

weed(s), 182, 197, 203, 204, 214, 215, 216, 217, 220, 229, 255, 269, 274, 283, 286, 287; milkweed, 227

wheat, 8, 22, 23, 25, 50, 57, 59, 70, 84, 85, 88, 89, 90, 91, 92, 94, 96, 97, 98, 99, 182, 199, 202, 205, 206, 208, 209, 211, 212, 214, 215, 216, 217, 220, 221, 223, 224, 225, 226, 233, 234, 235, 236, 237, 239, 241, 242, 243, 245, 247, 248, 249, 250, 251, 254, 257, 258, 260, 261, 262, 279

wicked / wickedness, 52, 62, 63, 80, 115, 153

wine, 56, 57, 59, 96, 132, 134, 136, 278, 279, 280

witness, 53, 61, 82, 92, 102, 103, 104, 105, 109, 116, 139, 186, 192, 198, 248, 270, 277

wood / wooden, 95, 96, 98, 108; woodland, 92; see also tree

worship / worshipful, 49, 51, 52, 65, 77, 79, 83, 114, 116, 130, 132, 133, 136, 139, 272, 279

wrath, 60, 80, 112, 188

yield(s), 43, 48, 49, 56, 60, 66, 92, 94, 123, 151, 202, 204, 211, 212, 214, 216, 217, 237, 254, 256, 261, 262, 283, 284, 285, 286

Zion, 62, 182, 185, 186, 187, 192

zōopoiēsis, 7, 10, 23, 24, 26, 110, 111, 112, 121, 123, 129, 141, 142, 143, 178, 194, 195, 196, 271, 273, 275, 276, 280

Modern Author Index

Adams, Edward, 114
Aldrete, Gregory S., 84, 97, 99, 107, 108
Alkon, Alison Hope, 199, 246, 247
Andersen, Francis I., 57, 58
Armstrong, Gail E., 81, 82
Ayres, Jennifer R., 267, 270

Bahnson, Fred, 264, 269, 270
Barclay, John M. G., 15, 16, 17, 18, 19, 103, 121, 122, 129, 130, 132, 134, 136, 137, 138
Bauckham, Richard, 35, 36, 43, 44, 140
Beard, Mary, 73, 76, 77, 78, 83
Beker, J. Christiaan, 170
Blatt, Harvey, 217
Blenkinsopp, Joseph, 62
Braaten, Laurie J., 183
Brown, Lester R., 211, 215, 216, 248, 249
Brueggemann, Walter, 62, 63
Burroughs, Bradley, xiv, xvi, 14
Burroughs, Presian, 31, 33, 109, 178, 283

Campbell, Douglas, xiii, 8, 9, 113, 122, 123
Casson, Lionel, 85, 87
Castriota, David, 72, 81, 82
Childs, Brevard, 62, 63
Christoffersson, Olle, 147
Collins, John J., 173
Conradie, Ernst, 11
Cranfield, C. E. B., 147, 160, 162, 164, 165, 171, 176

Davis, Ellen F., xiii, 32, 34, 35, 36, 39, 40, 41, 44, 46, 47, 48, 52, 54, 56, 57, 140, 141, 240
Dunn, James D. G., 113, 119, 121, 124, 162, 163
Dunstan, William E., 71, 78

Eastman, Susan, xiii, 148, 149, 151, 152, 172, 187
Eberhart, Timothy Reinhold, 120, 137, 200, 201, 279, 280
Elliott, Neil, 15, 16, 17, 18, 69, 71, 73, 78, 79, 84, 86, 88, 112, 136, 187
Erdkamp, Paul, 76, 85, 86, 87, 88, 90, 91, 99, 100

Fitzmyer, Joseph A., 154
Fredriksen, Paula, 118
Fretheim, Terence E., 32, 33, 38, 39, 40, 46, 48, 49, 52, 58, 59, 61, 66
Friedman, Richard Elliott, 1, 39
Friesen, Courtney, 191

Galen, Coen van, 86
Galinsky, Karl, 71, 73, 74, 76, 77, 78, 79, 80
Garnsey, Peter, 86, 99
Garr, W. Randall, 33
Gaventa, Beverly Roberts, 152, 180

Habel, Norman C., 2, 32, 33, 35, 40, 42
Hahne, Harry Alan, 41, 104, 181
Harink, Douglas, 121, 128, 131

Modern Author Index

Harper, Kyle, 89, 90, 91, 92, 93, 95, 107, 108
Harris, W. V., 92, 95, 97, 98, 106
Hays, Richard B., xiii, 7, 8, 9, 17, 56, 112
Horden, Peregrine, 75, 76, 86, 90, 93, 94
Horrell, David G., xv, 7, 9, 10, 138, 142, 146, 159, 165, 179, 188, 189, 192, 195, 269, 270
Hughes, J. Donald, 106
Hurt, R. Douglas, 202, 208, 209, 210, 234, 235, 236, 237, 238, 239, 240, 247

Jackson, T. Ryan, 22, 28, 29, 64, 65, 81, 152
Jackson, Wes, xiii, 6, 11, 14, 87, 197, 207, 208, 210, 211, 213, 250, 253, 257, 258, 259, 261, 264, 280
Jewett, Robert, 15, 16, 71, 73, 82, 104, 105, 109, 110, 111, 113, 114, 118, 121, 123, 124, 126, 128, 129, 132, 133, 134, 135, 136, 137, 152, 169, 170, 172, 173, 174, 187

Kaufman, David B., 99
Kaufman, Frederick, 214, 242, 247, 248, 249, 251
Keck, Leander E., 110, 113, 117, 118, 124, 129, 136, 172
Keesmaat, Sylvia C., xv, 6, 36, 47, 56, 106, 115, 116, 117, 158, 164, 173, 178, 183, 190, 194, 195
Kehoe, Dennis P., 85, 88, 92, 93, 94, 96, 97, 98
Kimbrell, Andrew, 5, 6, 200, 228, 232, 239, 243, 245, 248
Kimmerer, Robin Wall, 6, 9, 255, 267, 270, 275
Klawans, Jonathan, 53, 54, 55, 60, 61, 117, 118
Kleiner, Diana E. E., 78, 82
Kreitzer, Larry J., 75, 83, 84, 105

Laird, Margaret L., 83, 105
Legarreta-Castillo, Felipe de Jesús, 151, 152
Leopold, Aldo, 11, 12, 60, 259

Mart, Michelle, 202, 204, 216, 225, 237, 283, 284, 285, 286
Martyn, J. Louis, 184, 185
Matera, Frank J., 113, 173
Merchant, Carolyn, 140, 203, 207, 208
Middleton, J. Richard, 7, 28, 30, 31, 37, 38, 39
Milgrom, Jacob, 49, 50, 51, 52, 54
Montgomery, David R., 4, 209, 210, 212, 236, 244, 254, 255, 257, 263, 264, 265
Moo, Douglas J., 113, 155, 177
Moo, Jonathan, 65, 160, 164, 179, 189, 194
Murray, Robert, 37, 62
Myers, Ched, 203

O'Reilly, Matt, 61, 121, 122
Oswalt, John N., 186

Perkins, Pheme, 152
Pollan, Michael, 239, 264, 270

Rickman, Geoffrey E., 84, 85, 86, 87, 91, 96, 97, 98, 99
Rossing, Barbara R., 184

Sanders, E. P., xiii, 119, 151
Sarna, Nahum M., 32, 33
Scherrer, Peter, 79, 105
Schmid, H. H., 30, 45
Shahar, Meir Ben, 65, 111
Shiva, Vandana, 204, 239, 285
Stuart, Douglas, 57, 58, 59
Stulac, Daniel J., 64, 65
Sutherland, C. H. V., 98, 108

Theokritoff, Elizabeth, 278, 279
Tonstad, Sigve K., 2, 32, 34, 35, 36, 39, 42, 43, 84, 117, 119, 120, 122, 123, 126, 127, 128, 129, 130, 131, 134, 153, 169, 170, 172, 180, 201
Turcan, Robert, 76

von Rad, Gerhard, 33, 171

Modern Author Index

Wagner, J. Ross, 37
Wallace, Daniel B., xiii, 123, 155, 176, 177
Wenham, Gordon J., 32, 33
White Jr., Lynn, 140

White, Monica M., 255, 256, 270
Wirzba, Norman, xiii, 9, 37, 45, 110, 115, 120, 138, 250, 251, 264, 269, 270, 272, 274, 275, 278

Ancient Texts Index

ANCIENT NEAR EASTERN TEXTS

Atrahasis Epic
1.240–41	30
1.337–39	30

Code of Hammurabi	30

Enuma Elish
6.5–8	30
6. 31–38	30
6.113–18	30

Eridu Genesis	30

TANAKH

Genesis

	7, 8, 162
1	7, 24, 31, 32, 33, 36, 37, 38, 40, 41, 42, 44, 67, 146, 165, 203, 249
1–2	22, 27, 41, 141, 275
1–3	9, 161, 162
1–6	162
1–9	166
1:1	65
1:10	35
1:11	34
1:11–12	1, 34, 42, 165, 198
1:12	34, 35
1:14	32
1:16	58
1:18	35
1:20	33
1:20–21	213
1:20–22	35, 36, 198
1:21	33, 35
1:22	34, 35, 36, 165, 169
1:24	33
1:24–25	31, 165
1:24–30	198
1:25	33, 35
1:26	1, 29, 33, 36, 51, 265
1:26–28	31, 32, 121, 125, 140, 161, 178, 198
1:27	32
1:28	29, 35, 36, 151, 165, 169, 173, 265
1:28–30	28
1:29	1, 34, 42
1:29–30	34, 44, 228
1:30	1, 36, 165
1:31	35, 114
2	38, 39, 40, 62
2–3	152, 154, 160
2:5	39
2:7	38, 39
2:7–8	39, 40, 275
2:8–9	39
2:9	42
2:15	28, 39, 46, 51, 59, 173, 198, 265, 269
2:17	40, 42

Ancient Texts Index

Genesis (*cont.*)

2:18–20	38
2:19	38
2:19–20	38
3	24, 29, 41, 42, 43, 63, 120, 146, 154, 165, 182
3–6	22, 24, 28, 146
3–9	41, 163
3:1	42
3:6	42
3:11	40
3:16	42, 182, 185
3:17	1, 2, 42, 116
3:17–18	42, 165
3:17–19	42, 118, 128, 154, 169, 269, 275
3:18–19	43
3:19	42
4	37, 43
4:1	185
4:1–25	118
4:2	185
4:10	43
4:11	43
4:12	43
4:17	185
4:20	185
4:22	185
4:25	185
5:29	154
6	29, 37, 157, 158
6–9	28, 44
6:5	43, 158
6:11	23, 41, 43, 44, 158
6:11–12	43, 158
6:11–13	64, 156
6:12	44, 158
6:13	41, 44, 158
6:13a	44
6:13b	44
8:17	165
9:2–3	44
9:3	44
9:5	45
9:5–6	44
9:9–17	41, 44
9:10	44
12	45
12–50	31
12:1–3	28, 41, 45
12:1	45
12:7	45
16:11	185
16:15	185
16:16	185
17:19	185
18:18–19	45
22:18	45
26:4	45
30	185
36	185

Exodus

	22, 46, 47
1–15	46
2:2	185
2:22	185
2:23–24	182
3:12	130
6:5	182
8:1	130
12:13	50
12:23	50
15:11	170
19–23	41
19:5	40
19:6	67
20	28
20:6	40
20:10	49
22:24	57
23	28, 29
23:10–11	49
23:11	49
23:12	49
23:15	40
23:25	130
33:18–19	129
34:6–7	129
40:34	171

Ancient Texts Index

Leviticus

	22, 35, 46, 49, 52, 118
12:2	185
12:5	185
16:11–19	55
16:20–22	55
17:7	164
18:24	53, 118
18:24–30	53, 54
18:25	52, 53
18:28	53
19:9–10	49, 57
19:23–25	49
19:31	53
19:35–36	57
20:1–3	53
20:3	53
23	29
23:8	50
23:9–14	50
23:23–36	51
25	29, 47
25–26	28
25:3–7	49
25:7	49
25:11–12	49
25:23	47
25:55	47
26	29
26:3–7	48, 59
26:4	49
26:11–12	48
26:14–32	52
26:14–33	52
26:42	48, 66

Numbers

11:12	185
16:9	130
16:30	162
32:22	35
32:29	35
35:33–34	53, 54

Deuteronomy

	8, 22, 46
4:2	40
4:40	40
5:14	49
5:24	171
5:33	45
6:3	40
6:13	130
10:12	130
11	28, 29
11:13–15	48
11:13–17	53
11:16–17	52
20	29
20:19	46
20:19–20	49
22:4	46
22:6–7	46
24:19–21	47
25:4	46
28	28
28:1–14	48
28:15–68	52
28:57	185
29–30	41
30:19	53
31:28	53
32:21	172
32:43	172

Joshua

	8, 31
18:1	35
22:19	54

Judges

2:18	182
8:31	185

Ruth

4:15	185
4:17	185

Ancient Texts Index

1 Samuel

1:20	185
12	37

2 Samuel

7:14	19
8:11	35
11:27	185

1 Kings

13:2	185
14	29
14:15–16	52
16:13	164

2 Kings

	8
17:22	52

1 Chronicles

1	185
2	185
7	185
7:1–3	171
22:18	35

Nehemiah

5:5	35
9:6	119

Esther

7:8	35

Job

	62
31:38	182
31:38–40	182
36:6	119
38:41	40

Psalms

	8, 66, 115
2:7	19
4:3	163
7:15	185
11:6	182
19:1–4	114
28:1–3	171
38:6	164
72	22, 28, 56, 66
72:1–3	66
72:8	36, 66
72:9–11	66
72:12–13	66
72:13	66
72:16	66
72:17	67
77:33	164
101:16	171
104:30	40, 41
106:34–40	54
143:8	163

Proverbs

	8
3:9–10	50
10:23	185

Ecclesiastes

	8, 66
2:11	164
2:15	163
3:19	164
4:8	164
6:2	164
6:12	164
7:12	119

Song of Songs

8:5	185

Isaiah

	22, 55, 56, 60, 61, 127
1:4	52
1:26	62
2:1–4	62
2:2–4	65, 111

2:10	171	35:10	182
2:19	171	40–66	186
2:20	164	40:5	171
2:21	171	42:6	67
5	64	44:9	164
5:8	57	44:23	66
6:3	171	45:10	185
7:14	185	49:6	67
9:1	62	51:2	185
11	29, 37, 63, 66, 169	51:11	182
11:1	37, 62	54:1	185, 187
11:1–5	62	56:5–6	65, 111
11:1–9	28, 37, 61, 62, 63, 127	59:4	185
		60:3	67
11:1–10	128	65	29, 62, 65, 169
11:2	63	65–66	117
11:4	63	65:1–8	65
11:5–7	62	65:9–10	65
11:6	63	65:13–14	65
11:6–9	62, 63, 126	65:17	63, 65
11:10	18, 63, 126	65:17a	65
11:11	63	65:17–25	65
11:12	63	65:19–23	66
11:13–16	63	65:25	66
13:8	185	66:7	185
22	64	66:7–9	187
22:13	64	66:8	185, 186, 192
23:4	185	66:8–10	185, 186, 187
24	29, 64, 157, 158, 194	66:18–19	186
24–27	194	66:20	187
24:1	64, 158	66:20–21	186
24:1–5	156	66:22	186
24:1–7	64, 65		
24:3	64, 158	**Jeremiah**	
24:4	64	2:7	54
24:4–6	158	3	29
24:5	52, 64, 65	3:1	54
24:5–6	64	3:2–3	52
24:5–6a	64	4:31	182, 185
24:6	64	11	29
24:10	64	11:10	52
24:20	65	15:10	185
26:17	185, 192	30:16	185
26:18	185, 192	33:8	118
26:19	192	34:11	35
26:20	65		
26:21	192		

Ancient Texts Index

Ezekiel
	22, 55, 56, 59, 60
3:12	171
3:23	171
5:11	53
11:23	171
16:52	156
22:1–4	54
23:4	185
34:25–31	61
36	29, 60, 62, 118
36:8–9	60
36:8–12	61
36:11	60
36:17	53, 60
36:18	54, 60
36:19	53
36:25	118
36:25–30	60
37:1–14	61
37:12–13	193
37:14	193
37:23	118
39:16	118
44:4	171
44:30	50
47:7–12	61

Daniel
	8
1:8–13	134
12:1–3	61

Hosea
	59
1:3	185
1:6	185
1:8	185
2:1	172
4	29
4:1–3	52
4:1–7	53
9:9	156
14:1	52

Amos
	22, 56, 61
1:1	58
2:6–8	57
4:6–9	59
5:7–9	58
5:11	57
5:12	57
7:17	54
8	29
8:4–6	57
8:7–10	58
9:11–15	58
9:13–15	59, 63

Jonah
2:9	164

Micah
4:10	185
6:1–2	53

Habakkuk
	56, 59
2:4	56, 112
2:6	56
2:8	56
3:10	185

Zechariah
13:1	118
14:16–17	51

APOCRYPHA

Addition to Esther
14:17	134

Judith
10:5	134
12:1–4	134
12:17–19	134

Tobit

1:10–11	134

Wisdom of Solomon

	113
2:23	157

JEWISH PSEUDEPIGRAPHA

Apocalypse of Moses	41, 104
2 Baruch	41, 104, 152
39:7	147
1 Enoch	104
6–16	41
17–36	42
38:1	147
51:1	192
2 Enoch	41
4 Ezra	41, 104, 152
7:28	147
7:32	192
10:10	192
10:14	192
Joseph and Aseneth	
8.9	119
LAE / Life of Adam and Eve	152
Jubilees	42, 104

NEW TESTAMENT

Matthew

	192
1:21	185
1:23	185
1:25	185
5:5	284
27:50–52	191
27:52	191
27:53	191
28:2	191

Luke

1:31	185
1:57	185
2:7	185
2:11	185

John

6:63	119
16:21	185

Acts

2:29	188
13:14	85
14:15	164
20:15	107
20:16	50

Romans

	7, 15, 17, 20, 21, 23, 25, 37, 56, 63, 68, 103, 105, 110, 111, 112, 119, 136, 138, 141, 155, 249, 273, 277
1	56, 113, 153
1–4	111, 112
1–8	160
1:1	128, 150
1:1–6	194
1:3	126
1:4	112, 126, 172
1:5	20, 65, 128, 136, 149, 172
1:5–6	128
1:14	131
1:14–17	128
1:16	110
1:16–17	188
1:17	112, 128
1:18	56, 149

Romans (*cont.*)

1:18–21	149
1:19–21	113
1:19–23	173
1:19–32	113, 114
1:19–36	116
1:20	113, 126, 147, 149, 157
1:20–23	114
1:21	113, 114, 148, 149, 164
1:23	114, 157, 158, 160, 176, 179
1:24	118
1:25	114, 147
1:28–31	115
1:29	153
2	116
2:8	153
3	6, 112, 116, 117, 165, 203
3–5	145
3–8	115
3:1–20	117
3:5	110
3:9–18	6, 7, 117, 119
3:9–19	126
3:11	116
3:12b	153
3:13	116
3:15	116, 117
3:15–17	153
3:16	116
3:18	116
3:19–22	117
3:21–22	188
3:21–26	28, 117, 118, 188
3:21–30	167
3:22	112, 113, 118
3:24	172
3:26	110, 189
3:29–30	65, 128
3:30	118
4	112
4:5	110
4:11–12	128
4:13	121, 128
4:16	113
4:17	110, 119, 165
4:17–18	128
4:17–21	119
4:24	119
5	24, 42, 118, 120, 146, 150, 152, 153, 154, 157, 161, 162, 165
5–6	16, 20, 154, 160, 163, 165
5–8	111, 112, 119, 120, 123, 124, 126, 162
5:1	113
5:1–2	28, 173
5:2	176, 177
5:5–8	137
5:6–9	7
5:6–10	137
5:6–21	120
5:8	120, 128
5:9	188
5:9–11	126
5:10	149
5:11	118, 188
5:12	120, 152, 154, 158, 163
5:12–14	128, 150
5:12–21	6, 7, 13, 24, 28, 41, 43, 68, 102, 110, 120, 126, 130, 138, 146, 167
5:12—7:7	151
5:14	119, 120, 150, 163, 178
5:15	120
5:15–21	68
5:17	13, 19, 37, 68, 119, 120, 121, 123, 130, 140, 167, 173, 174, 194, 275
5:17–21	28
5:18	120
5:19	120, 152
5:21	119, 120, 130, 152, 163, 173
6	121, 122, 124, 140, 150, 153

6–8	175	8:11	7, 122, 123, 148, 165, 168, 190
6:1–4	28, 121	8:12–14	194
6:1–5	122	8:13	168
6:1–11	120	8:14	125, 147
6:1–23	174	8:14–16	148
6:3	153	8:15	147, 150, 154
6:4	172, 177	8:16	125, 147
6:4–5	171	8:17	19, 121, 124, 125, 126, 147, 168, 170, 177, 180, 194
6:6	68, 121, 150		
6:6–23	120		
6:8–11	135		
6:11	139	8:17–18	28, 124
6:11–13	122	8:18	147, 168, 169, 170, 171, 172, 177, 178, 189
6:12	119, 153		
6:12–13	153		
6:12–19	194	8:18–39	173
6:13	127, 199	8:19	13, 19, 20, 24, 103, 124, 125, 126, 139, 144, 146, 147, 148, 149, 166, 167, 168, 169, 170, 172, 174, 177, 189, 193, 281
6:16	150		
6:16–18	119		
6:17	68, 150, 152		
6:17–23	28		
6:18	13, 37, 130, 150, 153, 175, 194, 275		
		8:19–21	20, 124, 138, 146, 166, 168, 179
6:19	118, 150, 188		
6:20	150	8:19–22	7, 8, 19, 22, 23, 24, 25, 27, 28, 42, 65, 102, 103, 104, 109, 116, 120, 124, 125, 143, 144, 145, 146, 147, 149, 153, 154, 157, 160, 165, 168, 170, 173, 188, 191, 194, 195, 196, 276
6:22	13, 124, 126, 139, 150, 175, 188, 194, 275		
7	123, 165, 188		
7:6	150, 188		
7:11	34		
7:14–19	165		
7:16–24	188		
7:25	150, 188	8:19–23	148, 154, 179
8	147, 151, 154, 165, 172, 179, 190, 194	8:20	2, 24, 28, 114, 145, 146, 147, 149, 160, 161, 162, 163, 164, 165, 166, 174, 189
8:1	125, 188		
8:1–11	28		
8:2	123, 124, 126, 139, 148, 153, 154, 175, 274	8:20a	162
		8:20b	144, 161, 162
		8:20–21	8, 20, 68, 70, 103, 126, 146, 161, 167, 174, 222
8:3	7		
8:4	123		
8:6	123	8:20b–21	178
8:2–14	122	8:20–22	174
8:10–11	124		

333

Romans (*cont.*)

8:21	2, 6, 7, 13, 16, 20, 24, 28, 44, 64, 66, 68, 104, 110, 121, 123, 124, 125, 126, 139, 144, 145, 146, 147, 148, 150, 156, 157, 158, 159, 161, 162, 167, 168, 170, 172, 174, 175, 176, 178, 179, 189, 193, 194, 198, 199, 233, 249, 251, 259, 273, 274, 281
8:21a	176
8:21b	160
8:21–22	189
8:21–23	139
8:22	25, 146, 147, 149, 165, 168, 179, 180, 181, 182, 183, 184, 185, 187, 188, 190, 191, 193
8:23	28, 122, 124, 147, 148, 170, 171, 172, 178, 180, 183, 184, 189, 190
8:24	182
8:24–25	189
8:26	149, 165, 182, 183, 184
8:27	148
8:28–30	128
8:29	21, 28, 121, 125, 126, 140, 160, 184, 190
8:29–30	178
8:29–34	28
8:30	124, 147, 171, 173, 178
8:31–39	190
8:32	194
8:33	110
8:33–39	173
8:35	190
8:35–36	168
8:35–39	139
8:37	194
8:38–39	149
8:39	137, 147
9–11	111, 112, 127, 145
9:3	128
9:4	127, 128, 148
9:6	127
9:12	150
9:30	113
10:9	128
10:14–17	128
11:1	129
11:5	189
11:13	129
11:14	128
11:15	127, 128
11:28	148
11:30	189
11:31	189
11:36	114, 126
12	122
12–15	111, 142
12–16	111, 112, 126, 129
12:1	49, 130, 131, 139
12:1–2	199, 251, 273, 276
12:2	20, 21, 130, 137
12:4–8	134, 199
12:9	130, 131, 132
12:11	130, 150
12:16	130, 139
12:17	130
12:18	130, 139
12:20	131, 139, 235
12:21	130, 131
13	21, 131
13:1	131
13:1–7	130, 131
13:3	130
13:3–4	131
13:4	221, 276
13:8	131
13:8–10	137
13:9–11	189
13:10	249
13:11	132, 189
13:13	132
14	122, 133, 154, 243
14–15	133, 138, 143, 273

14:1	132, 133
14:3a	135
14:3b	135
14:5	51
14:5–6	133
14:6	135, 198, 279
14:7	135
14:9	136
14:14	134
14:15	134, 135, 136, 137, 138, 139, 198, 199, 222, 233, 279
14:15a	137
14:15b	137
14:17	137, 138, 139
14:18	150, 151
14:20	139, 199
14:20–21	136
14:21	133, 136
14:23	136
15	122, 127, 128
15:1	136, 137
15:1–3	137
15:1–13	134
15:2–3	137
15:3	19, 128, 136
15:7	127, 133
15:7–13	18
15:8	37, 127
15:8–9	19, 126
15:8–21	65
15:9–12	194
15:12	19, 37, 61, 63, 126
15:15–19	128
15:16	187
15:18	20, 136, 149
15:19	128
16:5	82
16:16	137
16:18	150
16:25–26	189
16:25–27	65
16:26	172

1 Corinthians

1:8	189
3:17	157
4:11	188
5:7	118
9:16	131
10:24	137
10:26	137
11:21–22	133
11:23–24	135
15:22	152
15:23	124
15:36	119
15:42	157

2 Corinthians

3:6	119
3:14	188
4:4	37
7:21	118
12:21	118

Galatians

	184
3:21	119
4:2	187
4:8–11	51
4:9	164
4:19	185, 187
4:27	185, 187
5:16–26	122
5:19	118
6:2	137
6:8	159

Ephesians

4:17	163

Philippians

1:5	188
1:6	189
1:10	189
1:20	169
2:1–11	21
2:5–11	19
2:11	16
2:16	189

Ancient Texts Index

Colossians
1:15	37, 190
1:18	190
2:16	51

1 Thessalonians
2:19	124
3:13	124, 147
4:7	118
4:15	124, 147
5:23	124

2 Thessalonians
1:17	147
2:1	124
2:8	124

Hebrews
6:7	185

James
1:15	185

Revelation
	7
12:2	185
12:4	185
12:5	185
12:13	185

RABBINIC TEXTS

Tosefta Sukkot
3:18	50

Mekilta
Bo' par. 7	50

CLASSICAL GREEK AND LATIN TEXTS

Augustus
Res Gestae
	85
5	84
7	77
13	72
15	84, 85
25	87
34	79
35	86

Columella
On Agriculture
2.6.4	90

Euripides
	191

Heraclitus
	191

Hesiod
Theogony
	191

Horace
	77, 81
Odes	
4.15	80, 81

Ovid
Metamorphoses	70, 71
77	70
89–90	70
100–101	70
103	71
109–10	70
113–14	71
114	71
125	71
127	71
128–43	71

Ancient Texts Index

Plato
Critias
111 B–D   106

Pliny the Elder
                88, 89, 90, 191
Natural History
18.12.63–66   89–90
18.35   88

Siculus
Eclogue
1   88

Virgil
Aeneid   77
6.913–16   78

Eclogues   71
4.13–14   71
4.21–22   72
4.38–40   72

Georgics   72

www.ingramcontent.com/pod-product-compliance
Lightning Source LLC
Chambersburg PA
CBHW020109010526
44115CB00008B/753